# AUTO-BIOGRAPHY

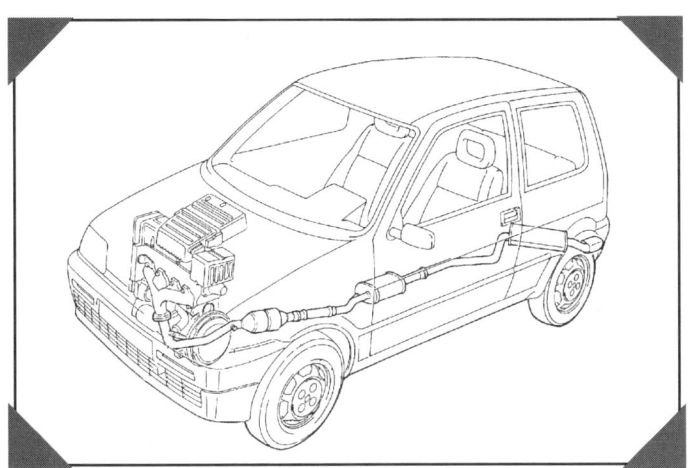

This page enables you to compile a list of useful data on your car, so that whether you're ordering spares or just checking the tyre pressures, all the key information - the information that is 'personal' to your car - is easily within reach.

Registration number: ..................................................
Model: ......................................................................
Engine type/size: .....................................................
Fuel type/grade: ......................................................
Body colour: ............................................................
Paint code number: ................................................
Date of first registration: .......................................
Date of manufacture (if different): ........................
VIN (or 'chassis') number: ....................................
Engine number: .....................................................
Ignition key/key tag number: ................................

Door lock key/s number/s: ....................................
Fuel locking cap key number (if fitted): ................
Alarm remote code (if fitted): ................................
Radio/cassette security code (if fitted): ...............

*Tyre size*
Front: ...............................Rear: ...............................
*Tyre pressures (normally laden)*
Front: ...............................Rear: ...............................
*Tyre pressures (fully laden)*
Front: ...............................Rear: ...............................

*Insurance*
    Name and address of insurer: ....................................................................................................
..........................................................................................................................................................................
    Policy number: ..............................................................................................................................
*Modifications*
    Information that might be useful when you need to purchase parts: ..................................
..........................................................................................................................................................................
*Suppliers*
    Address and telephone number of your local dealership: ...................................................
..........................................................................................................................................................................
..........................................................................................................................................................................

**VEHICLE DETAILS**

First published in 1998 by: **Porter Publishing Ltd.**
The Storehouse
Little Hereford Street
Bromyard
Hereford HR7 4DE
England

Tel: 01885 488800
Fax: 01885 483012

© Copyright Lindsay Porter
and Porter Publishing Ltd, 1998.

All rights reserved. No part of this publication may be reproduced, stored in a retrieval system, or transmitted in any form including electronic, electrical, mechanical, optical, photocopying, recording or by any other means without prior written permission of the publisher. All enquiries should be addressed to the publisher at the address shown on this page.

British Library Cataloguing in Publication Data.

A catalogue record for this book is available from the British Library.

ISBN 1-899238-25-5

*Series Editor:* Lindsay Porter
*Front cover design:* Crazy Horse 1842 Ltd and Porter Publishing Ltd.
*Back cover design:* Porter Publishing Ltd.
*Layout and Typesetting:* Mark Leonard at Porter Publishing Ltd.
Printed in England by The Trinity Press, Worcester.

### GREAT CARS ON VIDEO

PP Video has a truly great range of video tapes, mostly original 'archive' footage, and covering the finest cars ever built. We present the official Jaguar Cars Archive, Dunlop Archive, Audi AG Archive films, among others. There are profiles on the greatest classic cars, motor racing from the '30s, the '50s, the '60s and '70s, and much more besides. For a FREE VIDEO CATALOGUE, please write to: PP Video Ltd, at the address shown at the top of this page.

## MORE TOP-SELLING
### Step-by-Step
# PORTER MANUALS
**All with 100s of clear illustrations!**

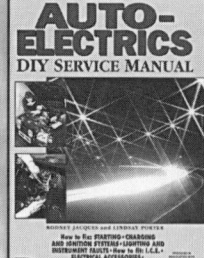

**AUTO-ELECTRICS DIY Service Manual**
Covers every electrical component on the car. Explains how it works AND how to fix it! Packed with simple instructions. Comprehensive and easy to follow.

**The Complete TRAILER MANUAL**
The ONLY complete trailer manual! How to build your own; how to use, service and repair; the towing and weight laws. All trailer types covered. Car tow limits listed car-by-car.

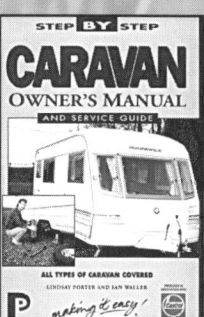

**THE CARAVAN MANUAL**
Keep your caravan in super, safe condition with the help of this book. Every aspect of servicing electrics, brakes, hitch, interior, accessories and more. User's guide and car tow limits listed, car-by-car.

**THE MOTOR CARAVAN MANUAL**
Step-by-Step service jobs on every type of petrol and diesel Motor Caravan; every type of body and all interior fittings. Buyer's guide; user's guide; step-by-step servicing and much more besides.

**DIESEL CAR ENGINES Service Guide**
See how your car's Diesel engine works; follow the step-by-step service instructions; fix it when it goes wrong. Thorough, comprehensive step-by-step DIY service manual, covering all Diesel car types.

**ABSOLUTE BEGINNERS Service Guide**
If you've never serviced a car before, this manual 'holds your hand' through every step, from topping-up and changing oil to overhauling brakes and bodywork.

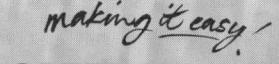

## PORTER MANUALS:

● Packed with information.
● The best for quality.
● The **easiest** to use!

From your local stockist, or contact us at the address at the top of this page for availability and a full list of titles.

**CLASSIC 'BIKE Service Guide**
For all those enthusiasts of old British motor bikes. The complete step-by-step guide to Buying, Selling, Running, Servicing and Maintaining every model of classic British 'bike.

*There's a great range of PORTER MANUALS covering most popular vehicles. However, those not covering FIAT cars - are not necessarily FIAT approved.*

# FIAT Cinquecento

## Repair Manual and Service Guide

by
**Lindsay Porter
and Michael Gascoigne**

Every care has been taken to ensure that the material in this book is correct. However, should any matter not be clear after reading this book, you are advised to consult your nearest franchised dealer. Liability cannot be accepted for damage, loss, accidents or injury, due to failure to follow instructions or to consult expert advice if this is required.

# CONTENTS

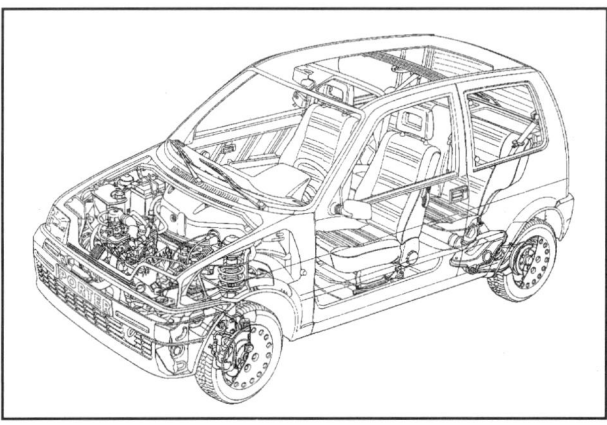

*Detailed Contents are shown at the start of each chapter.*

## CONTENTS

|  | Auto-Biography | i |
|---|---|---|
| **CHAPTER 1:** | Safety First! | 1-1 to 1-4 |
| **CHAPTER 2:** | Using Your Car | 2-1 to 2-8 |
| **CHAPTER 3:** | Facts and Figures | 3-1 to 3-6 |
| **CHAPTER 4:** | Getting Through the MoT | 4-1 to 4-4 |
| **CHAPTER 5:** | Servicing Your Car | 5-1 to 5-26 |
| **CHAPTER 6:** | Repairs and Replacements | 6-1 to 6-65 |
| **CHAPTER 7:** | Wiring Diagrams | 7-1 to 7-9 |
|  | Index |  |

 **FACT FILE: 'LEFT AND 'RIGHT' SIDES OF THE CAR**

● Throughout this manual, we refer to the 'left' and 'right' sides of the car. They refer to the sides of the car that you would see if you were sitting in the driver's seat, looking forwards.

iv

*Please be sure to read the whole of this Chapter before carrying out any work on your car.*

# CHAPTER 1
# SAFETY FIRST!

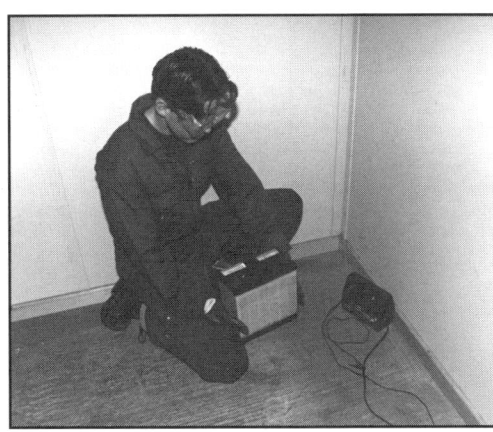

You must always ensure that safety is the first consideration in any job you carry out. A slight lack of concentration, or a rush to finish the job quickly can easily result in an accident, as can failure to follow the precautions outlined in this manual.

Be sure to consult the suppliers of any materials and equipment you may use, and to obtain and read carefully any operating and health and safety instructions that may be available on packaging or from manufacturers and suppliers.

## GENERAL

### Raising the Car Safely

ALWAYS ensure that the vehicle is properly supported when raised off the ground. Don't work on, around, or underneath a raised vehicle unless axle stands are positioned under secure, load bearing underbody areas, or the vehicle is driven onto ramps, with the wheels remaining on the ground securely chocked to prevent movement.

NEVER work on a vehicle supported on a jack. Jacks are made for lifting the vehicle only, not for holding it off the ground while it is being worked on.

ALWAYS ensure that the safe working load rating of any jacks, hoists or lifting gear used is sufficient for the job, and that lifting gear is used only as recommended by the manufacturer.

NEVER attempt to loosen or tighten nuts that require a lot of force to turn (e.g. a tight oil drain plug) with the vehicle raised, unless it is safely supported. Take care not to pull the vehicle off its supports when applying force to a spanner. Wherever possible, initially slacken tight fastenings before raising the car off the ground.

ALWAYS wear eye protection when working under the vehicle and when using power tools.

### Working On The Vehicle

ALWAYS seek specialist advice unless you are justifiably confident about carrying out each job. The safety of your vehicle affects you, your passengers and other road users.

DON'T lean over, or work on, a running engine unless it is strictly necessary, and keep long hair and loose clothing well out of the way of moving mechanical parts.

NOTE that it is theoretically possible for fluorescent striplighting to make an engine fan appear to be stationary - double check whether it is spinning or not! This is the sort of error that happens when you're really tired and not thinking straight. So...

...DON'T work on your car when you're over tired.

ALWAYS work in a well ventilated area and don't inhale dust - it may contain asbestos or other harmful substances.

NEVER run the engine indoors, in a confined space or over a pit.

REMOVE your wrist watch, rings and all other jewellery before doing any work on the vehicle - and especially when working on the electrical system.

DON'T remove the radiator or expansion tank filler cap when the cooling system is hot, or you may get scalded by escaping coolant or steam. Let the system cool down first and even then, if the engine is not completely cold, cover the cap with a cloth and gradually release the pressure.

1-1

NEVER drain oil, coolant or automatic transmission fluid when the engine is hot. Allow time for it to cool sufficiently to avoid scalding you.

ALWAYS keep antifreeze, brake and clutch fluid away from vehicle paintwork. Wash off any spills immediately.

TAKE CARE to avoid touching any engine or exhaust system component unless it is cool enough not to burn you.

## Running The Vehicle

NEVER start the engine unless the gearbox is in neutral (or 'Park' in the case of automatic transmission) and the hand brake is fully applied.

NEVER run catalytic converter equipped vehicles without the exhaust system heat shields in place.

TAKE CARE when parking vehicles fitted with catalytic converters. The 'cat' reaches extremely high temperatures and any combustible materials under the car, such as long dry grass, could be ignited.

## Personal Safety

NEVER siphon fuel, antifreeze, brake fluid or other such toxic liquids by mouth, or allow contact with your skin. Use a suitable hand pump and wear gloves.

BEFORE undertaking dirty jobs, use a barrier cream on your hands as a protection against infection. Preferably, wear suitable gloves, available from DIY outlets.

WEAR IMPERVIOUS GLOVES for sure when there is a risk of used engine oil coming into contact with your skin. It can cause cancer.

WIPE UP any spilt oil, grease or water off the floor immediately.

MAKE SURE that spanners and all other tools are the right size for the job and are not likely to slip. Never try to 'double-up' spanners to gain more leverage.

SEEK HELP if you need to lift something heavy which may be beyond your capability. Don't forget that when lifting a heavy weight, you should keep your back straight and bend your knees to avoid injuring your back.

NEVER take risky short-cuts or rush to finish a job. Plan ahead and allow plenty of time.

BE METICULOUS and keep the work area tidy - you'll avoid frustration, work better and lose less.

KEEP children and animals right-away from the work area and from unattended vehicles.

ALWAYS tell someone what you're doing and have them regularly check that all is well, especially when working alone on, or under, the vehicle.

# HAZARDS

## Fire!

Petrol (gasoline) is a dangerous and highly flammable liquid requiring special precautions. When working on the fuel system, disconnect the vehicle battery earth (ground) terminal whenever possible and always work outside, or in a very well ventilated area. Any form of spark, such as that caused by an electrical fault, by two metal surfaces striking against each other, by a central heating boiler in the garage 'firing up', or even by static electricity built up in your clothing can, in a confined space, ignite petrol vapour causing an explosion. Take great care not to spill petrol on to the engine or exhaust system, never allow any naked flame anywhere near the work area and, above all, don't smoke.

Invest in a workshop-sized fire extinguisher. Choose the carbon dioxide type or preferably, dry powder but NEVER a water type extinguisher for workshop use.

DON'T disconnect any fuel pipes on a fuel injected engine without following the advice in this manual. The fuel in the line is under very high pressure - sufficient to cause serious injury. Remember that many injection systems have residual pressure in the pipes for days after switching off. If necessary seek specialist advice.

## Fumes

Petrol (gasoline) vapour and that given off by many solvents, thinners, and adhesives are highly toxic and under certain conditions can lead to unconsciousness or even death, if inhaled. The risks are increased if such fluids are used in a confined space so always ensure adequate ventilation. Always read the maker's instructions and follow them with care.

Never drain petrol (gasoline) or use solvents, thinners adhesives or other toxic substances in an inspection pit. It is also dangerous to park a vehicle for any length of time over an inspection pit. The fumes from even a slight fuel leak can cause an explosion when the engine is started.

## Mains Electricity

Avoid the use of mains electricity when working on the vehicle, whenever possible. Use rechargeable tools and a

DC inspection lamp, powered from a remote 12V battery - both are much safer. However, if you do use mains-powered equipment, ensure that the appliance is wired correctly to its

plug, that where necessary it is properly earthed (grounded), and that the fuse is of the correct rating for the appliance. Do not use any mains powered equipment in damp conditions or in the vicinity of fuel, fuel vapour or the vehicle battery. Always use an RCD (Residual Current Device) circuit breaker with mains electricity. Then, if there is a short, the RCD circuit breaker minimises the risk of electrocution by instantly cutting the power supply.

## Ignition System
Never work on the ignition system with the ignition switched on, or with the engine being turned over on the starter, or with the engine running.

Touching certain parts of the ignition system, such as the HT leads, distributor cap, ignition coil etc., can result in a severe electric shock or physical injury as a hand is pulled sharply away. Voltages produced by electronic ignition systems are much higher than those produced by conventional systems and could prove fatal, particularly to people with cardiac pacemaker implants. Consult your handbook or main dealer if in any doubt.

## Cooling Fan
On many vehicles, the electric cooling fan can switch itself on even with the ignition turned off. This is especially likely after driving the car and parking it before turning off, after which heat rises to the top of the engine and turns the fan on, suddenly and without warning. If you intend working in the engine bay, it's best to do so when the engine is cold, to disconnect the battery, or keep away from the fan, if neither of these are possible.

## Battery
Never cause a spark, smoke, or allow a naked light near the vehicle's battery, even in a well ventilated area. Highly explosive hydrogen gas is given off as part of the charging process.

Battery terminals on the car should be shielded, since a spark can be caused by any metal object which touches the battery's terminals or connecting straps.

IMPORTANT NOTE: Before disconnecting the battery earth (ground) terminal read the relevant FACT FILE in Chapter 5 regarding saving computer and radio settings.)
When using a battery charger, switch off the power supply before the battery charger leads are connected or disconnected. If the battery is not of the 'sealed-for-life' type, loosen the filler plugs or remove the cover before charging. For best results the battery should be given a low rate trickle charge overnight. Do not charge at an excessive rate or the battery may burst. Always wear gloves and goggles when carrying or when topping up the battery. Acid electrolyte is extremely corrosive and must not be allowed to contact the eyes, skin or clothes.

## Brakes and Asbestos
Obviously, a car's brakes are among its most important safety related items. ONLY work on your vehicle's braking system if you are trained and competent to do so. If you have not been trained in this work, but wish to carry out the jobs described in this book, we strongly recommend that you have a garage or qualified mechanic check your work before using the car.

Whenever you work on the braking system components, or remove front or rear brake pads or shoes: i) wear an efficient particle mask; ii) wipe off all brake dust from the brakes after spraying on a proprietary brand of brake cleaner (never blow dust off with compressed air); iii) dispose of brake dust and discarded shoes or pads in a sealed plastic bag; iv) wash your hands thoroughly after you have finished working on the brakes and certainly before you eat or smoke; v) replace shoes and pads only with asbestos-free shoes or pads. Note that asbestos brake dust can cause cancer if inhaled; vi) always replace brake pads and/or shoes in complete 'axle' sets of four - never replace the pads/shoes on one wheel only.

## Brake Fluid
Brake fluid absorbs moisture rapidly from the air and can become dangerous resulting in brake failure. You should change the fluid in accordance with your vehicle manufacturer's recommendations or as advised in this book. Never store (or use) an opened container of brake fluid. Dispose of the remainder at your Local Authority Waste Disposal Site, in the designated disposal unit, not with general waste or with waste oil.

## Engine Oils
Always wear disposable plastic or rubber gloves when draining the oil from your engine. i) Note that the drain plug and the oil are often hotter than you expect. Wear gloves if the plug is too hot to touch and keep your hand to one side so that you are not scalded by the spurt of oil as the plug comes away; ii) There are very real health hazards associated with used engine oil. In the words of one manufacturer's handbook "Prolonged and repeated contact may cause serious skin disorders, including dermatitis and cancer." Use a barrier cream on your hands and try not to get oil on them. Always wear gloves and wash your hands with hand cleaner soon after carrying out the work. Keep oil out of the reach of children; iii) NEVER, EVER dispose of old engine oil into the ground or down a drain. In the UK, and in most EC countries, every local authority must provide a safe means of oil disposal. In the UK, try your local Environmental Health Department for advice on waste disposal facilities.

## Plastic Materials
Many of the materials used (polymers, resins, adhesives and materials acting as catalysts and accelerators) contain dangers in the form of poisonous fumes, skin irritants, and the risk of fire and explosions. Do not allow resin or 2-pack adhesive hardener, or that supplied with filler or 2-pack stopper, to come into contact with skin or eyes. Read carefully the safety notes supplied on the can, tube or packaging and always wear impervious gloves and goggles when working with them.

## Fluoroelastomers
Fluoroelastomers are commonly used for oil seals, wiring and cabling, bearing surfaces, gaskets, diaphragms, hoses and 'O' rings. If they are subjected to temperatures greater than 315 degrees C, they will decompose and can be potentially

hazardous. Some decomposition may occur at temperatures above 200 degrees C, and it is obvious that when a car has been in a fire or has been dismantled with the assistance of a cutting torch or blow torch, the fluoroelastomers can decompose in the manner indicated above.

According to the Health and Safety Executive, "Skin contact with this liquid or decomposition residues can cause painful and penetrating burns. Permanent irreversible skin and tissue damage can occur". Damage can also be caused to eyes or by the inhalation of fumes created as fluoroelastomers are burned or heated.

After a vehicle has been exposed to fire or high temperatures:

1. Do not touch blackened or charred seals or equipment.

2. Preferably, don't handle parts containing decomposed fluoroelastomers, but if you must, wear goggles and PVC (polyvinyl chloride) or neoprene protective gloves whilst doing so. Never handle such parts unless they are completely cool.

3. Contaminated parts, residues, materials and clothing, including protective clothing and gloves, should be disposed of by an approved contractor to landfill or by incineration according to national or local regulations. Oil seals, gaskets and 'O' rings, along with contaminated material, must not be burned.

## WORKSHOP

1. Always have a fire extinguisher of the correct type at arm's length when working on the fuel system. If you do have a fire, DON'T PANIC. Use the extinguisher effectively by directing it at the base of the fire.

2. NEVER use a naked flame anywhere in the workplace.

3. KEEP your inspection lamp well away from any source of petrol (gasoline) such as when disconnecting a carburettor float bowl or fuel line.

4. NEVER use petrol (gasoline) to clean parts. Use paraffin (kerosene), white spirits, or, a proprietary degreaser.

5. NO SMOKING. There's a risk of fire or of transferring dangerous substances to your mouth and, in any case, ash falling into mechanical components is to be avoided.

6. BE METHODICAL in everything you do, use common sense, and think of safety at all times.
The used oil from the sump of just one car can cover an area of water the size of two football pitches, cutting off the oxygen supply and harming swans, ducks, fish and other river lift.

**When you drain your engine oil - don't oil the drain!**
Pouring oil down the drain will cause pollution. It is also an offense.
Don't mix used oil with other materials, such as paint and solvents, because this makes recycling difficult.
Take used oil to an oil recycling bank. Telephone FREE on 0800 663366 to find the location of your nearest oil bank, or contact you local authority recycling officer.

*Please read the whole of the CHAPTER 1, SAFETY FIRST! before carrying out any work on your car.*

# CHAPTER 2
# USING YOUR CAR

This Chapter is taken from FIAT's own official Handbooks on the Cinquecento. It contains important and helpful information for the operation of your FIAT Cinquecento.

We recommend that you read this chapter carefully, so that you will become familiar with your vehicle's controls and instruments.

## KEYS AND LOCKS

### ❏ 1. DOORS AND BONNET

#### DOOR LOCKS
Most FIAT Cinquecentos have manual locking. You turn the key in the lock in the normal way to lock and unlock the door.

#### EARLY KEYS TO 6/95
**1A-1.** Early models are supplied with one key (and duplicate) for the ignition, side doors, hatchback and the fuel filler cap. An adhesive tag included with the keys bears a code number which is necessary for requesting duplicates. Put the tag in a safe place (never on your key ring).

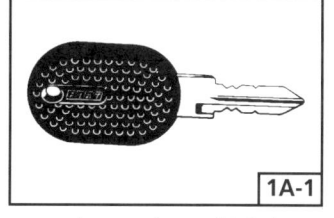

**New keys cannot be issued unless you supply your FIAT dealer with the key code number.**

#### KEYS FROM 6/95 ON
**1A-2.** There are three types of key supplied, which are:
● Key with burgundy grip is the 'Master' key. Only one is supplied and is used to store the codes of the other keys in the memory. Keep this key in a safe place and only use when necessary.
● Key with blue grip is for general use and is supplied with a duplicate. This key will start the engine, lock/unlock the doors and glove compartment.
● Key with remote button in blue grip has the same function as key and operates the electronic alarm (if fitted).

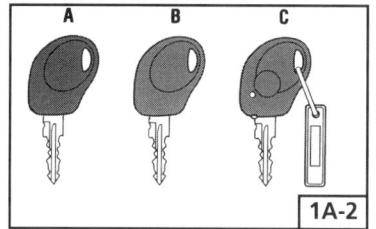

IMPORTANT NOTE: No repairs can be carried out on the FIAT CODE (electronic alarm) system or the engine control unit if the burgundy grip key is lost.

**1B.** Models produced before April 1996 are supplied with two FIAT CODE cards, which provide the following information:
● **D** - the electronic code to be used for emergency startup.
● **E** - the mechanical key code.
● **F**, **G** - Spaces for the remote control code stickers.

IMPORTANT NOTE: At the request of UK motor insurance companies, the two FIAT CODE cards, and replacement keys, are not provided with UK models produced after April 1996. If you need assistance please contact your nearest FIAT dealer.

#### REMOTE LOCKING/UNLOCKING
**1C.** A directional signal is emitted when you press button **1** on your remote unit/ignition key.

IMPORTANT NOTE: The presence of dirt, snow or ice on the side windows may prevent operation.

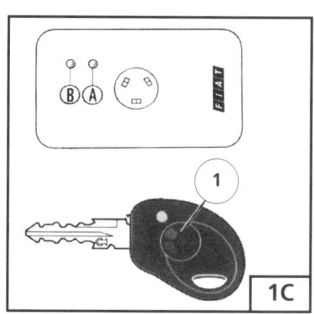

#### To Store the Code of Your Transmitter:
● Press and hold down button **A** with a ball-point pen. The red LED **B** illuminates, indicating that the receiving unit is ready to store the code.
● Hold down button **1** on your remote unit/ignition key.
● The LED at **B** stays ON, indicating that the receiver has stored the code.
● Release Button **A**. Red LED **B** flashes for about 8 seconds to confirm that the code has been stored.

CHAPTER 2 USING YOUR CAR

The control unit will store up to 4 different remote control codes.
If extra remote control/ignition keys are requested in addition to those already supplied, carry out the previous procedure for all 4 remote control keys.

If you ever need a new remote control unit, go to your nearest FIAT dealership, taking with you the remote control keys that you already have, plus the codes supplied with the car.

IMPORTANT NOTE: If the LED does not illuminate when remote unit/ignition key button (illustration **1C**, button **1**) is pressed, change the battery in the remote unit.

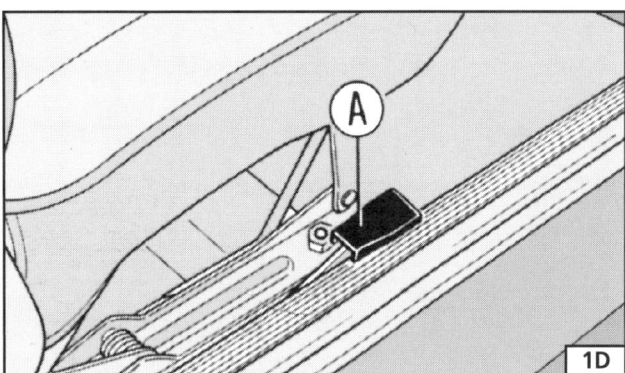

**LOCKING/UNLOCKING THE HATCHBACK DOOR:**
**1D.** Most hatchback models have manual locking. You turn the key in the lock in the normal way to lock and unlock the door. Some models are fitted with a hatchback door release lever **A** located at the side of the driver's seat which, when pulled upwards, can be used to open the hatchback door.

IMPORTANT NOTE: The gas-filled cylinders that assist the opening of the hatchback door are calibrated for the factory weight. The addition of any accessories such as speakers or a spoiler may prevent the door from operating properly.

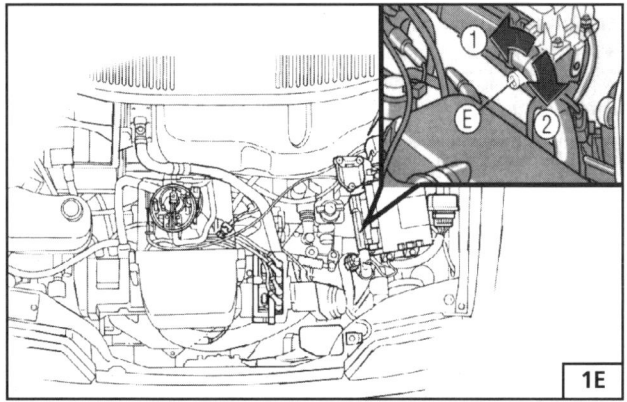

**HOW TO EXCLUDE THE ALARM**
**1E.** If the remote is faulty or the remote control batteries are flat:
• Insert one of two emergency keys supplied into the emergency switch slot **E**, which is located in the engine compartment, underneath the fuel injection control unit. Turn the key to the position **1** to switch the alarm OFF (see inset).

• Turn the key back towards its original position **2** to switch the alarm system back ON.

IMPORTANT NOTE: As the alarm system absorbs energy, if you are not planning on using the car for a long period of time, turn the alarm exclusion key to the OFF position, so as not to run the battery down.

## 2. IGNITION SWITCH AND STEERING COLUMN LOCK

### IGNITION SWITCH
**2.** The ignition/steering column lock key, once inserted in the ignition lock, can be placed in any of the following four positions:

• **PARK** - With the key in this position the side and tail lights can be turned on, the steering column locked and the keys can be removed. Press button **A** to turn the key to PARK.

• **STOP** - When the key is turned to the STOP position the steering column will be locked, and the keys can be removed.

• **MAR** - This is the driving position. When the key is in this position all the electrical devices are energised.

• **AVV** - Turning the key to this position starts the engine.

### STEERING COLUMN LOCK
• **LOCKING** - To apply the steering wheel lock turn the steering wheel slightly to the left or right when the key is at STOP, PARK or removed.

**SAFETY FIRST!**

• *Never remove the key when the car is moving. If you do, the steering wheel will lock the first time you turn it.*

• *If the ignition lock has been tampered with or shows any sign of damage (e.g. attempted theft), have the lock checked at your nearest FIAT Service Centre.*

• **UNLOCKING** - Turn the ignition key to MAR to unlock the steering wheel. If necessary, rock the steering wheel gently back and forth while dong so.

# DASHBOARD

## ❏ 3. PANEL INDICATORS

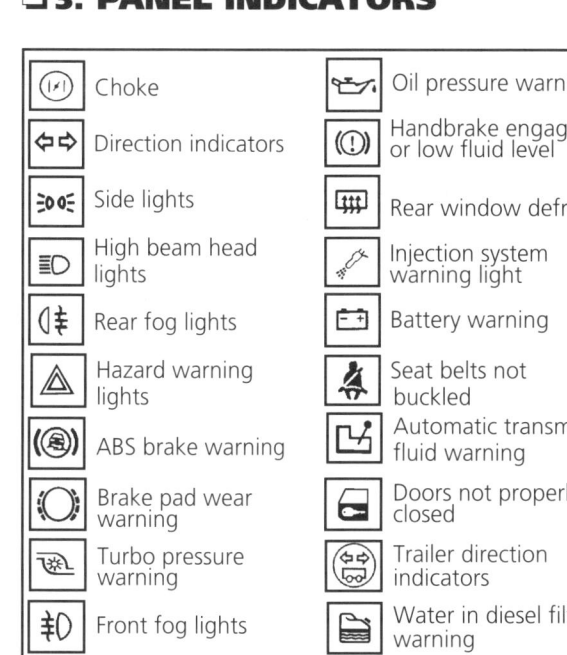

| | | | |
|---|---|---|---|
| ⓘ | Choke | 🛢 | Oil pressure warning |
| ⇦⇨ | Direction indicators | (!) | Handbrake engaged or low fluid level |
| ≡O≣ | Side lights | ⊞ | Rear window defroster |
| ≡D | High beam head lights | | Injection system warning light |
| ⫞ | Rear fog lights | 🔋 | Battery warning |
| ⚠ | Hazard warning lights | | Seat belts not buckled |
| ((⊙)) | ABS brake warning | | Automatic transmission fluid warning |
| | Brake pad wear warning | | Doors not properly closed |
| | Turbo pressure warning | | Trailer direction indicators |
| ⫬O | Front fog lights | | Water in diesel filter warning |
| | Diesel heater/glow plugs | | Air bag malfunction |

### INSTRUMENT DISPLAY PANEL

**3.** These are the instrument panel warning LED indicators for all FIAT Cinquecento models. Your vehicle will only have panel indicators relevant to your particular model.

## ❏ 4. HEATING AND VENTILATION CONTROLS

### 4A. CONTROLS

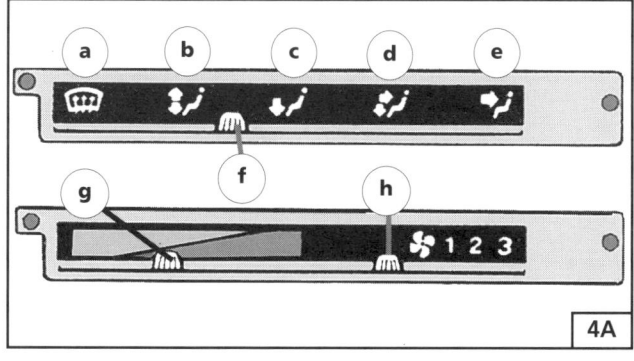

• **Air Distribution Control** - Adjust the air distribution by sliding lever **f** to the desired setting.

• **Air Temperature Control** - The temperature will increase the further you slide the air temperature lever **g** to the right (red zone).

• To decrease temperature slide the temperature control lever **2** to the left (blue zone).

• **Three Speed Fan Control** - Slide the fan speed control lever **h** to select the desired fan speed (operates only when the key is at MAR).

## HEATING
### HEAT DISTRIBUTION

With the air temperature lever (*illustration* **4A**, *control* **g**) in the red zone and the air volume control lever (**h**) turned to the desired fan speed, slide the air distribution lever (**f**) to:

• **a** - Demist the windows.
• **b** - For air directed to footwell and windscreen.
• **c** - To direct heating to footwell vents.
• **d** - Directs air to footwell an dashboard vents.
• **e** - For air directed to the side and centre vents.

When the car is moving the volume of the air entering the passenger compartment can be reduced by sliding the fan lever to the left of speed setting 1.

### AIR CONDITIONING (NOT AVAILABLE IN THE UK)

Air conditioning is an optional extra fitted to some models of Cinquecento.

### AIR CONDITIONING SWITCH

**4B.** To turn the air conditioning ON/OFF press switch.

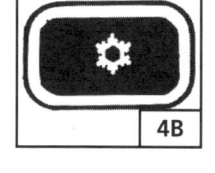

### AIR RECIRCULATION SWITCH

**4C.** When pressed, no outside air enters the passenger compartment. Use the recirculation feature for fast cooling or heating. Select recirculation whenever you drive in heavy traffic, in a tunnel or under any conditions where the air is heavily polluted.

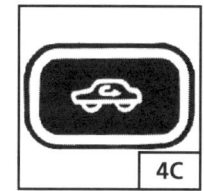

### AIR CONDITIONER COOLING

• Slide the air temperature adjustment lever (*illustration* **4A**, *control* **g**) to the blue zone.
• Turn the air conditioner switch **4B** ON.
• Switch the air volume control lever **h** to fan speed 3.
• Slide the air distribution control lever **f** to the desired setting.

### AIR CONDITIONER HEATING

Sliding the air temperature adjustment lever (*illustration* **4A**, *control* **g**) to the red zone:

• Switch the air volume control lever **h** to the desired fan speed.
• Slide the air distribution control lever **f** to the desired setting.

**IMPORTANT NOTE:** The air conditioner and heater may be used at the same time during winter or whenever the weather is particularly humid, for optimal demisting.

### DEFROSTING THE WINDSCREEN AND WINDOWS

• Slide the air temperature adjustment lever (*illustration* **4A**, *control* **g**) to the red zone.
• Select fan speed 2 or 3.
• Slide the air distribution control lever to its far left position (**a**).
• Press the air conditioner switch for efficient demisting.

CHAPTER 2  USING YOUR CAR

## VENTILATION
- Slide the air temperature control lever **g** to the blue zone.
- Select the fan speed desired.
- Slide the air distribution control lever **f** to the desired setting.

# CONTROLS

## 5. LIGHTS AND INDICATORS

### LIGHT CONTROL SWITCH
**5A.** With the ignition key at MAR, press the external light control switch (arrowed) to the first click to switch on:
- The tail lights and panel indicator.
- Number plate lights.
- Instrument panel light.

### LOW BEAM HEADLIGHTS
Press the light control switch **5A** to the second click to:
- Switch on all of the above and the headlights.

### FULL BEAM HEADLIGHTS
**5B.** The left-hand light control stalk has two settings:
- DOWN - to switch on the full beam headlights.
- UP - returns the headlight to the low beam position.
- All control

buttons light up when the lights are switched ON.
- When the key is at PARK the parking lights remain on no matter what other selections have been made.

### DIRECTION INDICATORS
**5C.** Move the indicator stalk:
- UP - for right turn.
- DOWN - for left turn.

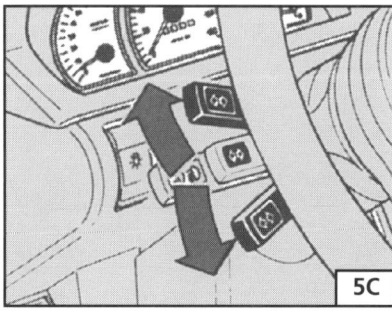

The panel direction indicator flashes when the direction indicators are operating. The stalk return to the central position after completing the turn.

### LIGHT CONTROL STALK (MODELS WITH AIR BAG)
**5D.** On models fitted with an air bag, the panel mounted light control switch is replaced by a single left-hand control stalk. The operation controls for this type of control lever are:

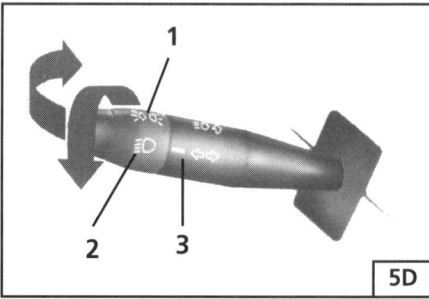

- **Side Lights** - turn the knurled switch at the end of the stalk, so that symbol **1** lines up with notch **3** to switch the side lights ON.
- **Low Beam Headlights** - turn the knurled switch so that symbol **2** lines up with notch **3** to turn on the low beam headlights.
- **Full Beam Headlights** - to turn the full beam headlights ON push the stalk towards the dashboard, pull the stalk back towards the steering wheel to turn the fullbeam OFF.
- **Indicators** - move the stalk upwards to turn on the right indicator, move the stalk down to turn on the left indicator.

## 6. WINDSCREEN WASHER/WIPER

### WINDSCREEN WASHER/WIPER STALK
**6A.** The washer/wiper will only work with the ignition key at MAR.

To operate the windscreen washer/wiper move the stalk to position:

- **0** - Washer/wiper OFF.
- **1** - intermittent wipe.
- **2** - Continuous operation.

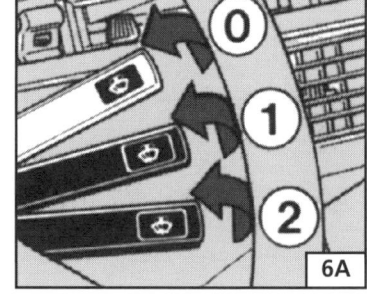

Pull the stalk towards the steering wheel to turn on the windscreen washer.

### WINDSCREEN WASHER/WIPER STALK (MODELS FITTED WITH AIR BAG)
**6B.** To operate the washer/wiper stalk on models fitted with an air bag, position the stalk at:

**0** - Windscreen wiper OFF.
**1** - Intermittent wipe.
**2** - Slow continuous wipe.
**3** - Fast continuous wipe.
**4** - For a temporary action.

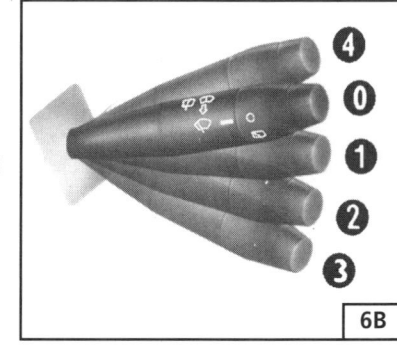

Pulling the stalk towards the steering wheel operates the windscreen washer.

### REAR WINDOW WASHER/WIPER (MODELS FITTED WITH AIR BAG)
**6C.** Rotate the knurled end of the washer/wiper stalk so that **B** lines up with notch **A** to operate the rear window wiper.

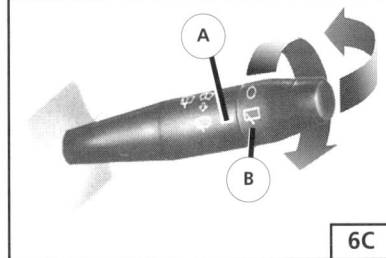

Push the stalk towards the dashboard to operate the temporary action rear window washer.

## ❏ 7. SWITCH BANK
Press the following control bank switches to:

- **1** - switch ON/OFF the hazard lights.
- **2** - turn the rear windscreen washer ON/OFF.
- **3** - turn ON/OFF the rear windscreen wiper.
- **4** - turn ON/OFF the rear foglights.
- **5** - activate the rear screen defrost/demister.

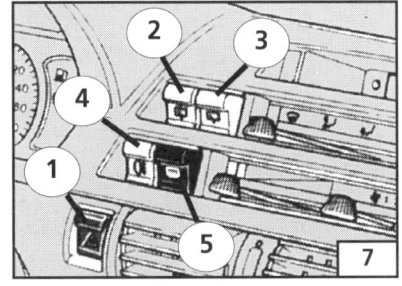

## ❏ 8. FUEL CUT-OFF SWITCH
This safety device switches off the fuel supply to the engine in the event of a head on collision. If the car is involved in a collision and there are no signs of fuel leaks, and the car is in good enough condition to set off again,

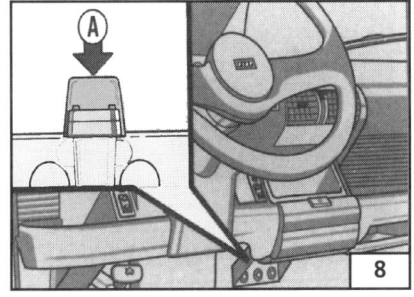

reactivate the fuel feed system by pressing button **A** (arrowed), which is situated under the centre of the dashboard on the engine compartment bulkhead.

# INDIVIDUAL SETTINGS

## ❏ 9. FRONT SEAT ADJUSTMENT

### LEGROOM ADJUSTMENT
Lift lever **A** and exert body pressure in the direction desired to set the seats fore-and-aft position:

- Release lever **A**, when the seat is locked in the desired position.

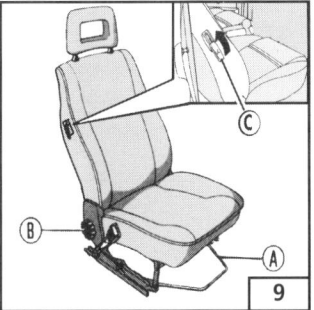

### FRONT SEAT ANGLE ADJUSTMENT
- To adjust the angle of the front seats backrest cushion rotate the adjustable knob **B**.

### ACCESS TO THE BACK SEATS
The front seats can be released and folded forwards by lifting lever **C** (illustration **9**, inset) to gain access to the back seats.

# ACCESSORIES

## ❏ 10. DOOR MIRROR ADJUSTMENT

### MANUAL TYPE
**10A.** Move the internal knob **B** (attached to the door mirror **A**) to adjust the mirror. Move the mirror in the direction arrowed if extra clearance is needed.

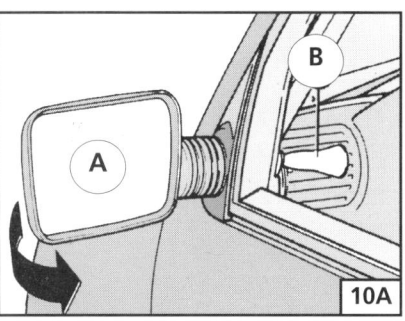

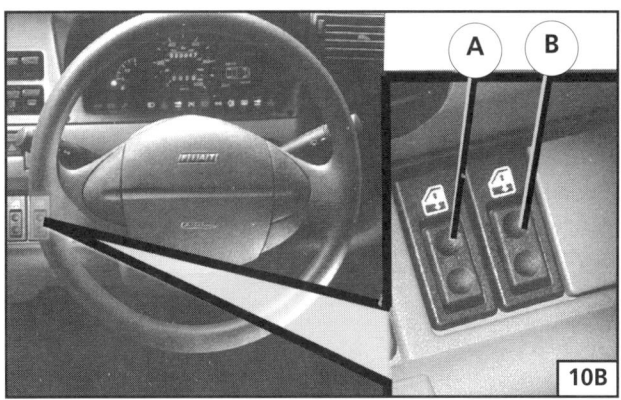

### ELECTRIC WINDOWS
**10B.** There are two switches situated on the dashboard that operate the front electric windows (if fitted) when the key is at MAR:

- **A** - Open and close the front left window.
- **B** - Open and close the front right window.

## ❏ 11. AIR BAG

### AIR BAG SAFETY DEVICE
As an extra safety device, some models are fitted with an air bag, which is stored in the steering wheel. The air bag inflates immediately to protect the driver's chest and face in the event of a head on collision.

IMPORTANT NOTE: All diagnosis, repair and replacement of the air bag device is a specialist job and is potentially dangerous. It must only be carried out by your FIAT Service Centre.

# CHAPTER 2 — USING YOUR CAR

> **SAFETY FIRST!**
> If an air bag has been fitted to your vehicle:
> • DO NOT apply stickers or any other objects to the steering wheel as this may restrict the operation of the air bag.
> • NEVER travel with anything on your lap or in front of your chest.
> • NEVER drive with a cigarette, pipe, pen or any other object in your mouth.

## ❏ 12. SUNROOF OPERATION

### SUNROOF CONTROLS
As an optional extra some models are fitted with a removable sunroof. To operate the manually operated sunroof:

OPENING AND CLOSING THE SUNROOF
**12A.** • Turn knob **A** anti-clockwise to open the sunroof or clockwise to close it.

**Sunscreen Removal**
• Unscrew screw **B** to remove the sunscreen.

A rubber strap which is attached to the rear seats backrest is provided for the storage of the removed sunroof and sunscreen.

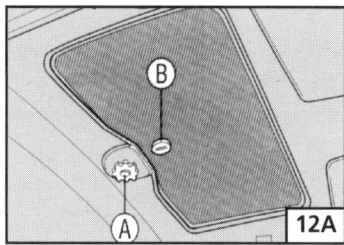

SUNROOF REMOVAL
**12B.** • With the sunroof closed insert a screwdriver into the centre slot of knob **A** (illustration **12A**) and turn the fastening pin.
• Open the sunroof and press lever **C** (arrowed).
• Lift the sunroof and release it from the front springs.

Reverse this procedure to replace the sunroof.

### CANVAS SUNROOF
**12C.** A long electrically operated canvas sunroof can be factory fitted as an optional extra to your Cinquecento and was fitted as standard to Cinquecento 'Soleil'.

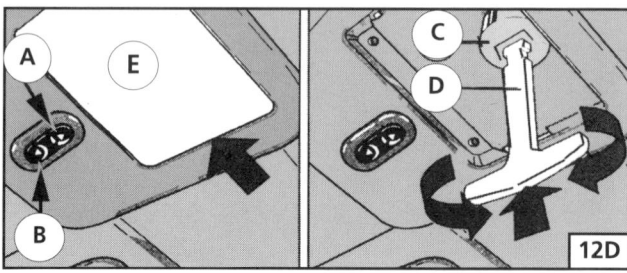

### ELECTRIC SUNROOF
**12D.** To operate this type of electric sunroof:
• Press button **A** to open.
• Press button **B** to close.

If the sunroof motor is faulty:
• Remove the press fitted cover **E** by prising it off with a screwdriver.
• Insert key **D** (which is kept in the document pocket) into the sunroof motor slot **C** and rotate to open or close the sunroof manually.

IMPORTANT NOTE: DO NOT attempt to open this type of sunroof if it is covered with snow or ice as this could damage the sunroof.

## BONNET AND LUGGAGE COMPARTMENT

### ❏ 13. BONNET

**OPENING THE BONNET**
**13A.** Pull the bonnet release lever **A**, toward the steering wheel to release the bonnet catch.

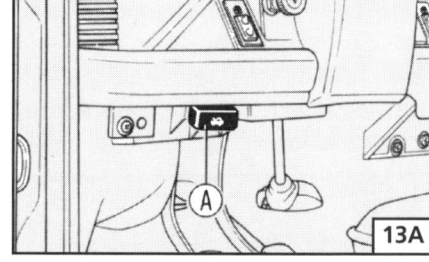

**13B.** Positioned at the front of the bonnet is a release catch **B**. Lift the catch up to release.

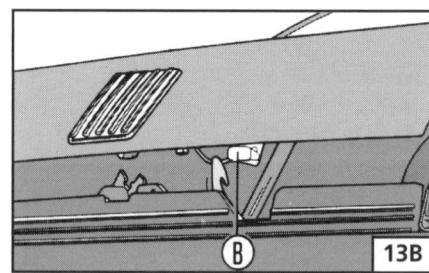

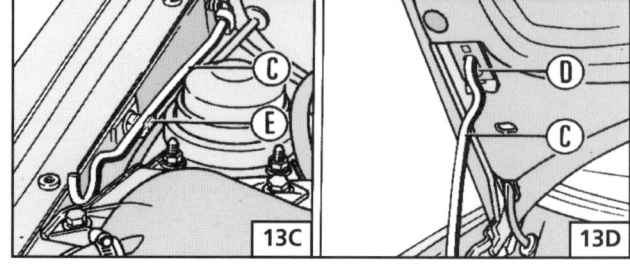

**13C.** Lift the bonnet and pull the support rod **C** out of its holder **E**.

**13D.** When the bonnet is fully raised, place the tip of the rod **C** in to the recess **D** located in the bonnet.

2-6

## ❏ 14. LUGGAGE COMPARTMENT

### FOLDING THE BACK SEATS
Use the following procedure to fold the rear seat forwards:

• Pull the strap at the centre of the backseat cushion in an upwards direction to swing up the seat cushion.

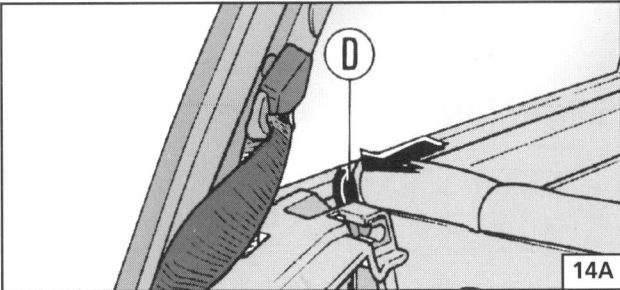

**14A.** Pull lever **D** up to release the seat backrest.

**14B.** Fold the backrest cushion forwards. (N.B. UK cars not fitted with split rear seats.)

To repositioning the back seats, reverse the order described above.

## WHEEL CHANGING

### ❏ 15. CHANGING THE WHEEL IN AN EMERGENCY

#### CHANGING A WHEEL
Whenever possible park the car on firm level ground. Put the car into reverse gear and pull on the handbrake. Keep chocks or pieces of wood in the boot of your car, which can be wedged in front and behind the diagonally-opposite wheel to the one being removed to prevent the car from rolling. If you haven't got a piece of wood handy, use large rocks or stones.

**15A.** The location of the spare wheel, jack and tools is in the luggage compartment under the mat.

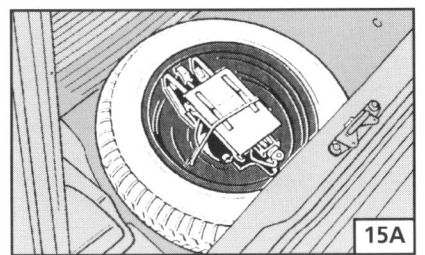

Undo the elastic retaining strap to release the tools and jack from within the spare wheel.

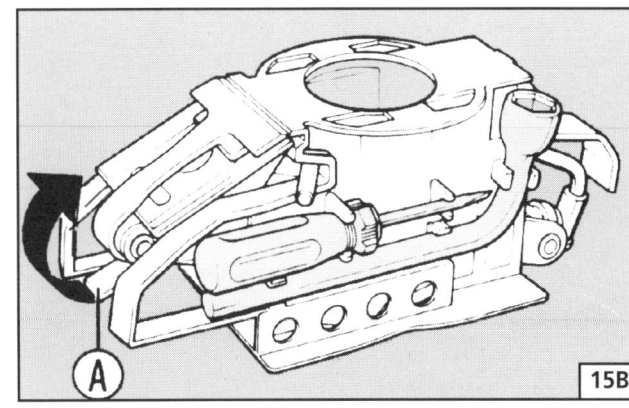

**15B.** Release the jack from the tool stand by lifting tab **A** in the direction arrowed.

### ❏ 16. RAISING THE VEHICLE

**16A.** To raise the vehicle, position the jack under the side member at position **A** or **B**.

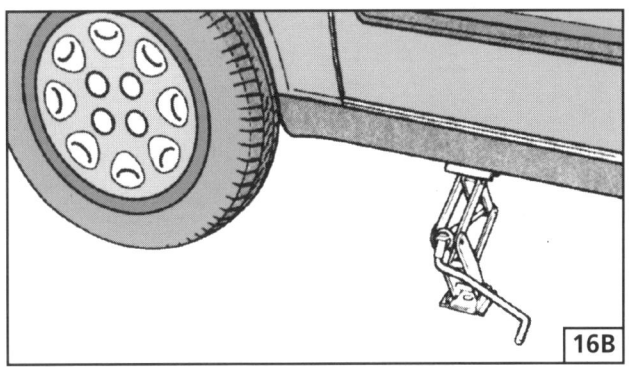

**16B.** Turn the jack handle until its grooved head fits the flange at the base of the sill.

#### REMOVING A WHEEL

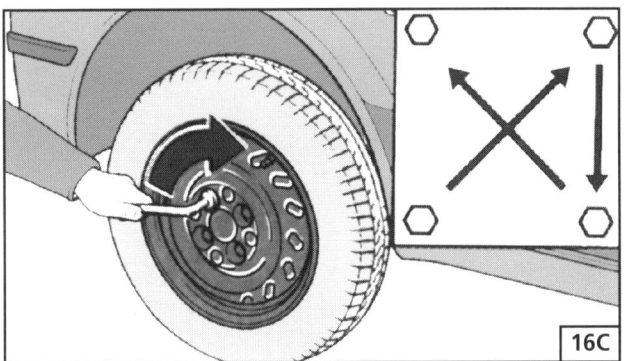

**16C.** Loosen all the wheel bolts in the order shown in the inset illustration.

**CHAPTER 2 USING YOUR CAR**

**2-7**

- Lift the car until the tyre is off the ground.
- Remove the hub cap, then unscrew the fourth wheel bolt, and remove the wheel.
- Put the spare wheel on, making sure that the aligning peg or pegs on the hub fits into the hole/s in the rim.
- Tighten the wheel bolts finger tight.
- Lower the car so that enough wieght is placed on the wheel to stop it spinning.
Tighten the wheel bolts evenly in a criss-cross fashion (see illustration **16C**, inset).
- Completely lower the vehicle and remove the jack.

IMPORTANT NOTES: If the spare wheel is a safety (space-saver) wheel:-
- DO NOT fit the the hub cap on to the spare wheel.
- DO NOT drive the vehicle at more than 50 mph (80 kph).
- Only inflate the tyre to 32 psi (2.2 bar).
- Remember that the wheel only has a life-span of 1,800 miles (3,000 km).
- Never drive with more than one space-saver wheel fitted.

### RAISING THE VEHICLE WITH A TROLLEY JACK

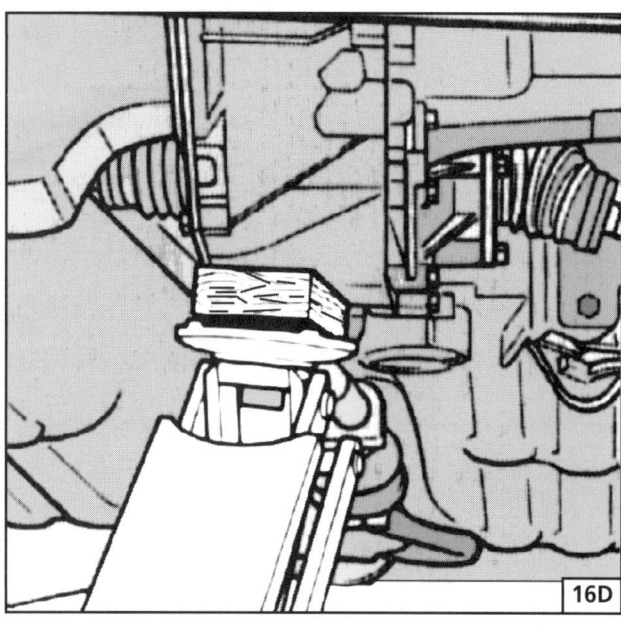

- **16D.** FROM THE FRONT: Place a hardwood block between the jack and the car. The jack must only be positioned under the gearbox case support with the short end of the block facing the front of the car.

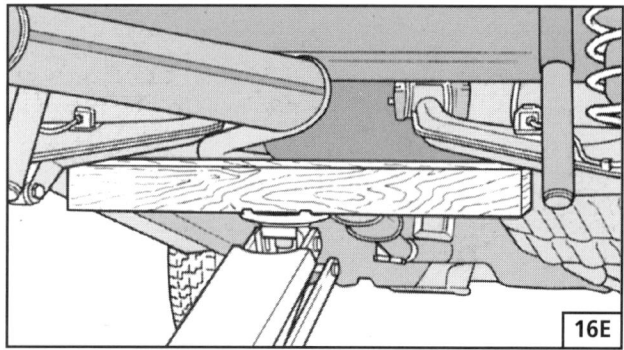

- **16E.** FROM THE REAR: Put a hardwood block between the jack and the car positioned only between the two suspension struts.

# EMERGENCY STARTING

## ❏ ENGINE STARTING

### JUMP STARTING YOUR CAR
Choose a fully charged battery with the same or higher capacity than the flat battery in your car, then . . .

- Make sure that the car with the flat battery has its electrical equipment turned off and that the ignition key is removed.

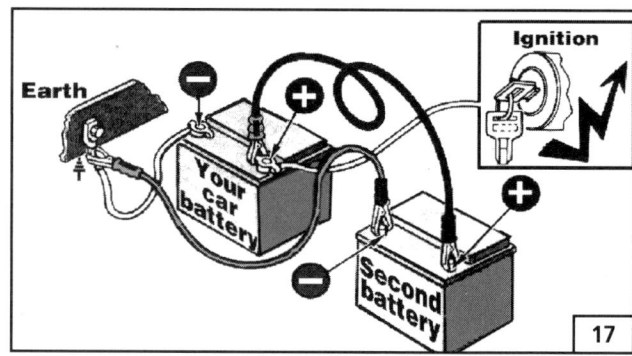

- **17.** Connect one of the jump lead clamps to the positive battery post of your flat battery. Then clamp the other end of the same lead on to the positive post of the second (charged) battery.
- Connect one end of the second jump lead to the negative pole of the charged battery, and attach the other end to the metal terminal (as shown) of the earth cable from your car's flat battery.
- Run the engine of the car with the charged battery at a medium to slow speed.
- Start the engine of the car with the flat battery, and run the engines of both cars for about three minutes.
- To reduce voltage peaks when disconnecting the jump leads, turn on the air fan and the heated rear screen of the car that had the flat battery.
- Remove the jumpleads, starting with the negative clamp from the car with the flat battery.

IMPORTANT NOTE: When disconnecting the jump leads DO NOT switch on the headlights in place of the heated rear screen, as the peak voltage may blow the headlight bulbs.

### BUMP STARTING
IMPORTANT NOTE: Never bump start a car fitted with a catalytic converter, as the sudden rush of unburnt fuel into the catalytic converter could damage the converter beyond repair. All UK Cinquecentos are fitted with catalytic converters.

# CHAPTER 3
# FACTS AND FIGURES

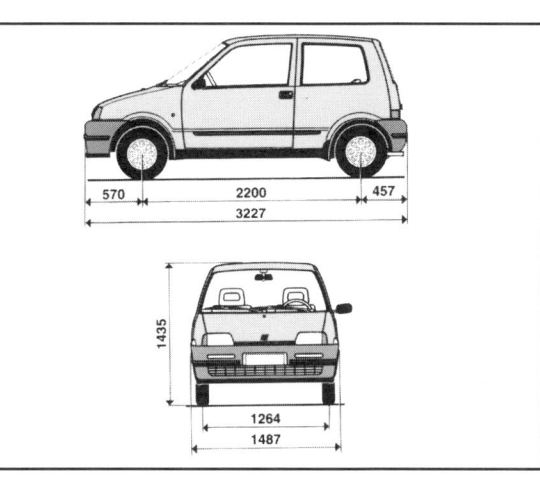

This chapter provides you with all the information you will need about your car, especially in connection with servicing and repairing it. First, you'll need to identify the engine type. If you don't know it already, see *Chapter 6, Repairs and Replacements*.

Before buying parts, be sure to take your vehicle's chassis (VIN) and spares numbers with you - see *Auto-Biography* on *page i* and *PART G: IDENTIFICATION NUMBERS* in this chapter.

## Chapter Contents

|  | Page No. |  | Page No. |
|---|---|---|---|
| PART A: MAJOR MILESTONES | 3-1 | PART E: REPAIR DATA | 3-3 |
| PART B: VITAL STATISTICS | 3-2 | PART F: TORQUE WRENCH SETTINGS | 3-4 |
| PART C: CAPACITIES | 3-2 | PART G: IDENTIFICATION NUMBERS | 3-6 |
| PART D: SERVICE DATA | 3-2 |  |  |

IMPORTANT NOTE: Many detail changes take place over the production life of a vehicle available. The following information will be true of most cases but can only be taken as a general guide. Consult your local FIAT dealer for confirmation.

## PART A: MAJOR MILESTONES

**Overview** The 'new 'FIAT 500', introduced into the UK in May 1993, is a successful attempt to combine the cheeky attractiveness and tiny size of the original 500 with modern efficiency and reliability. There is only one body style - 3-door hatchback - although there are different levels of body trim, according to model, and all are front-drive only (no Panda-like 4x4 option), with five-speed manual transmission. All cars were well equipped at introduction, with tinted glass, rear wash-wipe, remote tailgate release and stereo radio/cassette player. Three very different engine types are fitted - two of them on offer in the UK: the OHV 900 and the 1.1 with OHC FIRE (Fully-Integrated Robotised Engine) unit. In Italy and some other markets, the flat-twin 704cc engine carries echoes of the original FIAT 500.

**May 1993** *Cinquecento 900* introduced: Known as *S* and *SX* in the UK. Fitted with mildly developed version of the well-established iron-block OHV engines, inherited from the 127, Panda and Uno, with the same (903cc) capacity* for Italy, but with slightly reduced capacity (899cc) for the UK and other export markets. All 899cc engines with quieter, hydraulic valve tappets. *900 SX* also has electric front windows, glass sunroof and remote central locking.

**January 1994** Changed fascia - now 2-tone - with illuminated switches and brighter interior trim. *SX* retains central locking but no longer remote.

**January 1995** *Cinquecento Sporting* with 1.1 litre FIRE engine and 54 bhp launched in the UK. Alloy wheels with low-profile tyres; body coloured bumpers/skirts and mirrors. Inside the car, sports seats, electric door widows and central locking fitted as standard, with sunroof optional.

**March 1995** VIN (Vehicle Identity Number) etched into the front and rear screens and chassis number into all other glass.

**June 1995** General range revision - still consisting of '*S*', '*SX*' and Sporting, all of which now get the FIAT code immobiliser system. '*SX*' gets body coloured bumpers, side rubbing strips, a centre console inside the car and wider (155/65R13) tyres. 899cc engine management system modified to meet more stringent exhaust emission limits..

**June 1996** *Cinquecento Soleil* special edition model available, based on the *SX* but with a large electric folding sunroof and unique trims.

## PART B: VITAL STATISTICS

### Fuel Tank

All models - 35 litres.

### Wheels and Tyres

| ENGINE | WHEEL RIM SIZE | RADIAL TUBELESS TYRE TYPE | TYRE PRESSURES (cold) FRONT | | REAR | |
|---|---|---|---|---|---|---|
| | | | average load | heavy load | average load | heavy load |
| 900 | 4.00 x 13H OR 4.5J x 13H (steel) | 155/65R 13 OR 145/70R 13 | 2.0 bar/29 psi 2.1 bar/30 psi | 2.2 bar/32 psi 2.2 bar/32 psi | 2.0 bar/29 psi 2.1 bar/30 psi | 2.2 bar/32 psi 2.2 bar/32 psi |
| 1.1 | 5.5J x 13H2 (alloy) | 165/55R 13 | | | | |
| Spare wheel (Speed limit 50 mph) | 4.50 x 13 | 135/70R 13 | 2.2/32 psi | | | |

### Weights and Dimensions

All weights in kg. All sizes in mm.

The addition of accessories will increase the kerb weight thus lowering the maximum laden weight. Figures below do not include air conditioning, sun roof, tow hitch etc.

Maximum roof load - 50 kg (all models)
Weight on towball, when fitted - 20-35 kg. According to FIAT, models with air conditioning (non-UK) must not be used for towing.

| VEHICLE | UNLADEN WEIGHT | MAXIMUM LADEN WEIGHT | TOWABLE LIMITS WITHOUT BRAKES | WITH BRAKES | OVERALL LENGTH | OVERALL WIDTH* | WHEEL BASE | FRONT TRACK | REAR TRACK | HEIGHT (unladen) |
|---|---|---|---|---|---|---|---|---|---|---|
| 900 | 710 | 1150 | 350 | 400 | 3227 | 1487 | 2200 | 1264 | 1257 | 1435 |
| 1.1 | 735 | 1150 | 350 | 400 | 3227 | 1487 | 2200 | 1264 | 1257 | 1425 |

* (not including mirrors)

## PART C: CAPACITIES

See **RECOMMENDED LUBRICANTS** on the *inside of back cover*.

## PART D: SERVICE DATA

**All settings in mm. unless stated otherwise.**

All '900' figures are for the 899cc engine used in the UK and export markets outside Italy.

### Engine

FIRING ORDER: All models: 1-3-4-2
IGNITION TYPE: Electronic Marelli-Weber static advance injection. Ignition determined by electronic control unit receiving information from engine sensors: rpm, piston position (TDC sensor) and intake manifold vacuum.

IGNITION TIMING in degrees Before Top Dead Centre - BTDC:
**900** 850 rpm - 6 to 10 degrees.
4,200 to 5,000 rpm - 40 to 44 degrees.
**1.1** Set by ECU - not adjustable.

RPM/TDC FLYWHEEL SENSOR GAP: 1.1 ONLY - 0.5 to 1.5

| SPARK PLUG TYPES AND GAPS | | | |
|---|---|---|---|
| Model | FIAT | Champion | Gap (mm) |
| 900 | 9FYSSR | RN9YCC | 0.85 to 0.95 |
| 1.1 | 9GYSSR | RC9YCC | 0.85 to 0.95 |

IDLE SPEED: 800 to 900 rpm.

CO CONTENT AT IDLE (MAX): 0.5% (899cc) 0.35% (1108cc)

| VALVE CLEARANCES (mm) (Check when engine cold) | Inlet | Exhaust |
|---|---|---|
| 900 | Hydraulic, not adjustable | |
| 1.1 | 0.35 to 0.45 | 0.45 to 0.55 |

### Other settings

CLUTCH ADJUSTMENT: Adjustable pedal position see **Chapter 5, Servicing Your Car**.
BRAKE DISC PAD MINIMUM THICKNESS: 1.5
BRAKE SHOE FRICTION LINING MINIMUM THICKNESS: 1.5

## PART E: REPAIR DATA

### Engine 'bottom end'

IMPORTANT NOTE: It appears that different piston and piston ring sizes (both with different clearances) were used on some versions. Have your supplier check the size of your original pistons and rings before buying replacements and check the information given below. Note that specifications (i) relates to Italian-built engines, pre-March 1995 with engine number above 8,600,000; (ii) relate to Yugoslavian-built engines, pre-March 1995 with engine numbers below 8,600,000; (iii) relate to engines, post-March 1995 with engine numbers above 9,107,830.

|  | 900 engines<br>All dimensions common to 899cc and 903cc except where shown. | 1.1 Litre |
|---|---|---|
| BORE: | 65-65.05 | 70 |
| STROKE: | 67.7 | 72 |
| REBORE SIZE: | Steps of 0.01 | Steps of 0.01 |

ENGINE CAMSHAFT BEARING DIAMETERS - FRONT (TIMING GEAR) END (OHV engines only):
| Grade B | 50.485-50.5 | - |
| Grade C | 50.495-50.51 | - |
| Grade D | 50.685-50.7 | - |
| Grade E | 50.695-50.71 | - |

PISTON SIZES:

Piston height: See illustration.
(i) x = 40
(ii) y = 13.35
(iii) y = 14

| Diameter A | (i) 64.94-64.95<br>(ii) 64.971-64.989<br>(iii) 64.95-64.96 | 69.96-69.97 |
| Diameter B |  | 69.97-69.98 |
| Diameter C | (i) 64.96-64.97<br>(ii) 64.991-65.009<br>(iii) 64.97-64.98 | 69.98-69.99 |
| Diameter E | (i) 64.98-64.99<br>(ii) 65.011-65.029<br>(iii) 64.99-65.0 |  |
| OVERSIZES: | 0.4 | 0.4 |
| PISTON CLEARANCES IN BORE: | (i) 0.05-0.07<br>(ii) 0.011-0.039<br>(iii) 0.04-0.06 | 0.03-0.05 |

PISTON RING THICKNESS:
| TOP | (i) and (ii) 1.728-1.74<br>(iii) 1.478-1.49 | 1.175-1.19 |
| SECOND | (i) and (ii) 1.978-1.99<br>(iii) 1.475-1.49 | 1.175-1.19 |
| BOTTOM | (i) and (ii) 3.925-3.937<br>(iii) 2.978-2.99 | 2.475-2.49 |

PISTON RING CLEARANCES - RING-TO-GROOVE:
| TOP | (i) 0.05-0.082<br>(ii) 0.045-0.077<br>(iii) 0.045-0.077 | 0.04-0.08 |
| SECOND | (i) 0.04-0.072<br>(ii) 0.025-0.057<br>(iii) 0.045-0.08 | 0.02-0.055 |
| BOTTOM | (i) 0.03-0.062<br>(ii) 0.02-0.052<br>(iii) 0.02-0.052 | 0.02-0.055 |

PISTON RING END GAP:
| TOP | (i) 0.25-0.45<br>(ii) 0.2-0.35<br>(iii) 0.25-0.45 | 0.25-0.45 |
| SECOND | (i) 0.2-0.35<br>(ii) 0.2-0.35<br>(iii) 0.2-0.4 | 0.25-0.45 |
| BOTTOM | (i) 0.2-0.45<br>(ii) 0.2-0.35<br>(iii) 0.2-0.45 | 0.2-0.45 |

PISTON RING OVERSIZES:
| | 0.4 | 0.4 |

CRANK MAIN JOURNAL DIAMETER:
| Size 1 | 50.795-50.805 | 43.994-44 |
| Size 2 | 50.785-50.795 | 43.994-43.998 |
| Size 3 | - | 43.982-43.998 |

|  | 900 cc | 1.1 Litre |
|---|---|---|
| CRANK, BIG-END DIAMETER: | 39.985-40.005 | 37.99-38.008 |

MAIN BEARING SHELL THICKNESS:
| Size 1 | 1.832-1.838 | 1.836-1.84 |
| Size 2 | 1.837-1.843 | 1.841-1.845 |
| Size 3 | - | 1.846-1.85 |

MAIN BEARING CLEARANCE:
|  | 0.026-0.061 | Size 1: 0.025-0.043<br>Size 2: 0.027-0.045<br>Size 3: 0.029-0.047 |

MAIN BEARING UNDERSIZES:
|  | 0.254, 0.508 | 0.254, 0.508 |

BIG-END BEARING SHELL THICKNESS (STANDARD):
|  | 1.807-1.813 | 1.544-1.548 |

BIG-END BEARING CLEARANCE:
|  | 0.026-0.074 | 0.024-0.06 |

BIG-END BEARING UNDERSIZES:
|  | 0.254, 0.508 | 0.254-0.508 |

THRUST WASHER THICKNESS:
|  | 2.31-2.36 | 2.31-2.36 |

THRUST WASHER OVERSIZE:
|  | 0.127 | 0.127 |

CRANKSHAFT END FLOAT:
|  | 0.06-0.26 | 0.055-0.265 |

### Engine 'top end' and valve gear

CAMSHAFT BEARING OUTER DIAMETERS (OHC Engines only): 1 = Front
| - | 1: 24.045-24.07 |
| - | 2: 23.545-23.57 |
| - | 3: 24.045-24.07 |

CAM FOLLOWER DIAMETER:
| - | 34.975-34.995 |

CAM FOLLOWER BORE CLEARANCE:
| - | 0.005-0.05 |

INLET VALVE HEAD SIZE:
| 28.8-29.1 | 31.2-31.5 |

EXHAUST VALVE HEAD SIZE:
| 25.8-26.1 | - |

VALVE SEAT RE-CUTTING ANGLE:
| 45 degrees 55'<br>to 45 degrees 5' | 45 degrees 55'<br>-45 degrees 5' |

VALVE FACE RE-CUTTING ANGLE:
| 45 degrees 25'<br>to 45 degrees 35' | 45 degrees 25'<br>-45 degrees 35' |

OHC VALVE SHIM THICKNESSES:
| - | Between 3.2 and 4.7 mm in shim increments of 0.05 mm |

### Cooling system

All figures in degrees Celsius unless stated otherwise.

THERMOSTAT:
| Starts to open | 85-89 | 85-89 |
| Fully open | 97-100 | 100 |
| Valve travel | up to 7.5 mm | up to 7.5 mm |

PRESSURE CAP RATING:
| | 0.98 bar | 0.98 bar |

COOLING FAN:
| Switches on | 90-94 | 90-94 |
| Switches off | 85-89 | 85-90 |

WATER TIGHTNESS PRESSURE CHECK:
| | 0.98 bar | 0.98 bar |

### Clutch

LINING, OUTER DIAMETER (1), mm:
| | 170 | 181.5 |

LINING, INNER DIAMETER (2), mm:
| | 120 | 127 |

## CHAPTER 3 FACTS AND FIGURES

|  | 900 cc | 1.1 Litre |
|---|---|---|
| **Brakes** | | |
| GAP - SERVO PISTON PUSHROD FROM SUPPORT PLATE: | 0.825-1.025 | 0.825-1.025 |
| MINIMUM ALLOWED FRONT DISC THICKNESS (mm): | 9.2 | 9.2 |
| MAXIMUM ALLOWED BRAKE DRUM INTERNAL DIAMETER (mm): | 186.83 | 186.83 |

### Running gear/suspension - front

All figures with vehicle in running order, up to 5 litres of fuel in tank and correct tyre pressures.

CAMBER (not adjustable):
  29 degrees 30' to 30 degrees 30'  —  29 degrees 55' to 30 degrees 5'
FRONT CASTER (not adjustable):
  1 degree 10' to 2 degrees 10'  —  1 degree 6' to -2 degrees 6'
TOE-IN (adjustable):
  -1 mm to +1 mm  —  -1 mm to +1 mm
FRONT SPRING HEIGHT RELEASED (mm):
  about 320  —  324
FRONT SPRING when the given load in Nm is applied, the spring height should the figure shown in brackets:
  2210-2430 Nm (172 mm)  —  2450-2650 Nm (153.7 mm)
REPLACEMENT FRONT SPRING COLOURS: If new springs fail to give the above heights, YELLOW springs give LOWER heights; GREEN springs give HIGHER. ALWAYS use them in pairs of same colour.

### Rear suspension

All figures with vehicle in running order, up to 5 litres of fuel in tank and correct tyre pressures.

CAMBER (not adjustable):
  0 degrees to 1 degree  —  -29' to +31'
TOE-IN (not adjustable):
  -3 mm to +3 mm  —  -4 mm to +2 mm
REAR COIL SPRING HEIGHT, RELEASED (mm):
  about 308  —  301
REAR SPRING when the given load in Nm is applied, the spring height should be the figure shown in brackets:
  2570-2830 Nm (195 mm)  —  2680-2800 Nm (185 mm)
REPLACEMENT REAR SPRING COLOURS: If new springs fail to give the above heights, YELLOW springs give LOWER heights; GREEN springs give HIGHER. ALWAYS use them in pairs of same colour.

## PART F: TORQUE WRENCH SETTINGS

IMPORTANT NOTE: All torque wrench settings shown in Newton-metres (Nm). Bolt, nut or screw sizes in brackets in left-hand column.

### 900cc ENGINE (OHV)

**Engine**

| 900cc Engine (OHV) | Torque (Nm) |
|---|---|
| Main bearing caps fixing, bolt (M10 x 1.25) | 69 |
| Sump to crankcase fixing, bolt (M6) | 10 |
| Sump to timing cover and to crankshaft support oil cover (fly-wheel side) fixing, nut (M6) | 10 |
| Cylinder head to crankcase fixing, bolt (M9) | 30 degrees + 90 degrees + 90 degrees |
| Engine mounting fixing, bolt and nut (M8) | 25 |
| Engine mounting flange fixing, nut (M10 x 1.25) | 49 |
| Flange to bodyshell fixing, bolt with unlosable, tapered flexible washer (M8) | 24 |
| Mounting bracket to bodyshell fixing, bolt (M8) | 24 |
| Mounting to bracket fixing, bolt with tapered end and unlosable washer (M10) | 49 |
| Mounting bracket to gearbox casing fixing, bolt (M8) | 24 |
| Mounting bracket to differential fixing, nut for bolt (M12 x 1.25) | 88 |

| 900cc Engine (OHV) | Torque (Nm) |
|---|---|
| Mounting to bracket fixing, nut for bolt (M10 x 1.25) | 49 |
| Mounting bracket to bodyshell fixing, bolt with tapered end and unlosable flexible washer (M8) | 24 |
| Bracket to differential support fixing, bolt (M10 x 1.25) | 70 |
| Bracket to mounting fixing, bolt (M10 x 1.25) | 50 |
| Flexible mounting to support fixing, nut (M10 x 1.25) | 40 |
| Exhaust manifold to cylinder head fixing, nut (M8) | 20 |
| Tappet cover fixing, nuts (M6) | 8 |
| Flywheel cover fixing, bolt (M6) | 10 |
| Big end bolt (M8 x 1) | 41 |
| Flywheel to crankshaft fixing, bolt (M8) | 44 |
| Oil pressure switch (M14 x 1.5) | 49 |
| Rocker arm supports to cylinder head fixing, nut for studs (M10 x 1.25) | 39 |
| Drive pulley fixing, nut (M18 x 1.5) | 98 |
| Fuel pump cam driven gear to camshaft fixing, bolt (M10 x 1.25) | 49 |
| Spark plugs (M14 x 1.25) | 28 |
| Water temperature sender unit (M16 tapered) | 35 |

3-4

## Engine exhaust

| 900cc Engine (OHV) | Torque (Nm) |
|---|---|
| Exhaust pipe to cylinder head fixing, nut (M8) | 20 |
| Flange to exhaust manifold fixing, nut (M8) | 18 |
| Exhaust pipe sections joining collar fixing, nut for bolts (M8) | 24 |

## Clutch

| | |
|---|---|
| Clutch mechanism to engine flywheel fixing, bolt (M6) | 10 |
| Clutch release fork fixing, bolt (M8) | 25 |

## Gearbox and differential

| | |
|---|---|
| Gearbox control lever support bridge fixing, nut (M6 x 1) | 4.4 |
| Selector pipe join to gear control lever, nut for bolt (M6 x 1) | 7.4 |
| Selector pipe support bracket fixing, bolt (M8 x 1.25) | 24 |
| Rod spring retaining cover fixing, bolt (M8 x 1.25) | 25 |
| Cover to gearbox casing fixing, bolt (M8 x 1.25) | 25 |
| Gearbox casing to bell housing fixing, bolt (M8 x 1.25) | 25 |
| Cover on bell housing to engine fixing, bolt (M6 x 1) | 10 |
| Flange retaining differential casing to gearbox casing fixing, bolt (M8 x 1.25) | 25 |
| Plate and cover to gearbox casing fixing, bolt (M8 x 1.25) | 25 |
| Speedometer mounting fixing, bolt (M6 x 1) | 12 |
| Tapered, threaded gearbox oil drain plug (M22 x 1.5) | 46 |
| Gear fork and selector fixing, bolt (M6 x 1) | 18 |

## External gearbox controls

| | |
|---|---|
| Upper mounting (rod side) to bodyshell fixing, bolt (M8) | 25 |
| Rear mounting (rod side) to bodyshell fixing, bolt (M8) | 25 |
| Upper reaction bracket to gearbox support fixing, bolt (M8) | 22 |
| Lower reaction bracket to gearbox support fixing, bolt (M8) | 22 |

## Braking system

| | |
|---|---|
| Brake caliper mounting bracket to steering knuckle fixing, bolt (M10 x 1.25) | 55 |
| Brake disc to hub fixing, bolt (M8) | 12 |
| Upper and lower brake back plate to stub axle fixing, bolt (M8) | 24 |
| Brake drum to hub fixing, bolt (M8) | 12 |
| Handbrake lever mounting fixing, bolt (M8) | 15 |
| Handbrake adjustment nut (M12 x 1.5) | 28 |
| Wheel cylinder to brake back plate fixing, bolt (M6) | 10 |
| Pressure regulators fixing, bolt (M8) | 24 |
| Brake pump and pressure regulator mounting brackets to brake servo fixing, nut (M8) | 20 |
| Brake servo to pedals mounting fixing, nut (M8) | 25 |
| Brake and clutch pedals mounting fixing, nut (M8) | 15 |
| Brake and clutch pedals fixing, nut (M8) | 32 |

## Steering

| | |
|---|---|
| Steering wheel to steering column fixing, nut (M16 x 1.5) | 50 |
| Universal joint fork to steering column fixing, nut (M8) | 20 |
| Steering track rod end to steering knuckle fixing, nut (M10 x 1.25) | 34 |

| 900cc Engine (OHV) | Torque (Nm) |
|---|---|
| Side steering rod fixing, nut (M12 x 1.5) | 34 |
| Steering column to bodywork mounting rear fixing, nut (M8) | 24 |
| Steering column to bodywork mounting front fixing, nut (M6) | 4.7 |
| Steering rack to bodywork fixing, bolt (M10 x 1.25) | 52 |

## Front suspension

| | |
|---|---|
| Upper shock absorber fixing, nut (M12 x 1.25) | 88 |
| Shock absorber mounting to bodyshell fixing, nut (M8) | 27 |
| Shock absorber to steering knuckle fixing, nut (M12 x 1.25) | 108 |
| Front track control arm to bodyshell fixing, nut (M12 x 1.25) | 88 |
| Rear track control arm to bodyshell fixing, bolt (M12 x 1.25) | 88 |
| Ball joint to steering knuckle fixing, nut (M10 x 1.25) | 49 |
| Wheel nut fixing, nut with collar (M22 x 1.5) | 24 |
| Wheel bolts/nuts (M12 x 1.25) | 86 |

## Rear suspension

| | |
|---|---|
| Track control arm to chassis fixing, nut (M12 x 1.25) | 88 |
| Shock absorber upper and lower fixing, bolt (M10 x 1.25) | 49 |
| Wheel hub fixing, nut (M20 x 1.5) | 225 |
| Chassis front and rear fixing, bolt (M12 x 1.25) | 88 |
| Buffer to chassis fixing, bolt (M8) | 10 |
| Wheel nuts/bolts (M12 x 1.25) | 86 |

## Bodywork

| | |
|---|---|
| Seat belt to adjuster fixing, bolt (7/16") | 40 |
| Sear belt to side member fixing, bolt (7/16") | 40 |
| Internal fixings on seat for seat belts, bolt (7/16") | 40 |
| Adjuster to steering knuckle upper fixing, bolt (M8) | 20 |
| Adjuster to steering knuckle lower fixing, bolt (M8) | 20 |

## 1.1 LITRE ENGINE (OHC)

(See **900cc ENGINE** for fixings common to both types and for running gear and bodywork.)

| 1.1 Litre Engine (OHC) | Torque (Nm) |
|---|---|
| Main bearing cap, bolt (M10 x 1.25) | 40 + 90 degrees |
| Cylinder head to crankcase fixing, bolt (M9) | 30 degrees + 90 degrees + 90 degrees |
| Flywheel to crankshaft fixing, bolt (M8) | 44 |
| Drive gear to crankshaft fixing, bolt (M10 x 1.25) | 10 |
| Camshaft driven gear fixing, bolt (M10 x 1.25) | 70 |
| Crankshaft front and rear covers to crankcase fixing, bolt (M6) | 10 |
| Camshaft caps fixing, bolt (M8 x 1.25) | 20 |
| (M8) | 10 |
| Belt tensioner fixing, nut (M8) | 28 |
| Pump coolant intake pipe fixing, bolt (M6) | 10 |
| Tappet cover fixing, bolt (M6) | 8 |
| Water pump to crankcase fixing, bolt (M6) | 8 |
| Water pump to crankcase fixing, bolt (M6) | 10 |
| Alternator drive pulley fixing, bolt (M8) | 25 |
| Plate to oil pump casing fixing, bolt (M6) | 7 |
| Oil sump to crankcase fixing, bolt (M6) | 10 |
| Oil sump to covers fixing, nut (M6) | 10 |
| Alternator to crankcase fixing and adjustment, bolt (M10 x 1.25) | 50 |
| Engine mounting fixing, nut (M10 x 1.25) | 59 |
| Engine mounting fixing, bolt (M10 x 1.25) | 59 |
| Mounting to support fixing, nut (M10 x 1.25) | 59 |

## 1.1 Litre Engine (OHC) — Torque (Nm)

Inlet manifold to cylinder head fixing,
bolt (M8) ................................................. 27
Accelerator bracket to inlet manifold
fixing, bolt (M8) ....................................... 25
Union on inlet manifold for brake servo
vacuum pick-up (14 x 1.5 tapered) ........... 35
Butterfly casing to inlet manifold fixing,
bolt (M6) ................................................... 7
Oil pressure switch (M14 x 1.5) ................ 32
Spark plugs (M14 x 1.5) ............................ 27
Exhaust manifold fixing, nut (M8) ............. 24
Flange to exhaust pipe fixing, nut (M8) .... 24
Pipe mounting bracket to differential side
power unit mounting fixing, bolt (M8) ...... 24
Bracket to bodyshell for exhaust pipe, front
section, fixing, nut (M10 x 1.25) ............... 45
Hot air intake fixing, bolt (M6) .................. 55
Controls support to gearbox casing fixing,
bolt with flange (M8) ................................ 20
Speedometer drive shaft fixing,
bolt with flange (M6) .................................. 5
Selector lever on controls support fixing,
bolt with flange (M8) ................................ 15

## 1.1 Litre Engine (OHC) — Torque (Nm)

Differential casing retaining flange to
complete support fixing, bolt (M8) ........... 20
Gearbox casing to bell housing fixing,
bolt (M8) ................................................. 20
Cover to gearbox casing fixing,
bolt with flange (M6) .................................. 5
Differential cover to bell housing fixing,
bolt with flange
(M8) .......................................................... 20
(M10 x 1.25) ............................................ 35
Gearbox oil filler plug (M22 x 1.5 tapered) .. 40
Gearbox oil drain plug (M16 x 1.5 tapered) .. 22
Engine/gearbox lower reinforcement to
gearbox fixing, nut (M10 x 1.25) ............. 35
Engine/gearbox lower reinforcement to
gearbox fixing, bolt (M12 x 1.25) ............ 50
Engine/gearbox upper reinforcement to
crankcase fixing, bolt (M8) ...................... 28
Gearbox to engine fixing,
stud bolt (M12 x 1.25) ............................. 40
Gearbox to engine fixing,
bolt (M12 x 1.25) ..................................... 85
Gearbox to engine fixing, nut (M12 x 1.25) .. 85
Starter motor fixing, bolt with flange (M8) .. 26

# PART G: IDENTIFICATION NUMBERS

## Vehicle Identification Numbers

**G1:** There are four sets of identification numbers in all. First, there is the Vehicle Identification (V.I.N.) Number, or chassis number found in the luggage compartment floor, next to the spare wheel recess.

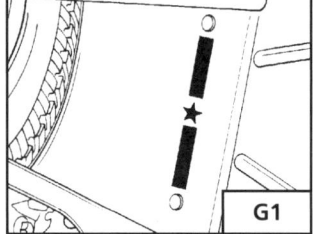

There are two groups of codes which are unique to your car. You should never buy a car without checking first that the V.I.N. shown on the car matches that on the vehicle registration document. The vehicle code is also shown at position **C** on the Model and Data Plate and the chassis serial number is also shown at position **D**.

## Engine Numbers

**G2A:** Second, is the engine number (**a**), in a similar position on both engine types. Also, see *G2B* and *G2C*. The numbers stamped on the plate stand for the following: **A** - Manufacturer; **B** - Homologation number; **C** - Vehicle identity code; **D** - Chassis serial number; **E** - Maximum authorised weight of vehicle, fully laden; **F** - Maximum authorised weight of vehicle, fully laden plus trailer; **G** - Maximum authorised weight on front axle; **H** - Maximum authorised weight on rear axle; **I** - Engine type; **L** - Body code (see below); **M** - Number for buying spares.

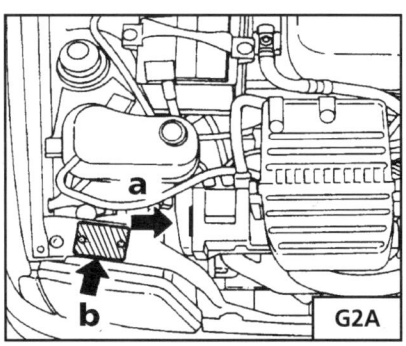

**G2B:** This is the position of the engine numbers on 900 OHV engines.

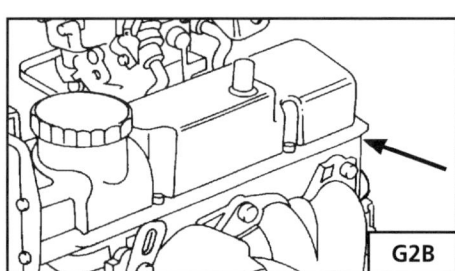

**G2C:** It's on the crankcase, above the water pump housing on all Sporting FIRE OHC engines.

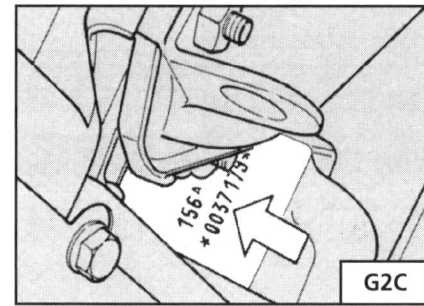

## Model and Data Plate

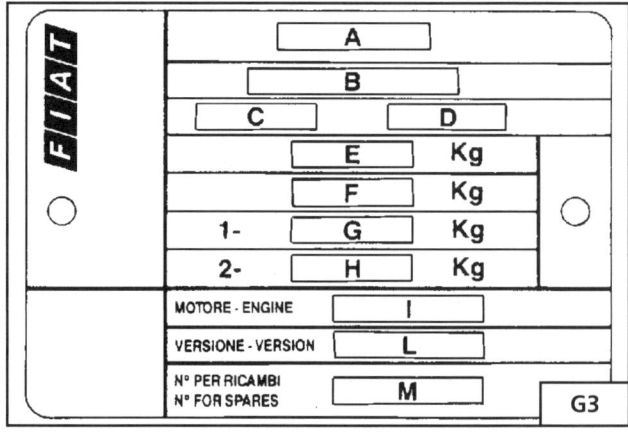

**G3:** Third, there is the Model and Data Plate see *G2A*, position **b**. (IMPORTANT NOTE: On later vehicles this may be on the luggage bay floor, opposite the VIN stamping.)

**G4:** Fourth, you will need the Paint Identification Plate if you need to buy paint. You'll find it on the inside of the hatchback door. The numbers shown on the plate give the following information: **1** - Paint manufacturer; **2** - Colour name; **3** - Colour code; **4** - Respray and touch-up code.

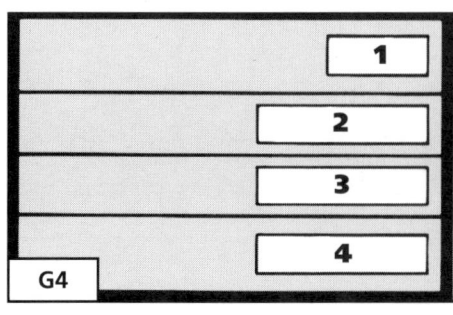

*Please read the whole of the CHAPTER 1, SAFETY FIRST! before carrying out any work on your car.*

# CHAPTER 4
# GETTING THROUGH THE MOT

This chapter is for owners in Britain whose vehicles need to pass the 'MoT' test. Obviously, you won't be able to examine your car to the same degree of thoroughness as the MoT testing station. But you can reduce the risk of being one of the 4 out of 10 who fail the test first time by following this check-list.

The checks shown below are correct at the time of writing but do note that they are becoming stricter all the time. Your local MoT testing station will have the latest information, should you need it.

## Chapter Contents

| | Page No. | | Page No. |
|---|---|---|---|
| PART A: INSIDE THE CAR | 4-1 | PART C: VEHICLE RAISED OFF THE GROUND | 4-3 |
| PART B: VEHICLE ON THE GROUND | 4-2 | PART D: EXHAUST EMISSIONS | 4-4 |

# PART A: INSIDE THE CAR

## Steering Wheel and Column

○ **1.** Try to move the steering wheel towards and away from you and then from side to side. There should be no appreciable movement or play. Check that the steering wheel is not loose on the column.

○ **2.** Lightly grip the steering wheel between thumb and finger and turn from side to side. **Cars with a steering rack:** free play should not exceed approximately 13 mm (0.5 in.), assuming a 380 mm (15 in.) diameter steering wheel. **Cars fitted with a steering box:** free play should not exceed approximately 75 mm (3.0 in.), assuming a 380 mm (15 in.) diameter steering wheel.

○ **3.** If there is a universal joint at the bottom of the steering column inside the car, check for movement. Place your hand over the joint while turning the steering wheel to-and-fro a little way with your other hand. If ANY free play can be felt, the joint must be replaced.

○ **4.** Ensure that there are no breaks or loose components on the steering wheel itself.

## Electrical Equipment

○ **5.** With the ignition turned on, ensure that the horn works okay.

○ **6.** Check that the front wipers work.

○ **7.** Check that the windscreen washers work.

○ **8.** Check that the internal warnings for the indicator and hazard warning lights work okay.

## Checks With An Assistant

○ **9.** Check that the front and rear side lights and number plate lights work and that the lenses and reflectors are secure, clean and undamaged.

○ **10.** Check the operation of the headlights (you won't be able to check the alignment yourself) and check that the lenses are undamaged. The reflectors inside the headlights must not be tarnished, nor must there be condensation inside the headlight.

○ **11.** Turn on the ignition and check the direction indicators, front and rear and on the side markers.

○ **12.** Check that the hazard warning lights operate on the outside of the vehicle, front and rear.

○ **13.** Check that the rear fog light/s, including the warning light inside the car, all work correctly.

○ **14.** Check that the rear brake lights work correctly. These checks are carried out all around the vehicle with all four wheels on the ground.

○ **15.** Operate the brake lights, side lights and each indicator in turn, all at the same time. None should affect the operation of the others.

### SAFETY FIRST!

● *Follow the Safety information in **CHAPTER 1, SAFETY FIRST!** but bear in mind that the vehicle needs to be even more stable than usual when raised off the ground.*

● *There must be no risk of it toppling off its stands or ramps while suspension and steering components are being pushed and pulled in order to test them.*

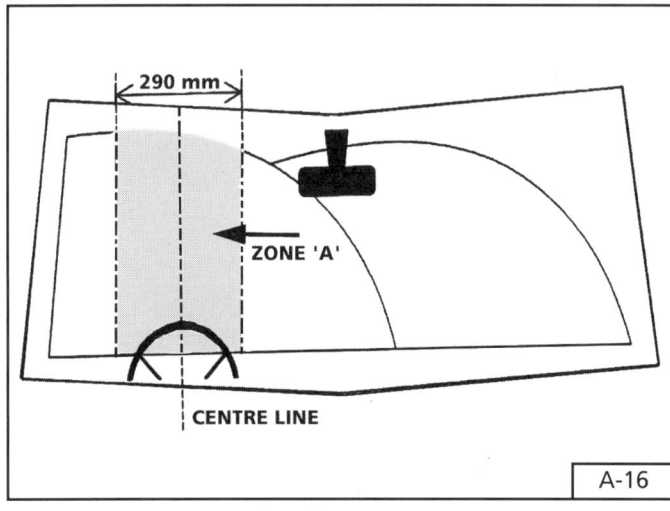

## Windscreen and Mirrors

○ 16. In zone 'A' of your windscreen, no items of damage larger than 10 mm in diameter will be allowed. In the rest of the area swept by the windscreen wipers, no damage greater than 40 mm in diameter will be allowed, nor should windscreen stickers or other obstructions encroach on this area.

○ 17. Check that the exterior mirror on the driver's side is in good condition.

○ 18. There must be one other mirror in good condition, either inside the car or an external mirror on the passenger's side.

## Brakes

○ 19. You cannot check the brakes properly without a rolling road brake tester but you can carry out the following checks:

○ 20. Pull on the handbrake. It should be fully ON before the handbrake reaches the end of its travel.

○ 21. Knock the handbrake from side to side and check that it does not then release itself.

○ 22. Check the security of the handbrake mountings and check the floor around it for rust or splits.

○ 23. Check that the brake pedal is in good condition and that, when you take hold of it and move it from side to side, there is not too much play.

○ 24. Push the footbrake down hard, with your foot. If it creeps slowly down to the floor, there is probably a problem with the master cylinder. Release the pedal, and after a few seconds, press down again. If the pedal feels spongy or it travels nearly to the floor, there is air in the system or another MoT-failing fault with the brakes.

○ 25. Check the servo unit (when fitted) as follows: Pump the pedal several times then hold it down hard. Start the engine. As the engine starts, the pedal should move down slightly. If it doesn't the servo or the vacuum hose leading to it may be faulty.

## Seat Belts and Seats

○ 26. Examine all of the webbing (pull out the belts from the inertia reel if necessary) for cuts, fraying or deterioration.

○ 27. Check that each inertia reel belt retracts correctly.

○ 28. Fasten and unfasten each belt to ensure that the buckles work correctly.

○ 29. Tug hard on each belt and inspect the mountings, as far as possible, to ensure that all are okay.

IMPORTANT NOTE: Checks apply to rear seat belts as much as front ones.

○ 30. Make sure that the seat runners and mountings are secure and that the back rest locks in the upright position.

## Doors and Door Locks

○ 31. Check that both front doors latch securely when closed and that both can be opened and closed from both outside and inside the car.

# PART B: VEHICLE ON THE GROUND

## Electrical Equipment

See *Part A: INSIDE THE CAR* for checks on the operation of the electrical equipment.

○ 1. Examine the wiper blades and replace those that show any damage.

## Vehicle Identification Numbers (VIN)

○ 2. The VIN (or chassis number on older vehicles) must be clearly displayed and legible.

○ 3. Number plates must be secure, legible and in good condition with correct spacing between letters and numbers. Any non-standard spacing will not be accepted.

## Braking System

○ 4. Inside the engine bay inspect the master cylinder, servo unit (if fitted), brake pipes and mountings. Look for corrosion, loose fitting or leaks.

## Steering and Suspension

○ 5. While still in the engine bay, have your assistant turn the steering wheel lightly from side to side and look for play in steering universal joints or steering rack mountings and any other steering connections.

○ 6. If your vehicle is fitted with power steering, check the security and condition of the steering pump, hoses and drivebelt, in the engine bay.

○ 7. Look and reach under the car while your assistant turns the steering wheel more vigorously from side to side. Place your hand over each track rod end in turn and inspect all of the steering linkages, joints and attachments for wear.

○ 8. Go around the vehicle and 'bounce' each corner of the vehicle in turn. Release at the lowest point and the vehicle should rise and settle in its normal position without continuing to 'bounce' of its own accord.

# PART C: VEHICLE RAISED OFF THE GROUND

## Bodywork Structure

◯ **1.** Any sharp edges on the external bodywork, caused by damage or corrosion will cause the vehicle to fail.

◯ **2.** Check all load bearing areas for corrosion. Open the doors and check the sills inside and out, above and below. Any corrosion in structural metalwork within 30 cm (12 in.) of seat belt mounting, steering and suspension attachment points will cause the vehicle to fail.

## Wheels and Tyres

*Illustration courtesy Dunlop/SP Tyres*

◯ **3.** To pass the test, the tread must be at least 1.6 mm deep throughout a continuous band comprising the central three-quarters of the width of the tread. The Tread Wear Indicators (TWI) will tell you when the limit has been reached, on most tyres.

IMPORTANT NOTE: Tyres are past their best, especially in wet conditions, well before this point is reached!

◯ **4.** Check that the front tyres match and that the rear tyres match each other - in terms of size and type but not necessarily make. They must be the correct size for the vehicle and the pressures must be correct.

◯ **5.** With each wheel off the ground in turn, check the inside and the outside of the tyre wall for cuts, lumps and bulges and check the wheel for damage. Note that tyres deteriorate progressively over a period of time and if they have degraded to this extent, replace them.

## Under the Front of the Car

You will need to support the front of the car on axle stands with the rear wheels firmly chocked in both directions.

◯ **6.** Have your helper turn the steering from lock to lock and check that the steering turns smoothly and that the brake hoses or pipes do not contact the wheel, tyre or any part of the steering or suspension.

◯ **7.** Have your assistant hold down the brake pedal firmly. Check each brake flexible hose for bulges or leaks.

◯ **8.** Inspect all the rigid brake pipes underneath the front of the vehicle for corrosion or leaks and also look for signs of fluid leaks at the brake calipers. Rigid fuel pipes need to be checked in the same way.

◯ **9.** At each full lock position, check the steering rack rubber gaiters for splits, leaks or loose retaining clips.

◯ **10.** Check the track rod end dust covers to make sure they are in place.

◯ **11.** Inspect each constant velocity joint gaiter - both inners and outers - for splits or damage. You will have to rotate each wheel to see the gaiters all the way round.

◯ **12.** Check all of the suspension rubber mountings, including the anti-rollbar mountings (when fitted). Take a firm grip on each shock absorber in turn with both hands and try to twist the damper to check for deterioration in the top and bottom mounting bushes.

◯ **13.** Underneath the front wheel arches, check that the shock absorbers are not corroded, that the springs have not cracked and that there are no fluid leaks down the body of the shock absorber.

◯ **14.** While under the front end of the car, check the front of the exhaust system for security of fixing at the manifold, for corrosion and secure fixing to the mounting points.

◯ **15.** Preferably working with a helper, grasp each front road wheel at the 12 o'clock and 6 o'clock positions and try rocking the wheel. Look for movement or wear at the suspension ball joints, suspension mountings, steering mountings and at the wheel bearing - look for movement between the wheel and hub. Repeat the test by grasping the road wheel at 3 o'clock and 9 o'clock and rocking once more.

◯ **16.** Spin each wheel and check for noise or roughness in the wheel bearing and binding in either the wheel bearing or the brake.

IMPORTANT NOTE: Don't forget that on front wheel drive cars, the gearbox must be in neutral. There will be a certain amount of noise and drag from the drivetrain components.

◯ **17.** If you suspect wear at any of the suspension points, try levering with a screwdriver to see whether or not you can confirm any movement in that area.

◯ **18.** Vehicles fitted with other suspension types such as hydraulic suspension, torsion bar suspension etc. need to be checked in a similar way with the additional point that there must be no fluid leaks or damaged pipes on vehicles with hydraulic suspension.

## Underneath the Rear of the Car

◯ **19.** Inspect the rear springs for security at their mounting points and for cracks, severe corrosion or damage.

◯ **20.** Check the rear shock absorbers in the same way as the checks carried out for the fronts.

◯ **21.** Check all rear suspension mounting points, including the rubbers to any locating rods or anti-rollbar that may be fitted.

◯ **22.** Check all of the flexible and rigid brake pipes and the fuel pipes just as for the front of the vehicle.

○ **23.** Have your assistant press down firmly on the brake pedal while you check the rear brake flexible hoses for bulges, splits or other deterioration.

○ **24.** Check the fuel tank for leaks or corrosion. Remember also to check the fuel filler cap - a correctly sealing filler cap is a part of the MoT test.

○ **25.** Examine the handbrake mechanism. Frayed or broken cables or worn mounting points, either to the bodywork or in the linkage will all be failure points.

○ **26.** Check each of the rear wheel bearings as for the fronts.

○ **27.** Spin each rear wheel and check that neither the wheel bearings nor the brakes are binding. Pull on and let off the handbrake and check once again to make sure that the handbrake mechanism is releasing.

**SAFETY FIRST!**
- Only run the car out of doors.
- Beware of burning yourself on a hot exhaust system.

○ **28.** While you are out from under the car, but with the rear end still raised off the ground, run the engine. Hold a rag over the end of the exhaust pipe and listen for blows or leaks in the system. You can now get back under the car and investigate further if necessary.

○ **29.** Check the exhaust system mountings and check for rust, corrosion or holes in the rear part of the system.

○ **30.** Check the rear brake back plate or calipers (as appropriate) for any signs of fluid leakage.

○ **31.** Check the insides and the outsides of the tyres as well as the tyre treads for damage, as for the front tyres.

## PART D: EXHAUST EMISSIONS

This is an area that is impossible to check accurately at home. However, the following rule-of-thumb tests will give you a good idea whether your car is likely to fail or not.

**i INSIDE INFORMATION:** If you feel that your car is likely to fail because of the emission test, have your MoT testing station carry out the emission part of the test first so that if it fails, you don't waste money on having the rest of the test carried out. *i*

○ **1. PETROL ENGINES BEFORE 1 AUGUST 1973 AND DIESEL ENGINES BEFORE 1 AUGUST 1979** only have to pass visible smoke check. Rev the engine to about 2,500 rpm (about half maximum speed) for 20 seconds and then allow it to return to idle. If too much smoke is emitted (in the opinion of the tester) the car will fail.

○ **2. DIESEL ENGINES FROM 1 AUGUST 1979** The engine will have to be taken up to maximum revs several times by the tester, so make certain that your timing belt is in good condition, otherwise severe damage could be caused to your engine. If the latter happens, it will be your responsibility!

### FACT FILE: VEHICLE EMISSIONS

*PETROL ENGINED VEHICLES WITHOUT CATALYSER*

**Vehicles first used before 1 August 1973**
- visual smoke check only.

**Vehicles first used between 1 August 1973 and 31 July 1986**
- 4.5% carbon monoxide and 1,200 parts per million, unburned hydrocarbons.

**Vehicles first used between 1 August 1986 and 31 July 1992**
- 3.5% carbon monoxide and 1,200 parts per million, unburned hydrocarbons.

*PETROL ENGINED VEHICLES FITTED WITH CATALYTIC CONVERTERS*

**Vehicles first used from 1 August 1992 (K-registration on)**

- All have to be tested at an MoT Testing Station specially equipped to handle cars fitted with catalytic converters whether or not the vehicle is fitted with a 'cat'. If the test, or the garage's data, shows that the vehicle was not fitted with a 'cat' by the manufacturer, the owner is permitted to take the vehicle to a Testing Station not equipped for catalysed cars, if he/she prefers to do so (up to 1998-only). Required maxima are - 3.5% carbon monoxide and 1,200 parts per million, unburned hydrocarbons. The simple emissions test (as above) will be supplemented by a further check to make sure that the catalyst is maintained in good and efficient working order.

- The tester also has to check that the engine oil is up to a specified temperature before carrying out the test. (This is because 'cats' don't work properly at lower temperatures - ensure *your* engine is fully warm!)

*DIESEL ENGINES' EMISSIONS STANDARDS*

- The Tester will have to rev your engine hard, several times. If it is not in good condition, he is entitled to refuse to test it. This is the full range of tests, even though all may not apply to your car.

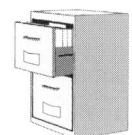

**Vehicles first used before 1 August, 1979**
- Engine run at normal running temperature; engine speed taken to around 2,500 rpm (or half governed max. speed, if lower) and held for 20 seconds. FAILURE, if engine emits dense blue or black smoke for next 5 seconds, at tick-over. (NOTE: Testers are allowed to be more lenient with pre-1960 vehicles.)

**Vehicles first used on or after 1 August, 1979**
- After checking engine condition, and with the engine at normal running temperature, the engine will be run up to full revs between three and six times to see whether your engine passes the prescribed smoke density test. (For what it's worth - 2.5k for non-turbo cars; 3.0k for turbo diesels. An opacity meter probe will be placed in your car's exhaust pipe and this is not something you can replicate at home.) Irrespective of the meter readings, the car will fail if smoke or vapour obscures the view of other road users.

- IMPORTANT NOTE: The diesel engine test puts a lot of stress on the engine. It is IMPERATIVE that your car's engine is properly serviced, and the cam belt changed on schedule, before you take it in for the MoT test. The tester is entitled to refuse to test the car if he feels that the engine is not in serviceable condition and there are a number of pre-Test checks he may carry out.

*Please read the whole of the Introduction to this Chapter before carrying out any work on your car.*

# CHAPTER 5
# SERVICING YOUR CAR

Everyone wants to own a car that starts first time, runs reliably and lasts longer than the average. And it's all a question of thorough maintenance!

If you follow the FIAT-approved Service Jobs listed here you can almost guarantee that your car will still be going strong when others have fallen by the wayside - or the hard shoulder.

## How To Use This Chapter

This chapter contains all of the servicing Jobs recommended by FIAT for all models of Cinquecento imported into the UK. To use the schedule, note that:
- Each letter code tells you the Service Interval at which you should carry out each Service Job.
- Look the code up in the Service Intervals Key.
- Each Service Job has a Job number.
- Look up the number in the relevant part of this chapter and you will see a complete explanation of how to carry out the work.

### SAFETY FIRST!

*SAFETY FIRST information must always be read with care and always taken seriously.*
- *In addition, please read the whole of **Chapter 1, Safety First!** before carrying out any work on your car.*
- *There are many hazards associated with working on a car but all of them can be avoided by adhering strictly to the safety rules.*
- *Don't skimp on safety!*

# SERVICE INTERVALS - INTRODUCTION

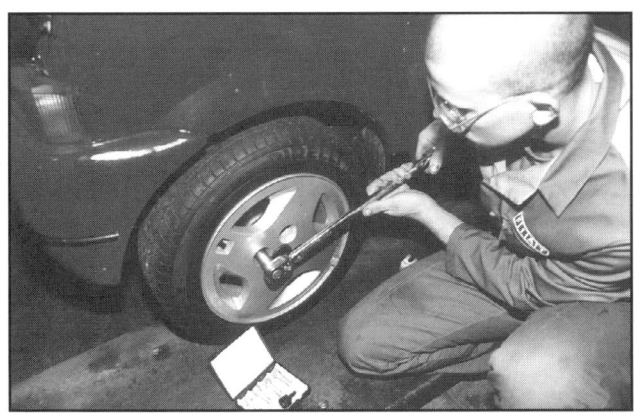

## Lubrication Advice from FIAT

FL VS MAX (a regular 15W/40 engine oil) should be changed every 9,000 miles, while **SELENIA** 15W/40 (a synthetic oil) should be changed every 13,500 miles. In any case, irrespective of the mileage, both types of oil should be changed after 12 months. The oil filter should be replaced at the same time as the engine oil is changed.

### HEAVY USE

If the vehicle is regularly subject to heavy use (such as town driving, journey in dusty areas, constant mountain driving, towing a trailer or caravan, harsh climatic conditions, a great deal of motorway driving at high speeds, etc.), oil and filter changes, **Regular Checks** and other safety related service jobs should be carried out at more frequent intervals.

*making it easy*
- We think it is very important to keep things as straight forward as possible.
- Where you see this heading, you'll know there's an extra tip to help 'make it easy' for you!

*Thanks are due to the excellent, knowledgeable and helpful staff at FIAT main dealers, **Ryauto** of Amblecote, in the West Midlands for supplying vehicles and for their assistance with this chapter. In particular, thanks are due to the efficient Maurice Hough, Service Manager, the experienced Foreman, Tony Morris, and young demon mechanic, Matthew Worsfold.*

Some of the suggested inspection/replacement intervals may not correspond to those shown in the original handbook. The suggested schedule shown here is based on FIAT's recommendations and takes into account the age of the vehicle and the annual MoT test in the UK.

IMPORTANT NOTE: Each service should be carried out at EITHER the recommended mileage OR the recommended time interval, whichever comes first.

# SERVICE INTERVAL CHART

### SERVICE INTERVALS: KEY

A - Every week, or before every long journey.
B - Every 6 months, or 4,500 miles.
C - Every 12 months, or 9,000 miles.
D - Every 18 months, or 13,500 miles.
E - Every 2 years or 18,000 miles.
F - Every 3 years or 27,000 miles.
G - Every 4 years or 36,000 miles.
H - Every 6 years or 54,000 miles.
I - Every 63,000 miles.
J - Every 72,000 miles.

## PART A: REGULAR CHECKS

| Job | Service Intervals |
|---|---|
| Job 1. Engine oil - check level | A |
| Job 2. Cooling system - check level | A |
| Job 3. Brake fluid - check level | A |
| Job 4. Battery - check electrolyte level | A |
| Job 5. Screen washer fluid - check level | A |
| Job 6. Tyres - check pressures and condition (road wheels) | A |
| Job 7. Check lights/change bulbs | A |

## PART B: THE ENGINE AND COOLING SYSTEM

| Job | Service Intervals |
|---|---|
| Job 8. Change engine oil and filter | C |
| Job 9. Check crankcase ventilation | H |
| Job 10. Check/adjust valve clearances | E |
| Job 11. Check camshaft timing belt (1108 cc) | G |
| Job 12. Change camshaft timing belt (1108 cc) | I |
| Job 13. Check/adjust drive belt | E |
| Job 14. Check cooling system | C |
| Job 15. Change engine coolant | F |

## PART C: TRANSMISSION

| Job | Service Intervals |
|---|---|
| Job 16. Check transmission oil level | E |
| Job 17. Change transmission oil | I |
| Job 18. Check driveshaft gaiters | C |
| Job 19. Check/adjust clutch | E |

## PART D: IGNITION AND ELECTRICS

| Job | Service Intervals |
|---|---|
| Job 20. Check/clean/gap spark plugs | B |
| Job 21. Change spark plugs | E |
| Job 22. Check/clean HT leads | E |
| Job 23. Check ignition timing/system | H |
| Job 24. Check electric fan operation | C |
| Job 25. Run diagnostic ignition/injection test | E |

## PART E: FUEL AND EXHAUST

| Job | Service Intervals |
|---|---|
| Job 26. Check fuel pipes for leaks | C |
| Job 27. Change air filter | E |
| Job 28. Change fuel filter | E |
| Job 29. Check/adjust engine idle and emissions (if necessary) | C |
| Job 30. Check emission/control systems | F |
| Job 31. Check Lambda sensor | F |
| Job 32. Check inlet and exhaust manifold fixings | E |
| Job 33. Check exhaust system | C |

## PART F: STEERING AND SUSPENSION

| Job | Service Intervals |
|---|---|
| Job 34. Check front wheel bearings | C |
| Job 35. Check front suspension | C |
| Job 36. Check steering column, joints and rack | C |
| Job 37. Check rear wheel bearings | C |
| Job 38. Check rear suspension | C |
| Job 39. Check wheel bolts for tightness | C |

## PART G: BRAKING SYSTEM

| Job | Service Intervals |
|---|---|
| Job 40. Check front brakes | C |
| Job 41. Check rear brakes | E |
| Job 42. Check/adjust handbrake | C |
| Job 43. Check brake pipes | C |
| Job 44. Change brake hydraulic fluid | E |

## PART H: BODYWORK & INTERIOR

| Job | Service Intervals |
|---|---|
| Job 45. Lubricate hinges and locks | C |
| Job 46. Check windscreen | C |
| Job 47. Check seat and seat belt mountings | C |
| Job 48. Check headlight alignment | C |
| Job 49. Check underbody | C |
| Job 50. Check spare tyre and jack | B |
| Job 51. Replace airbag gas generator | 10 years |

## PART I: ROAD TEST

Job 52. Road test and specialist check. *AFTER EVERY SERVICE*

# ENGINE BAY LAYOUTS

These are the engine bay layouts common to almost all Cinquecentos.

### 1 - 900 MODELS

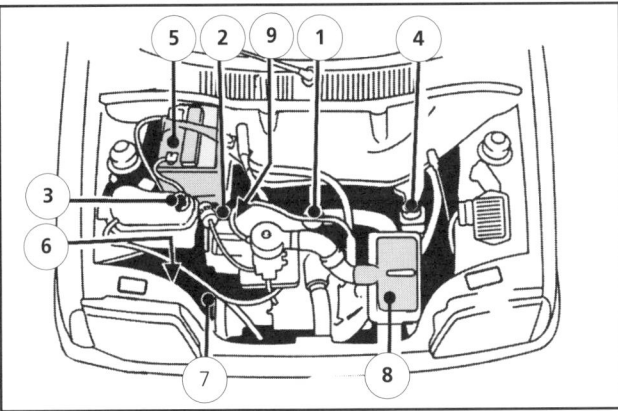

### 2 - SPORTING (1.1 LITRE) MODELS

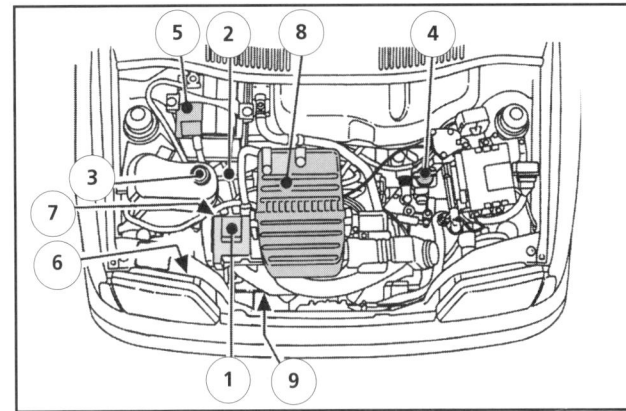

1 - oil filler cap
2 - engine oil dipstick
3 - coolant filler cap
4 - brake fluid reservoir
5 - battery
6 - screenwash reservoir filler
7 - alternator location
8 - air filter housing
9 - oil filter location

**FACT FILE: CINQUECENTO ENGINE TYPES**

- Cinquecento has been fitted with three engine types although one of them, the 704cc flat-twin engine, was never fitted to right-hand drive cars.

- The 900 engine is an overhead valve unit - a lightly modified version of the FIAT Panda 903cc engine. For the UK and other non-Italian markets, capacity was reduced to 899cc.

- Cinquecento 'Sporting' models were all fitted with an 1108cc FIRE (Fully Integrated Robotised Engine) unit. This single overhead camshaft engine is significantly more powerful (54 bhp compared with the 900's 39 bhp) and also weighs less.

- All Cinquecento engines are fitted with electronic SPI injection and solid state ignition, except some non-UK vehicles, fitted with a Webber carburettor.

# PART A: REGULAR CHECKS

We recommend that these Jobs are carried out on a weekly basis, as well as before every long journey. They consist of checks essential for your safety and for your car's reliability.

### ☐ Job 1. Engine oil - check level.

Check the engine oil level with the car on level ground. If the engine has been running, leave it turned off for several minutes to let the oil drain into the sump.

**1A.** The dipstick is located at the rear of the engine on the 900 unit, near the battery.

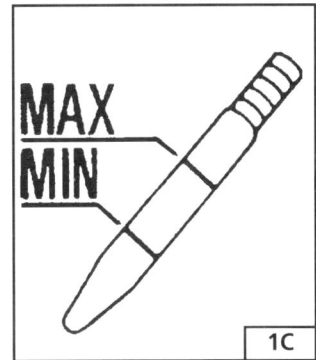

**1B.** The Sporting FIRE engine's dipstick is also at the back, in a similar location.

**1C.** Lift the dipstick out, wipe it dry and re-insert it. The oil level is correct when between the MAX and MIN marks.

*i* INSIDE INFORMATION: The difference between MIN and MAX marks is approximately one litre of oil. *i*

**CHAPTER 5 PART A: REGULAR CHECKS**

## TOPPING-UP

**1D.** On 900 OHV engines the round oil filler cap is at the right-hand end of the engine's valve cover (viewed from the front of the car). The cap unscrews anti-clockwise.

**1E.** On FIRE engines the oil filler cap is a square plastic moulding on the cam cover at the dipstick-end of the engine. Remove it by pulling upwards. It can need quite a tug!

Pour in the fresh oil carefully, ideally using a funnel. Pour particularly slowly into FIRE engines which can otherwise spit oil back, over the engine.

IMPORTANT NOTE: Regularly check the ground over which the car has been parked for traces of oil or other fluid leaks. If a leak is found, don't drive the car without first finding out where the leak is from, and repairing it if from a safety-related component.

❑ **Job 2. Cooling system - check level.**

### SAFETY FIRST!

- ALWAYS check the coolant level with the engine COLD
- If the engine is hot there is a real danger of scalding from boiling coolant gushing from the tank when the cap is removed.

Never allow the coolant level to fall below the MIN mark on the expansion tank. It is vitally important that all engines have the correct proportion of anti-freeze in the coolant all year round to prevent corrosion. A 50% mix of water with **FL Paraflu** coolant gives the best protection.

**2A.** The coolant should be between the MAX and the MIN marks (and best kept at MAX) on the header tank with the engine cold. The header tank is just in front of the battery on all models.

**2B.** Unscrew the coolant filler cap anti-clockwise and remove it. Top-up using a 50:50 mixture of **Paraflu** anti-freeze and water.

❑ **Job 3. Brake fluid - check level.**

### SAFETY FIRST!

- If brake fluid should come into contact with skin or eyes, rinse immediately with plenty of water.
- It is acceptable for the brake fluid level to fall slightly during normal use, but if it falls significantly below the MIN mark on the reservoir there is probably a leak or internal seal failure. Stop using the car until the problem has been put right.
- If you let dirt get into the hydraulic system it can cause brake failure. Wipe the filler cap clean before removing it.
- You should only ever use new brake fluid from a sealed container - FIAT recommend **FL Tutela DOT 3** brake fluid. Old fluid absorbs moisture and this could cause the brakes to fail when carrying out an emergency stop or during another heavy use of the brakes - just when you need them most and are least able to do anything about it, in fact!

If you live in a very humid climate, check with your FIAT dealer to see if your brake fluid needs changing more regularly than recommended in the *Service Interval Chart*.

**3A.** On all models the brake fluid reservoir is positioned above the master cylinder in the rear left-hand corner of the engine bay. The reservoir is semi-transparent so the level can be checked without disturbing the cap. The reservoir should be almost full (arrowed).

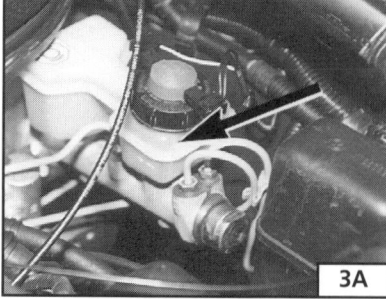
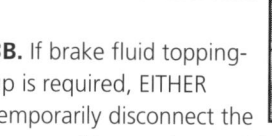

IMPORTANT NOTE: Ensure the fluid level is high enough to allow fluid to flow internally between front and rear sections of the reservoir.

**3B.** If brake fluid topping-up is required, EITHER temporarily disconnect the sensor cables, as shown, OR turn the cap without allowing the centre section to turn. This section, with two wires attached, swivels in the cap. Place the cap and float to one side - take care not to drip fluid from the float - and top up with **FL Tutela DOT 3**.

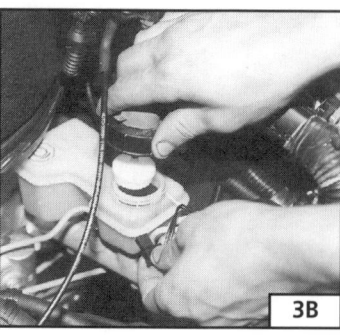

**3C.** Check that the brake fluid-level warning-light is operating. Turn the ignition key to the MAR (ignition-ON) position and press down the button (arrowed) between the two

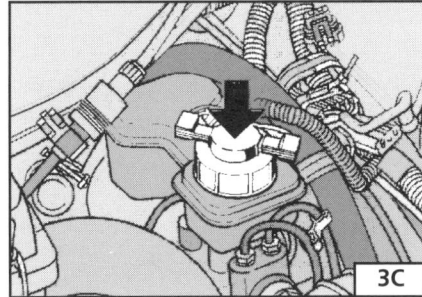

terminals on the reservoir cap. The warning light on the dash should light up. Check the bulb, check the fuse, or have your FIAT dealer repair the warning system, if faulty.

❑ **Job 4. Battery - check electrolyte level.**

FACT FILE: DISCONNECTING THE BATTERY
● Many vehicles depend on a constant power supply from the battery; with these you find yourself in trouble if you simply disconnect the battery. You might find the car alarm goes off, or that the engine management system forgets all it ever 'learned', making the car feel odd to drive until it has re-programmed itself. You might also find that the radio refuses to operate until its correct security code is keyed into it.
● On cars with engine management systems and/or coded radios, you must ensure the car has a constant electrical supply, even with the battery removed. You will need a separate 12 volt battery; put a self-tapping screw into the positive lead near the battery terminal before disconnecting it, and put a positive connection to your other battery via this screw.
● Be EXTREMELY CAREFUL to wrap insulation tape around the connection so that no short is caused. The negative terminal on the other battery must be connected to the car's bodywork.

**4.** Check the electrolyte level in the battery. MAX and MIN lines (arrowed) are moulded into the translucent battery casing. In the case of non-FIAT-supplied batteries, the cell caps or strip (**a**) may need to be removed to see the level.

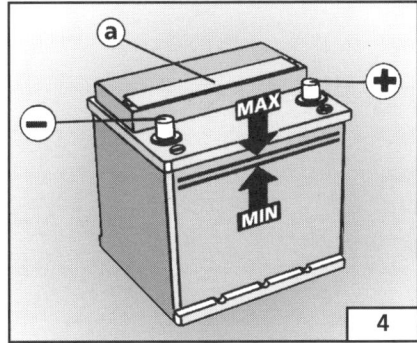

**SAFETY FIRST!**

● *The gas given off by a battery is highly explosive. Never smoke, use a naked flame or allow a spark in the battery compartment.*
● *Never disconnect the battery (it can cause sparking) with the battery caps removed.*
● *All vehicle batteries contain sulphuric acid. If the acid comes into contact with the skin or eyes, wash immediately with copious amounts of cold water and seek medical advice.*
● *Do not check the battery levels within half an hour of the battery being charged with a separate battery charger because the addition of fresh water could cause electrolyte to flood out.*

Original FIAT batteries are of the 'maintenance-free' type and usually do not need topping-up. However, if necessary, top up after prising off the cell sealing strip with a screwdriver. Top-up each cell ONLY with distilled or de-ionised water.

❑ **Job 5. Screen washer fluid - check level.**

**5.** Top up with a mixture of water and screen-wash additive, mixed according to the instructions on the container. The reservoir also

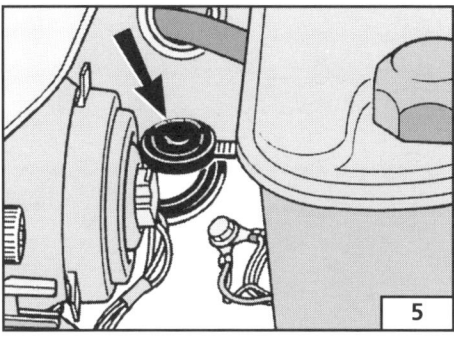

feeds the rear washer. The reservoir itself is not visible and so you'll have to top-up regularly.

❑ **Job 6. Tyres - check pressures and condition (road wheels).**

**6A.** Check the tyre pressures using a reliable and accurate gauge. Note that the recommended pressures (see **Chapter 3, Facts and Figures**) are given for COLD tyres. Tyres warm up as the car is used - and warm tyres give a false (high) reading. You should also check for wear or damage at the same time.

**SAFETY FIRST!**

● *If a tyre is worn more on one side than another, consult your FIAT dealer or a tyre specialist. It probably means the tracking needs re-setting, though it could indicate suspension damage, so have it checked.*
● *If a tyre is worn more in the centre or on the edges, this indicates incorrect tyre pressures.*
● *Incorrectly inflated tyres wear rapidly, can give dangerous handling, and can worsen fuel consumption.*

**6B.** Every few weeks, examine the tyre treads for wear using a tread-depth gauge. This will help you keep safe and on the right side of the law! Check

treads visually every time you check the pressures.

**CHAPTER 5 PART A: REGULAR CHECKS**

5-5

Every three months, raise each wheel off the ground and turn it slowly between your hands, looking and feeling for any bulges, tears or splits in the tyre walls, especially the inner sidewalls. (See **Job 50** for spare tyre checks.)

*i* INSIDE INFORMATION: In time, rubber deteriorates, increasing the risk of a blow-out. Keep your eye on the sidewalls of older tyres. If you see **any** cracking, splits or other damage scrap the tyre. If you're not sure, consult your FIAT dealer or tyre specialist. *i*

❑ **Job 7. Check lights/change bulbs.**

- Whenever a light fails to work, check its fuse before replacing the bulb.
- A blown bulb often causes a fuse to 'go' in sympathy.
- See **Job 7U to 7Z, FUSES AND RELAYS**.

### HEADLIGHTS

**7A.** Pull off the headlight multi-plug...

**7B.** ...and peel off the rubber cover...

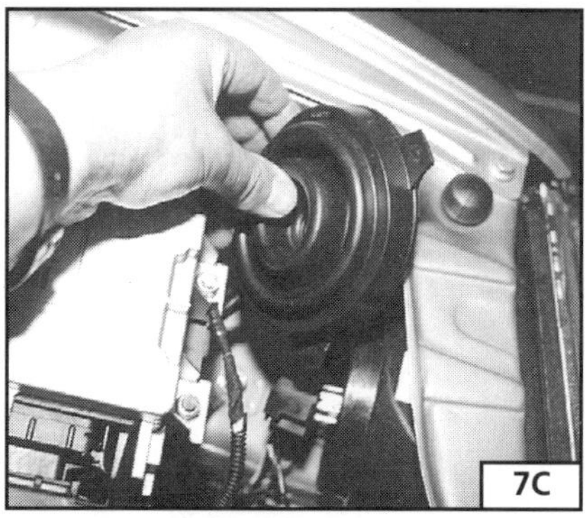

**7C.** ...removing it from the back of the headlight.

**7D.** Unhook the bulb securing spring arms (**C**)...

**7E.** ...and remove the bulb.

**7F.** Without touching the bulb glass, fit the new bulb and refit the spring clips.

**7G.** A locating tag (**E**) ensures the bulb (**D**) only goes in in the correct position. The bulb shown here is of the less efficient non-halogen type only fitted to some non-UK vehicles. Refit and reconnect in the reverse order.

- If you touch a halogen headlight or driving light bulb with bare fingers you will shorten its life, so handle with a piece of tissue paper.
- If the bulb is touched, wipe it carefully with methylated spirit.

### FRONT SIDE LIGHTS

**7H.** The side light bulb holder is under the main headlight bulb.

**7I.** The bayonet-type holder (**A**) is pushed in slightly, turned anti-clockwise and removed. The bulb is a push-fit within it.

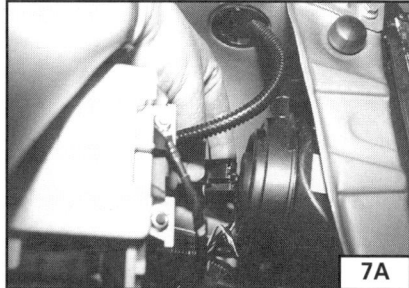
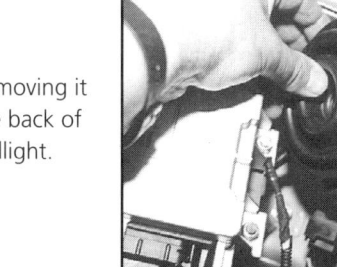
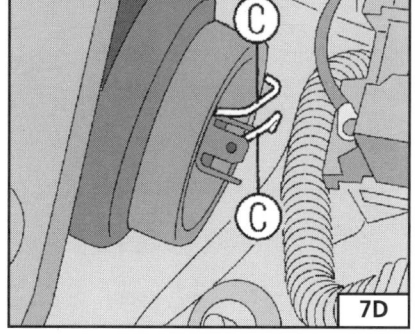
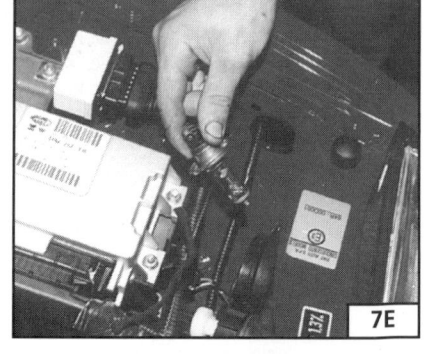

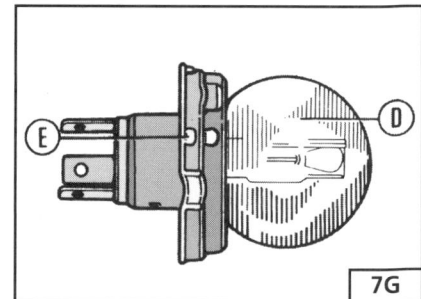

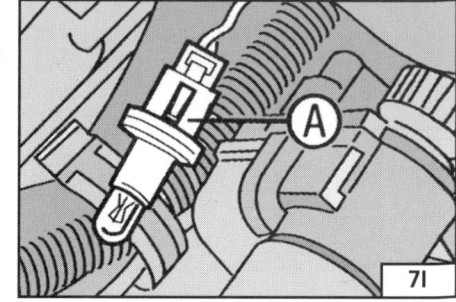

## FRONT DIRECTION INDICATORS

**7J.** Pull spring clip (**A**) until it releases from its location point (arrowed).

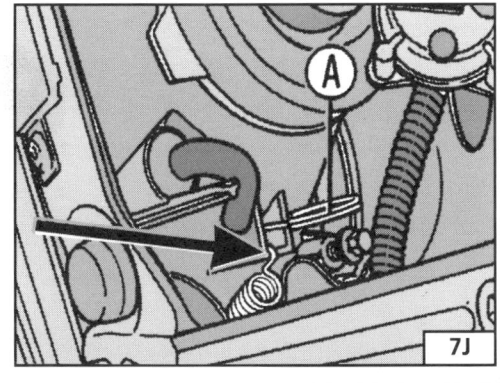

**7K.** Note the location of these two spring tabs.

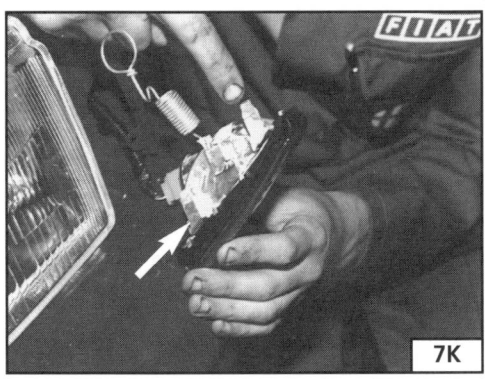

**7L.** Press the tabs (**B**) to release them from their locators (**C**), so that you can pull the light unit forwards and reach the bulb holder (**D**).

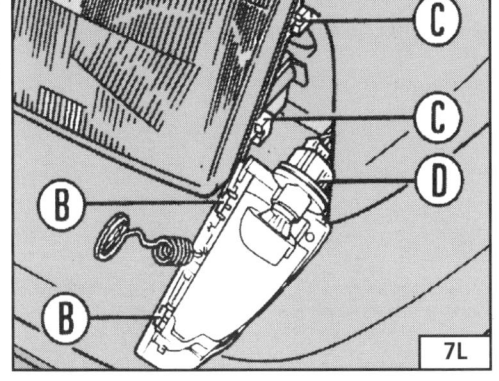

**7M.** Twist and remove the bulb holder; twist and remove the (coloured) 21W bulbs. Replace ONLY with the correct type.

## INDICATOR SIDE REPEATERS

**7N.** Turn the lens anti-clockwise and remove. The 5W capless bulb is a straightforward pull-out, push-in replacement.

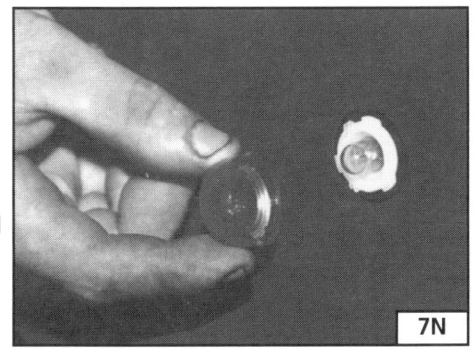

## REAR LIGHT UNIT

**7O.** Remove the two screws (**A**), pull the top of the light unit towards you and lift clear.

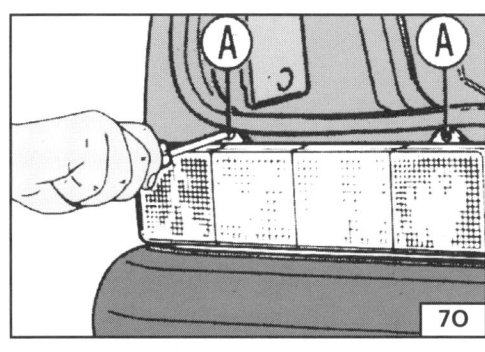

**7P.** Push in the tab and release the electrical connector.

**7Q.** Remove the screws (**B**) to free the light lens, then pull off the lens for access to the bulb holder.

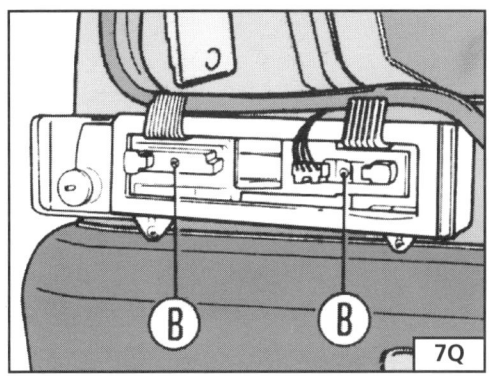

**7R.** All bulbs are of the bayonet type - push in slightly, turn anti-clockwise and withdraw. Ensure the pegs on the bulb are the right way round when attempting to refit - they only go one way. Bulb (**C**) is the direction indicator (21W - yellow except on S versions, when white), (**D**) is the 2-filament 5/21W tail/stop light, (**E**) is the 21W fog light on the driver's side, and 21W reversing light on the other side of the car.

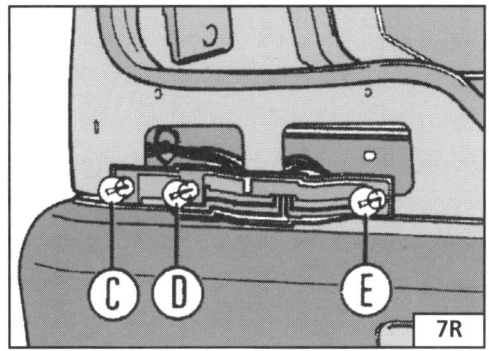

## NUMBER PLATE LIGHT

**7S.** Remove the two screws (arrowed) from whichever lens you want to remove and remove the 5W bayonet bulb from beneath.

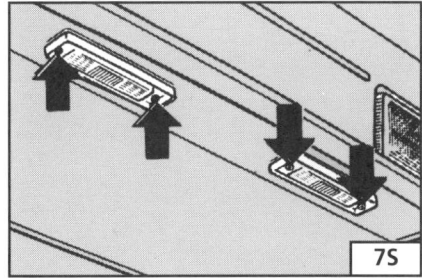

**CHAPTER 5 PART A: REGULAR CHECKS**

5-7

## INTERIOR LIGHT

**7T.** Remove the interior light lens (**A**) by pressing it at the point arrowed. Replace the 5W tubular bulb.

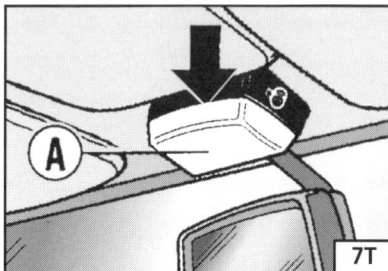

## DASH BULBS

See **Chapter 6, Repairs and Replacements** for details of instrument panel removal for access to its light bulbs. The bulbs are a quarter-turn fit in the back of the panel.

## FUSES AND RELAYS

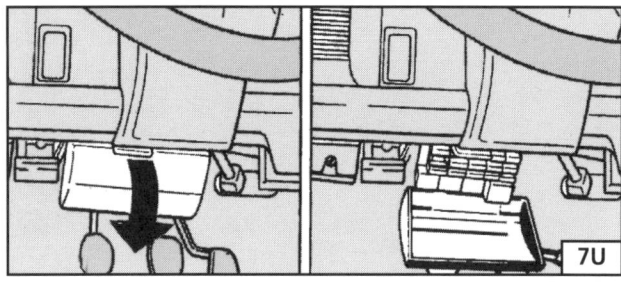

**7U.** The fuse and relay box is found behind a flap under the dashboard, beneath the steering column.

**Fuses:**

1. ⚠ (15A) Hazard lights and panel indicator, horn, courtesy light, cigar lighter, clock, sound system.
2. ▥ (15A) Rear window defroster and panel indicator.
3. ✼ (25A) Radiator fan.
4. ⇦⇨ (10A) Instrument power supply, direction indicators and panel indicator, FIAT CODE.
5. ≣◯ (10A) Left high-beam headlight.
6. ≣◯ (10A) Right high-beam headlight and panel indicator.
7. (15A) Rear window wash/wipe, panel switches lighting.
8. ≣◯ (10A) Right low-beam headlight.
9. ≣◯ (10A) Left low-beam headlight.
10. (7.5A) Rear foglight and panel indicator.
11. ∋◯≣ (7.5A) Cigarette lighter, clock, right tail light and front left side light, right number plate light and heater light.
12. ∋◯≣ (7.5A) Instrument lighting, left tail light/front right side light and panel indicator, left number plate light.
13. (7.5A) Reversing and stop lights and clock.
14. SERVIZI/SERVICES (20A) Windscreen wash/wipe.
15. ✼ (15A) Heater fan. Version with air conditioner: **25A**.

**7V.** A symbol above each fuse tells you which circuit it protects.

**Note: The following circuits are not protected by fuses:**
- battery charging circuit
- battery low panel indicator
- ignition and starter motor circuit.

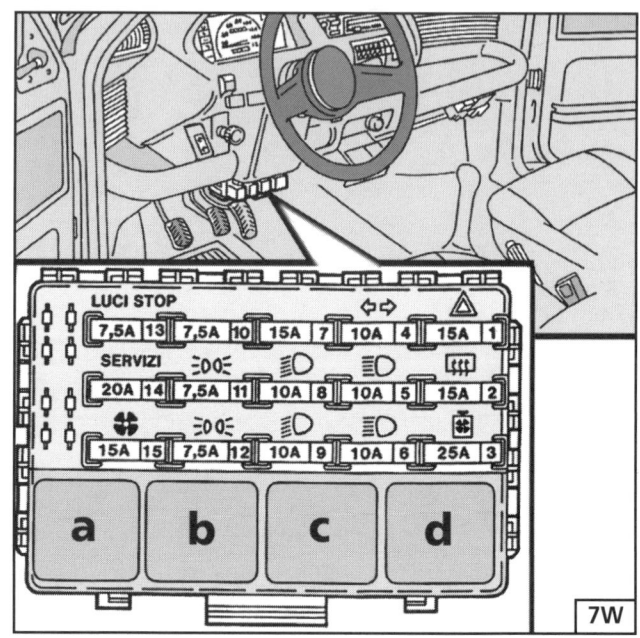

**7W.** The **amperage** is clearly marked on each fuse. ALWAYS replace a blown fuse with one of the correct amperage. NEVER 'fix' a fault by using a fuse of a higher amperage, nor 'bridge' a blown fuse - it could cause a fire!

**Relays:**
The main relays are:
**a.** dipped headlights and radiator fan
**b.** heated rear screen
**c.** horn
**d.** indicators/warning light 'flasher' box

Three fuses protecting optional devices are located on the side of the fuse box:
- (15A) Door lock.
- (25A) Electric windows.
- (7.5A) Dim-dip headlight feature (only for some right-hand drive models).

**7X.** When a fuse is 'blown' its conductor wire (**A**) has a gap in it.
- If a fuse blows, find out why and put it right before fitting a new fuse.

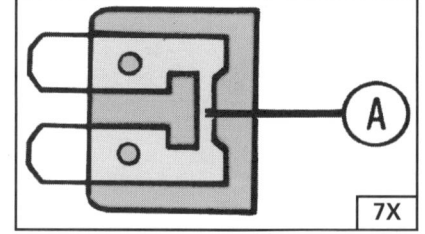

**7Y.** The injection system is protected by a 25A fuse near the left-hand strut, under the bonnet.

5-8

**7Z.** Cars with air conditioning (non-UK only) are protected by fuses on the left-side of the engine bay.
- Two more fuses are located under the dash: a 15A fuse protecting the car alarm (if fitted); a 20A fuse for the canvas sunroof (certain markets only).
- **A** - 7.5A, compressor
- **B** - 25A, condenser and heater fan

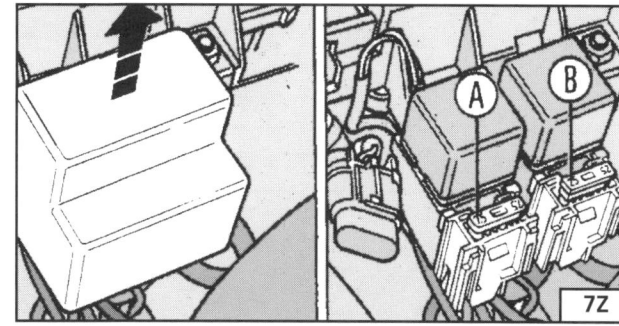

# PART B: ENGINE & COOLING SYSTEM

## ❏ Job 8. Change engine oil and filter.

### SAFETY FIRST!

- Refer to the section on **ENGINE OILS** and **RAISING THE CAR SAFELY** in **Chapter 1, Safety First!** before carrying out this work.
- You must wear plastic gloves when changing the oil. Used engine oil can severely irritate the skin and can be carcinogenic.
- Oil drain plugs are often over-tightened and those taper plugs are always tight anyway. So take care that the spanner does not slip.
- Take care that the effort needed to undo the drain plug doesn't tip the car off its supports - remember to use wheel chocks!

*making it easy!*
- Only drain the oil from a warm engine - but not so hot that the oil can scald!
- Allow the oil to drain for at least ten minutes before replacing the sump plug.
- You can use this time by renewing the oil filter.

**8A.** The sump drain plug is on the under-side of the sump, at the rear. The plug has a recessed hexagonal head and you will need either a sump plug spanner, a large Allen key, or a 'Hex' headed socket fitted to a socket wrench.

IMPORTANT NOTE: The plug is a taper-fit and can become very tight, necessitating the use of a long drive-bar for its removal, as used here at Ryauto.

**8B.** Once the initial tightness of the plug has been released, unscrew the last few turns by hand, holding the plug in place until the threads have cleared, then withdrawing it smartly to allow oil to flow into the receptacle beneath.

ℹ️ INSIDE INFORMATION: As the oil empties, the angle of 'spurt' will change, so be prepared to move the container. ℹ️

**8C.** The oil filter on 900 OHV engines is located on the rearward-facing side of the engine.

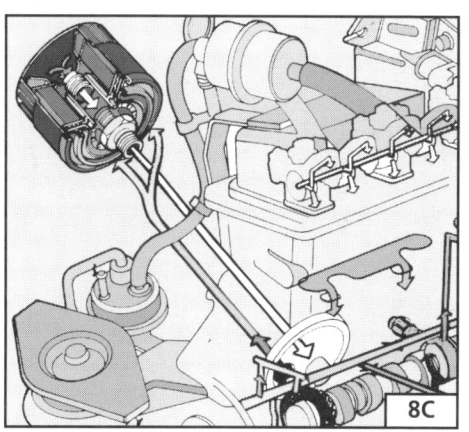

**8D.** On Sporting 1.1 engines, it is mounted low on the front of the engine block, towards the timing belt. In either case, use an oil filter wrench to unscrew the old filter. Note that there may be a lot of oil spilt as the filter seal is broken, so keep the drip tray beneath it.

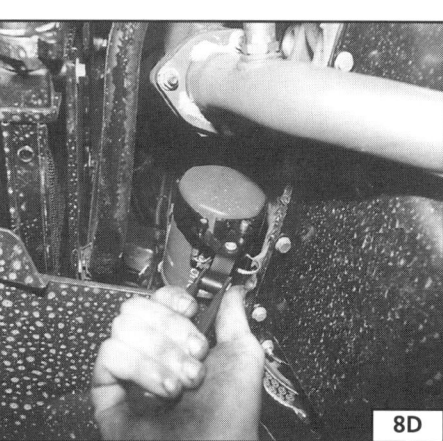

**8E.** To prevent the rubber sealing ring on the new filter from buckling or twisting out of shape while tightening, smear it with clean oil.

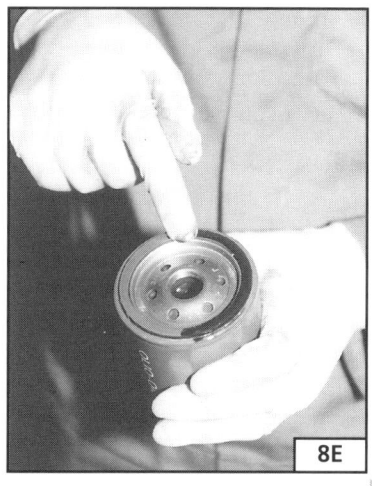

Screw the new filter onto the stub by hand. When the rubber sealing ring contacts its seat, continue to turn the filter a further 3/4 of a turn, *by hand only*. Over-tightening the filter makes it difficult to remove at the next oil change and can buckle the seal, causing a leak.

**ℹ 8F.** INSIDE INFORMATION: It isn't necessary to use excessive force when refitting the sump plug. Simply grip the regular length spanner so that the thumb rests on, or near, the spanner head, limiting the amount of leverage that can be applied. Use firm pressure only. Before refitting the plug, wipe around the drain hole with a piece of clean cloth to remove any dirt. ℹ

**8G.** Pour in the correct quantity of **Selenia** engine oil (see *Chapter 3, Facts and Figures*) and check the level against the dipstick.

**ℹ** INSIDE INFORMATION: 1.1 Sporting FIRE engines fill very slowly! If you're impatient, oil will spill over the top. ℹ

Note that the empty oil filter will cause the level to drop slightly when the engine is started and the oil flows into it. Before using the car, run the engine for two minutes, turn off, leave to stand for a few minutes and then recheck and correct the oil level.

### ❑ Job 9. Check crankcase ventilation.

**9.** Check the condition of the breather hose from the valve cover or cam cover to the air cleaner. The one shown has split lengthways because of oil contamination and needs replacing. If the pipe has become blocked or damaged, replace it, transferring the flame trap from inside the old pipe to the new one. On some

models, you will have to remove the air filter housing to get at the crankcase ventilation pipe beneath.

### ❑ Job 10. Check/adjust valve clearances (1108cc).

There are two types of valve gear, but only one needs valve clearances to be checked at intervals - always when the engine is cold.
● 900 OHV ENGINES have semi-conventional valve rockers but with hydraulic, non-adjustable tappets. See *Chapter 6, Repairs and Replacements* for information on setting when new.
● 'FIRE' OHC ENGINES have a belt-driven overhead camshaft with shim-and-bucket type tappets.

### 1.1 SPORTING (OHC) ENGINES

**10A.** Remove the air cleaner (see *Job 27*), then remove the bolts holding the camshaft cover in place and lift the cover off.

*making it easy!* ● To turn the camshaft, jack up one of the front wheels and put the car in gear. (Chock the rear wheels.)
● Take out the spark plugs. Make sure the ignition is OFF.
● As you turn the road wheel that is off the ground, the engine will turn over.

**10B.** The valve clearance is measured directly beneath the cam and must be checked when the high point of the cam is pointing directly upwards and away from the cam follower.

Try different feeler gauge thicknesses until you find one that's a tight sliding fit between cam and follower. Make a written

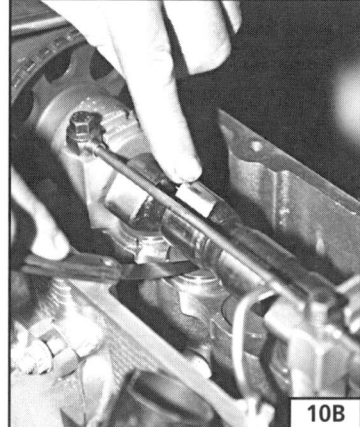

note of each clearance starting with number 1 at the timing belt end of the engine.

**ℹ** INSIDE INFORMATION: ● Remember that clearances for inlet and exhaust valves differ. See *Chapter 3, Facts and Figures*.
● Counting from the timing belt end the valves are: 1, 3, 6, 8 - exhaust; 2, 4, 5, 7 - inlet. ℹ

If a clearance is outside the tolerances shown in *Chapter 3, Facts and Figures*, the relevant shim will have to be changed. New shims are available from your FIAT dealer. This work is fully described in *Chapter 6, Repairs and Replacements*.

☐ **Job 11. Check camshaft timing belt (1108cc).**

## OHC ENGINES ONLY

Remove the camshaft belt outer cover. See **Chapter 6, Repairs and Replacements, PART A: ENGINE**.

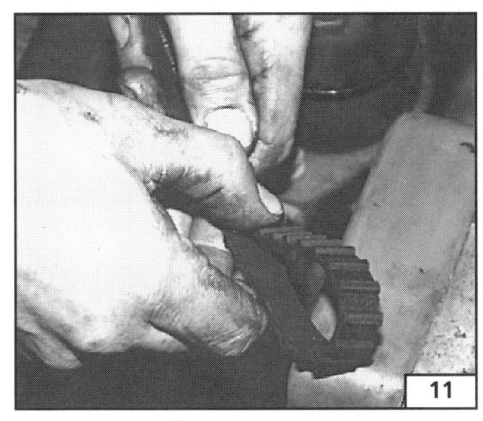

**11.** Examine the belt for wear. If there is any cracking, or if the toothed side appears worn, or any 'teeth' are missing, replace the belt straight away. If the belt breaks the valves may collide with the pistons, causing serious engine damage. Camshaft belt replacement is described in **Chapter 6, Repairs and Replacements**, or you may wish to have your FIAT dealer carry out the work for you.

☐ **Job 12. Change camshaft timing belt (1108cc).**

## OHC ENGINES ONLY

It is ESSENTIAL that you renew the camshaft drive belt at the recommended interval. See the **Service Interval Chart** at the start of this chapter. **Chapter 6, Repairs and Replacements** explains how to carry out the work.

☐ **Job 13. Check/adjust drive belt.**

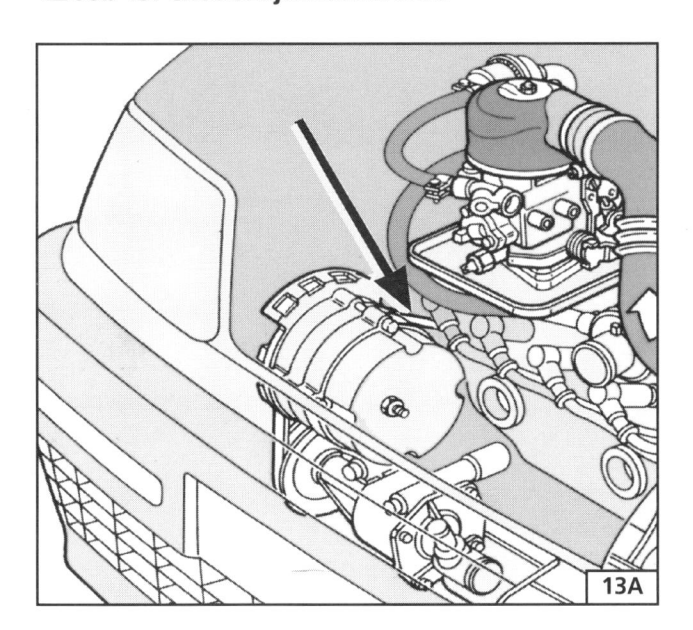

**13A.** On 900 models, access to the alternator belt (arrowed) and adjustment fixings may be difficult from the engine bay. If this is the case, raise and support the right-hand road wheel, remove it and detach the access panel by tapping the pins out from the centres of the plastic expansion plugs which secure it. Some models may have screws securing the panel.

**13B.** You can best check the Sporting FIRE engine's belt from beneath the car.

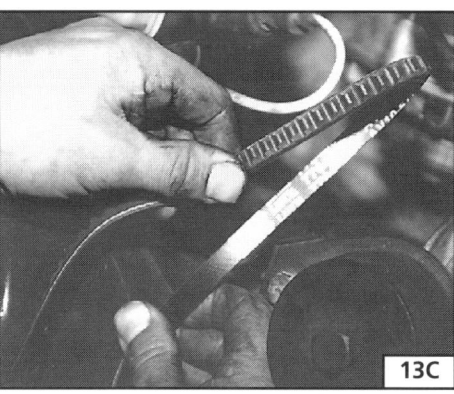

**13C.** Check the belt, and if there is any sign of cracking, 'polishing', fraying or severe wear on the inner face, replace it.

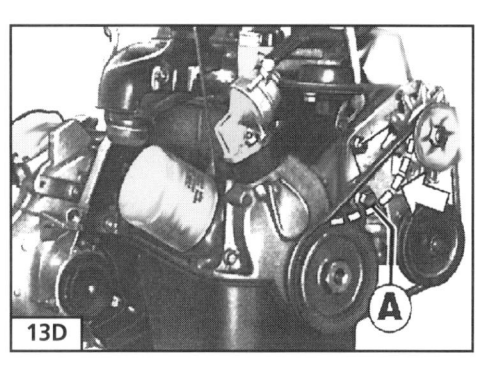

**13D.** The alternator drive belt should deflect no more than 10 mm when firm thumb pressure is applied to the belt between the pulleys in the direction of the arrow (**A**), with the dotted line showing the direction of deflection in exaggerated form. This is the 900's OHV engine.

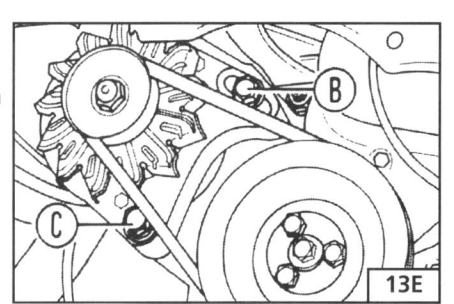

**13E.** If adjustment is necessary, slacken the upper pivot bolt (**B**) and the lower bolt (**C**), on all models. This is the Sporting's FIRE engine.

Use a length of wood to pivot the alternator away from the engine block but take great care not to damage the alternator casing. Tighten the bolts when the tension is correct.

☐ **Job 14. Check cooling system.**

### SAFETY FIRST!

- The coolant level should be checked - and the cooling system worked on, ONLY WHEN THE COOLANT IS COLD.
- If you remove the pressure cap or bleed screws when the engine is hot, scalding coolant will spurt out.

## SAFETY FIRST!

- Keep anti-freeze away from children. If it is accidentally swallowed or contacts skin or eyes, rinse immediately with plenty of water and seek immediate medical help.

Examine the cooling system hoses, looking for signs of splitting, chafing and perishing. Squeeze the top and bottom radiator hoses. Any hard, brittle areas or crackling sounds tell you that the hoses are decomposing from the inside - replacements needed!

*making it easy* 
- If original FIAT hose clips are fitted, cut them off (taking great care not to damage the stub beneath!)
- Replace with screw-tight clips, when fitting a new hose. Ensure that hose clips are secure and firm but not over-tightened.

### ☐ Job 15. Change engine coolant.

## SAFETY FIRST!

- See **SAFETY FIRST** at the start of **Job 14**.

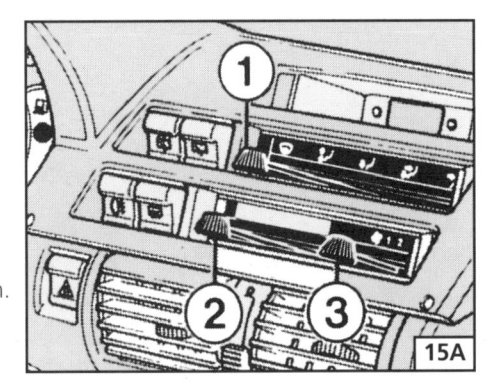

**15A.** Remove the expansion tank filler cap. Move the heater control (**2**) to the red (open) position.

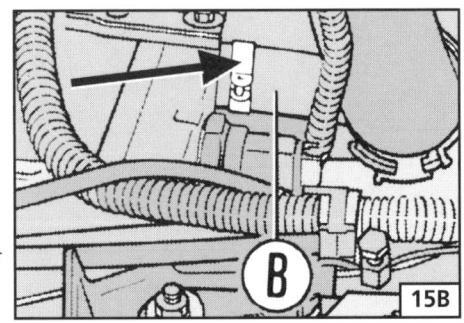

**15B.** Loosen the worm-drive clip (arrowed) or cut off the FIAT clip (see **Job 14**) and pull off the bottom radiator hose (**B**).

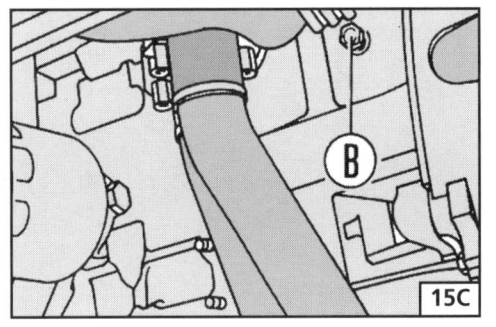

**15C.** Also open the drain plug or tap (**B**) at the centre of the rear flank of the engine block, when fitted. Drain the coolant into a container. On models with a separate expansion tank, detach the hose from the expansion tank and drain the tank.

*i* INSIDE INFORMATION: From time to time it's a good idea to flush the cooling system. With the bottom hose re-connected, disconnect and remove the top hose from the radiator. Insert the end of a garden hose first into the hose (packing the gap with a rag) and then the radiator inlet, flushing the system in both directions until the water comes out clear. *i*

IMPORTANT NOTE: Flush first with the heater control turned OFF until the engine and radiator are clear, so that you don't flush sediment into the heater. Then with the heater turned ON, flush the heater system out.

### ALL LATER VEHICLES

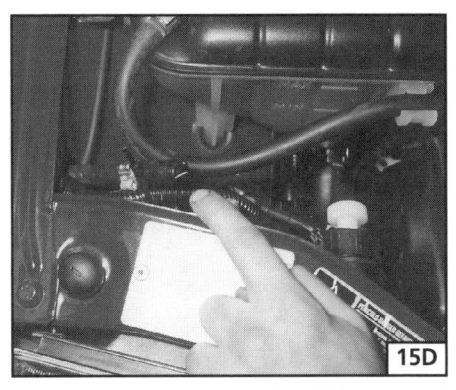

**15D.** To prevent air-locks forming in the cooling system as it is refilled (all hoses and the drain plug reconnected, of course!), 1.1 Sporting models have two air-bleed screws strategically positioned in the system. These should be opened before refilling. The first, not fitted to 900 models, it seems, is located in a tube in the front right-hand side of the engine bay...

**15E.** ... and the second, fitted to all models, is found on the heater hose in front of the bulkhead. Only undo the screws by two or three turns. Retighten both screws when air-free coolant emerges.

IMPORTANT NOTE: Don't worry if there is only one bleed screw, or if - as is the case with some FIATs - there are no bleed screws. In the first case, just bleed from the one point. In the second, detach the small-diameter top-hose from the thermostat housing and bleed air from there, reconnecting only when bubble-free coolant emerges.

Refill the cooling system with a 50/50 mixture of clean water and fresh **Paraflu** anti-freeze. Tighten the bleed screws when coolant, and not air, comes out steadily. Run the engine for a few minutes and bleed again.

IMPORTANT NOTE: It is highly likely that more air will be dislodged when you first use the car. Keep your eye on the coolant level (See **Job 2**) - perhaps carrying some 50/50 diluted coolant with you for the first few journeys.

# PART C: TRANSMISSION

❑ **Job 16. Check transmission oil level.**

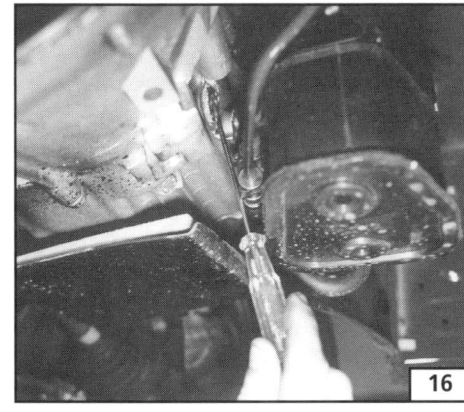

**16.** The combined oil level and filler plug is on the forward-facing side of the gearbox, tucked right behind the charcoal canister when fitted. Check the level with the car on level ground.

Wipe around the filler plug with a rag to prevent dirt contamination. Remove the plug - using a 10 mm Allen key - and top-up if necessary, using the specified **Tutela** transmission oil (see *Chapter 3, Facts and Figures*), until oil just dribbles from the filler hole. Refit the plug.

❑ **Job 17. Change transmission oil.**

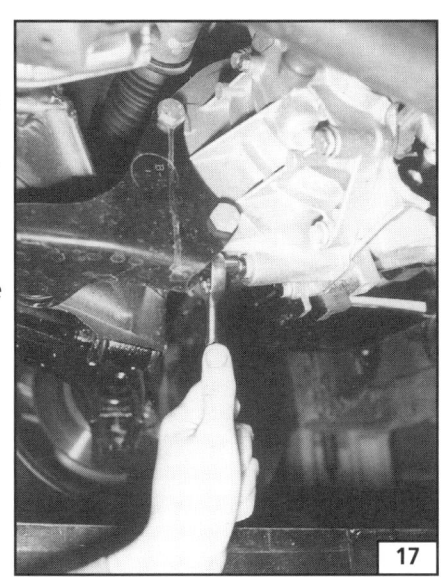

**17.** The combined gearbox and final drive oil should be drained at the time shown in the *Service Interval Chart*. Do so only after the car has been used and the gearbox oil is warm, so that it flows well. Remove the drain plug (near the transmission mounting, accessed from beneath the car) and drain the oil into a container. Leave for 10 minutes to drain completely, and refill with the correct grade of **Tutela** transmission oil through the level/filler plug, as described in *Job 16*.

❑ **Job 18. Check driveshaft gaiters.**

**18.** Grasp and turn the driveshafts, checking both inner and outer gaiters, checking for signs of gaiter splitting or damage that could allow grease out or - worse still - water in. Ensure the gaiter clips are secure.

IMPORTANT NOTE: Change any split, damaged or suspect gaiter as soon as possible - preferably before using the car again. See *Chapter 6, Repairs and Replacements* for full instructions.

❑ **Job 19. Check/adjust clutch.**

The clutch mechanism is self-adjusting, although the cable linkage can stretch over a period of time and may need adjustment.

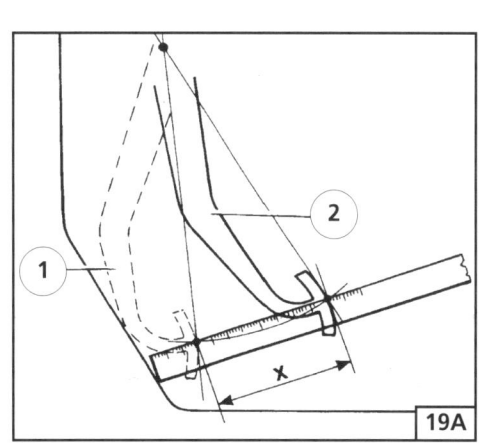

**19A.** To adjust the position of the clutch pedal:
● Work the clutch pedal two or three times;
● Check that the travel "**X**" is between 122 and 132 mm.
● Use a rule by the pedal to measure the difference (**X**) between the pedal in contact with the bulkhead partition (**1**) and the pedal in the rest position (**2**).

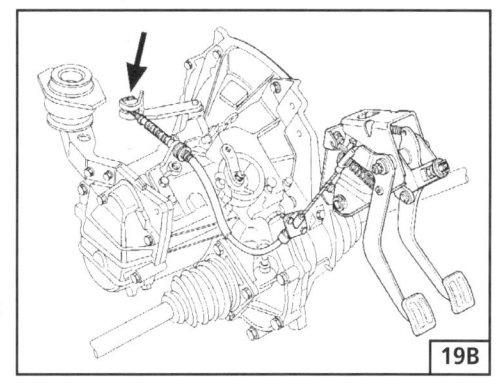

**19B.** Any adjustment of the travel should be carried out via the nut and the lock nut (arrowed) on the clutch control cable, on the gearbox top, inside the engine bay.

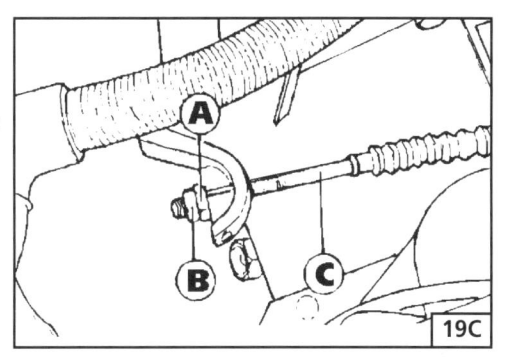

**19C.** Slacken the outer lock-nut (**B**) from the inner adjusting nut (**A**) using two spanners in opposition. Note that turning the adjusting nut inwards along the threaded rod (**C**) will increase pedal travel. Tighten lock-nut against inner nut after adjustment.

See **FACT FILE: DISCONNECTING THE BATTERY**, page 5-5.

CHAPTER 5 PART C: TRANSMISSION

5-13

# PART D: IGNITION AND ELECTRICS

❏ **Job 20. Check/clean/gap spark plugs.**

### SAFETY FIRST!

• You may minimise the risk of shock when the engine is running by wearing thick rubber gloves and by NEVER working on the system in damp weather or when standing on damp ground. Read **Chapter 1, Safety First!** before carrying out any work on the ignition system.
• ELECTRONIC IGNITION SYSTEMS INVOLVE VERY HIGH VOLTAGES! All manufacturers recommend that only trained personnel should go near the high-tension circuit (coil, distributor and HT wiring) and it is ESSENTIAL that anyone wearing a medical pacemaker device does not go near the ignition system.
• Stroboscopic timing requires the engine to be running - take great care that parts of the timing light or parts of you don't get caught up in moving components!
• Don't wear loose clothing or long, loose hair.

GENERAL. On OHV engines the spark plugs face forwards, allowing easy working access. On the FIRE OHC engines they are on the back of the engine.

**20A.** INSIDE INFORMATION: On the Sporting (FIRE-engined) cars, it is necessary to remove the air cleaner. The (rectangular) air cleaner housing is released by levering off the two plastic caps (arrowed) and undoing the air filter housing nuts, releasing the clips on the front,...

**20B.** ...and unclipping the small-bore hoses, which allows the housing to be pushed carefully to one side.

**20C.** Carefully remove the spark plug caps, being careful to pull only on the cap and not the HT lead. If you can't be sure to remember which HT lead belongs to which spark plug, number them from one end of the engine to the other.

**20D.** Unscrew the plug using the correct type of spark plug socket. Take care to keep the spanner strictly in line with the plug so as not to crack the electrode. This is the Sporting 1.1 engine; the plugs are on the front of the 900 engine.

If the electrodes of the plugs look rounded and worn, replace the plugs.

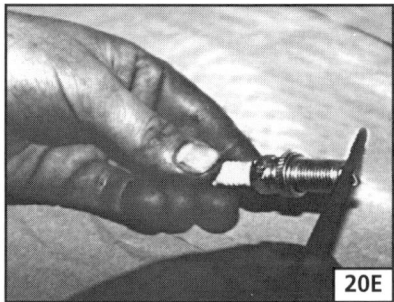

**20E.** It is essential that the plug is gapped correctly. See **Chapter 3, Facts and Figures**. Use a feeler blade of the correct thickness, sliding it between the electrodes. It should be a firm sliding fit. Use a gapping tool or carefully wielded pliers to bend the curved electrode towards or away from the centre electrode. Take GREAT CARE not to damage the insulator near the tip of the plug.

INSIDE INFORMATION: With all Cinquecento engines, the spark plugs screw into aluminium, which is easily damaged if the spark plugs do not engage their threads properly. It is important therefore to screw in the plugs by hand initially - by, say, two or three turns - before using the plug spanner. A light smear of copper grease on the plug threads will enable them to turn more freely and also make them easier to remove next time. Finally, don't over-tighten the plugs - firm hand-pressure on the spanner is sufficient.

❏ **Job 21. Change spark plugs.**

Spark plugs 'tire' and lose efficiency over a period of time, even if they look okay. See **Job 20** for information on their removal and replacement.

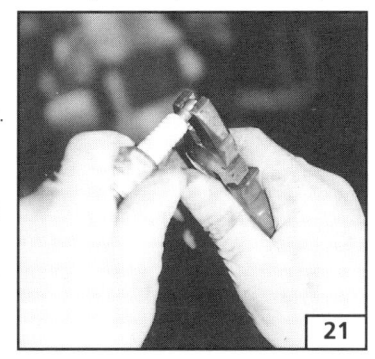

🅘 **21. INSIDE INFORMATION:** To stop the cap coming loose, 'nip' it tight with pliers before fitting. 🅘

❏ **Job 22. Check/clean HT leads.**

**SAFETY FIRST!**

• See **SAFETY FIRST!** at the start of this section and **Chapter 1, Safety First!**

**FACT FILE: IGNITION TYPES**
• Both 4-cylinder engines are fitted with non-adjustable electronic ignition.
• There is no conventional distributor - the ECU does the job electronically - and each engine has a non-repairable pair of coils mounted on the left-hand end of the cylinder head.

• Remove each plug lead from the spark plugs, pulling only on the plug caps, not on the HT cables.
• Clean the caps and cables with a clean rag, applying a little aerosol water-dispellant spray to help shift oil and grime.

IMPORTANT NOTE: DO NOT spray water dispellant or apply lubricant to any part of an electronic ignition distributor. (It's okay to clean/wipe the coils, however.)

❏ **Job 23. Check ignition timing/system.**

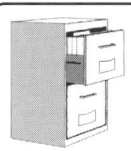

**FACT FILE: IGNITION TIMING**
• With both engine types, the ignition timing is one of the parameters controlled by the ECU, taking information from the flywheel sensor. The bracket onto which the sensor is mounted is set in position at the factory and should never need to be moved. In theory, the sensor can be removed from the bracket and replaced without the setting being affected.
• With the type of ignition system used on the 900 engine, it does not appear to be possible to check the timing, other than by using the FIAT diagnostic tester - see **Job 25**.
• On the Sporting 1.1 engine, it is possible to check the timing, as described below.

## SPORTING 1.1 FIRE ENGINES ONLY

*making it easy!* • Use typists' correction fluid to highlight the timing marks and make them easier to see in the timing light beam.

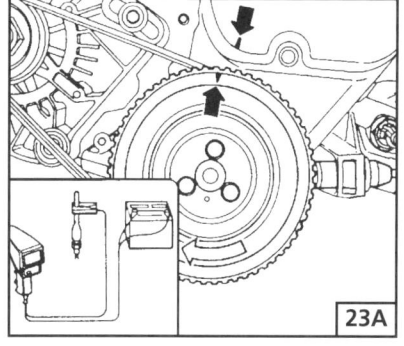

**23A.** Connect a timing light, with inductive clips (i.e. NOT in the HT lead) according to the maker's instructions, making sure none of the wires can come into contact with any hot or moving parts of the engine. Check the timing by directing the flashing beam of the timing light at the timing marks on the engine (arrowed), which will appear 'frozen'.

With all the electrical equipment turned off and the cooling fan not operating, and at an idling speed of between 850 and 950 rpm, the advance should be between 5 degrees and 11 degrees Before Top Dead Centre.

IMPORTANT NOTE: Fluctuations in the ignition advance should be considered normal since the electronic control unit constantly corrects its value to keep the engine speed stable.

It is not possible to adjust the advance and under no circumstances should you attempt to move the flywheel sensor in order to compensate for an incorrect reading. Your FIAT dealer will need to use the special FIAT diagnostic equipment to analyse the cause of any problem that you may identify.

### CHECKING RPM AND TDC SENSOR

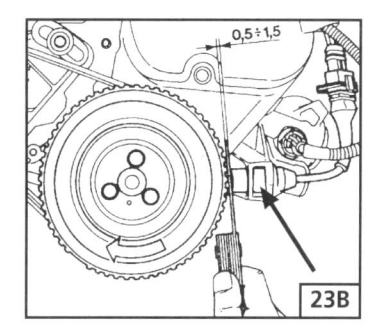

**23B.** The sensor is on the alternator-end of the engine. The gap between the sensor and the rotor must be between 0.5 and 1.5 mm. This is the position of the sensor (arrowed) on the Sporting 1.1 engine; on the 900 engine, the sensor is at approximately 10 o'clock on the rotor.

IMPORTANT NOTE: The sensor position cannot be adjusted and if the gap is outside the accepted tolerances, it suggests that some damage may have taken place. If so, refer to your FIAT dealership.

❏ **Job 24. Check electric fan operation.**

**24.** Drive the car until it is at normal operating temperature. Park outdoors and, with the gearbox in neutral (or 'P' in the case of an automatic) leave the engine running. At just above normal temperature the electric cooling fan should

**CHAPTER 5 PART D: ELECTRICS**

5-15

come on, and then go off again when the temperature drops. If the fan doesn't behave, you will need to check the thermo-switch on the radiator, pointed out here (*illustration 24*) from under the car, along with all connections and wires in its circuit with the fan motor. See **Chapter 6, Repairs and Replacements**.

❏ **Job 25. Run diagnostic ignition/injection test.**

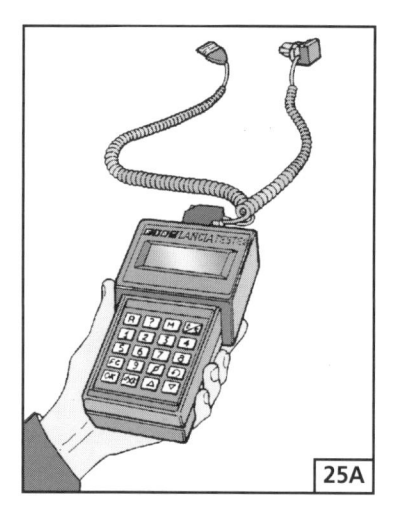

**25A.** Faults can only be accurately diagnosed with a FIAT diagnostics tester.

**25B.** It is connected to the diagnostic socket found here (arrowed) in 900 engine bays...

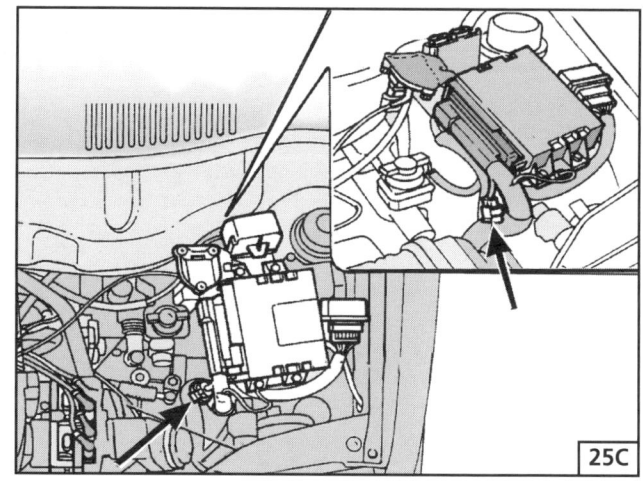

**25C.** ...and here on the Sporting engine (arrowed).

## PART E: FUEL AND EXHAUST

### SAFETY FIRST!

- *The high pressure pipework on a (non-SPI) fuel injection system can retain its pressure for days even after the engine has been switched off.*
- *When you disconnect the pipework, a jet of fuel can be emitted under very high pressure - strong enough to penetrate the skin or damage the eyes.*
- *NEVER work on the fuel pipework when the engine is running.*
- *ALWAYS place a rag over a union while it is being undone until all the pressure has been let out of the system.*
- *You are recommended to wear strong rubber gloves and goggles when disconnecting the fuel injection system's high pressure pipework. Always disconnect VERY slowly, letting pressure out progressively.*
- *See the apprpriate vehicle documentation for details of how to depressureise the system. Usually it means removing the fuel pump relay and running the engine until it 'dies'.*
- *Disconnect the battery negative earth before working on the fuel system.*
- *Work outdoors and away from sources of flame or ignition.*
- *ALWAYS wear rubber gloves - don't let your skin come into contact with fuel.*

❏ **Job 26. Check fuel pipes for leaks.**

Check the fuel lines, looking for signs of chafing, splits and perishing of the rubber and plastic parts. Ensure any worm-drive hose clips used on the connections are firm and secure.

❏ **Job 27. Change air filter.**

### SPORTING (FIRE) OHC ENGINES

**27A.** Release the two plastic spring clips (arrowed), one on each side of the air cleaner housing, by pulling outwards. Pull the front part of the housing forwards so that the filter element can be pulled out and replaced. When you push the new element into position, make sure the outer seal is properly fitted to the channel. Replace the front of the housing and secure the clips.

### 900 (OHV) ENGINES

**27B.** Release the four steel spring clips...

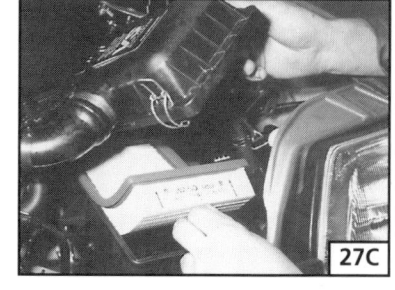

**27C.** ...lift the housing cover and remove the filter from the housing.

IMPORTANT NOTE: In dusty conditions, the element should be checked and, if necessary replaced, more often than normal. A blocked element will cause poor fuel consumption, take emissions out of the legal limit and could pollute the catalytic converter.

☐ **Job 28. Change fuel filter.**

### 900 CARBURETTOR ENGINES ONLY (NON-UK)

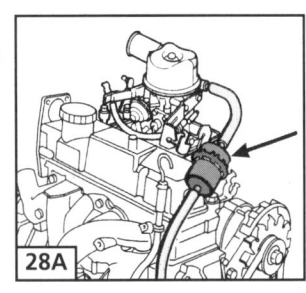

**28A.** If your (carburettor) engine's fuel supply hose to the carburettor is equipped with a disposable in-line fuel filter (arrowed), renew it by disconnecting the battery earth lead, undoing the fuel hose clips at either side of the filter unit, and removing the filter. Absorb spilt fuel with a rag. Discard the filter, and fit the new one with its arrow pointing in the direction of fuel flow. Refit/reconnect in the reverse order. If the original hose clips have to be cut off, fit new worm-drive clips.

IMPORTANT NOTES:
● Wear plastic gloves and goggles and have a large rag and a suitable fire extinguisher ready.
● Place a container beneath the filter to catch fuel spillage.

### FUEL INJECTION MODELS

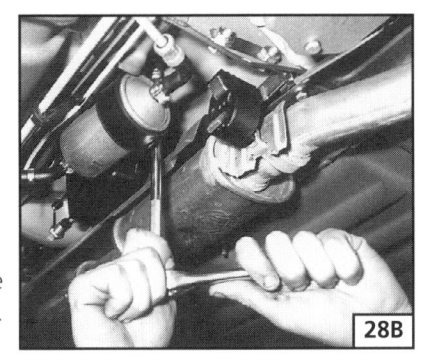

**28B.** The filter - beneath the car, adjacent to the exhaust - must be renewed at the specified service interval to prevent damaging sediment from getting into the injection mechanism. It should be released from its mounting bracket, but only after the inlet and outlet hose clips have been removed. Cut them off, if they are the original FIAT crimped type and replace with screw-tight clamps.

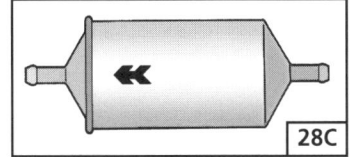

**28C.** The new filter must be fitted with its arrow in the direction of fuel flow.

IMPORTANT NOTE: After clamping the new filter in place, refit the hoses, tighten the unions, ensure no traces of fuel are left in the engine bay, reconnect the battery and restart the engine. Check carefully to ensure there are no leaks.

☐ **Job 29. Check/adjust engine idle and emissions (if necessary).**

Setting the idle speed and mixture is not just a matter of making the car run smoothly and economically; it's also a question of allowing it to run within the legal hydrocarbon (HC), Nitrous Oxide (NO) and carbon monoxide (CO) emission limits. If it is outside limits, the car will fail the annual test. (However, a worn engine will fail even if the carburettor or injection system is correctly set up.)

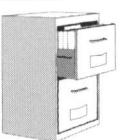

> **FACT FILE: ESSENTIAL PREPARATIONS**
> ● When tuning the engine you should adjust the carburettor or injection last of all, as their settings will be affected by the state of tune of the rest of the engine.
> ● Ignition dwell angle and timing must be correct (in other words, the ECU must function correctly on these cars), the air filter should be clean, there should be no air leaks on the induction system, and all electrical consumers and the air conditioning (if fitted) should be switched off.
> ● Get the engine to full operating temperature before checking and adjusting.
> ● If you warm the engine on tick-over (instead of on a journey), it won't be hot enough until you have heard the electric cooling fan cut in and out again twice.

*i* INSIDE INFORMATION: These jobs require the use of a tachometer (rev-counter) and an exhaust gas analyser to achieve any degree of accuracy. If you don't own them - and relatively inexpensive tools are now available - you may wish to have the work carried out by your local FIAT dealer. *i*

*ROUGH GUIDE: Within each section is a description of how you can get the car running tolerably well without any specialist equipment, so that you can take it to your FIAT dealership for accurate (and MoT-able!) tuning.*

### 900 MODELS WITH WEBER CARBURETTORS ONLY (NON-UK)

IMPORTANT NOTE: Some non-UK Cinquecentos were fitted with an adjustable Weber carburettor.

TAMPER PROOFING: All these carburettors originally had a tamper-proof seal (some plastic, some aluminium) placed over the mixture adjustment screw. These seals are to prevent anyone unauthorised from altering the mixture and exhaust emissions. In certain countries these seals must be retained by law.

If the seal is a plastic cap placed over the adjuster screw, it can be broken off with pliers. If it is a plug within the screw recess, force it out with a sharp object.

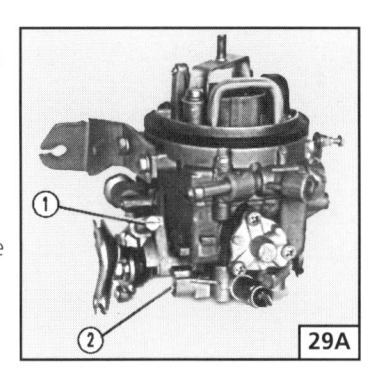

**29A. IDLE SPEED ADJUSTMENT:** Connect a rev-counter according to the maker's instructions, and check the idle speed. Turning the butterfly adjustment screw (**1**) clockwise increases the idle speed, anti-clockwise reduces it. Set the idle speed to 800-900 rpm.

*ROUGH GUIDE: Turn the screw until the engine is running at the slowest speed at which it runs smoothly and evenly.*

CHAPTER 5 PART E: FUEL AND EXHAUST

MIXTURE ADJUSTMENT: Check that the idle speed is correct and make sure that the engine is at full operating temperature. Connect an exhaust gas analyser to the end of the tailpipe, as instructed by the maker. If the CO reading is outside the range 0.5% to 1.5% CO (carbon monoxide), adjustment is required as follows:

Use a narrow-blade screwdriver and turn the mixture screw (*illustration 29A, part 2*) clockwise to weaken (reduce) or anti-clockwise to richen (increase) the reading.

***ROUGH GUIDE:*** *Turn the mixture screw inwards (clockwise). As you do so, the tick-over speed will increase, until the point comes where the engine starts to run 'lumpily'. Back off the screw until the engine runs smoothly again, and then some more until the speed just starts to drop. At this point, screw the adjuster back in by a quarter-turn and you'll be somewhere near the optimum setting for smooth running.*

**IMPORTANT NOTE:** After setting the mixture adjustment, re-check and, if necessary, re-adjust the idle speed.

### 900 AND SPORTING ENGINES WITH FUEL INJECTION

The idle speed and mixture settings are controlled by the Electronic Control Unit (ECU) which is 'self-learning' and is programmed to adjust itself to give the ideal settings under all conditions. No manual adjustment is possible, nor provided for. If there is a problem, you will need to take your car to a FIAT dealer, with the appropriate diagnostic equipment.

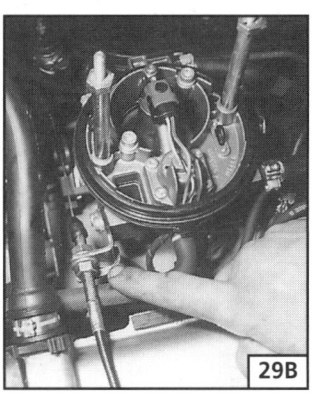

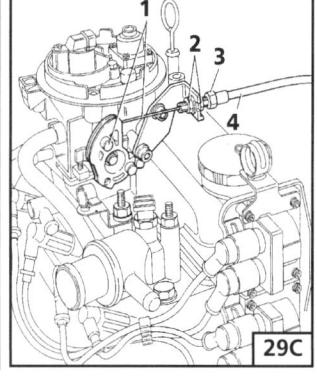

**29B.** You must NOT try to adjust tick-over with the cable adjustment, but a too-tight cable will give an excessively fast tick-over. This is the 1.1 FIRE engine.

**29C.** The system on the 900 OHV engine is identical. The cable (**1**) should be adjusted so that there is no tension in the quadrant with foot-off the throttle, but so that the butterfly is fully open on full throttle. Slackening the locknuts (**2**) allows you to screw the adjuster (**3**) in or out, altering the tension on the outer cable (**4**).

☐ **Job 30. Check emission control systems.**

**PETROL INJECTION MODELS ONLY**

On petrol-injected Cinquecentos, sophisticated emission control equipment is fitted.

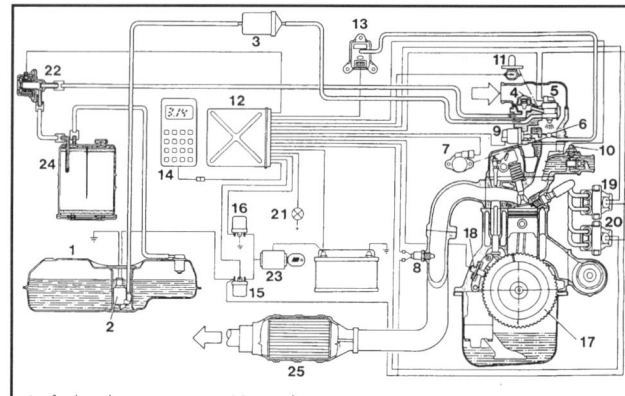

1 - fuel tank
2 - immersed petrol pump
3 - fuel filter
4 - petrol pressure regulator
5 - injector
6 - butterfly valve
7 - butterfly position sensor
8 - oxygen sensor, or Lambda sensor
9 - actuator for adjusting idle speed and when the engine is warming up from cold
10 - coolant temperature sensor
11 - intake air temperature sensor
12 - injection/ignition control unit
13 - absolute pressure sensor
14 - diagnostic socket for Fiat-Lancia tester
15 - ignition/injection system power relay
16 - injection/ignition control unit relay
17 - crankshaft pulley
18 - RPM and TDC sensor
19 - ignition coil for cylinders 3 and 2
20 - ignition coil for cylinders 4 and 1
21 - failure and autodiagnosis warning light
22 - petrol vapour cut-out valve
23 - ignition switch with key
24 - activated carbon filter
25 - trivalent catalytic silencer

**30A.** This is the single point injection (SPI) system fitted to 900 cars...

**FACT FILE: EMISSION CONTROL SYSTEM**

The main features of the system are:

• an **Electronic Control Module Unit or (ECU)** - the 'computer brain', which is programmed to alter the car's fuel and ignition settings according to information received from various sensors.

• a **catalytic converter** in the exhaust system, to convert CO and other gases to less harmful gases.

• a **Lambda sensor** in the exhaust manifold or front pipe (according to model) to detect the 'tune' of the exhaust gases and give a signal to the ECU.

• a petrol **evaporation control system**, to cut down on petrol vapour emissions from the fuel tank.

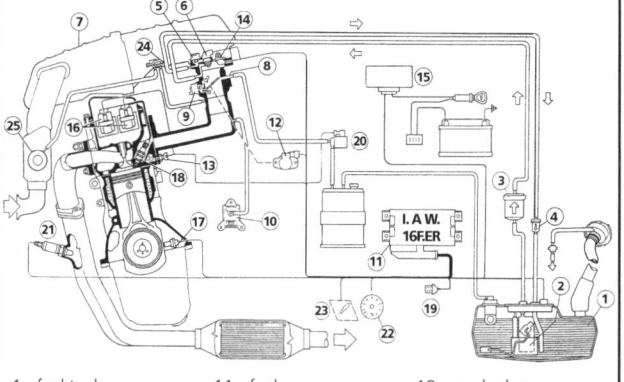

1 - fuel tank
2 - electric fuel pump
3 - fuel filter
4 - anti-backflow valve
5 - fuel pressure regulator
6 - fuel injector
7 - air cleaner
8 - fuel vapours connector
9 - engine idle speed actuator
10 - absolute pressure sensor
11 - fuel injection/ignition electronic control unit
12 - throttle position sensor
13 - engine coolant temperature sensor
14 - intake air temperature sensor
15 - double relay for fuel injection/ignition system
16 - ignition coils
17 - RPM and TDC sensor
18 - spark plugs
19 - diagnostic socket for FIAT/LANCIA tester
20 - vapour recirculation solenoid
21 - Lambda probe
22 - Rev counter (if present)
23 - I.A.W. system fault warning light
24 - thermostatic valve
25 - mixer unit

**30B.** ...and this the SPI system fitted to Sporting 1.1 engines.

5-18

**ELECTRONIC CONTROL MODULE:** This is not an item that requires any servicing. If you think it might be faulty, ask your FIAT dealer or fuel injection specialist to check it for you. This must be done by someone with the correct FIAT plug-in diagnostic equipment and data.

**CATALYTIC CONVERTER:** The CAT is not serviceable. If it fails, you will be told at the MoT test. Replacement is expensive, so we recommend you obtain a second opinion before replacing the 'cat'.

**LAMBDA SENSOR:** For information concerning the sensor, see *Job 31*.

**CHARCOAL CANISTER:** This unit is located behind the cars' front panel, and does not need regular servicing. Check the canister one-way valve (see **Chapter 6, Repairs and Replacements, Part E, FUEL AND EXHAUST** for illustration) by disconnecting it and trying to blow through both ends. You should only be able to blow air towards the canister, not away from it. If the valve is faulty, renew it, making sure that it is fitted the right way round.

*i* INSIDE INFORMATION: If the canister is flooded with petrol, it is probable that one of the **purge valves** or **purge valve floats** is faulty. Get this investigated and rectified by a FIAT dealer. If the engine cuts out and then restarts after a while, it could be the **breather hose valve**, fitted under the fuel filler neck. This one-way valve allows air to enter the tank as the fuel level falls, otherwise an air lock can prevent fuel reaching the engine. To test the valve, take off the pipe clips, remove the valve and test it as for the canister one-way valve, above. It should allow air to pass into the tank, but not the other way. *i*

☐ **Job 31. Check Lambda sensor.**

**PETROL INJECTION MODELS ONLY**

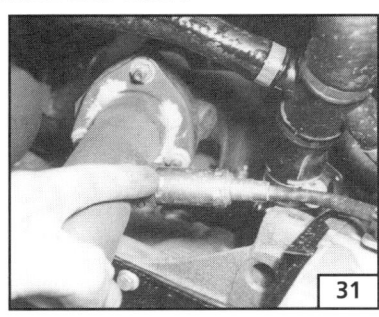

**31.** For a description of how the Lambda sensor (fitted in the exhaust downpipe) works, see *Job 30*, **FACT FILE: EMISSION CONTROL SYSTEM**. It should be checked at the recommended interval - the cost of checking and replacing the sensor is far less than that of having to replace the catalytic converter because it has been polluted due to a sensor fault.

*making it easy* • Replacement of the sensor is a simple job, but it can only be tested by your FIAT dealer with the correct equipment.
• If the sensor is faulty, have it renewed by your dealer.
• Lambda sensors are very delicate and easily damaged. It is not likely that you would be able to return one to the supplier if you fitted it yourself.
• Lambda sensors are only fitted to cars with a catalytic converter.

☐ **Job 32. Check inlet and exhaust manifold fixings.**

**32A.** Check that the inlet and exhaust manifold nuts and bolts are tightened to the correct torque. See **Chapter 3, Facts and Figures**. Check the exhaust-to-manifold flange (arrowed) from beneath the car. This is the Sporting FIRE engine; it's on the back of the 900 unit.

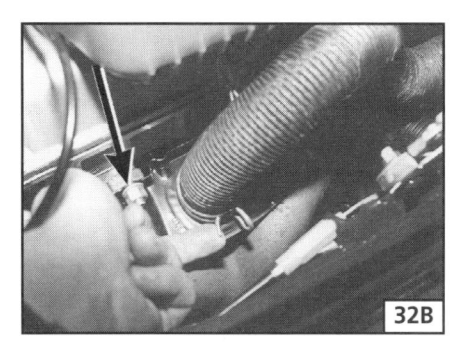

**32B.** Check the manifold-to-head fixing (arrowed).

*i* INSIDE INFORMATION: While in the vicinity, check the condition of the heated air hose from exhaust manifold to air intake. It *can* deteriorate and it *can* affect running. *i*

☐ **Job 33. Check exhaust system.**

**33A.** Examine the silencer and exhaust pipes and joints for corrosion and signs of leaking, indicated by a 'sooty' deposit at the point of the leak.

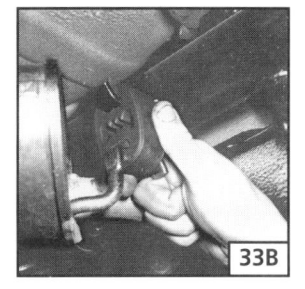

**33B.** Also check the condition of the rubber 'hangers' that hold the system to the car. If any are missing or broken, the exhaust system can fracture due to extra stresses. Stretch the rubber, and look for cracks.

*making it easy* • If you suspect a leak but its location isn't obvious, start the engine and pressurise the system by holding a piece of board against the tailpipe.
• Under pressure, the leak should be more noisy and obvious.
• Don't burn yourself on the exhaust!

# PART F: STEERING AND SUSPENSION

☐ **Job 34. Check front wheel bearings.**

In order to check for wear:
* raise the front of the car on axle stands (see *Chapter 1, Safety First!*);
* place the gearbox in neutral;
* pull the handbrake securely on and chock the rear wheels.

**34A.** Try spinning each wheel (as far as possible with a front-drive car), feeling for rough rotation. Rock the wheel about its centre in the vertical plane...

**34B.** ...and in the horizontal plane, feeling for excess bearing play.

*i* **INSIDE INFORMATION:** If a wheel bearing is worn, you will normally hear a noise on the outer, loaded bearing when cornering. *i*

☐ **Job 35. Check front suspension.**

## BOTTOM BALL JOINT

Jack up the car underneath the suspension lower arm (wishbone), so that the wheel is two inches off the ground. See *Chapter 1, Safety First*.

**35A.** Place a long, rigid bar between the ground and the bottom of the tyre tread, and gently 'jog' the wheel upwards repeatedly...

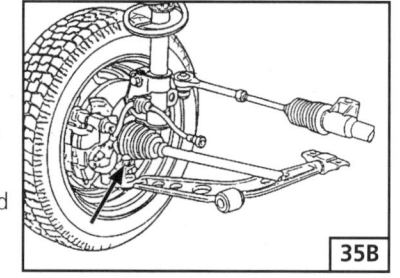

**35B.** ...while a helper looks at and feels the lower balljoint (arrowed) for vertical movement. The helper should NOT lie under the car, and you should be careful not to rock the car off the jack.
Also examine the ball joint gaiter for any damage or leakage of grease - a simple, visual examination. You will have to replace the wishbone assembly if the gaiter is damaged. See *Chapter 6, Repairs and Replacements* for information.

## TRACK CONTROL ARM INNER BUSHES

**35C.** Raise the car off the ground and support it on an axle stand under the subframe so that the suspension on the side being checked can hang free. Lever between the arm and its mounting, looking for excessive movement of the bushes. Some cushioned flexing is normal. See *Chapter 6, Repairs and Replacements* for bush replacement information.

## SUSPENSION STRUT/SHOCK ABSORBER

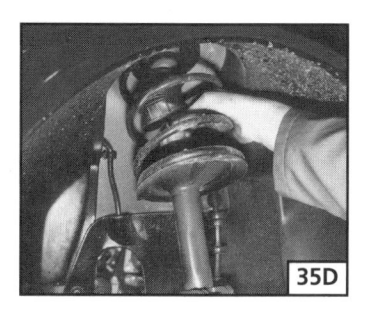

**35D.** Examine the shock absorber, which is enclosed inside the coil spring, for leaks, looking for signs of a 'damp' oil stain seeping from underneath the top half of the shock absorber body. Pull back the rubber shroud.

The top of the strut/shock absorber is mounted in a rubber bush which can be checked for softness, cracking or deterioration from inside the engine bay.

**BOUNCE TEST:** Try 'bouncing' each front corner of the car in a rhythmical motion, pressing down as hard as you can. When you let go, the movement should continue for no more than one-and-a-half rebounds. If it does so, this is a sure indication that the shock absorber is worn and should be replaced. If one of the front shock absorbers needs replacing, replace both, for safety reasons.

## ANTI-ROLL BAR BUSHES

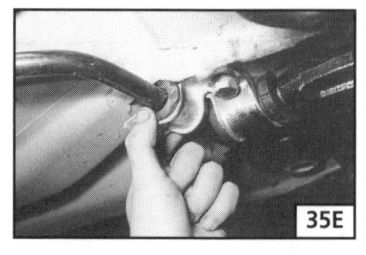

**35E.** Over time, anti-roll bar bushes soften and, eventually, disintegrate. Examine them and check the mountings on the wishbones, as well.

☐ **Job 36. Check steering column, joints and rack.**

## TRACK ROD ENDS

**36A.** Drive the car on to car ramps, firmly apply the handbrake and chock the rear wheels. Get your helper to sit inside the car, turn the ignition key to the 'MAR' (ON) position to release the steering column lock. Now, move the steering wheel repeatedly about 100 mm (4 in.) each way while someone checks for free movement in each track rod end (TRE). Also, look out for a split gaiter. Replace the TRE if the gaiter is split, or it will rapidly fail.

**ℹ INSIDE INFORMATION:** Try placing your hand over the TRE as the steering is moved. If there are any signs of wear, replace the TRE. ℹ

## STEERING COLUMN

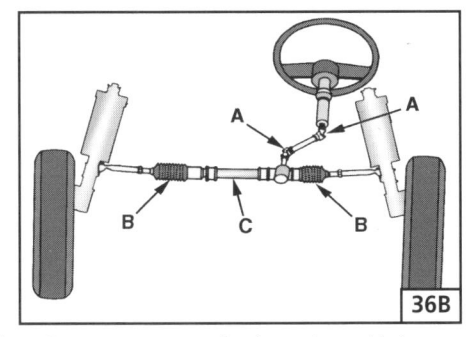

**36B.** The steering column has two universal joints (**A**) which need to be checked for wear. While your assistant is turning the steering wheel, check to see if there is any movement in the universal joints.

**ℹ INSIDE INFORMATION:** Place your hand over the joint - you can usually feel the movement better than you can see it. If there is ANY movement at all, play at the steering wheel will be greatly exaggerated - replace the faulty universal joint. ℹ

## STEERING RACK GAITERS

**36C.** Turn the ignition key to the 'MAR' (ON) position but take care not to start the engine. Turn the steering wheel to full right lock. From underneath the bonnet, examine the gaiter (see illustration **Job 36B, part B**) on the left-hand side, which will now be fully extended. Check visually for splits or oil leakage. Turn the steering wheel to the opposite lock and examine the gaiter on the other side of the rack. If necessary, replace IMMEDIATELY - the rack will rapidly be ruined if the gaiter is split.

**36D.** Also, watch the steering rack body (see illustration **Job 36B, part C**) to see if it is firmly attached. If there is any movement between the rack and its two mountings, shown here, check the securing bolts for tightness.

☐ **Job 37. Check rear wheel bearings.**

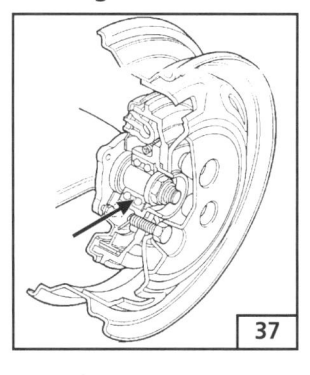

**37.** Cinquecento rear wheel bearings are sealed in their hubs and are usually very long lived. See the checking procedures described in **Job 34**, but remember not to apply the handbrake! Also note that the rear wheels will be easier to spin than the fronts.

☐ **Job 38. Check rear suspension.**

Chock the front wheels, jack the rear of the car under the rear suspension (see **Chapter 2, Using Your Car**), and place stands under the rear wheel-change jacking points. Lower the car onto the axle stands.

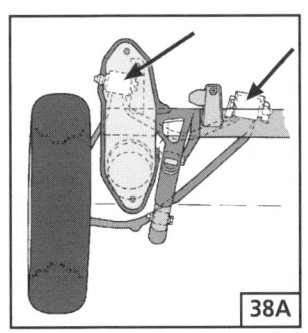

**38A.** Check the rear wishbone bush pivots (arrowed). Replace if excessive movement or bush deterioration are noticed. See **Chapter 6, Repairs and Replacements**.

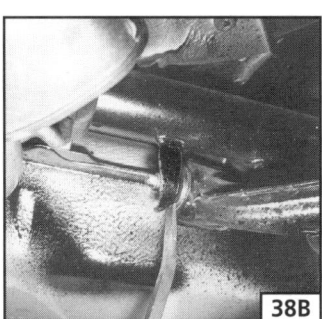

**38B.** Use a lever, such as a strong screwdriver, on each inner...

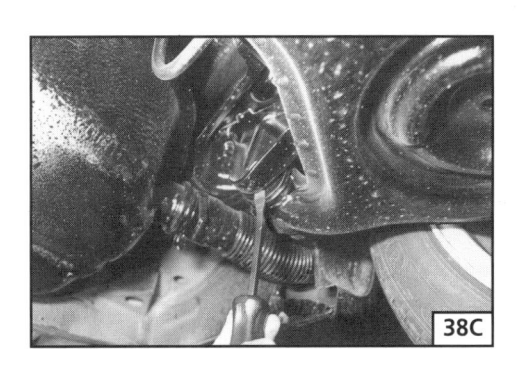

**38C.** ...and each outer mounting point.

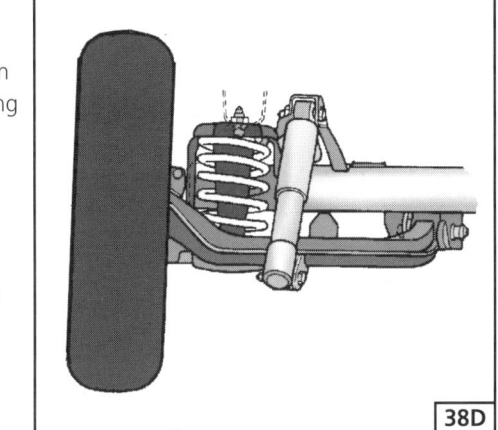

**38D.** Check the condition of each spring and the seatings for corrosion. Check that the bump stops, inside the springs, are present and correct.

5-21

**38E.** Look for signs of leaks coming from underneath the top part of each rear shock absorber and replace if necessary. Check the top and bottom rubber mounting bushes. If any are soft or split they must be replaced.

**BOUNCE TEST:** Bounce-test the shock absorbers as in **Job 35**.

❑ **Job 39. Check wheel bolts for tightness.**

**39.** Remove each wheel bolt in turn and ensure that they run smoothly. Clean the threads, if necessary. Refit and check that all are tightened to the correct torque - see **Chapter 3, Facts and Figures** - using a torque wrench.

## PART G: THE BRAKING SYSTEM

### SAFETY FIRST!

• Before raising the car, see **Chapter 1, Safety First!**
• Also, be sure to read the section on **BRAKES AND ASBESTOS** in **Chapter 1, Safety First!** for further important information.
• Your car's brakes are among its most important safety-related items. Do NOT attempt any work on the braking system unless you are fully competent to do so.
• If you have not been trained in this work, but wish to carry it out, we strongly recommend you have a garage or qualified mechanic check your work before using the car on the road.
• Always start by washing the brakes with a proprietary brand of brake cleaner - brake drums removed where appropriate - and never use compressed air to clean off brake dust.
• Always replace brake pads and/or shoes in complete 'axle' sets of four - never replace them on one wheel only.
• After fitting new brake shoes or pads, avoid heavy braking for the first 150 to 200 miles (250 to 300 km), except in an emergency.

Start by raising the wheel to be worked on and supporting it on an axle stand. Remove the road wheel - see **Chapter 1, Safety First!**

❑ **Job 40. Check front brakes.**

It is possible to visually check the thickness of the brake pads without carrying out any dismantling. However, if you are not experienced in carrying out this work, you may find it easier to work out how much life is left in the pads by removing them, as shown in this job. It is also excellent practice to clean out the brake dust and corrosion from inside the caliper housing from time to time and to check the condition of the piston seals.

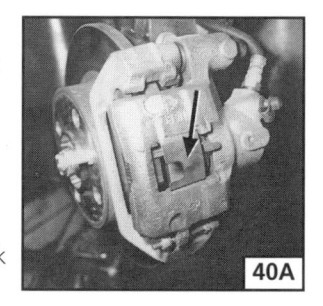

**40A.** With the wheel removed, take out the cover plate (arrowed) so that you can check the thickness of the pads.

**40B.** For the reasons given earlier, you are strongly advised to swing the caliper free. Use a pair of long-nosed pliers to pull out the clip (arrowed)...

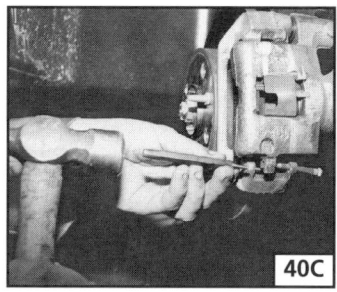

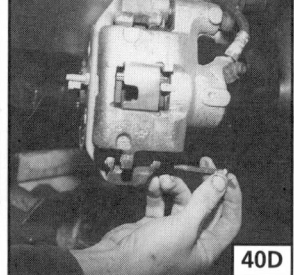

**40C.** ...tap out the retaining pin with a suitable drift...

**40D.** ...pull the pin straight out and push the clip back in to the end of the pin so that you don't lose it.

**40E.** You can now swing the caliper up and remove the pads for checking. Use a proprietary brand of spray-on brake cleaner to wash all brake dust from the brake components.

**40F.** You can now check the thickness of the brake disc which should not be less than the minimum specified in **Chapter 3, Facts and Figures**. Any scabbing of the brake disc or deep scoring will also mean that it should be replaced. If in doubt, check with your FIAT dealer.

> **FACT FILE: BRAKE DISC WEAR SYMPTOMS**
> There are certain essential checks you should carry out for yourself, with brake pads removed:
> - Look for any obvious grooves worn into the disc. Slight undulations are acceptable, but anything worse and the disc should be replaced.
> - Look and feel for any wear-ridge on the outer edges of the disc. The depth will give an indication of wear.
> - Check for corrosion of the disc surface. If any is found, the brake caliper is probably faulty, and needs checking.
> - If any surface flaking is found on either side of the disc, replace them both.
> - If you are not certain whether any wear is acceptable, ask your specialist or FIAT dealer to check.

Before reassembling the brake, check the condition of the brake caliper. Have an assistant VERY SLOWLY AND GENTLY apply pressure to the brake pedal while you watch the piston which should move outwards. If it doesn't easily move, it is seized and the caliper should be replaced. DO NOT allow the piston to project more than 10 mm or it may be forced from the caliper - use a G-clamp as an 'end stop'.

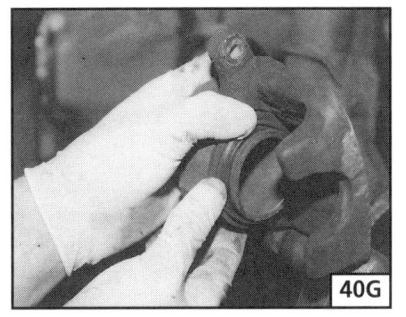

**40G.** Check inside the caliper housing for signs of corrosion. If any is found, or the seal is damaged, the caliper should be exchanged for a new or overhauled unit from your FIAT dealership. Examine the piston's protective gaiter for splitting and fluid leaks. This one is in poor condition and the caliper requires immediate replacement.

> *making it easy!*
> - In order to fit new pads, the caliper piston must be pushed back into the bore.
> - Use an old battery hydrometer to draw about half of the fluid from the master cylinder.
> - Push the piston back into the caliper, using a G-clamp.
> - Keep an eye on the master cylinder so that it doesn't overflow as fluid is pushed back up the pipe.

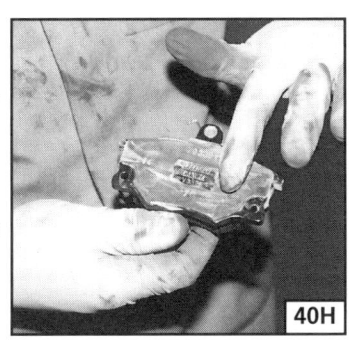

**40H.** Before fitting the pads, put a light smear of brake grease (NOT ordinary grease) on the pads' metal backplates at the points shown. Be VERY sparing or grease could migrate to the friction linings!

Replace the caliper. Refit the retaining pin and clip in the reverse order shown earlier.

IMPORTANT NOTE: After fitting the pads, and before driving the car, apply the brakes firmly several times to adjust them.

## ❏ Job 41. Check rear brakes.

> **SAFETY FIRST!**
> - Read **SAFETY FIRST!** at the start of **Job 40** before proceeding!

Slacken the wheel bolts, raise the wheel, remove it and support the car with an axle stand. Make sure that the wheels remaining on the ground are chocked in both directions and that the handbrake is off.

### DRUM REAR BRAKES

> *making it easy!* If the drum sticks, try:
> - disconnecting the handbrake cable from beneath the car.
> - screw a pair of bolts into the two threaded holes in the drum. Evenly tightening the bolts will force the drum off the shoes.
> - tap carefully around the drum with a hide mallet to help loosen it.

**41A.** Remove the two bolts (one of them the wheel positioning stud)...

**41B.** ...and remove the drum.

**41C.** Clean the inside of the drum and the brake components with aerosol brake cleaner. If the drum is badly scored or cracked, replace it.

CHAPTER 5 PART G: BRAKING SYSTEM

5-23

**41D.** Fold back each of the two rubbers on the wheel cylinder. Any fluid found inside requires a new cylinder.

IMPORTANT NOTE: For information on replacing missing or damaged springs, rear brake shoes or wheel cylinders, see **Chapter 6, Repairs and Replacements**.

### SAFETY FIRST!

- Raise the rear of the car to adjust the handbrake. It is ESSENTIAL to ensure the front wheels are securely chocked in both directions, and that axle stands or ramps are used to support the car.

☐ **Job 42. Check/adjust handbrake.**

The handbrake is intended to 'set' itself in use as the rear brake self-adjusters operate. If the handbrake seems not to work, even though lever travel is not excessive, remove the rear drums and examine the brake shoes (see **Job 41**) rather than over-tighten the handbrake cable. The handbrake may need adjusting when, after a time, the handbrake cable stretches or if the rear brake friction materials are replaced.

Apply the handbrake lever by two 'clicks' of the ratchet.

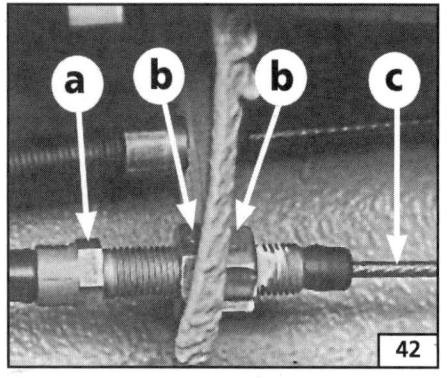

**42.** From underneath the car, slacken the lock-nuts (**b**) and turn the adjusting rod (**a**) until the cable (**c**) is drawn taut. Check that both rear wheels are 'locked' when the handbrake is ON (no more than three 'clicks'), and that both rear wheels are completely free when it is fully OFF. When everything works properly, tighten the lock-nuts (**b**) and grease the adjuster mechanism and cable ends. Lower the car to the ground, and check again that moving the handbrake through no more than three notches is sufficient to hold the car stationary. A proper check of handbrake efficiency can only be carried out by a garage with a 'rolling road' brake tester.

☐ **Job 43. Check brake pipes.**

### FLEXIBLE HOSES

Check the flexible brake pipes that connect the calipers to the metal pipes on the body. Try bending back on themselves those that are not contained in a protective coil, and look for any signs of cracking, particularly at the bends. Check them all for signs of rubbing, splitting, kinks and perishing of the rubber. Check hoses for 'ballooning' with the brake pedal pressed hard.

### RIGID PIPES

Check all rigid pipes for signs of damage or corrosion and check that all of the locating clips are sound and in place.

☐ **Job 44. Change brake hydraulic fluid.**

Change the brake fluid at the recommended interval. See **Chapter 6, Repairs and Replacements, PART G: BRAKES**.

*i* INSIDE INFORMATION: Brake fluid absorbs water from the air. This corrodes brake components and can cause total brake failure. With brakes applied heavily, the fluid can heat to above 100 degrees Celsius, the water vaporises, and the pedal goes to the floor! *i*

Examine the brake shoes for wear or oil contamination. If the latter, the wheel cylinder is probably leaking (see **41D**) and the shoes will have to be scrapped. FIAT recommend a **minimum** 1.5 mm shoe lining thickness, but it's advisable to replace shoes well before they're this thin.

## PART H: BODYWORK & INTERIOR

☐ **Job 45. Lubricate hinges and locks.**

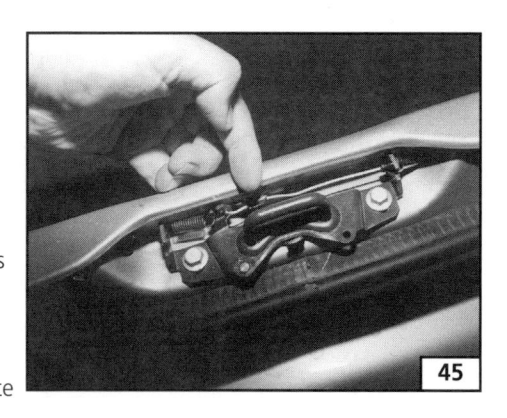

**45.** Apply a few drops of light oil (from either an aerosol or oil can) to the hinges of the bonnet, doors and tailgate. Dip the door/tailgate key in graphite powder and insert the key to lubricate the lock barrels, not forgetting the fuel filler cap. Grease the door and tailgate latch mechanism (aerosol grease is handy), the bonnet release mechanism (and the tailgate's, if applicable) and the cable end.

☐ **Job 46. Check windscreen.**

Clean the windscreen with a proprietary glass cleaner and examine it for stone chips, cracks and scoring. While some degree of damage is acceptable, the strict MoT Test regulations limit the amount and position of such defects. Some screen chips can be repaired and made invisible.

❑ **Job 47. Check seat and seat belt mountings.**

Your car's seat and safety belt mountings and backrest adjustment locking mechanism will be checked as part of the annual test, but it pays to check them beforehand. Also, regularly check that the seat belts: a) retract easily and smoothly, and b) 'hold' when you snatch them, or under sharp braking.

❑ **Job 48. Check headlight alignment.**

Have the headlight alignment checked by your FIAT dealer, who will have the necessary beam-setting equipment to carry out the work accurately. This job will also be carried out as part of the annual MoT Test in the UK.

## MANUAL ADJUSTERS

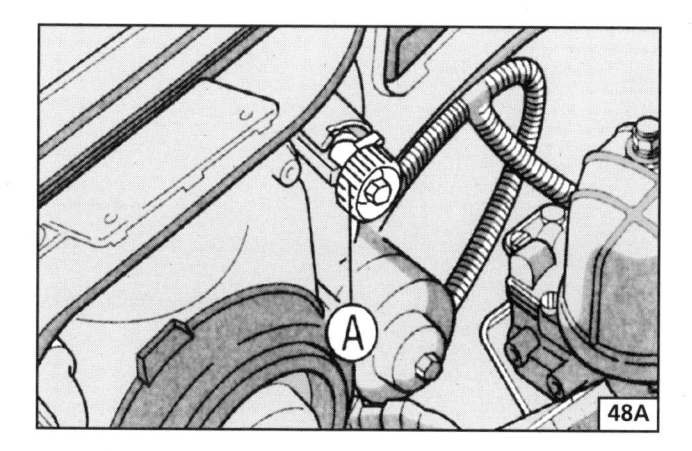

**48A.** On cars with manual adjusters, ensure that the beam correction knurled knobs (**A**) at the top corner of each headlight, inside the engine bay - are in the light-load position (turned clockwise) before headlight alignment is carried out. Otherwise the beams will aim too high if unladen.

## ELECTRIC ADJUSTERS

**48B.** Some cars have a beam adjuster on the dash panel. Set it to position '**0**' before the beams are aligned.

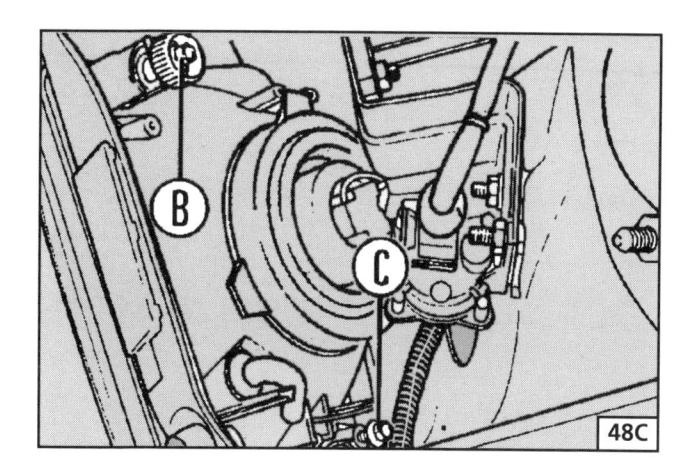

**48C.** In an emergency, you may need to temporarily set the beams yourself to avoid dazzling oncoming traffic. Screw (**B**) - in the centre of the manual adjuster knob, when fitted; otherwise by itself in the same position - adjusts the beam up-and-down. Screw (**C**) adjusts it from side to side. Have the setting checked with a garage beam setter as soon as possible.

❑ **Job 49. Check underbody.**

Check the condition of the underbody for damage and corrosion. Take a tin of waxy underbody seal and a brush under the car and replace any missing underbody seal.

❑ **Job 50. Check spare tyre and jack.**

This job should ideally be carried out every month or two - you never know when you're going to need that spare! But if you haven't remembered, do it at the time shown on the **Service Interval Chart** at the latest.

ℹ INSIDE INFORMATION: Lift the spare out and check the 'hidden' lower side wall for cracking. Also check that the wheel-changing tools are all present and correct and lubricate the jack screw with light oil. ℹ

❑ **Job 51. Replace airbag gas generator.**

If your car is fitted with an airbag, have your FIAT dealer replace the gas generator 10 years after the car was built. There may be a reminder inside the glove compartment door.

# PART I: ROAD TEST

❏ **Job 52. Road test and specialist check - after every service.**

Before you can claim to have 'finished' working on your car, you must check it, test it, and, if necessary, have a qualified mechanic check it over for you.

If you are not a qualified mechanic, we strongly recommend having someone who is a properly qualified mechanic - your FIAT dealership perhaps - inspect all of the car's safety-related items after they have been worked on at home and before using the car on the road.

- Before setting out, check that the lights, indicators and in-car controls, as well as seat belts and seat adjustments, all work correctly.
- Run the car for several minutes before setting out then turn off, check fluid levels and check underneath for leaks.
- Check that the steering moves freely in both directions and that the car does not 'pull' one way or the other when driving in a straight line - but do bear in mind the effect of the camber on the road.
- Make sure that the brakes work effectively, smoothly and without the need for 'pumping'. There should be no juddering or squealing.
- Check that the car does not 'pull' from one side to the other when you brake firmly from around 40 mph. (Don't cause a skid and don't try this if there is any following traffic.)

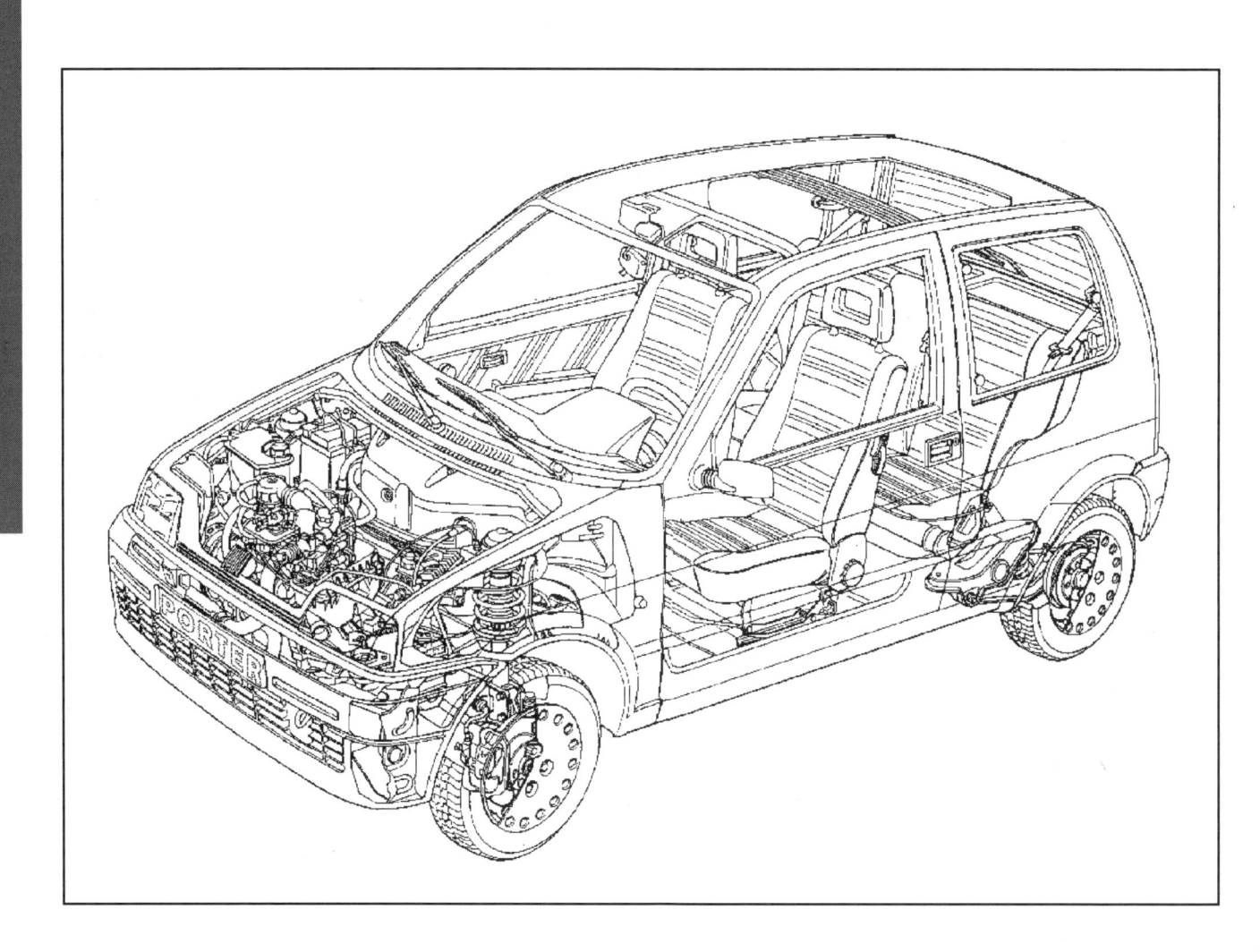

*Please read the whole of CHAPTER 1, SAFETY FIRST before carrying out any work on your car.*

# CHAPTER 6
# REPAIRS AND REPLACEMENT

This chapter shows you how to remove and overhaul all the major 'wearing' parts of the car. We deliberately *don't* show how to rebuild major components, such as the gearbox, or differential. You are much better off, in terms of time, cost and the provision of a guarantee, to buy a replacement unit.

The same applies to major electrical components, such as alternator and starter motor. If as we recommend you stick to 'original' FIAT replacement parts, you will maintain the original quality of your car.

## How To Use This Chapter

- In this chapter, each area of the car is dealt with in a different PART of the chapter, such as, **PART A: ENGINE**.
- Each Job in each PART has a separate identifying number. For example, **Job 1. OHV cylinder head removal**.
- Every Job is broken down into easy-to-follow Steps, numbered from 1-on.
- Illustrations are numbered so that you can see at a glance where they belong!
- The illustration **Job 1-4** (in PART A) for example, relates to the text in **Job 1, Step 4**.

## Chapter Contents

| | Page No. |
|---|---|
| PART A: ENGINE | 6-1 |
| PART B: TRANSMISSION AND CLUTCH | 6-24 |
| PART C: COOLING SYSTEM | 6-30 |
| PART D: ELECTRICAL AND INSTRUMENTS | 6-32 |
| PART E: FUEL AND EXHAUST SYSTEMS | 6-38 |
| PART F: STEERING AND SUSPENSION | 6-45 |
| PART G: BRAKES | 6-52 |
| PART H: BODY AND INTERIOR | 6-58 |

### FACT FILE: CINQUECENTO ENGINE TYPES

FIAT Cinquecentos available in the UK use two main engine types:

**A. The OHV (Overhead Valve) engine.** This engine is 899cc (903cc with some non-UK engines) but is considered to have a nominal capacity of 900cc. Since there is only one engine of this type in the Cinquecento range it is simply referred to as the OHV engine. It can be recognised by the circular injector turret cover on top of the engine, connected to the air cleaner at one side. See illustration *PART A: Job 1-1*.

**B. The 1.1 litre FIRE OHC engine (Fully Integrated Robotised Engine, Overhead Camshaft)** is recognised by the large rectangular air cleaner mounted directly on top of the engine. See illustration *PART A: Job 12-1*.

The OHV and FIRE OHC engines are both mounted transversely with the clutch and gearbox units at the left side, but the engines have the appearance of being the 'opposite way' round from each other.

6-1

# CHAPTER 6
# PART A: ENGINE

*...FACT FILE Continued*

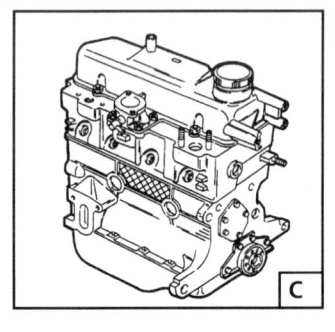

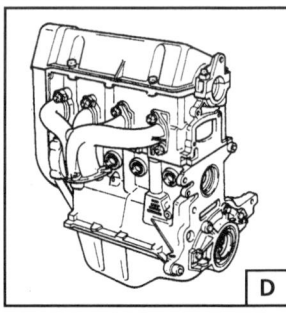

**C.** The OHV engine has the spark plugs at the front and the exhaust manifold at the back.

**D.** The FIRE OHC engine has the spark plugs at the back and the exhaust manifold at the front.

The following engines belong to models that are not available in the UK and are not covered in this manual. See your FIAT dealer if you require maintenance for either of these engines:

- The 704cc two-cylinder OHV engine, mounted longitudinally.
- The 903cc four-cylinder OHV engine, mounted transversely. This looks similar to the 899cc engine. If in doubt about your engine type, check the engine code. Models with the 899cc engine have the engine code 1170A1.046 displayed on a bodywork panel above the right headlight. The 903cc engines have different engine codes, depending on the model of vehicle.

## SAFETY FIRST!

- *Before carrying out any of the work in this chapter, be sure to read and understand **Chapter 1, Safety First!***
- *Be sure to read any safety notes supplied with any of the materials for equipment you purchase in connection with the work described in this chapter.*
- *If you are not sure about your competence or skills in carrying out any of the work described in this chapter, have the work carried out by your FIAT dealership.*

## PART A: ENGINE

### PART A: Contents

Job 1. OHV cylinder head - removal.
Job 2. OHV cylinder head - refitting.
Job 3. OHV cylinder head - dismantling and overhauling.
Job 4. OHV hydraulic tappets - removal, refitting and refilling.
Job 5. OHV engine - hydraulic tappet pre-loading adjustment.
Job 6. OHV engine - timing chain and sprockets - removal.
Job 7. OHV engine - timing chain and sprockets - refitting.
Job 8. OHV engine - dismantling.
Job 9. OHV engine - reassembly.
Job 10. FIRE OHC cylinder heads, valve clearance adjustment.
Job 11. FIRE OHC engine - timing belt, removal and replacement.
Job 12. FIRE OHC cylinder head - removal.
Job 13. FIRE OHC cylinder head - refitting.
Job 14. FIRE OHC cylinder head - dismantling and overhauling.
Job 15. FIRE OHC engine - dismantling.
Job 16. FIRE OHC engine - reassembly.
Job 17. Engine and transmission, all types - removal.
Job 18. Engine and transmission, all types - refitting.
Job 19. Engine/transmission (removed from car), all types - separation.
Job 20. Engine/transmission, all types - reconnection.
Job 21. Engine/transmission mountings, all types - replacement.

### FACT FILE: PISTON/CONROD ASSEMBLIES

a - direction of rotation
b - bore no. stamp (FIRE OHC engines)
c - bore no. stamp (OHV engines)
d - piston centre-line
e - conrod centre-line

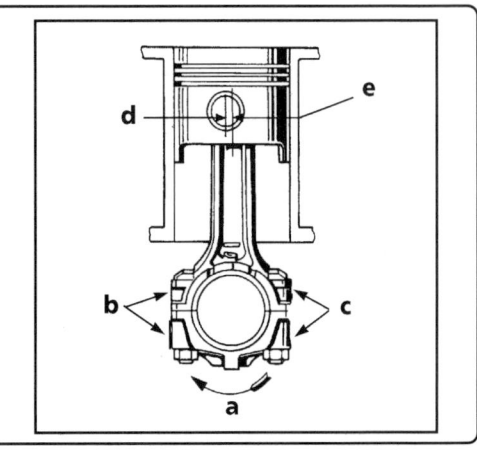

- On all Cinquecento engines, the piston and conrod have to be assembled with the offset the right way round.
- We recommend that your FIAT dealer assembles the pistons onto the conrods for you.
- Although the amount of offset differs, this is the direction of offset on all engines.

6-2

## Job 1. OHV cylinder head - removal.

**ℹ INSIDE INFORMATION:** Allow the engine to cool right down before starting work, or you will run the risk of causing cylinder head distortion. ℹ

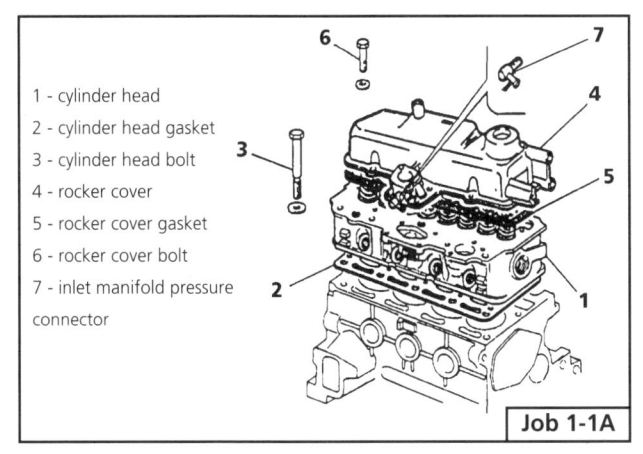

1 - cylinder head
2 - cylinder head gasket
3 - cylinder head bolt
4 - rocker cover
5 - rocker cover gasket
6 - rocker cover bolt
7 - inlet manifold pressure connector

**Job 1-1A**

☐ **Step 1A:** These are the major cylinder head components.

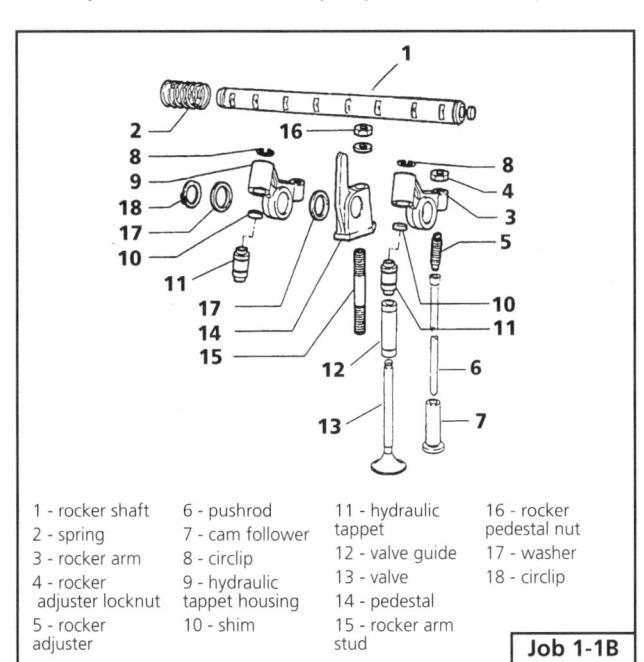

1 - rocker shaft
2 - spring
3 - rocker arm
4 - rocker adjuster locknut
5 - rocker adjuster
6 - pushrod
7 - cam follower
8 - circlip
9 - hydraulic tappet housing
10 - shim
11 - hydraulic tappet
12 - valve guide
13 - valve
14 - pedestal
15 - rocker arm stud
16 - rocker pedestal nut
17 - washer
18 - circlip

**Job 1-1B**

☐ **Step 1B:** Some of these valve-gear components will have to be dismantled when removing the head. See **Step 14-on**.

### SAFETY FIRST!

• *Disconnect both battery leads, negative terminal first before carrying out any dismantling.*

☐ **Step 2:** Drain the cooling system while the engine is cold, by loosening the bottom radiator hose. Remove the cap on the expansion tank so that the coolant will flow out more easily. Drain into a bowl if you intend re-using it.

☐ **Step 3:** Remove the air filter assembly and injector turret. See **PART E: FUEL, IGNITION AND EXHAUST**.

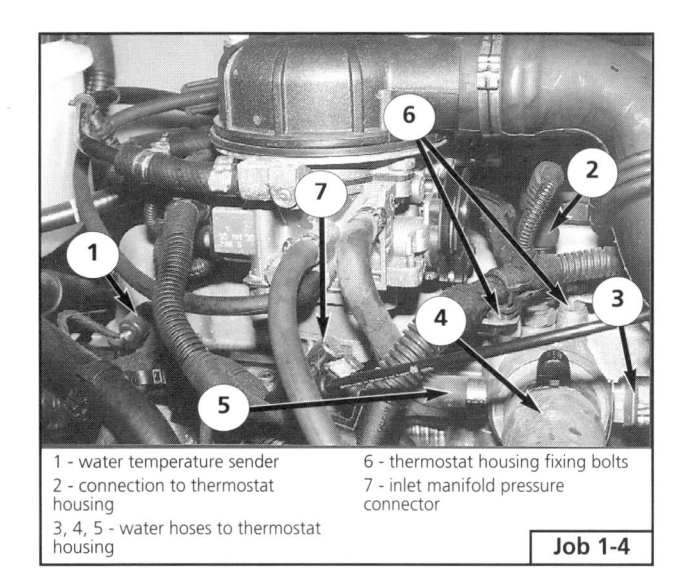

1 - water temperature sender
2 - connection to thermostat housing
3, 4, 5 - water hoses to thermostat housing
6 - thermostat housing fixing bolts
7 - inlet manifold pressure connector

**Job 1-4**

☐ **Step 4:** Remove the electrical connections from the water temperature sender (**1**) and thermostat housing (**2**).

☐ **Step 5:** Disconnect the water hoses from the thermostat housing. See illustration **Job 1-4 parts 3, 4** and **5**.

☐ **Step 6:** Remove the thermostat housing by undoing the bolts. See illustration **Job 1-4, part 6**.

☐ **Step 7:** Unscrew the water temperature sender unit. See illustration **Job 1-4, part 1**.

☐ **Step 8:** Remove the vacuum hoses to the absolute pressure sensor and servo brake unit. Both of these connect the same fitting on the inlet manifold. See illustration **Job 1-4, part 7**.

☐ **Step 9:** Remove the electrical connections (marked by the arrows) from the ignition coils mounted on the end of the rocker cover.

**Job 1-9**

☐ **Step 10:** Disconnect the HT leads from the spark plugs.

☐ **Step 11:** Undo the nut (**1**) and remove the bracket retaining the engine oil level dip stick.

☐ **Step 12:** Undo the nuts **Job 1-11, part 2** and disconnect the exhaust manifold from the cylinder head. See illustration **Job 1-11, part 2**. There are five nuts, and one of them secures the warm air inlet duct.

**Job 1-11**

**CHAPTER 6 PART A: ENGINE**

6-3

**making it easy** • An alternative method is to jack up the car and disconnect the exhaust manifold from the downpipe.
• Then you can remove the cylinder head with the manifold attached. It's up to you!
• The advantage of disconnecting the manifold from the cylinder head is to make the cylinder head fit more easily on your workbench while you are working on it.

☐ **Step 13:**
Remove the rocker cover bolts (including those around the small inlet manifold - arrowed), then lift off the rocker cover and gasket, complete with ignition coils and spark plug cables.

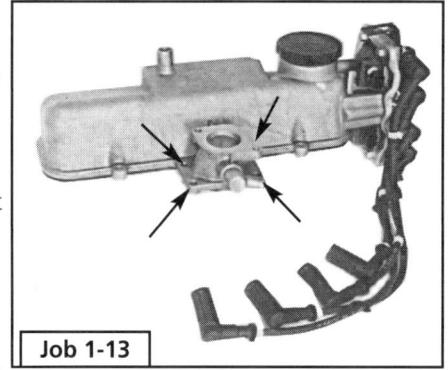

*Job 1-13*

☐ **Step 14:**
Unscrew the four rocker post nuts evenly, a few turns at a time, until all are loose, then remove the nuts and spring washers. This is the cylinder head assembly with the rocker cover removed.

*Job 1-14*

**IMPORTANT NOTE:** Sometimes the complete stud might come out of the cylinder block. If this occurs, make sure the stud is fully screwed into the block when refitting.

☐ **Step 15:** Pull the rocker shaft assembly clear of the studs. The whole assembly comes off, complete with the hydraulic tappets.

*Job 1-15*

**IMPORTANT NOTE:** The hydraulic tappets are full of oil and should not be turned upside down, otherwise the oil will come out and air will get in, causing the hydraulic element to become flexible and noisy. If this occurs they will have to be refilled. See **Job 4**.

☐ **Step 16:**
Remove the eight pushrods (**1**), keeping them in the correct order.

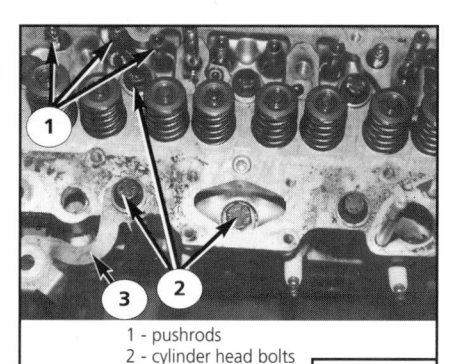

1 - pushrods
2 - cylinder head bolts
3 - water pipe bracket

*Job 1-16*

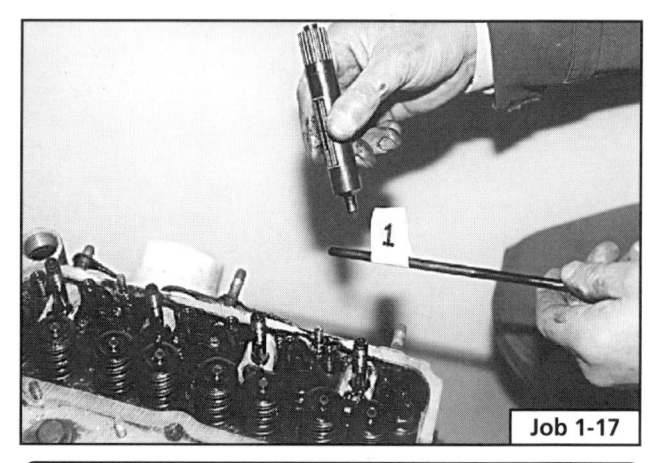

*Job 1-17*

**making it easy** ☐ **Step 17:** • So that you don't confuse the order in which the pushrods were fitted, put masking tape around the end of each one as it is removed and number it. No. 1 is at the timing chain end.

☐ **Step 18:**
Unscrew the ten cylinder head bolts half a turn at a time in the order shown. Nine of the bolts are on the upper face of the cylinder head and one is inside the inlet manifold. See illustration **Job 1-16, part 2**. When free, remove all bolts and washers. You will also need to remove the water pipe bracket which is held by two of the bolts. See illustration **Job 1-16, part 3**.

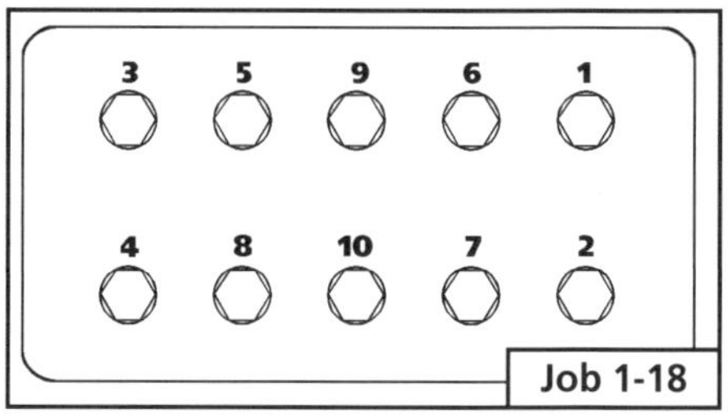

| 3 | 5 | 9 | 6 | 1 |
| 4 | 8 | 10 | 7 | 2 |

*Job 1-18*

☐ **Step 19:**
Remove the cylinder head.

*Job 1-19*

**making it easy** • If the head is stuck, use a wooden hammer shaft or something similar, as a lever in one of the exhaust ports to break the seal.
• If you are removing the cylinder head complete with the exhaust manifold, just pull upwards on the manifold.

☐ **Step 20:**
Remove the cylinder head gasket. Carefully clean the gasket facing surfaces on the cylinder head and cylinder block, and protect the bores and main waterways by plugging with clean rags.

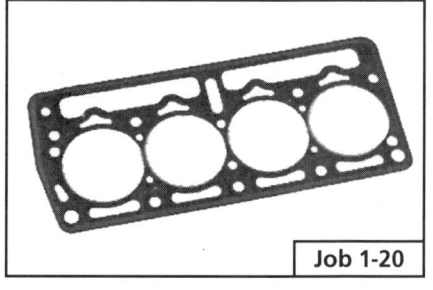

*Job 1-20*

For cylinder head overhaul, see **Job 3**.

## Job 2. OHV cylinder head - refitting.

☐ **Step 1:** Make sure you have all the gaskets (arrowed) you will need, from your FIAT dealership. All the gaskets should be renewed.

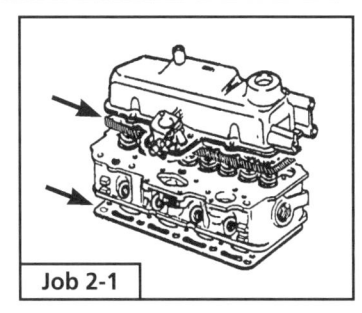

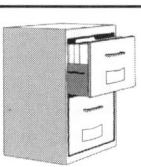

Job 2-1

### FACT FILE: CYLINDER HEAD GASKETS AND BOLTS

- The cylinder head gaskets are the ASTADUR type. These are made of a special material which undergoes a polymerisation process during the operation of the engine and hardens considerably during usage.
- To enable the polymerisation to take place it is necessary to keep the gasket in its sealed nylon container until it is ready for use. It is important not to use oil or grease on the gasket or the mating surfaces.
- ASTADUR type gaskets are matched to cylinder head fixing bolts of the yield point type. These bolts should be replaced after they have been used four times.

☐ **Step 2:** Carefully clean the cylinder head and block surfaces. Remove the rag from the cylinder bores and clean the bores and piston crowns. Apply a coating of new engine oil to the cylinder walls.

☐ **Step 3:** Make sure that the two cylinder head locating dowels are properly fitted in the recessed bolt holes at the front and rear of the cylinder block.

Job 2-3

☐ **Step 4:** Remove the cylinder head gasket from its sealed nylon container and place it over the dowels with the word "ALTO" facing upwards.

Job 2-4

☐ **Step 5:** Carefully lower the cylinder head into position.

☐ **Step 6:** Fit the securing bolts and washers loosely onto the cylinder head. There are ten bolts, including the one that fits inside the inlet manifold. See illustration *Job 1-16, part 2*.

IMPORTANT NOTE: Remember to fit the water pipe bracket which is held by the two bolts next to the water temperature sender unit. Also see illustration *Job 1-16, part 3*.

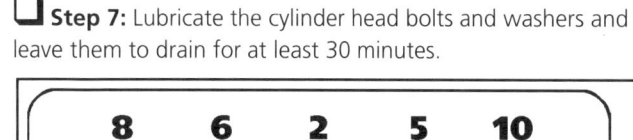

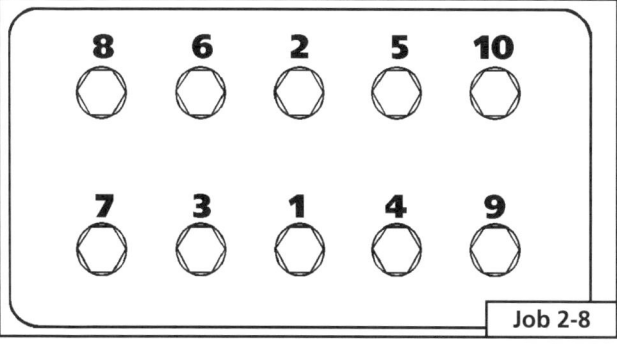

☐ **Step 7:** Lubricate the cylinder head bolts and washers and leave them to drain for at least 30 minutes.

Job 2-8

☐ **Step 8:** Using a torque wrench tighten the cylinder head bolts a little at a time in the order shown until all reach their specified torque requirement. See *Chapter 3, Facts and Figures*.

IMPORTANT NOTE: The cylinder head bolts must be tightened in the special sequence described in *Job 13, Steps 9A, 9B and 9C on page 6-18*.

☐ **Step 9:** Lubricate the pushrod ends with new engine oil and fit the pushrods in the same order as they were removed.

☐ **Step 10:** Fully unscrew the rocker arm adjusters and lower the rocker assembly carefully onto the four studs in the cylinder head, ensuring that all the rocker ball ends are located in the pushrod cups.

**ℹ INSIDE INFORMATION:** Spinning the pushrods between your fingers helps to ensure proper location in the tappets. **ℹ**

☐ **Step 11:** Refit the nuts and washers to the studs and tighten progressively to the specified torque. See *Chapter 3, Facts and Figures*.

☐ **Step 12:** Adjust the pre-loading of the hydraulic tappets. See *Job 5*.

☐ **Step 13:** Refit the exhaust manifold and ducting, oil level dipstick bracket, water temperature sender and the thermostat housing.

☐ **Step 14:** Refit the rocker cover, using a new gasket.

**ℹ INSIDE INFORMATION:** Avoid distortion of the rocker cover by not over-tightening the bolts. Over-tightening distorts the cover and causes leaks! **ℹ**

☐ **Step 15:** Refit the injector turret, including all electrical connections and hoses, then refit the air filter. See *PART E: FUEL, IGNITION AND EXHAUST*.

☐ **Step 16:** Reconnect all remaining hoses and electrical connections, then connect the battery.

☐ **Step 17:** Refill the cooling system, using the correct **FL Paraflu** anti-freeze solution. See *Chapter 3, Facts and Figures*.

## Job 3. OHV cylinder head - dismantling and overhauling.

1 - valve head (seating area)
2 - valve guide
3 - valve stem
4 - valve spring cap
5 - collets
6 - oil seal
7 - valve spring
8 - valve spring seat
9 - hydraulic tappets
10 - rocker shaft

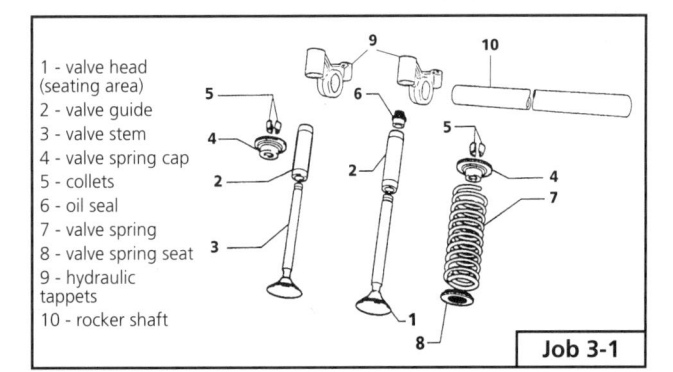

*Job 3-1*

□ **Step 1:** Familiarise yourself with the valve components shown in this illustration. They relate to the parts shown in illustration **Job 1-1B**, where the valve operating gear is shown.

*making it easy* • Storage and handling of the cylinder head is made easier by removing the exhaust manifold, thermostat housing and water temperature sender unit.

□ **Step 2:** Use a suitable valve spring compressor to compress each spring in turn to allow the removal of the split collets from the valve stems. Take care not to lose the collets when releasing the spring compressor.

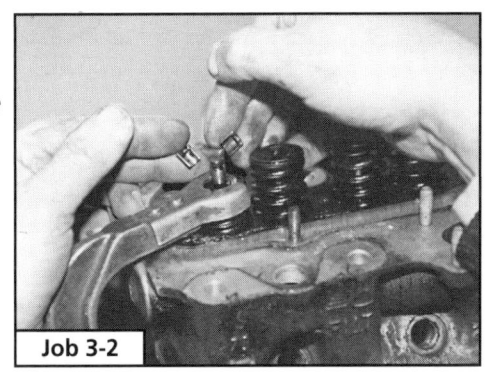

*Job 3-2*

*making it easy* • Keep the valves in their correct order by pushing their stems through some cardboard and numbering them, No. 1 being at the timing chain end.
• Another means of identification is to label each valve with masking tape which you can write on with a biro or felt pen.

□ **Step 3:** The valve spring caps, springs and spring seats can all be lifted clear and the valves withdrawn from their guides.

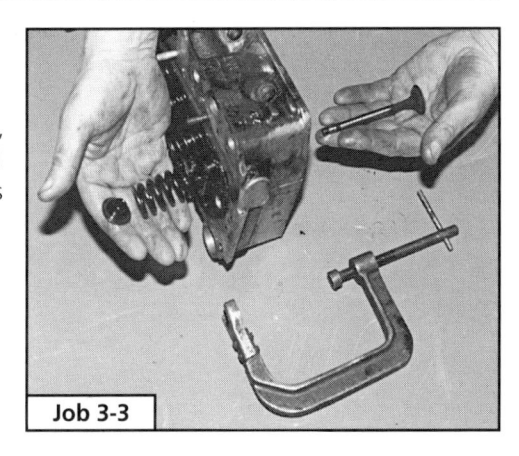

*Job 3-3*

□ **Step 4:**
ℹ INSIDE INFORMATION: The valves should slide freely out of their guides. Any resistance may be caused by a build-up of carbon, or a slight burr on the stem where the collets engage. This can usually be removed by careful use of fine wet-or-dry paper, allowing you to withdraw the valves without scoring their guides. ℹ

*Job 3-4*

□ **Step 5:** Re-insert each valve into its guide, in the correct order, keeping hold of the valve end. Try to move the valve from side to side. Try again from the other end of the valve guide. If *any* movement can be felt, the guide is worn and must be replaced by your FIAT dealer or specialist workshop.

□ **Step 6:** The cylinder head is made of light alloy and is easily damaged when being cleaned. Use a rotary wire brush from the combustion chambers and ports, but no sharp objects such as screwdrivers should be used. The machined surfaces must have all traces of old gasket removed by use of a straight edge - take great care not to dig it in! Then wash down with paraffin to remove old oil and dirt, and dry off with a clean rag.

At *all* costs, avoid gouging the cylinder head. This can be very expensive to put right!

*making it easy* • Try using carburettor cleaner or proprietary gasket remover, to loosen old gasket material.

□ **Step 7:** Clean the carbon from the valves with a rotary wire brush and wash them in paraffin. This is a cleaned-up valve next to a typically carboned-up one. Wash the valve springs, caps, seats and collets and dry.

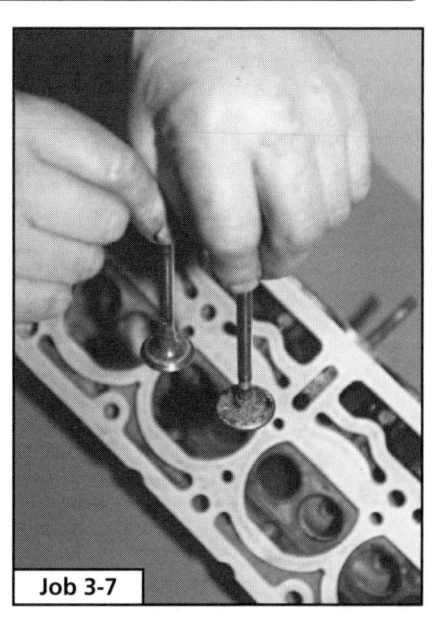

*Job 3-7*

*making it easy* • Clean the flat ends of the valve heads back to the shiny metal!
• Now the sucker on the end of your valve grinding stick won't keep falling off when you grind-in the valves!

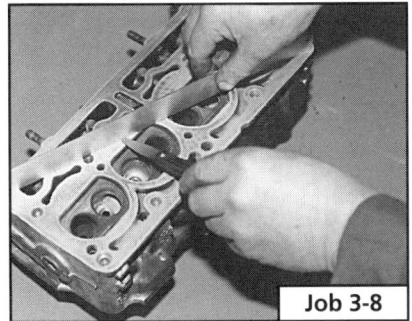

☐ **Step 8:** The cylinder head should be checked for distortion by use of a straight edge and feeler gauge. At the same time check for excessive corrosion. If you are in doubt, or if the old gasket has blown, have the cylinder head refaced by your FIAT agent or engine specialist.

*Job 3-8*

☐ **Step 9:** Examine the valve seats for pitting or burning. Also, check the valve seats in the cylinder head. Small pits can be removed by grinding the valves onto their seats. The seats in the cylinder head will have to be recut (again, by your local FIAT agent if the pitting is too deep), and new valves fitted.

### FACT FILE: VALVE GRINDING

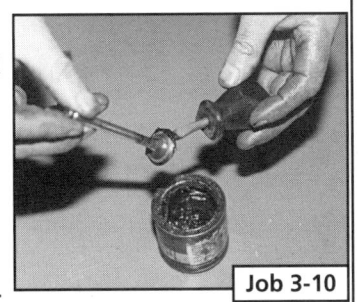

☐ **Step 10:** Apply a small quantity of coarse grinding paste evenly round the valve seat. A valve grinding stick with a suction pad slightly smaller than the valve head should be selected. Put a dab of moisture onto the suction pad and press the grinding stick to the first valve.

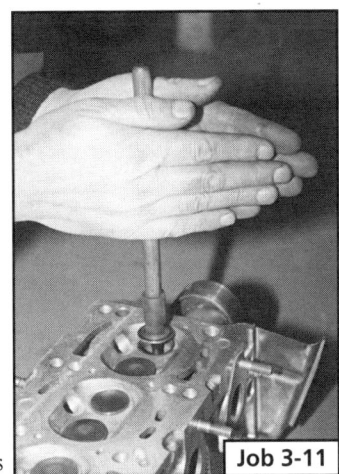

*Job 3-10*

☐ **Step 11:** Lower the valve stem into its guide and, holding the grinding stick between the palms of your hands, rub your hands together (like a bushman making a fire), rotating the valve and grinding the two seats together. Lift the valve regularly, say every ten or so turns, to allow the grinding paste to be redistributed. When you can feel the paste wearing smooth, remove the valve and wipe all the surfaces clean.

*Job 3-11*

IMPORTANT NOTE: Make sure that no paste is allowed to enter the guide. This would cause a lot of wear to the valve stem and guide.

• A complete ring of grey contact area should be visible on the valve head and its seat in the cylinder head. If necessary, start off with coarse paste to remove the deeper pits, and finally use fine paste to obtain a smooth finish. If pitting is too bad, you could have the valve face and the valve seats resurfaced or, in worst cases, the valve and/or valve seat (in the cylinder head) will have to be replaced. Consult your FIAT dealer or engine specialist if in doubt.

• **Now repeat this operation on the remaining seven valves.**

*i* INSIDE INFORMATION: A narrow contact band means more seat pressure and longer life. A wide band allows rapid valve burning. *i*

### SAFETY FIRST!

• *Treat compressed air with respect. Always wear goggles to protect your eyes.*
• *Never allow the airline nozzle near any of the body apertures.*

☐ **Step 12:** Wash the whole cylinder head again using paraffin and an old brush, making sure that all traces of grinding paste are removed, then dry off. Use compressed air if available.

☐ **Step 13:** The valve stems must be amply lubricated with clean engine oil and then located in their respective guides, after pushing new oil seals onto the tops of the guides. Temporarily wrap sellotape around the tops of the valve stems so that the seal slides over the collets groove.

☐ **Step 14:** *i* INSIDE INFORMATION: Check the valve springs' heights against new ones if possible, but if not, check them against each other. If any are shorter than the others, play safe and replace the complete set. After a long time in use, they are bound to have suffered fatigue which could cause complete valve failure. *i*

☐ **Step 15:** Place the valve spring seat over the guide, and then position the spring, with the tighter coils towards the seat, followed by the cap. Compress the spring enough to allow you to engage the split cotters with the valve stem.

*i* INSIDE INFORMATION: Use a little grease to keep the collets in place. Slowly release the compressor, checking that the collets are correctly located. Tap the end of each valve stem with a soft hammer to bed the collets in. With all the valves in place, the cylinder head is ready for refitting as described in **Job 2**. *i*

## Job 4. OHV hydraulic tappets - removal, refitting and refilling.

### FACT FILE: HYDRAULIC TAPPETS

• OHV engines fitted to Cinquecento models have hydraulic tappets that are self-adjusting so that you do not have to adjust the clearances between the valves and rockers during regular servicing.
• However, you will have to adjust the pre-loading of the hydraulic tappets if they have been replaced, or if any maintenance has been carried out that involves removal of the rocker arm, as shown, for example in *Job 1*.
• For details of pre-loading adjustment, see *Job 5*.

*FACT FILE Continued...*

## CHAPTER 6 PART A: ENGINE

*FACT FILE Continued...*

### Operation

The contact gap is maintained by the circulation of oil between the upper chamber **a** and the lower chamber **b**. The circulation route is as follows:

- Up the rocker arm duct (**1**).
- Through the slots (**2**) in the shim (**3**) and into the upper chamber (**a**) within the piston (**4**).
- Through the one-way ball valve (**5**) into the lower chamber (**b**). The valve opens when the engine has been switched off for some time with the tappet casing (**6**) in contact with the valve stem and then the engine is re-started causing a slight vacuum in the lower chamber.
- Through the clearance between the tappet casing (**6**) and piston (**4**), when the engine is switched off with the tappet casing in contact with the valve stem. The oil passing through the clearance goes back to the upper chamber (**a**) through the holes (**7**) in the piston, and any excess oil goes back to the rocker arm duct (**1**).

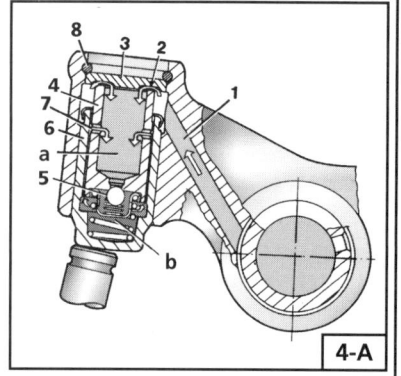

IMPORTANT NOTE: The hydraulic tappets should not be turned upside down, when removed, otherwise the oil will come out and air will get in, causing the hydraulic element to become flexible and noisy. If this occurs, the tappets will have to be re-filled, as described in this Job.

Job 4-A

☐ **Step 1:** Disconnect the battery negative earth lead.

☐ **Step 2:** Remove the air filter and injector turret. See **PART E: FUEL, IGNITION AND EXHAUST**.

☐ **Step 3:** Remove the rocker cover as described in **Job 1** to expose the rocker arms and hydraulic tappets.

Job 4-3

☐ **Step 4:** Undo the four rocker post nuts and remove the rocker arm.

*making it easy*
- It's possible to carry out this Job with the rocker arm in place but it's not recommended.
- You are advised to remove it to avoid dropping small components into or around the engine when dismantling the rocker arm.

☐ **Step 5:** Use circlip pliers, or a screwdriver to remove the circlip (*illustration 4-A, part 8*) from the top of the hydraulic tappet.

☐ **Step 6:** Remove the shim (see illustration **Job 4-A, part 3**)...

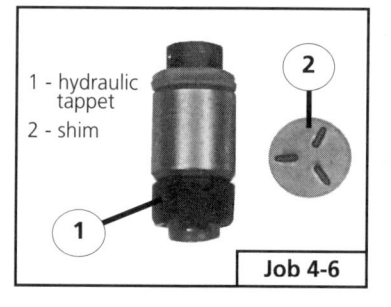

1 - hydraulic tappet
2 - shim

Job 4-6

☐ **Step 7:** ...then slide, or drift, the hydraulic tappet upwards, out of its housing.

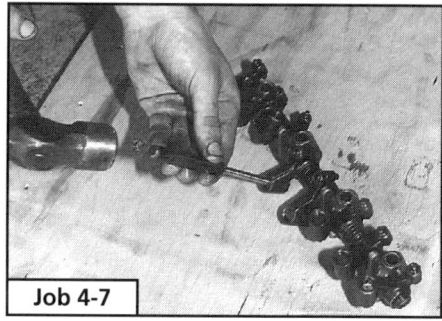

Job 4-7

☐ **Step 8:** Inspect the hydraulic tappet for wear, and if necessary replace it with a new one. Insert the tappet into the rocker arm and make sure it can slide freely up and down. It should be able to slide under gravity.

☐ **Step 9:** Fill the upper chamber (illustration **Job 4-A, part a**) with engine oil.

☐ **Step 10:** Replace the shim and circlip.

☐ **Step 11:** When you have finished replacing hydraulic tappets, refit the rocker arm and tighten to the correct torque. See **Chapter 3, Facts and Figures**.

☐ **Step 12:** Adjust the pre-loading of the hydraulic tappets. See **Job 5**.

### Job 5. OHV engine - hydraulic tappet pre-loading adjustment.

The hydraulic tappets need to be adjusted whenever the tappets or rocker arm have been removed and replaced, but they do not normally need to be adjusted during regular servicing of the vehicle.

IMPORTANT NOTE: Hydraulic tappets are NOT the same as conventional OHV tappets. Do not follow the usual procedure for adjusting conventional tappets. Use the procedure described here.

☐ **Step 1:** Bring the piston for the cylinder concerned to top dead centre during the explosion stroke. To achieve this:
- Remove the spark plugs.
- Put the gearbox into neutral.
- Turn the engine by hand so that the inlet valve goes down (open) and then comes up again (closed), and the corresponding exhaust valve is also up.

The valves are numbered as follows, from the timing chain end:

| | | |
|---|---|---|
| 1 - exhaust | 4 - exhaust | 7 - inlet |
| 2 - inlet | 5 - exhaust | 8 - exhaust |
| 3 - inlet | 6 - inlet | |

6-8

☐ **Step 2:** Loosen the lock-nut (illustration *Job 5-3, part a*) retaining the rocker adjuster.

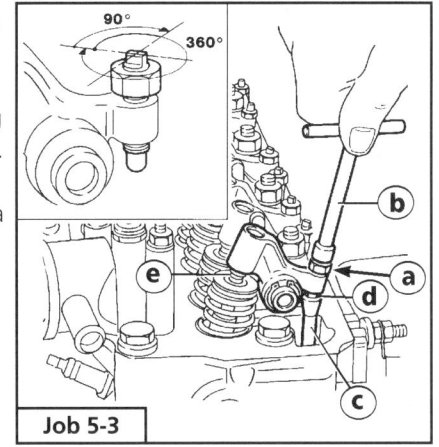

☐ **Step 3:** Using a suitable spanner (**b**), slowly turn the adjuster to bring it into contact with the push rod (**c**). While the gap is closing, turn the push rod with your fingers, until you are sure that the clearances (**d** and **e**) have just disappeared.

☐ **Step 4:** Set the pre-loading of the hydraulic tappet by tightening the adjuster by 1¼ turns (450 degrees or 1.25).

☐ **Step 5:** Tighten the lock nut while holding the adjuster in position so that it does not become disturbed.

☐ **Step 6:** Repeat these instructions for all other tappets that have been replaced. If you have removed and replaced the rocker arm, you need to adjust all the tappets.

## Job 6. OHV engine - timing chain and sprockets - removal.

*making it easy* • *The timing system components can be removed while the engine is in the car, by working under the right-front wheel arch.*

a - woodruff key
b - dowel peg
c - camshaft sprocket
d - camshaft
e - fuel pump drive cam
f - camshaft securing bolt
g - timing chain tensioner
h - TDC-and-RPM sensor
i - sensor mounting bracket*
j - bracket fixing bolt*
k - bracket fixing shear bolt*

*Do not remove!

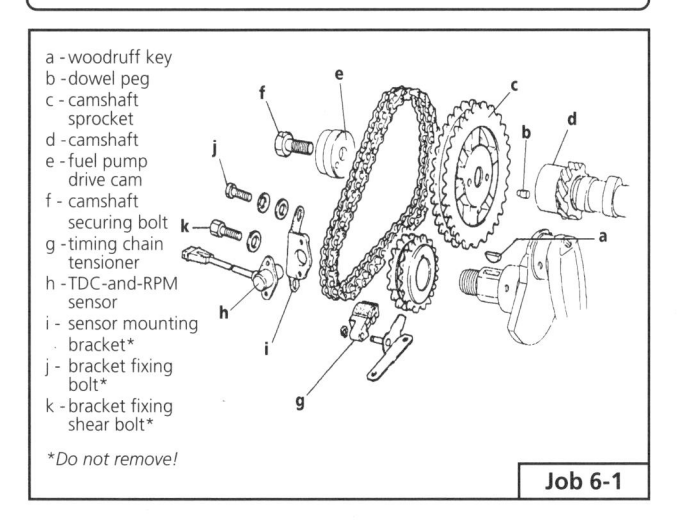

☐ **Step 1:** These are the timing chain and tensioner components.

ℹ **INSIDE INFORMATION:** The fuel pump drive cam is 'left over' from an earlier engine type and doesn't actually do anything. Earlier engines used to have a mechanical fuel pump driven by the camshaft, instead of an electric pump inside the tank. ℹ

☐ **Step 2:** Disconnect the battery negative earth lead. Jack up the car and remove the right front wheel. Support the front of the car on axle stands.

☐ **Step 3:** Remove the shield from underneath the radiator - fixing points (arrowed).

☐ **Step 4:** Remove the right front plastic wheel arch liner - fixing points (arrowed).

☐ **Step 5:** Slacken the alternator mounting bolts and remove the drive belt.

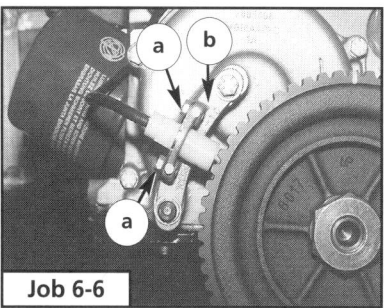

☐ **Step 6:** Undo the bolts (**a**) and remove the RPM-and-TDC sensor from the bracket (**b**) on the timing cover.

**IMPORTANT NOTE:** Do NOT attempt to remove the bracket. Its position has been factory set and is crucial for accurate timing and efficient engine running.

☐ **Step 7:** Remove the flywheel shield - fixing points (arrowed).

☐ **Step 8:** Unscrew the crankshaft pulley bolt and remove the pulley.

ℹ **INSIDE INFORMATION:** Prevent the engine turning by engaging a low gear and asking a helper to apply the foot brake firmly. If this fails, try either of the following:
• Use a large screwdriver to prevent the flywheel ring gear from turning.
• Fit a flywheel lock. (FIAT part No. 1867029000), if available. ℹ

**CHAPTER 6 PART A: ENGINE**

6-9

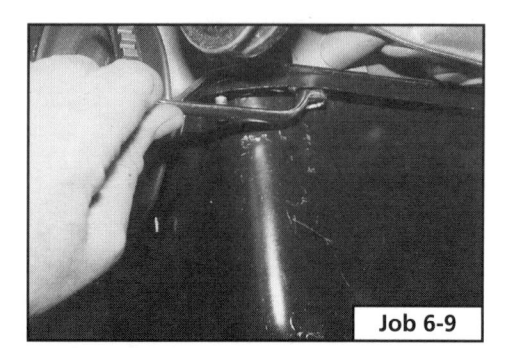

## CHAPTER 6 PART A: ENGINE

☐ **Step 9:** Drain the oil, then loosen the sump bolts.

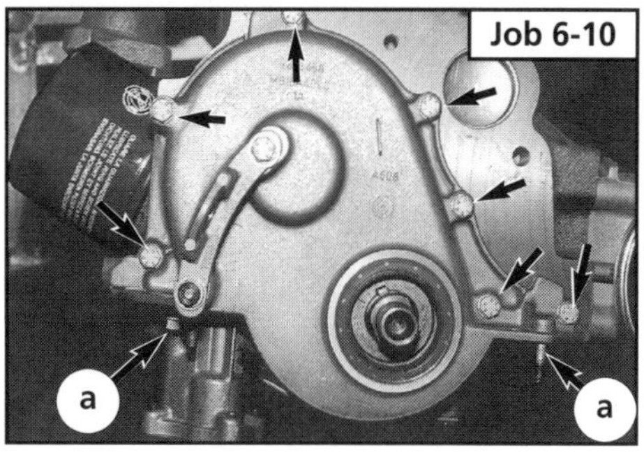

*Job 6-9*

☐ **Step 10:** Do one of the following:
● EITHER: Remove the sump completely.
● OR: Loosen the sump bolts so that the sump drops down sufficiently to clear the two (**a**) bolts at the bottom of the timing cover. (The sump has been removed in this illustration.)

*Job 6-10*

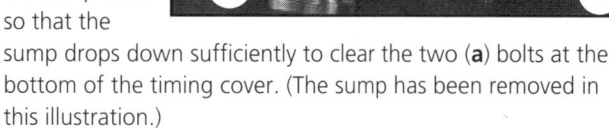

☐ **Step 11:** Unscrew the seven timing cover bolts (see illustration **Job 6-10, arrowed**) and remove the cover and gasket. The sump bolts referred to in **Step 10** can clearly be seen here (**a**). Remove and replace the oil seal (**b**).

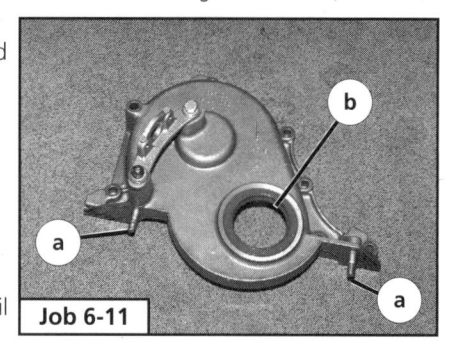

*Job 6-11*

☐ **Step 12:** Note the timing marks (arrowed) on both chain sprockets. If the chain is correctly fitted, it will be possible to rotate the sprockets so that the dot on the camshaft pulley coincides with the line on the crankshaft pulley. At this position the following also occurs:
● The woodruff key (see illustration **Job 6-1, part a**) on the crankshaft will be at the top.
● Cylinders 1 and 4 will be at top dead centre. If you have removed the rocker cover, you will see that tappets 1, 2, 7 and 8 are in their uppermost position.

*Job 6-12*

☐ **Step 13:** The chain tensioner has a locking device so that you can release the tension on the chain. Push the plunger to compress the spring and turn the lever to lock it in position.

*Job 6-13*

*Job 6-14*

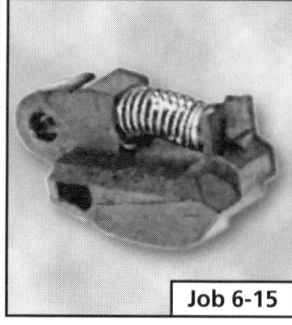

*Job 6-15*

☐ **Step 14:** Remove the circlip (arrowed) from the chain tensioner mounting bracket...

☐ **Step 15:** ...and remove the chain tensioner assembly. Then unlock it so that the spring is not left compressed. Examine the slipper surface for excessive wear and make sure the spring is intact. If necessary, obtain a replacement assembly. It is usually best to replace the chain tensioner assembly if you are replacing the timing chain and sprockets.

☐ **Step 16:** Undo the camshaft sprocket bolt. You will need to use a suitable method to prevent the engine from turning, just as when you removed the crankshaft pulley in **Step 7**.

*Job 6-16*

☐ **Step 17:** Remove the fuel pump drive cam. See illustration **Job 6-1, part e**.

☐ **Step 18:** Use two large screwdrivers as levers to release the camshaft and crankshaft sprockets, then carefully pull the sprockets off their shafts, together with the timing chain.

☐ **Step 19:** Remove the woodruff key from the crankshaft and the dowel peg from the camshaft and keep them in a safe place. See illustration **Job 6-1, parts a and b**.

*Job 6-18*

☐ **Step 20:** Inspect the timing chain, camshaft sprocket and crankshaft sprocket for wear. If one of these components is worn, you need to replace all of them. Don't replace any of them individually.

### Job 7. OHV engine - timing chain and sprockets - refitting.

This Job is basically the reverse of **Job 6**, which is carried out with the front of the car on axle stands and the right front wheel arch removed to gain access to the timing components. See the **Job 6** illustrations for details of the components referred to in this Job.

6-10

❑ **Step 1:** Turn the crankshaft until the woodruff key slot is uppermost. Insert the key and lightly tap fully home, if it is a tight fit, leaving the forward edge slightly lower than the back.

❑ **Step 2:** Insert the dowel peg into the camshaft.

❑ **Step 3:** Mount the timing chain onto the sprockets and turn the assembly so that the two timing marks come alongside each other.

❑ **Step 4:** Mount the chain and sprockets onto the shafts, so that the crankshaft sprocket goes over the woodruff key and the camshaft sprocket goes over the dowel peg. To make this possible, you might have to first mount the camshaft sprocket by itself and turn the camshaft to the correct position. When the chain and sprockets are mounted, make sure the two timing marks are alongside each other, (see illustration *Job 6-12*) then tap the crankshaft sprocket so it fits firmly over the woodruff key.

❑ **Step 5:** Fit the fuel pump drive cam and the retaining bolt and tighten to the specified torque. See **Chapter 3, Facts and Figures**.

❑ **Step 6:** Lock the chain tensioner so that it will not exert tension on the chain when fitted.

❑ **Step 7:** Mount the chain tensioner on its bracket and secure it with the circlip, then unlock the tensioner.

❑ **Step 8:** Remove the seal from the timing cover by levering it out from the inside. See illustration *Job 6-11, part b*. Clean off all traces of old gasket and sealant from the cover.

❑ **Step 9:** Fit a new seal squarely into its hold and tap home.

❑ **Step 10:** Clean the mating surface on the cylinder block.

❑ **Step 11:** Smear a little grease on the timing cover to locate the gasket and fit the timing cover to the block. Screw the bolts in finger-tight.

❑ **Step 12:** Clean the crankshaft pulley hub and coat with clean engine oil. Push the pulley onto the crankshaft and carefully locate its groove over the woodruff key (the same woodruff key that holds the crankshaft sprocket).

❑ **Step 13:** Centralise the cover seal on the pulley and tighten the cover securing bolts.

❑ **Step 14:** Tighten the crankshaft pulley nut to the correct torque. See **Chapter 3, Facts and Figures**.

❑ **Step 15:** Refit the TDC-and-RPM sensor on its mounting bracket and make sure it is positioned the correct distance from pulley teeth. See **Chapter 3, Facts and Figures**.

❑ **Step 16:** Refit the sump and refill with oil.

❑ **Step 17:** Refit the alternator drive belt.

❑ **Step 18:** Refit the right front wheel arch, radiator shield and front wheel, then lower the car to the ground.

❑ **Step 19:** Re-connect the battery negative earth lead.

## Job 8. OHV engine - dismantling.

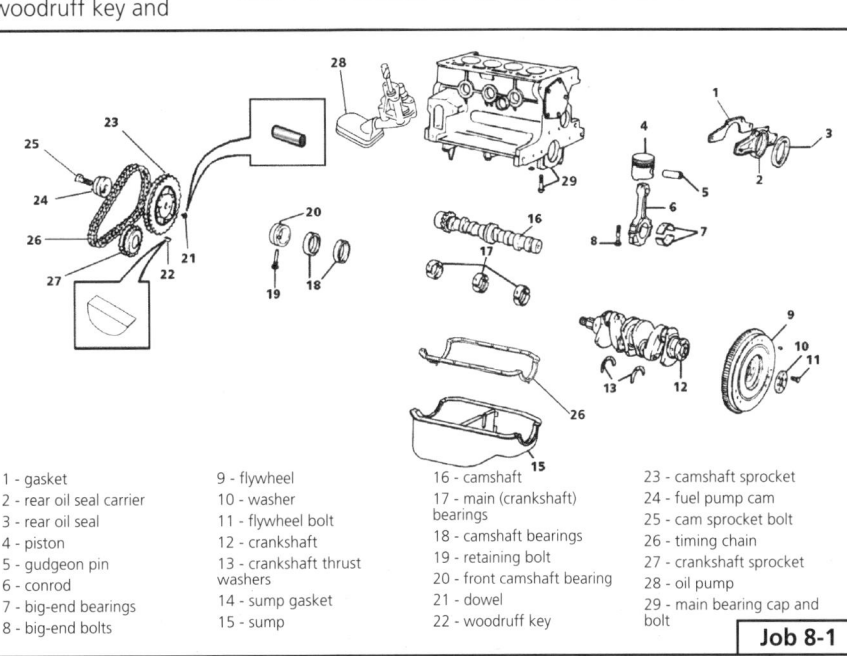

1 - gasket
2 - rear oil seal carrier
3 - rear oil seal
4 - piston
5 - gudgeon pin
6 - conrod
7 - big-end bearings
8 - big-end bolts
9 - flywheel
10 - washer
11 - flywheel bolt
12 - crankshaft
13 - crankshaft thrust washers
14 - sump gasket
15 - sump
16 - camshaft
17 - main (crankshaft) bearings
18 - camshaft bearings
19 - retaining bolt
20 - front camshaft bearing
21 - dowel
22 - woodruff key
23 - camshaft sprocket
24 - fuel pump cam
25 - cam sprocket bolt
26 - timing chain
27 - crankshaft sprocket
28 - oil pump
29 - main bearing cap and bolt

**Job 8-1**

❑ **Step 1:** Familiarise yourself with the major bottom-end engine components shown here.

❑ **Step 2:** Remove the engine from the vehicle. See **Job 17**.

❑ **Step 3:** Remove the water pump. See **PART C: COOLING SYSTEM**.

❑ **Step 4:** Unbolt and remove the clutch from the flywheel.

❑ **Step 5:** Remove the cylinder head as described in **Job 1**.

❑ **Step 6:** Remove the dipstick and guide tube.

❑ **Step 7:** With the engine lying on one side, unbolt and remove the sump.

❑ **Step 8:** Check the connecting rods (see illustration *Job 8-1, part 6*) and their big end bearing caps to make sure that each is marked with matching numbers or punch marks, starting with No. 1 at the timing cover end. Mark if necessary. Undo the big-end bolts and remove the caps, loosen them if stubborn with a soft faced mallet. Keep the caps in their original order.

❑ **Step 9:** *i* INSIDE INFORMATION: Remove the shell bearings by pressing on the side opposite the location slot in the connecting rod and cap. Keep them in their correct order if they are to be reused. *i*

☐ **Step 10:** Withdraw the piston/conrod assemblies from the top of their bores, keeping them in order.

☐ **Step 11:** Position a block of wood inside the crankcase to stop crankshaft movement. Undo the crankshaft pulley nut and remove the pulley.

☐ **Step 12:** Remove the timing chain and sprockets. See *Job 6*.

☐ **Step 13:** Unbolt and remove the oil pump.

☐ **Step 14:** Remove the locking screw from the camshaft front bearing and withdraw the camshaft. Take care that the cam lobes do not damage the bearings as the camshaft is pulled through.

☐ **Step 15:** Remove the cam followers, keeping them in their correct order.

☐ **Step 16:** Undo the securing bolts, remove the flywheel and the rear engine plate.

☐ **Step 17:** Stand the block in the upside down position, unbolt and remove the crankshaft rear oil seal carrier.

☐ **Step 18:** Make sure the main bearing caps are numbered and note which way round they are fitted, then undo their bolts and remove them. Keep the bearing shells with their caps and the centre thrust washers in their correct positions.

☐ **Step 19:** Lift the crankshaft away from the cylinder block and recover the other halves of the main bearing shells.

## Job 9. OHV engine - reassembly.

*i* INSIDE INFORMATION: It is good policy to change the oil pump when carrying out an engine overhaul. A faulty or worn pump will cause a new or rebuilt engine to wear out again very quickly! *i*

IMPORTANT NOTE: All bearings, shells, piston rings and ALL seals that bear on moving parts MUST be copiously lubricated with fresh engine oil as the engine is being reassembled. Work ONLY in clean conditions, with clean components and clean hands.

## Checking for Wear

### GENERAL

All parts must be thoroughly cleaned for inspection - still keeping them in the right order for reassembly in case they are to be re-used. Check each component as follows:

### CYLINDER BLOCK

Look for any cracks in the casting, particularly at bolt holes and between cylinders. Check the bores for score marks, caused by burned pistons or broken rings. Check for a wear ridge just below the top of the bore where the top piston ring ends its travel. If any of these defects are present in any of the cylinders, they will have to be rebored. Ask your FIAT agent or engine specialist to inspect and measure the bores for wear if you are unsure. It is sometimes possible to 'glaze bust' the bores and fit new piston rings, assuming the pistons to be in good condition. All of this work can be carried out by your FIAT agent, who will supply the pistons when reboring and who should also fit the pistons to your connecting rods as the gudgeon pins are a press fit into the connecting rod small ends - which have to be heated - not a DIY job.

### CRANKSHAFT

Check all the mains journals and crankpins for any signs of wear ridges round the circumference or scoring of the surface. Check for ovality with a suitable micrometer, 0.025 mm being the maximum permissible amount. Check the shell bearings, which should have an even, dull grey finish. If this has worn through to the copper coloured backing, or if the crankshaft has any of the previously mentioned faults, the crankshaft should be reground by your specialist who will also supply the new shell bearings and thrust washers.

### CAMSHAFT

Check the bearings in the cylinder block and replace if there are excessive wear signs. Once installed, the centre and rear bearings should be reamed out to size by your FIAT agent. The front bearing is already reamed. Check each cam lobe for wear, which can be quite rapid once started. The cam followers should also be checked, particularly where they contact the cam lobe. If you are replacing the camshaft, fit new followers as well.

### TIMING CHAIN AND SPROCKETS

The timing chain, sprockets and tensioner should be changed as a matter of course during a complete overhaul.

### CYLINDER HEAD

See *Job 3*.

### ROCKER SHAFT AND ROCKERS

Check the shaft for wear at the rocker pivot points.

*i* INSIDE INFORMATION: Check the rocker bushes for wear by positioning the rockers on a 'new' part of the shaft and rocking sideways. *i*

Check the hydraulic tappets for damage to the contact caps, where they contact the valve stem. Check the thread on the pre-loading adjustment nut and bolt. Check the pushrods for straightness and the ball and sockets for wear.

### OIL PUMP

Unscrew the bolts holding the two parts of the pump body together. Wash all the parts in paraffin and dry them. Check the gear teeth for wear:
- Check visually and by rocking the gears together.
- Using a feeler gauge, check the clearance between the gear teeth and the pump body.
- With a straight edge across the top of the body, use a feeler

gauge to check the clearance between the upper side of the gears and the pump body. See **Chapter 3, Facts and Figures**. If either of the clearances is outside the specified limits, fit a new pump.

**ℹ INSIDE INFORMATION:** It is good policy to change the oil pump when carrying out an engine overhaul. An engine supplied by your FIAT agent would include a new pump. **ℹ**

# Engine Reassembly

## SECTION A - CRANKSHAFT

☐ **Step A1:** Make sure the bearing seats in the block are perfectly clean and locate the shells so that their tabs engage with the slots.

☐ **Step A2:** Apply some grease to the smooth side of the thrust washers (see illustration **Job 8-1, part 13**) and place them in position either side of the centre main bearing.

☐ **Step A3:** Oil the shells liberally with fresh engine oil and lower the crankshaft into position.

☐ **Step A4:** Fit the remaining halves of the shells into the bearing caps and position the remaining halves of the thrust washers on either side of the centre main cap with grease.

☐ **Step A5:** Oil the crank journals and position the caps the right way round and in the correct order.

☐ **Step A6:** Screw the bolts in finger tight and check that the crankshaft rotates freely and smoothly.

☐ **Step A7:** Tighten the bolts evenly and progressively until the specified torque setting is reached. See **Chapter 3, Facts and Figures**. Check again that the crankshaft rotates smoothly.

☐ **Step A8:** Check the crankshaft end float by using a feeler gauge between the thrust washer and the crankshaft. Thicker washers are available if required - see **Chapter 3, Facts and Figures**.

☐ **Step A9:** Fit the rear oil seal carrier (with its new seal), using a new gasket. Lubricate the seal.

☐ **Step A10:** Fit the rear engine plate.

☐ **Step A11:** **ℹ INSIDE INFORMATION:** Check the flywheel for score marks or micro cracking on the clutch contact surface. Deep score marks or cracking would be too much to machine out, making a new flywheel necessary. **ℹ**

Position Nos. 1 and 4 big-end crankpins at TDC, then fit the flywheel with the TDC mark facing upwards. Tighten the bolts to their specified torque - see **Chapter 3, Facts and Figures**.

## SECTION B - CAMSHAFT

☐ **Step B1:** Oil the cam followers and refit in their original positions.

☐ **Step B2:** Oil the camshaft bearings (see illustration **Job 8-1, parts 18** and **20**) and install the camshaft with care, avoiding damaging the bearings with the cam lobes.

☐ **Step B3:** Fit the front bearing (see illustration **Job 8-1, part 18**), chamfer first, and secure with the locking bolt. Lubricate the cam lobes.

## SECTION C - OIL PUMP

☐ **Step C1:** Position the gasket on the crankcase mounting.

☐ **Step C2:** Locate the drive-shaft in the pump and offer the assembly to the crankcase allowing the drive-shaft and camshaft gears to mesh. Fit the mounting bolts.

☐ **Step C3:** Fit the oil return pipe.

**ℹ INSIDE INFORMATION:** The sump cannot be fitted until the timing cover is in place and the pistons and connecting rods fitted. **ℹ**

## SECTION D - TIMING CHAIN AND SPROCKETS

See **Job 7**.

## SECTION E - PISTON/CONNECTING ROD ASSEMBLIES

IMPORTANT NOTE: The pistons and connecting rods are to be fitted as assemblies. Their dismantling and reassembly is a job for your FIAT agent - not a DIY job.

☐ **Step E1:** Make sure the bores and pistons are clean. Position the piston ring gaps at equal intervals round the piston's circumference and lubricate well. Make sure the rings are fitted with the word TOP upwards.

*Job 9-E1*

☐ **Step E2:** Locate the upper half of the big end shell bearing in the conrod, making sure that the mating surfaces are clean.

☐ **Step E3:** Locate a ring clamp over the piston rings and tighten enough to close the ring gaps, but not too tight! Lubricate the rings so that they compress and slide easily within the clamp.

☐ **Step E4:** Position the assembly in its correct bore with the piston arrow pointing towards the timing cover and the connecting rod number facing away from the camshaft.

PISTON RING COMPRESSOR

☐ **Step E5:** With the ring clamp touching the cylinder block, use a hammer shaft to carefully tap the piston through the clamp and into the bore.

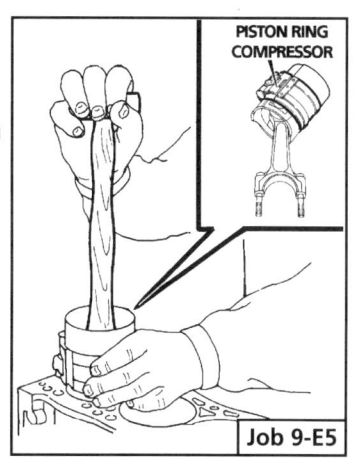

*Job 9-E5*

☐ **Step E6:** Lubricate the crankpin and the big-end shell and draw the conrod down the bore so that the big end locates with the crankpin.

☐ **Step E7:** Fit the other half of the big-end shell to the bearing cap and lubricate. Offer the cap to the connecting rod and make sure that the numbers match. Screw in the fixing bolts and tighten progressively to the correct torque. See *Chapter 3, Facts and Figures*.

☐ **Step E8:** Fit the remaining piston/conrod assemblies.

☐ **Step E9:** Fit the sump and gasket, and tighten the bolts progressively. Check that the drain plug is tight.

### SECTION F - CYLINDER HEAD

☐ **Step F1:** Stand the engine on its sump and fit the cylinder head. See *Job 2*.

### SECTION G - ANCILLARY COMPONENTS

☐ **Step G1:** Refit the exhaust manifold and ducting, the alternator and the thermostat housing.

☐ **Step G2:** Refit the rocker cover (to which is attached the ignition coils and spark plug cables).

☐ **Step G3:** Fit a new oil filter.

☐ **Step G4:** Refit the coolant pump. Check for play in the bearings and for any sign of leaking. Replace if suspect.

☐ **Step G5:** Refit the dipstick tube.

☐ **Step G6:** Fit the clutch. See **PART B: TRANSMISSION**.

### SECTION H - INSTALLATION AND INITIAL START UP

☐ **Step H1:** Reconnect the engine to the transmission. See *Job 20*.

☐ **Step H2:** Refit the complete unit to the car. See *Job 18*.

☐ **Step H3:** Refit the injector unit and air filter assembly. Remake the electrical connections to the ignition coils. See **PART E: FUEL, IGNITION AND EXHAUST**. Fit the spark plugs.

☐ **Step H4:** Run the engine in neutral, slightly faster than its normal idling speed, until it reaches its working temperature, then slow it down to normal idling speed.

☐ **Step H5:** Stop the engine and allow it to cool, check the oil and coolant levels and look for any leaks.

☐ **Step H6:** Avoid over-revving or overloading the engine during its settling down period of 600 miles, then retighten the head as follows:
• Using the correct sequence, slacken each head bolt by one quarter of a turn.
• Immediately retighten it to the specified torque. See *Chapter 3, Facts and Figures*.

• Adjust the pre-loading of the hydraulic tappets. See *Job 5*.

IMPORTANT NOTE: Modern FIAT cylinder head gaskets do NOT need re-torquing after a bedding-down interval. Check with your supplier.

## Job 10. FIRE OHC cylinder heads, valve clearance adjustment.

**i** INSIDE INFORMATION: Adjustment should always be made with the engine cold. **i**

☐ **Step 1:** Remove the camshaft cover and the spark plugs. Jack up a front wheel and engage top gear. Turning the wheel will rotate the engine and therefore the camshaft. (If the cylinder head is detached and on the bench, turn the camshaft by gripping the camshaft sprocket.)

☐ **Step 2:** The inlet and exhaust valves use different clearances which are checked when each cam lobe is pointing directly away from its follower. See *Chapter 3, Facts and Figures*.

☐ **Step 3:** The order in which the valves are fitted in the cylinder head is:
• *Inlet: 2-3-6-7*
• *Exhaust: 1-4-5-8*
from the timing cover end.

☐ **Step 4:** Select a feeler blade which is about the thickness of the correct valve clearance and insert it between the heel of the cam and the cam follower shim when the cam lobe is uppermost. If necessary, select different thicknesses of feeler blade until a small amount of drag can be felt as the blade is pushed in and out. Record the total blade thickness. This is the valve clearance for this valve.

*Job 10-4*

☐ **Step 5:** Rotate the camshaft and repeat this operation on each of the remaining seven valves, noting their respective clearances. Those which have clearances within limits obviously don't need any further attention.

☐ **Step 6:** The remaining valves will now need to have their shims (arrowed) changed for thicker or thinner ones, bringing their clearances to within the specifications shown in *Chapter 3, Facts and Figures*.

*Job 10-6*

❑ **Step 7:** In theory, a special tool is needed to depress the cam follower and allow extraction of the shim. This is available to your FIAT dealer, or you will have to make a lever with a fork that locates nicely on the rim of a cam follower allowing removal of the shim by prising it from the follower.

**ℹ INSIDE INFORMATION:** In practice, you would probably spend longer making the tool than following this procedure:
● Measure and note all of the valve clearances.
● Calculate the amount of increase or decrease in shim thickness needed.
● Remove the camshaft and change the necessary shims.
● Refit, re-check the clearances and repeat if necessary.
● You should also note that some shims can be *extremely* awkward to shift, even with the camshaft removed - and far more awkward with it in place!
● We recommend camshaft removal! ℹ

❑ **Step 8:** The thickness of a shim is engraved on it in 'mm'. If this is worn away, you will have to measure the thickness with a metric micrometer - or have your FIAT dealer do it for you.

❑ **Step 9:** Where a clearance is too small with the thinnest shim in position, the valves should be removed and the stem ground just sufficiently to make the correction. Your FIAT dealer can do this, keeping the end square and retaining a smooth finish.

## Job 11. FIRE OHC engine - timing belt, removal and replacement.

❑ **Step 1:** These are the principal components concerned with timing belt removal and replacement.

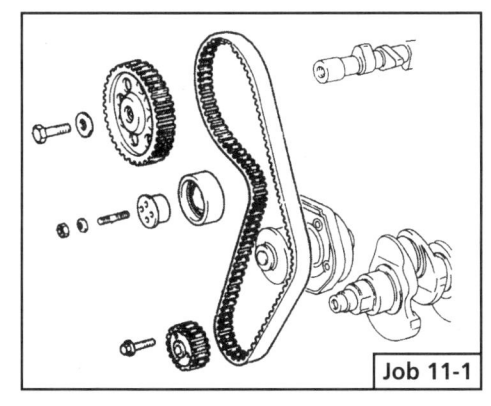

Job 11-1

IMPORTANT NOTE: FIAT strongly recommend that you should NEVER re-use a timing belt. Removal and re-application of the belt's tension can lead to premature failure. ALWAYS fit a new one!

❑ **Step 2:** Disconnect the battery earth. Remove the air cleaner, remove the spark plugs and take off the alternator drive belt.

❑ **Step 3A:** Remove the timing cover, not forgetting the bolt at the bottom.

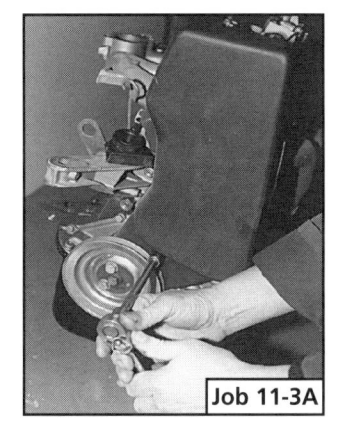

Job 11-3A

❑ **Step 3B:** Take note of the different cover types used on different models.

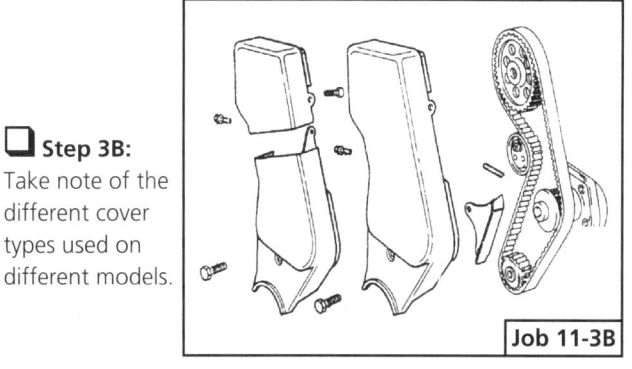

Job 11-3B

❑ **Step 4:** Unbolt and remove the crankshaft pulley.

Job 11-4

❑ **Step 5:** Using a spanner on the crankshaft bolt, turn clockwise until the camshaft sprocket timing mark (arrowed) is aligned with the mark on the cylinder head.

Job 11-5

❑ **Step 6:** Also, make sure that the timing mark on the crankshaft pulley is aligned with the mark on the oil pump cover (see arrows).

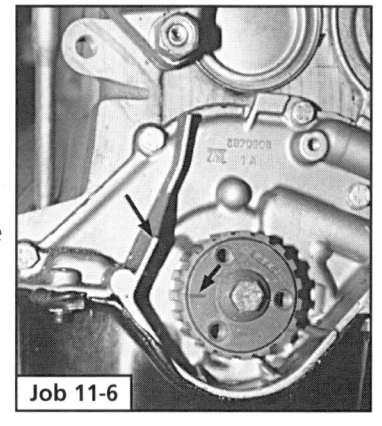

Job 11-6

❑ **Step 7:** Slacken the timing belt tensioner nut...

Job 11-7

**CHAPTER 6 PART A: ENGINE**

**6-15**

☐ **Step 8:** ...and move the pulley away from the belt by turning it.

**ℹ INSIDE INFORMATION:** Retighten the nut to temporarily retain the 'slackened' position, to make it easier to refit the belt, later. ℹ

☐ **Step 9:** Remove the old belt.

*Job 11-8*

☐ **Step 10:** The new belt must be fitted with the arrows, printed on the outside of the belt, pointing in the direction of engine rotation. Ensure that the timing marks are still aligned.

☐ **Step 11:** Engage the belt with the crankshaft sprocket first, then in turn, the coolant and camshaft sprockets. Finally, feed it round the tensioner pulley. Also, as a double-check that the belt is not 'out', ensure that the yellow lines on the belt align exactly with the timing marks on the camshaft sprocket and crankshaft sprocket.

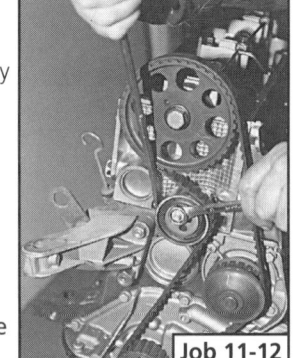

*Job 11-11*

☐ **Step 12:** Slacken the tensioner nut and push the pulley onto the belt until taut. Check that the timing marks are still correctly aligned. Still pressing the pulley against the belt, tighten its locking nut.

**ℹ INSIDE INFORMATION:** If you can't put enough pressure on the tensioner with your fingers, carefully use a long screwdriver as a lever. Alternatively, push a pair of bolts into the two holes in the tensioner and lever between them to turn the tensioner. ℹ

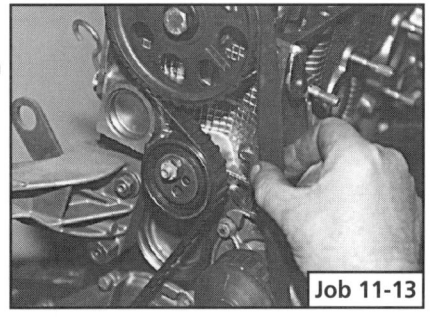

*Job 11-12*

☐ **Step 13:** Turn the engine through two complete turns clockwise. If correctly tensioned, you should just be able to twist the belt through a quarter of a complete turn

*Job 11-13*

(i.e. through 90 degrees) with your thumb and finger at the centre of its longest run. Re-adjust if necessary.

## Job 12. FIRE OHC cylinder head - removal.

**ℹ INSIDE INFORMATION:** Allow the engine to cool right down before starting work, or you will run the risk of causing cylinder head distortion. ℹ

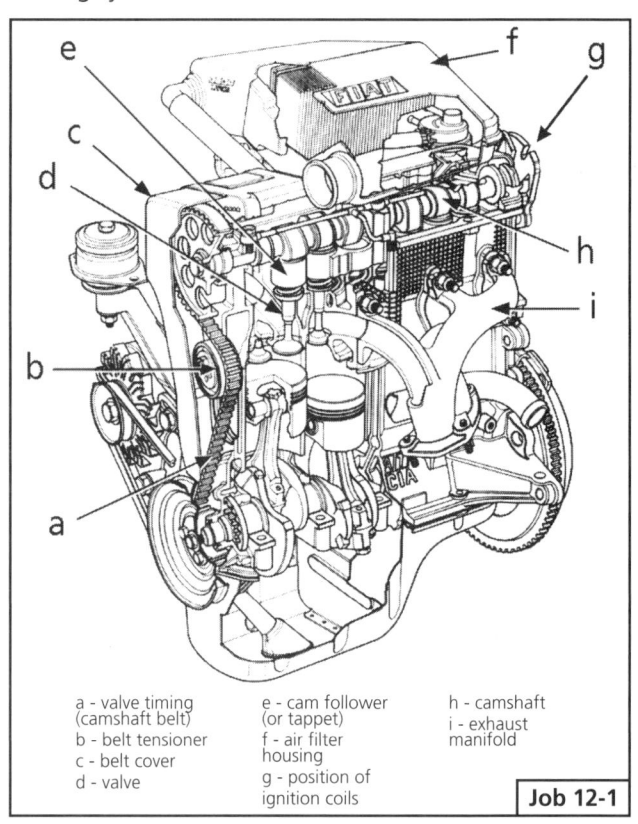

a - valve timing (camshaft belt)
b - belt tensioner
c - belt cover
d - valve
e - cam follower (or tappet)
f - air filter housing
g - position of ignition coils
h - camshaft
i - exhaust manifold

*Job 12-1*

☐ **Step 1:** This illustration shows the layout of the major components of the FIRE Overhead Camshaft (OHC) engine.

☐ **Step 2:** Disconnect the battery negative earth lead.

☐ **Step 3:** Drain the cooling system while the engine is cold.

☐ **Step 4:** Remove the air filter, disconnect the accelerator cable, and remove all electrical connections and hoses from the injector turret and inlet manifold. Plug the ends of the fuel hoses. See *PART E: FUEL, IGNITION AND EXHAUST*.

☐ **Step 5:** Remove the electrical control connections from the ignition coils, then remove the coils complete with the spark plug leads.

☐ **Step 6:** Disconnect the water return hose from the thermostatic housing on the end of the cylinder head.

☐ **Step 7:** Remove the camshaft cover and gasket.

☐ **Step 8:** Unbolt the timing belt cover and remove. See *Job 11*.

☐ **Step 9:** Put No. 1 piston at TDC as described in *Job 11, Steps 5* and *6*.

☐ **Step 10:** Slacken the timing belt tensioner and remove the belt from the sprockets.

☐ **Step 11:** Unbolt the inlet manifold and, if you prefer, remove it complete with the injector turret.

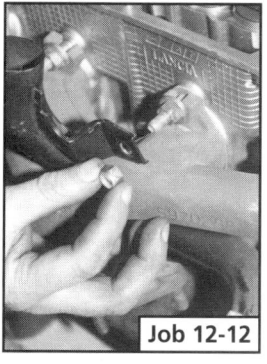

Job 12-11

Job 12-12

Job 12-13

☐ **Step 12:** On the opposite side of the engine, take off the hot air ducting from the exhaust manifold studs - two locknuts.

☐ **Step 13:** Disconnect the exhaust downpipe bracket. Unbolt the manifold from the cylinder head and tie to one side (in the engine bay), or remove if you prefer.

☐ **Step 14:** Unscrew the cylinder head bolts half a turn at a time in the order shown, until all are loose.

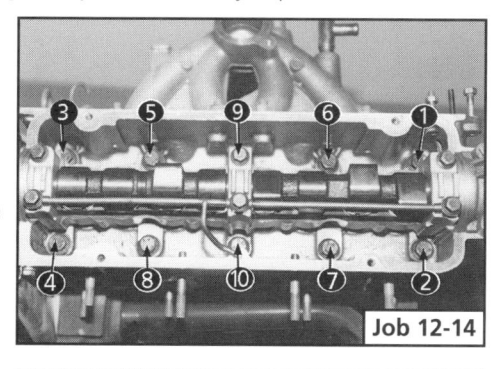

Job 12-14

☐ **Step 15:** Now remove the bolts and their washers from the cylinder head.

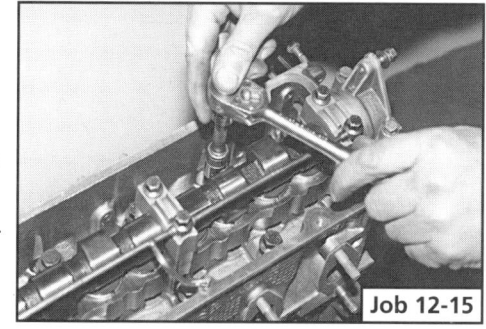

Job 12-15

☐ **Step 16:** The cylinder head is now ready for removal. Never attempt to use a wedge between the cylinder head and block. This causes a lot of damage.

Job 12-16

*making it easy* • If the head is stuck, use a wooden hammer shaft or something similar, as a lever in the exhaust ports to break the seal.

## Job 13. FIRE OHC cylinder head - refitting.

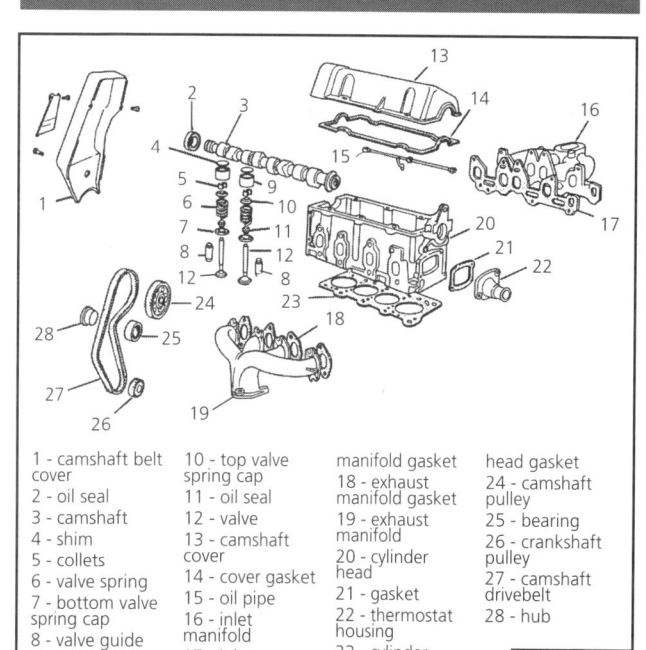

1 - camshaft belt cover
2 - oil seal
3 - camshaft
4 - shim
5 - collets
6 - valve spring
7 - bottom valve spring cap
8 - valve guide
9 - tappet
10 - top valve spring cap
11 - oil seal
12 - valve
13 - camshaft cover
14 - cover gasket
15 - oil pipe
16 - inlet manifold
17 - inlet manifold gasket
18 - exhaust manifold gasket
19 - exhaust manifold
20 - cylinder head
21 - gasket
22 - thermostat housing
23 - cylinder head gasket
24 - camshaft pulley
25 - bearing
26 - crankshaft pulley
27 - camshaft drivebelt
28 - hub

Job 13-1

☐ **Step 1:** This shows the layout of the cylinder head components. The camshaft cover gasket is reusable unless damaged, compressed or brittle, in which case it must be replaced.

☐ **Step 2:** Before refitting, make sure that the cylinder head and block surfaces have been thoroughly cleaned and that the bolt holes in the cylinder block are clear to their bottoms.

☐ **Step 3:** Align the camshaft sprocket timing mark (arrowed) with the one on the cylinder head.

Job 13-3

☐ **Step 4:** Make sure that the two aligning dowels are in place, at opposite ends of the block.

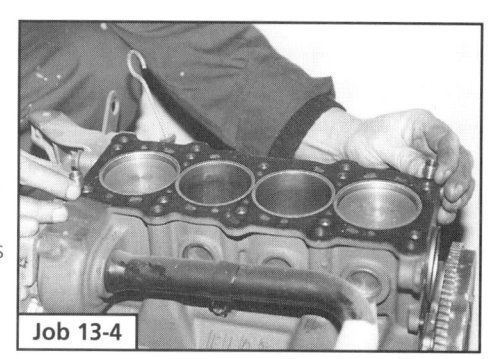

Job 13-4

**CHAPTER 6 PART A: ENGINE**

6-17

☐ **Step 5:** The new cylinder head gasket must be fitted dry. Any gasket sealer, oil or grease could cause it to blow. Place it over the dowels on the cylinder block with the word 'ALTO' facing upwards.

*Job 13-5*

☐ **Step 6:** Place the cylinder head carefully on the block, locating it on the positioning dowels.

☐ **Step 7:** *i* INSIDE INFORMATION: The cylinder head bolts must be cleaned, dipped in engine oil and drained for thirty minutes before fitting. This stops them 'hydraulicing' when being screwed home and allows them to be 'torqued' down evenly. *i*

*Job 13-6*

☐ **Step 8:** Fit the cylinder head bolts and their washers finger tight, then tighten them in the sequence shown here using the following procedure:

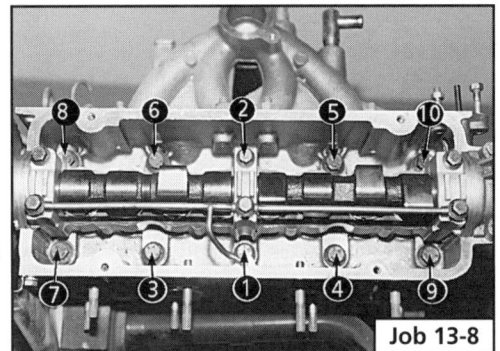

*Job 13-8*

☐ **Step 9A:** First, tighten each bolt to 20 Nm with a torque wrench...

*Job 13-9A*

☐ **Step 9B:** ...followed by a second stage, further tightening each bolt.

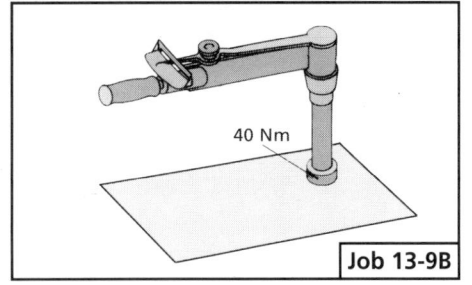

*Job 13-9B*

☐ **Step 10:** Tighten each bolt once again in the correct order, by a further 90 degrees. Then finally, turn each bolt by a (second) 90 degrees.

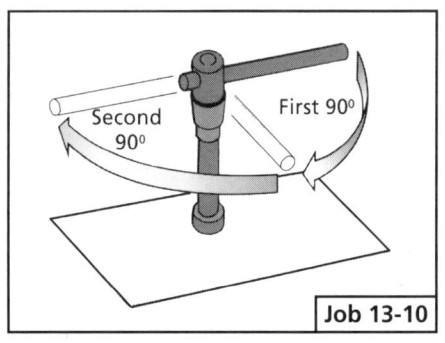

*Job 13-10*

☐ **Step 11:** Refit the inlet manifold using a new gasket and be careful to position the accelerator cable bracket 14 to 16 mm from the alternator terminal clamp. Before the manifold nuts are tightened, insert the large serrated washer (if one is fitted) between the bracket and the manifold. Tighten the manifold nuts evenly to the correct torque. See **Chapter 3, Facts and Figures**.

☐ **Step 12:** Refit the exhaust manifold with a new gasket and tighten to the correct torque. The downpipe bracket can now be reconnected.

☐ **Step 13:** Making sure the timing marks are aligned, follow the instructions in **Job 11** for fitting a new timing belt. DON'T re-use the old one!

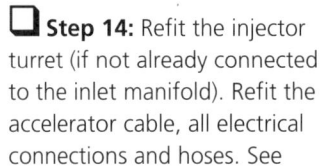

☐ **Step 14:** Refit the injector turret (if not already connected to the inlet manifold). Refit the accelerator cable, all electrical connections and hoses. See **PART E: FUEL, IGNITION AND EXHAUST**.

*Job 13-13*

☐ **Step 15:** Refit the coils, spark plugs and spark plug leads, and remake the electrical control connections.

☐ **Step 16:** Refit the camshaft cover and timing belt cover.

☐ **Step 17:** Reconnect all remaining hoses and electrical connections.

☐ **Step 18:** Fill the cooling system with the correct dilution of new **FL Paraflu** anti-freeze solution. See **Chapter 3, Facts and Figures** and **Chapter 5, Servicing Your Car**.

☐ **Step 19:** Refit the air cleaner and re-connect the battery negative earth lead.

## Job 14. FIRE OHC cylinder head - dismantling and overhauling.

☐ **Step 1:** The cylinder head has to be partly stripped as it is being removed from the engine. See **Job 12**. Only the camshaft and valves remain to be dismantled at this stage.

*Job 14-1*

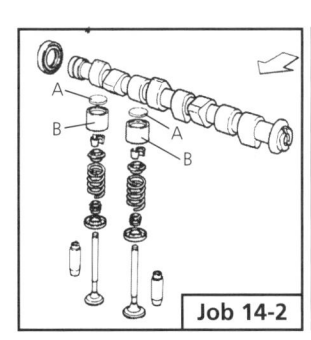

**Step 2:** This is the general layout of the valve gear. Take careful note of the tappet shims (**A**) and valve collets (**B**).

**Step 3:** Undo the camshaft sprocket fixing bolt and remove the sprocket.

> *making it easy*
> • Pass a steel bar through one of the sprocket holes to prevent rotation when undoing the camshaft sprocket bolt.
> • Avoid damage to the cylinder head by putting a piece of wood under the end of the bar.

**Step 4:** Mark the camshaft bearing caps, so that you can refit them in the same positions.

**Step 5:** Unbolt and remove the oil feed pipe - carefully prise out the stub using a screwdriver, as shown after removing the relevant bolts.

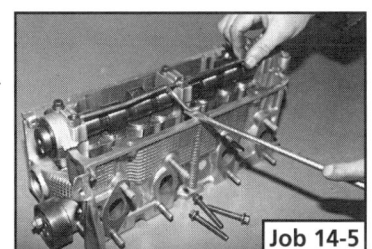

**Step 6:** Undo the remaining bolts and remove the bearing caps. Carefully remove the camshaft from the cylinder head, without disturbing the shims and cam followers beneath.

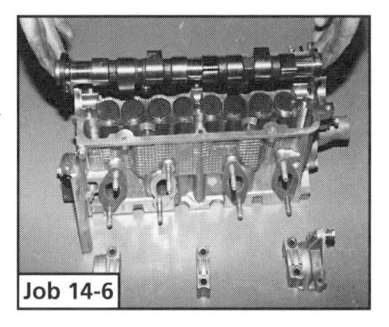

*i* INSIDE INFORMATION: • Note that the oil in the engine will tend to make the cam followers tricky to lift. Try prising carefully with a pair of screwdrivers, one each side and lift evenly.
• If valve grinding or seat cutting has taken place, or the valves, camshaft or cam followers have been changed, the original shims will no longer give the correct clearances. See **Job 10** for adjustments. *i*

**Step 7:** Now remove cam followers (or tappets), keeping them in the correct order for refitting. They will be complete with their shims at this stage.

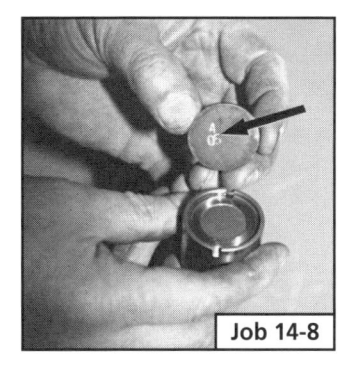

**Step 8:** The shims can each be removed, if necessary, but be sure to keep them with their correct 'partners'. Each shim is marked with its thickness (arrowed).

**Step 9:** Use a suitable valve spring compressor to compress each spring in turn to allow the removal of the split collets from the valve stems. Take care not to lose the collets when releasing the spring compressor.

**Step 10:** The valve spring caps, springs and spring seats can all be lifted clear and the valves withdrawn from their guides. Keep the valves in their correct order.

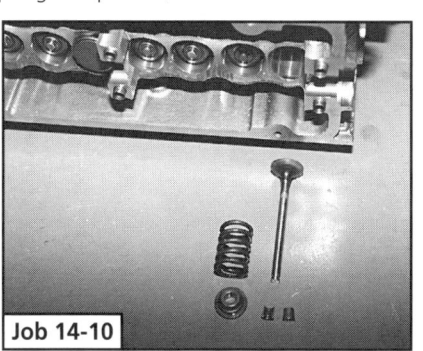

> *making it easy*
> • Keep the valves in their correct order by pushing their stems through some cardboard and numbering them, No. 1 being at the timing belt end.
> • An alternative means of identification is to label each valve with masking tape and write on it.

**Step 11:** *i* INSIDE INFORMATION: The valves should slide freely out of their guides. Any resistance may be caused by a build up of carbon, or a slight burr on the stem where the collets engage. This can usually be removed by careful use of fine wet-or-dry paper, allowing you to withdraw the valves without scoring their guides. *i*

**Step 12:** The cylinder head is made of light alloy and is easily damaged when being cleaned. Use a rotary wire brush for the combustion chambers and ports, but no sharp objects such as a screwdriver should be used. The machined surfaces must have all traces of old gasket removed by use of a straight edge. Then wash down with paraffin to remove old oil and dirt and dry with clean rag. **At all costs**, avoid gouging the cylinder head. This can be very expensive to put right.

> *making it easy*
> • Try using carburettor cleaner or proprietary gasket remover, to loosen old gasket material.

❑ **Step 13:** Carry out the following checks:
- The cylinder head must be checked for distortion by use of a straight edge and feeler gauge.
- At the same time check for excessive corrosion. If you are in doubt, or if the old gasket has blown, have the cylinder head refaced by your FIAT agent or engine specialist.
- The valves should be checked for side movement in their guides. Anything but the very slightest tells you that the valve guides are in need of replacement. Your local FIAT agent or engine specialist should do this job.
- Examine the valve seats for pitting or burning, and also check their mating seats in the cylinder head. Small pits can be removed by grinding the valves onto their seats.
- If the pitting is too deep, the seats in the cylinder head will have to be recut, again, by your local agent and new valves fitted.

*making it easy*
- Clean the valve heads back to shiny metal.
- Now the sucker on the end of your valve grinding stick won't keep falling off!

- IMPORTANT NOTE: 'Unleaded' engine valve seats are too hard for hand 'powered' valve grinding to make much impression on them. You can only grind out the smallest of blemishes by hand.

❑ **Step 14:** Clean the carbon from the valves with a rotary wire brush and wash them in paraffin. Wash the valve springs, caps, seats and collets and dry them.

❑ **Step 15:** Grind in the valves. The process is the same as on OHV cylinder heads. See *Job 3*.

❑ **Step 16:**
*i* INSIDE INFORMATION: It can be tricky to re-fit the collets. Put a dab of grease on the collet, put a dab on the end of your screwdriver, pick up the collet and 'stick' it in place on the stem of the valve. *i*

Job 14-16

❑ **Step 17:** Reassemble the rest of the cylinder head in the reverse order. Remember to oil the camshaft bearings and use a new camshaft oil seal. See your FIAT agent if there is any pitting or burning visible on the valve faces or seat.

## Job 15. FIRE OHC engine - dismantling.

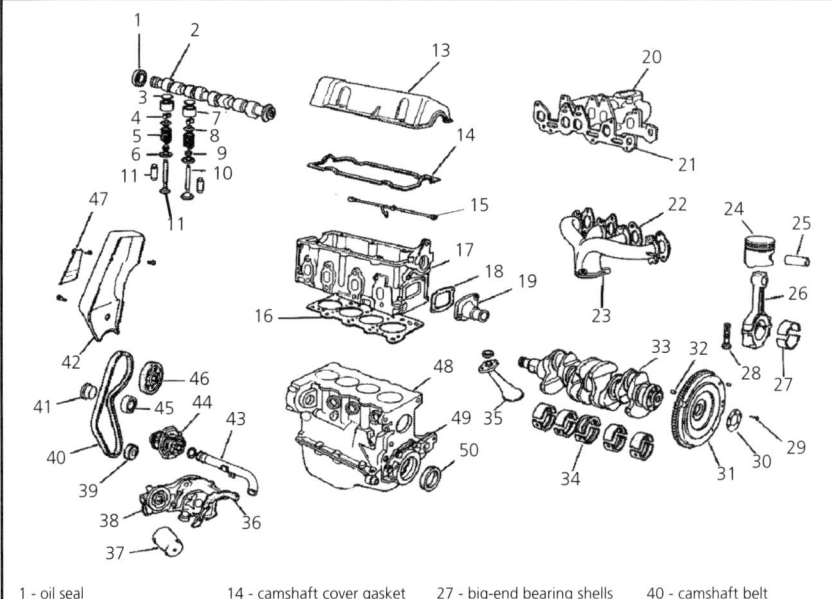

1 - oil seal
2 - camshaft
3 - shim
4 - collets
5 - valve spring
6 - bottom spring cap
7 - tappet
8 - top spring cap
9 - oil seal
10 - inlet valve
11 - valve guides
12 - exhaust valve
13 - camshaft cover
14 - camshaft cover gasket
15 - oil pipe
16 - cylinder head gasket
17 - cylinder head
18 - thermostat gasket
19 - thermostat/housing
20 - inlet manifold
21 - gasket
22 - gasket
23 - exhaust manifold
24 - piston
25 - gudgeon pin
26 - conrod assembly
27 - big-end bearing shells
28 - conrod bolt
29 - bolt
30 - washer
31 - flywheel
32 - dowel
33 - crankshaft
34 - crankshaft bearings
35 - oil pump pick-up
36 - gasket
37 - oil filter
38 - oil pump
39 - crankshaft pulley
40 - camshaft belt
41 - hub
42 - camshaft belt cover
43 - coolant pipe
44 - coolant pump
45 - cam belt tensioner
46 - camshaft pulley
47 - rear cover
48 - cylinder block
49 - oil seal housing
50 - oil seal

Job 15-1

❑ **Step 1:** Familiarise yourself with the layout of the FIRE engine components, shown here.

❑ **Step 2:** Remove the engine from the vehicle. See *Job 17*.

❑ **Step 3:** Remove the cylinder head. See *Job 12*.

❑ **Step 4:** Remove the thermostat housing.

❑ **Step 5:** Remove the distribution pipe from the coolant pump and remove the pump.

❑ **Step 6:** Remove and discard the oil filter.

❑ **Step 7:** Remove the alternator and drive belt.

❑ **Step 8:** Lock the flywheel and undo the crankshaft nut. Pull off the crank pulley.

❑ **Step 9:** Remove the clutch and then the flywheel.

❑ **Step 10:** Unbolt and remove the sump.

❑ **Step 11:** Remove the oil pump and pickup assembly.

❑ **Step 12:** Remove the engine back plate and timing index plate.

❑ **Step 13:** Lie the engine on its side and undo the big-end bolts.

☐ **Step 14:** Remove the bearing caps and half shells and keep them in order.

🛈 INSIDE INFORMATION: Make sure the caps have numbers matching those on their mating conrods. It is essential they are kept together. 🛈

☐ **Step 15:** Withdraw the piston/conrod assemblies from their bores and keep them strictly in the order they were fitted in.

☐ **Step 16:** Turn the cylinder block upside down and remove the rear crankshaft seal and carrier.

☐ **Step 17:** Undo the main bearing cap bolts and remove the caps. They are numbered from the front (timing belt end), the centre one being identified by the letter 'C'.

☐ **Step 18:** Lift out the crankshaft and retrieve the bearing shells and thrusts, keeping them in order in case they are re-used.

## Job 16. FIRE OHC engine - reassembly.

## Checking for Wear

### GENERAL

As the checks carried out on the cylinder block and crankshaft are common to most engines, read **Job 9, OHV Engine Reassembly, Checking for Wear**. Whenever rebuilding an engine, it is best to fit a new oil pump.

## Engine Reassembly

### SECTION A - CRANKSHAFT

☐ **Step A1:** Make sure the bearing seals in the block are perfectly clean and locate the main bearing shells so that their tabs engage with the slots.

☐ **Step A2:** Position the thrust washers either side of the centre web - they are held in place by the bearing shell. Then carry out **Job 9, Section A, Steps A3 to A8**.

☐ **Step A3:** Fit the rear oil seal carrier (**8**) (with its new seal **9**) - see illustration **Job 15-1, parts 49 and 50**), using RTV instant silicone gasket (**3**) on the oil seal carrier gasket (**5**). Lubricate the 'bearing' surfaces of the oil seal with fresh engine oil.

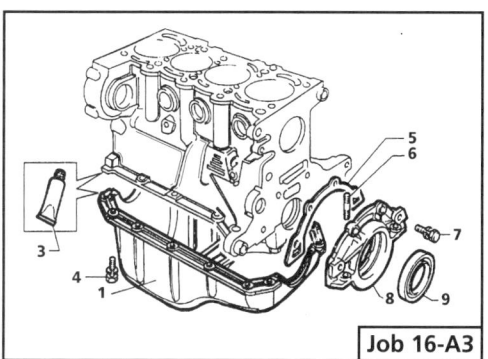

### SECTION B - PISTON/CONNECTING ROD ASSEMBLIES

Refer to **Job 9, Section E** and carry out **Steps E1 to E3**, noting that the arrow on the piston crown must point to the camshaft drivebelt end. Continue with **Steps E5 to E8**.

### SECTION C - COMPLETE THE REASSEMBLY

☐ **Step C1:** Fit a new seal to the oil pump and fit the pump, using a new gasket.

☐ **Step C2:** Fit the pump pickup/filter assembly using a new sealing washer.

☐ **Step C3:** Fit the engine backplate and fit the flywheel. Use a locking fluid on the flywheel bolts and tighten them to their correct torque. See **Chapter 3, Facts and Figures**.

☐ **Step C4:** Refit the sump (see illustration **Job 16-A3, parts 1** and **4**) using a smear of 'silicone gasket' on the gasket and refit the flywheel housing cover plate.

☐ **Step C5:** Fit the crankshaft sprocket, locating it on its integral key. Tighten the securing bolt to its specified torque. See **Chapter 3, Facts and Figures**.

☐ **Step C6:** Fit the new clutch. See **PART B: TRANSMISSION, Job 3**.

☐ **Step C7:** Refit the cylinder head. See **Job 13**.

☐ **Step C8:** Refit the coolant pump using silicone gasket.

☐ **Step C9:** Refit the timing belt rear cover. Refit the tensioner and lock it away from the tensioned position.

☐ **Step C10:** Fit the new timing belt. See **Job 11**.

☐ **Step C11:** Refit the crankshaft pulley.

☐ **Step C12:** Refit the alternator and a new drive belt.

☐ **Step C13:** Refit the oil dipstick.

☐ **Step C14:** Refit the thermostat housing, using a new gasket.

☐ **Step C15:** Using a new seal, fit the coolant pipe to the back of the coolant pump.

☐ **Step C16:** Lubricate the sealing ring and screw on a new oil filter cartridge.

☐ **Step C17:** Follow **Job 9, INSTALLATION AND INITIAL START-UP; Steps H1 to H6**, to complete the installation and initial start up.

IMPORTANT NOTE: Some FIAT cylinder head gaskets do NOT need the head bolts re-torquing after a bedding-down interval. Check with your supplier.

## Job 17. Engine and transmission, all types - removal.

IMPORTANT NOTE: See **PART B: TRANSMISSION** for gearbox removal by itself.

*i* INSIDE INFORMATION: The complete engine/transmission unit is removed and replaced from under the car - and this applies to all types. Make sure you can raise the front of the car high enough (and support it safely and securely!) to allow the power unit to be pulled clear from underneath, before starting work! *i*

☐ **Step 1:** Open the bonnet and disconnect the windscreen washer tube.
☐ **Step 3:** Disconnect the battery negative earth lead.

> *making it easy* ☐ **Step 2:** • Mark the bonnet hinge positions with a felt pen round the edge of the hinges, for easy alignment when refitting.
> • With someone helping you to support the bonnet's weight, undo the hinge bolts and remove the bonnet from the car.

☐ **Step 4:** Drain the cooling system and engine oil.

☐ **Step 5:** Remove the air filter, then remove all connections from the injector turret. Plug the ends of the fuel hoses. See **PART E: FUEL, IGNITION AND EXHAUST**.

☐ **Step 6:** Disconnect all hoses and electrical connections from the cylinder head, thermostatic housing and inlet manifold.

☐ **Step 7:** Disconnect the control cables from the ignition coils, but leave the spark plug leads in place.

☐ **Step 8:** Disconnect the leads from the starter motor and alternator.

☐ **Step 9:** Disconnect the lead from the oil pressure warning light switch, on the cylinder block.

☐ **Step 10:** Remove the hose from the water pump, under the alternator.

☐ **Step 11:** From the timing cover end, disconnect the electrical connector and earth cable from the RPM-and-TDC sensor.

☐ **Step 12:** From the transmission end, disconnect the clutch cable, speedometer cable, reversing lamp switch and earth strap.

☐ **Step 13:** With the road wheels on the ground, remove the front hub caps and slacken the drive-shaft hub nuts but don't remove them until the front of the car has been raised.

> *making it easy* • As the drive-shaft nuts are very tight, use a long bar to give extra leverage and ask a helper to plant his or her foot firmly on the brake pedal to prevent hub rotation.

☐ **Step 14:** Raise the front of the car, remove the front wheels and support on axle stands.

☐ **Step 15:** Remove the coolant radiator shield from under the right headlight by undoing the fixings (arrowed).

Job 17-15

☐ **Step 16:** Remove the plastic wheel arch liners (fixings arrowed) from both sides of the car.

☐ **Step 17:** Disconnect the electrical cable from the Lambda sensor at its junction, then remove the exhaust front downpipe, including the catalytic converter.

Job 17-16

☐ **Step 18:** Disconnect the gear selector and engagement rods from the levers on the gearbox. Remove the clips fixing the outer cables to the support bracket, then remove the cables and rods from the bracket

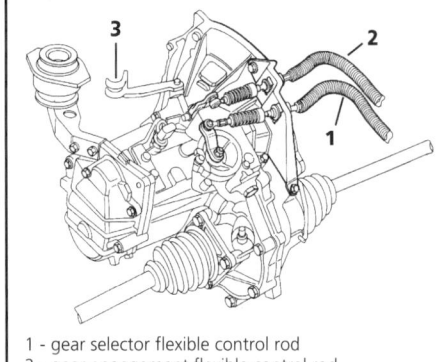

1 - gear selector flexible control rod
2 - gear engagement flexible control rod
3 - clutch lever

Job 17-18

and place them in the engine compartment. This illustration shows the gear linkage for OHV engines. On FIRE OHC engines there is also a reverse gear inhibitor that needs to be removed. See **PART B: TRANSMISSION**.

☐ **Step 19:** Remove the previously loosened hub nuts.

☐ **Step 20:** Disconnect the complete steering knuckle from the left and right shock absorbers.

Job 17-20

☐ **Step 21:** Pull the wheel hubs away from the drive shafts. Tie back the drive shafts to the transmission bodyshell to prevent them from coming out of the differential housing.

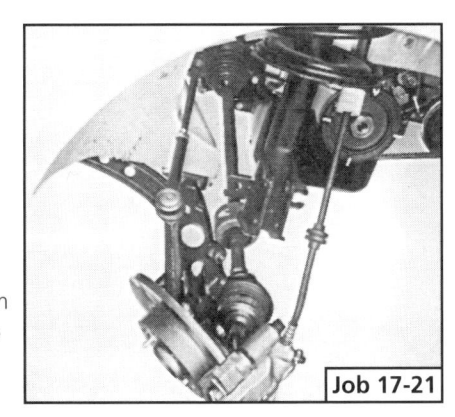

Job 17-21

☐ **Step 22:** Support the weight of the engine from above with suitable lifting gear, or from beneath with a trolley jack.

☐ **Step 23:** Disconnect the three engine mountings. See illustration **Job 21-1** for the positions of the mountings.

☐ **Step 24:** Carefully lower the engine to the ground. Raise the front of the car high enough to clear the engine, then pull the engine out from under the car.

Job 17-24

## Job 18. Engine and transmission, all types - refitting.

This is a reversal of **Job 17 - Removal**, plus these extra points:

☐ **Step 1:** Lower the car to the ground and fully tighten the front suspension, drive-shaft and engine mounting bolts. (Always use new driveshaft hubnuts.)

☐ **Step 2:** Fill the cooling system, using the correct 50/50 **Paraflu** anti-freeze solution.

☐ **Step 3:** Put fresh **Selenia** oil in the engine.

☐ **Step 4:** Top up the transmission oil.

☐ **Step 5:** Adjust the clutch free travel. See **Chapter 5: Servicing Your Car**.

For **Steps 1** to **4**, see **Chapter 3, Facts and Figures** for correct torque settings and quantities.

## Job 19. Engine/transmission, (removed from car), all types - separation.

*making it easy* / ☐ **Step 1:** ● Clean the whole unit with a proprietary degreaser - and dry off before starting work.
● This makes these heavy components easier and safer to handle and greatly reduces the risk of contamination when you strip them down

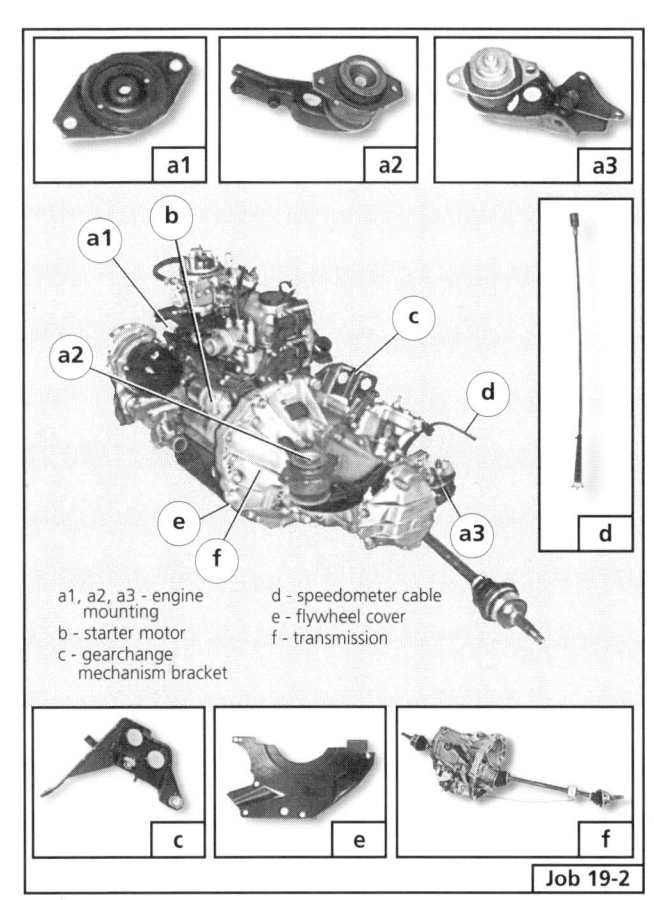

a1, a2, a3 - engine mounting
b - starter motor
c - gearchange mechanism bracket
d - speedometer cable
e - flywheel cover
f - transmission

Job 19-2

☐ **Step 2:** Undo and remove the following components:
● engine mounting brackets (**a1, a2** and **a3**)
● starter motor (**b**)
● gearchange mechanism bracket (**c**)
● speedometer cable (**d**) if not already removed
● flywheel cover (**e**)

☐ **Step 3:** Support the weight of the transmission (illustration **Job 19-2, part f**) and withdraw it from the engine in a straight line.

## Job 20. Engine/transmission, all types - reconnection.

Refer to **Job 19** for the location of components referred to here.

☐ **Step 1:** Offer the transmission to the engine. The input shaft should slide easily through the splined hub of the driven plate, as long as this is still centralised. Re-centre the clutch if necessary.

*making it easy* / ● If the input shaft and hub splines are not aligned, ask a helper to turn the crankshaft pulley nut while you apply gentle pressure to bring the two units together.

☐ **Step 2:** Once the input shaft is properly engaged, use two bolts, tightened evenly to draw the units together. DON'T force it! If the units don't come together easily, separate them, check clutch centring and try again. Fit the remaining bolts, not forgetting the lifting eyes and brackets.

☐ **Step 3:** Refit the flywheel cover, gearchange bracket and engine mounting brackets.

☐ **Step 4:** Refit the starter motor.

**CHAPTER 6 PART A: ENGINE**

6-23

## CHAPTER 6 — PART B: TRANSMISSION

## Job 21. Engine/transmission, all types - replacement.

This Job describes how to replace the engine mountings while the engine is in the car.

☐ **Step 1:** Support the weight of the engine with a jack until there is no upward or downward pressure on the mounting to be changed.

*making it easy!*
- Change one mounting at a time.
- The others will help keep the power unit correctly positioned.

☐ **Step 2:** Undo the securing bolts and fit the new mounting. Remove the supporting jack. Note the parts (**b**) are the transmission mountings. The method of attaching the engine mounting (**a**) to the FIRE OHC engine (see inset **d**) differs slightly from the OHV engine mounting (**c**).

ℹ **INSIDE INFORMATION:** If you unbolt the whole of the rear mounting bracket, be sure to replace the two bolts (**e**) into the transmission casing to prevent oil leakage. ℹ

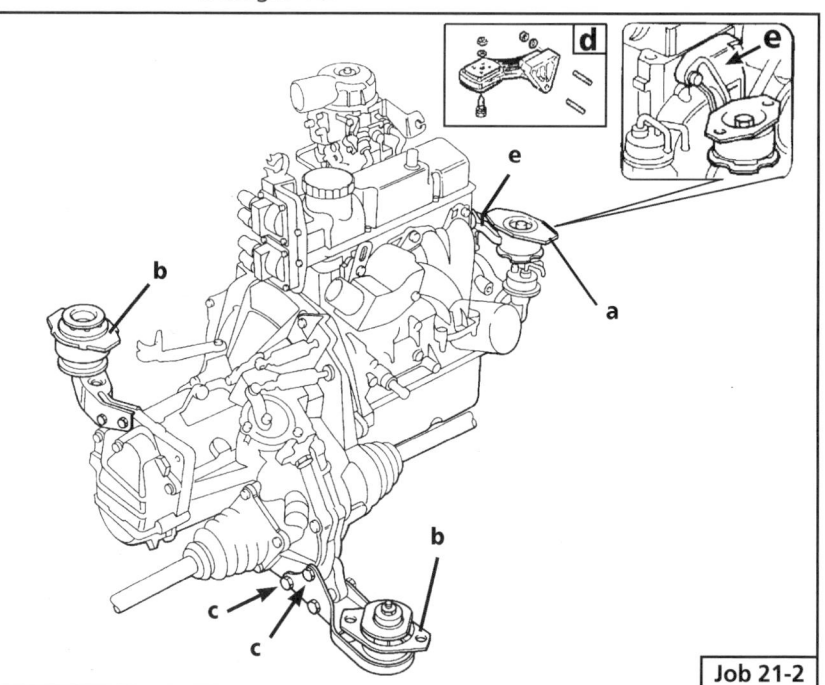

Job 21-2

# PART B: TRANSMISSION AND CLUTCH

### PART B: Contents

Job 1. Transmission - removal (with engine in car).
Job 2. Transmission - refitting (with engine in car).
Job 3. Clutch - replacement.
Job 4. Clutch cable - removal and refitting.
Job 5. Gear lever and linkage - removal and refitting.
Job 6. Drive-shaft - removal and refitting.
Job 7. Outer drive-shaft constant velocity joint - replacement.
Job 8. Left inner spider joint - replacement.
Job 9. Right inner spider joint - replacement.
Job 10. Front hub bearings - replacement.

## Job 1. Transmission - removal (with engine in car).

It is possible to remove the gearbox without removing the engine, for example if you want to replace the clutch or fit an exchange gearbox. The advantages of leaving the engine in the car are that there will be less dismantling to carry out and less weight to manhandle. Refer to **PART A: ENGINE, Jobs 17 and 18** for further information on removal of some of the components mentioned here. Ensure that you can support the car sufficiently high off the ground for the gearbox to be removed from beneath.

☐ **Step 1A:** This is the OHV engine's transmission unit and fixings.

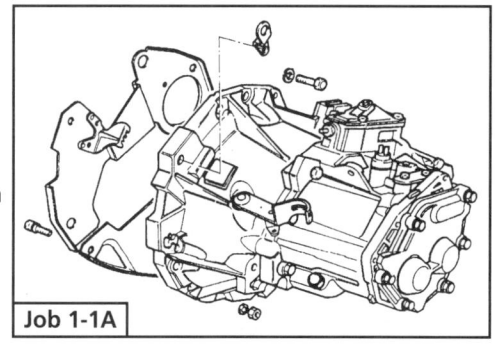

Job 1-1A

☐ **Step 1B:** This is the FIRE OHC engine's transmission unit and fixings.

☐ **Step 2:** Remove the air filter.

☐ **Step 3:** Disconnect the battery.

Job 1-1B

☐ **Step 4:** Disconnect the following items from the transmission:
- earth cable
- speedometer cable
- leads from reversing light switch

☐ **Step 5:** Disconnect the clutch cable from the transmission. See **Job 4, Step 1**.

☐ **Step 6:** Disconnect the gear change linkage from the transmission. See **Job 5, Steps 1 to 3**.

6-24

❏ **Step 7:** Undo the bolts (arrowed) and remove the starter motor from the bellhousing.

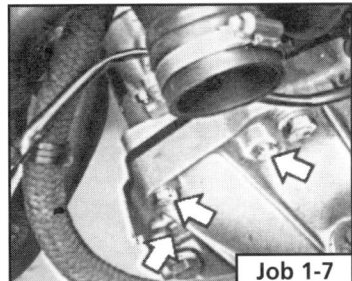

❏ **Step 8:** Undo the upper bolts (arrowed) holding the gearbox to the engine.

❏ **Step 9A:** Remove the bonnet and use suitable lifting gear to support the weight of the engine at the gearbox end. You can use the FIAT engine supporting cross member 1870595000...

❏ **Step 9B:** ...and positioning hooks, if available.
• Alternatively: you might be able to make your own home-made version.
• you could use a trolley jack or stand carefully placed beneath the car.
• you could use an engine hoist or crane from above the car.

❏ **Step 10:** Disconnect both the left and right front wheel hubs from the drive-shafts. See **Job 6, Steps 2 to 6**.

### SAFETY FIRST!

• Do NOT attempt to slacken the hub nuts while the car is on a jack or on axle stands.
• These require an enormous force to be tightened or released (see **Chapter 3, Facts and Figures**) and they will have been staked.
• There is a severe risk of pulling the car off the supports.
• Slacken the front hub nuts while the wheels are on the ground, then raise the front of the car, support it securely, and remove the wheels.

*making it easy* ❏ **Step 11:** Remove the plastic wheel arch liner to gain easier access to components underneath the car.

❏ **Step 12:**
• EITHER: Tie back the drive shafts to the transmission to prevent them from falling out.
• OR: Drain the transmission oil, then remove the drive shafts from the transmission. See **Job 6, Steps 8 and 9**.

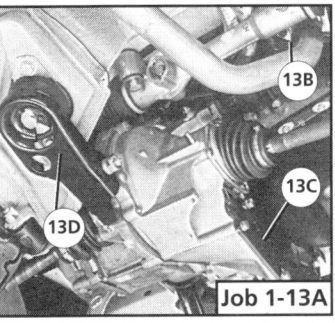

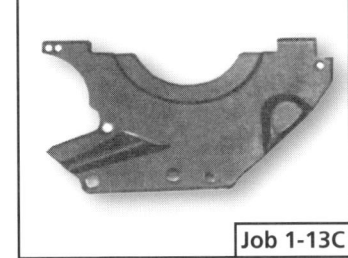

❏ **Step 13A:** Disconnect the following components from underneath the car:

❏ **Step 13B:** Disconnect the exhaust front downpipe from the manifold.

❏ **Step 13C:** Remove the flywheel cover.

❏ **Step 13D:** Remove the engine/transmission mounting from the centre-rear of the transmission. If you have not drained the transmission oil, refit the bolts into the transmission casing to prevent leaks.

❏ **Step 14:** Remove the following components:
• The bolts (**a**) from the gearchange cable support bracket.
• The rear nut (**b**) connecting the gearbox-differential to the engine.

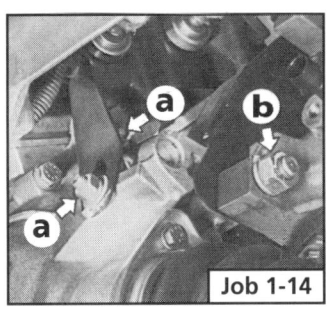

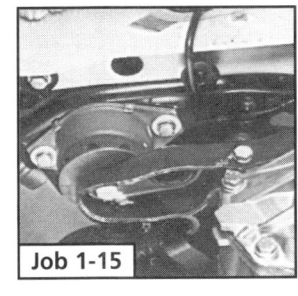

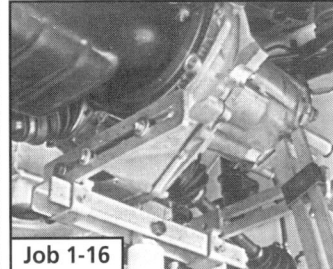

❏ **Step 15:** Remove the bolts from the front engine/transmission mounting.

❏ **Step 16:** Support the weight of the gearbox-differential carefully on a trolley jack or stand.

*making it easy* • Use a FIAT gearbox-differential support, if available - or make up something similar.
• The support fits onto your jack, giving better support to the transmission while you separate it from the engine.

**CHAPTER 6 PART B: TRANSMISSION**

☐ **Step 17:** Remove the last bolt (arrowed) fixing the transmission unit to the engine, at the front.

*Job 1-17*

☐ **Step 18:** With the transmission unit carefully supported, slide it free of the engine without putting any pressure on the clutch or the gearbox first motion shaft, then lower it to the ground and remove it from beneath the car.

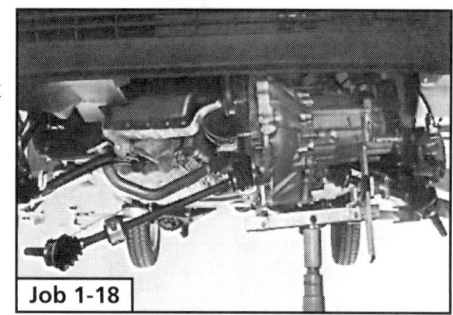

*Job 1-18*

## Job 2. Transmission - refitting (with engine in car).

IMPORTANT NOTE: Refer to the illustrations in **PART A: ENGINE, Jobs 17 and 18** in connection with this Job.

☐ **Step 1:** Refitting is the reverse of removal. Before starting, make sure that the clutch driven plate is still centralised. See **Job 3**.

☐ **Step 2:** Fill the transmission with the correct grade of new FL oil. See **Chapter 3, Facts and Figures**.

☐ **Step 3:** Check the clutch adjustment. See **Chapter 5, Servicing Your Car, Job 19**.

☐ **Step 4:** When the brake calipers have been refitted, pump the brake pedal until its normal solid feel is restored.

☐ **Step 5:** Use a self-grip wrench to reconnect the gear rod balls and sockets.

☐ **Step 6:** When refitting the driveshaft, use new drive-shaft nuts, tightened to the correct torque and staked into the shaft grooves with a punch. See **Job 6**.

## Job 3. Clutch - replacement.

☐ **Step 1:** These first three numbered parts are the parts you will need to obtain, from your FIAT dealership.

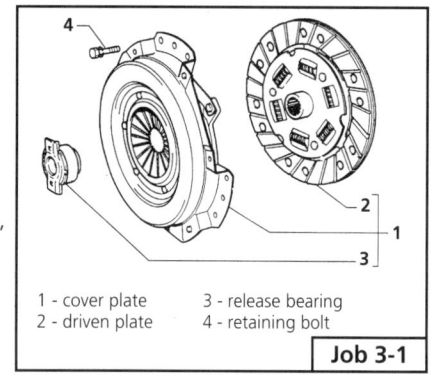

1 - cover plate
2 - driven plate
3 - release bearing
4 - retaining bolt

*Job 3-1*

**FACT FILE:**
● We strongly recommend that all three main components: clutch cover, driven plate and release bearing are replaced after a high mileage, ensuring longer life and smoother operation.
● If one is worn, they are all likely to be, so save yourself another big stripdown in the near future!

☐ **Step 2:** Remove the transmission. See **Job 1**.

☐ **Step 3:** Unscrew the clutch cover retaining bolts (see illustration **Job 3-1, part 4**) progressively - each one a little at a time - until the spring pressure is released, then remove the bolts.

☐ **Step 4:** Ease the cover off its dowels and catch the driven plate as it falls.

☐ **Step 5:** *i* INSIDE INFORMATION: Check the inside of the clutch bellhousing for contamination by oil. This indicates a leak from either the crankshaft rear seal or the gearbox input shaft seal (illustrated). A faulty seal should be replaced without delay. Oil can cause judder and slip. Here, the seal (inset) is being replaced. See **PART A: ENGINE, Job 15** for the position of the crankshaft seal. *i*

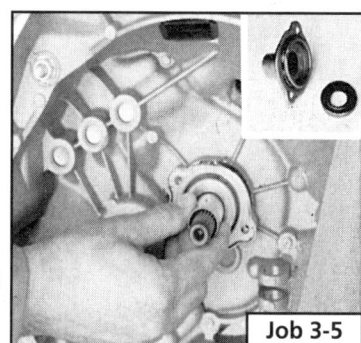

*Job 3-5*

☐ **Step 6:** Check the surface of the flywheel that mates with the clutch, for scoring, or significant micro cracking caused by excessive heat generated by clutch slip. Replace the flywheel if in doubt.

☐ **Step 7:** Check the release fork pivot, inside the bellhousing, for wear. Replace the bushes (see inset) if necessary, lubricating with a small quantity of molybdenum disulphide grease.

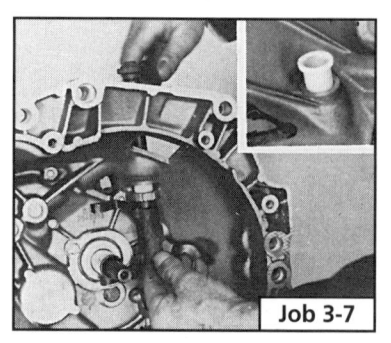

*Job 3-7*

☐ **Step 8:** Clean the oil (or the protective film) from the clutch cover and flywheel faces.

☐ **Step 9:** Offer the driven plate to the flywheel with the side having the greatest hub projection facing outwards.

☐ **Step 10:** Locate the clutch cover on the flywheel dowels and screw in the fixing bolts, finger tight.

☐ **Step 11:** Use an aligning tool to make sure that the clutch is centralised, otherwise the gearbox will not relocate on the engine and damage can be caused to the centre plate.

**ℹ INSIDE INFORMATION:** There is no spigot bush or bearing in the crankshaft end, but there is an indentation which you can 'feel' with a normal clutch alignment tool, allowing you to centralise the driven plate between the clutch cover release fingers. ℹ

☐ **Step 12:** Tighten the cover bolts evenly to the correct torque. See **Chapter 3, Facts and Figures**.

☐ **Step 13:** Smear a little 'copper' grease on the release bearing guide and the gearbox input shaft.

☐ **Step 14:** Refit the transmission. See **Job 2**.

## Job 4. Clutch cable - removal and refitting.

### PART A: CABLE OPERATED CLUTCH

☐ **Step A1:** From under the bonnet, slacken the cable adjusting nut and disconnect the cable from the release lever (**1**). Disconnect the outer cable from its mounting bracket (**2**).

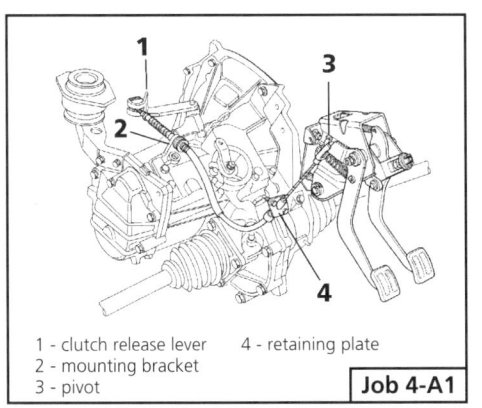

1 - clutch release lever
2 - mounting bracket
3 - pivot
4 - retaining plate
Job 4-A1

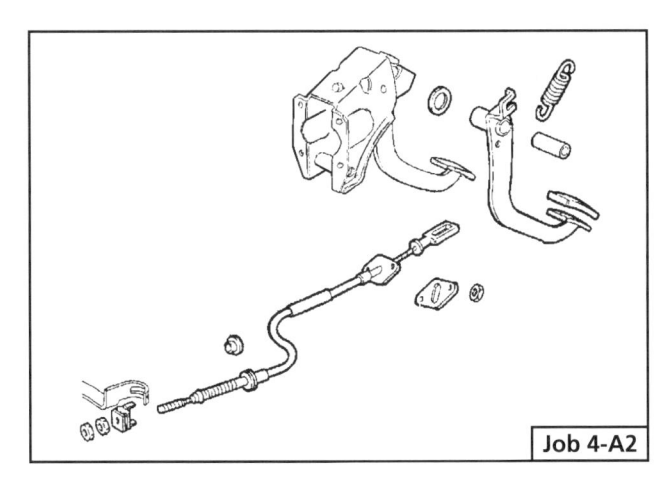

Job 4-A2

☐ **Step A2:** From inside the car, disconnect the cable from the foot pedal by removing the securing clip and pulling the cable end off its pivot (also, see illustration **Job 4-A1, part 3**).

☐ **Step A3:** Unbolt the cable retaining plate (illustration **Job 4-A1, part 4**) from the firewall. Pull the cable out from inside the car.

☐ **Step A4:** Fit the new cable in the reverse order.

☐ **Step A5:** Adjust the clutch cable. See **Chapter 5, Servicing Your Car, Job 19**.

### PART B: ROD AND CABLE OPERATED CLUTCH

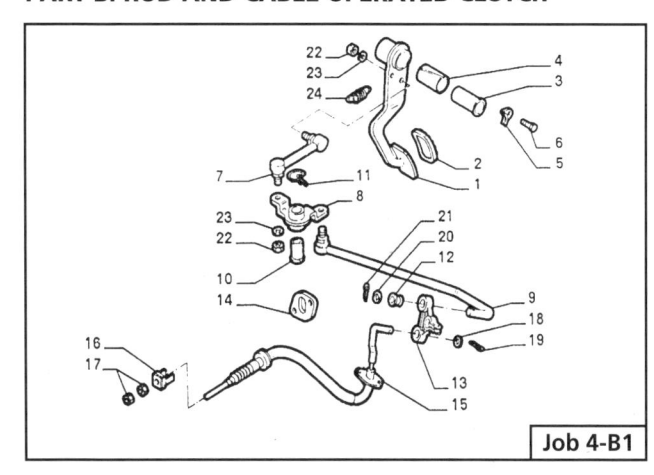

Job 4-B1

☐ **Step B1:** These are the components of the rod and cable mechanism.

☐ **Step B2:** The rod (illustration **Job 4-B1, part 7**) passes through the firewall and is held at each end with a nut and spring washer.

☐ **Step B3:** The pivot bush (illustration **Job 4-B1, parts 3 and 4**) can be replaced after removing the pivot pin clips (**part 11**) and dismantling the pivot.

☐ **Step B4:** The intermediate rod (illustration **Job 4-B1, part 9**) is connected to the operating cable (**part 15**) at the connector (**part 13**). Both are held with split-pins (**parts 19** and **21**).

☐ **Step B5:** Adjust the clutch cable at the clutch as shown in **Chapter 5, Servicing Your Car, Job 19**.

## Job 5. Gear lever and linkage - removal and refitting.

The assemblies for both engine types are the same, except that the FIRE OHC engine has a third cable called the reverse gear inhibitor cable.

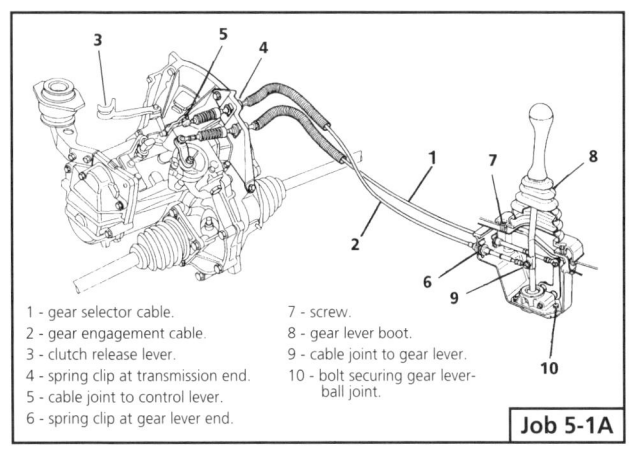

1 - gear selector cable.
2 - gear engagement cable.
3 - clutch release lever.
4 - spring clip at transmission end.
5 - cable joint to control lever.
6 - spring clip at gear lever end.
7 - screw.
8 - gear lever boot.
9 - cable joint to release lever.
10 - bolt securing gear lever-ball joint.
Job 5-1A

☐ **Step 1A:** Familiarise yourself with the components of this illustration, which shows the complete assembly at the transmission for BOTH engine types - and the gear lever ends for the OHV engine-type.

**6-27**

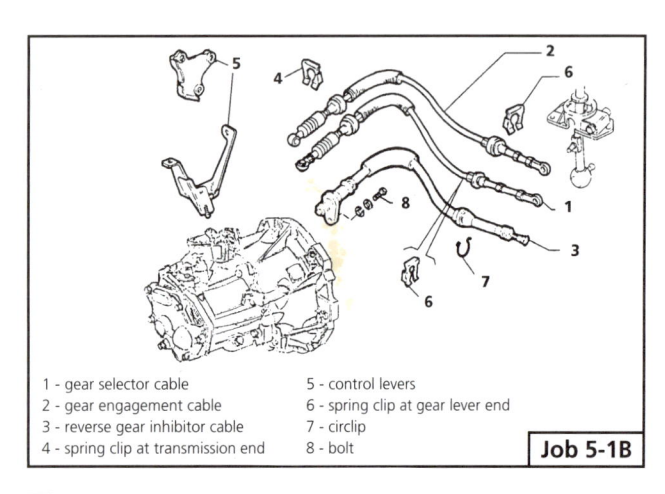

**Job 5-1B**

1 - gear selector cable
2 - gear engagement cable
3 - reverse gear inhibitor cable
4 - spring clip at transmission end
5 - control levers
6 - spring clip at gear lever end
7 - circlip
8 - bolt

☐ **Step 1B:** This is an expanded view of the cables and fittings for the FIRE OHC engine.

☐ **Step 2:** Disconnect the gear and selector engagement cables from the control levers (illustration **Job 1A** or **Job 1B, part 5**) and spring clips (illustration **Job 1A** or **Job 1B, part 4**) at the transmission end. Immediately above the control levers there is a brake hydraulic pressure adjuster that needs to be unbolted to get the gearchange cables away from their levers.

☐ **Step 3: FIRE OHC ENGINES ONLY:** Disconnect the reverse gear inhibitor cable from the transmission by removing the bolt (illustration **Job 5-1B, part 8**).

☐ **Step 4:** If you wish to remove the complete cables, remove the screws and pull up the gear lever boot (illustration **Job 5-1A, parts 7 and 8**), then undo the spring clips and joints (illustration **Job 5-1A, parts 6 and 9**). On FIRE OHC engines, remove the circlip (illustration **Job 5-1B, part 7**).

☐ **Step 5:** If you wish to remove the gear lever, undo the bolts (illustration **Job 5-1A, part 10**) from underneath the car, then withdraw the lever and ball joint from inside the car.

☐ **Step 6:** Refit in reverse order, using a self-grip wrench to reassemble the balljoints.

## Job 6. Drive-shafts - removal and refitting.

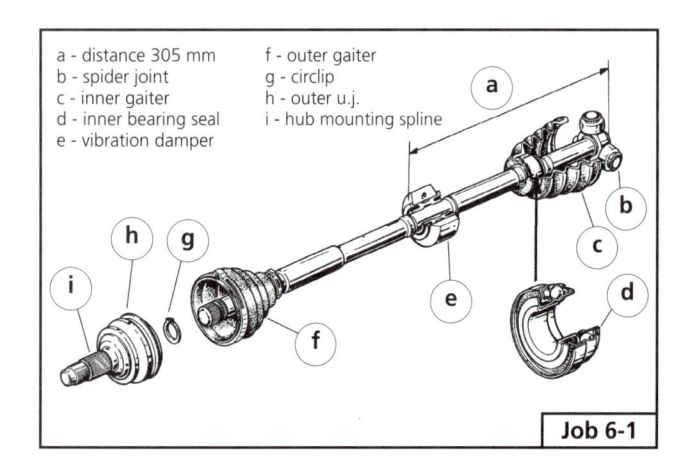

a - distance 305 mm
b - spider joint
c - inner gaiter
d - inner bearing seal
e - vibration damper
f - outer gaiter
g - circlip
h - outer u.j.
i - hub mounting spline

**Job 6-1**

☐ **Step 1:** Take note of the layout of the driveshaft components.

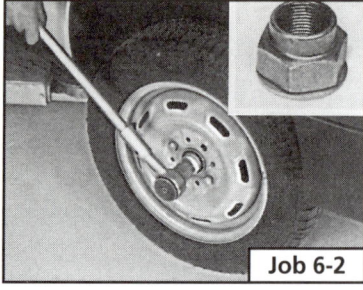

☐ **Step 2:** Open out the staking on the hub nut (inset), as far as possible. Ask a helper to apply the footbrake very firmly and slacken the nut, using a long bar for good leverage. DON'T do it with the car off the ground because the very large force needed could pull it off its stands. Leave the slackened hub nut in place for the time being.

**Job 6-2**

☐ **Step 3:** Jack up the front of the car, support it on axle stands and remove the roadwheel. Drain the transmission oil.

**Job 6-4** 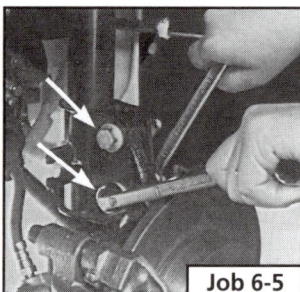   **Job 6-5**

☐ **Step 4:** Disconnect the track rod end from the steering arm using a suitable splitter tool.

☐ **Step 5:** Remove the hub carrier securing bolts (arrowed) from the base of the front suspension strut and tap the carrier down and out of the clamp. Pull the top of the stub carrier outwards.

☐ **Step 6:** Remove the hub nut and push or tap the drive-shaft splines (arrowed) out of the hub carrier, taking care not to damage the thread.

**Job 6-6**

*making it easy!* ☐ **Step 7:** Remove the plastic wheel arch liner to gain easier access to components underneath the car.

☐ **Step 8:** Support the drive-shaft while undoing the flange bolts (arrowed) at the transmission end, (non-Sporting model illustrated).

**Job 6-8**

**Step 9:** Withdraw the shaft from the transmission.

**Step 10:** Refit in the reverse order, using a new hub nut tightened to the specified torque. See **Chapter 3, Facts and Figures**. Stake the nut into the drive shaft groove as shown. See **PART F: STEERING AND SUSPENSION, Job 9, Step 13**.

**Step 11:** Refill the transmission with oil. See **Chapter 3, Facts and Figures**.

## Job 7. Outer drive-shaft constant velocity joint - replacement.

**Step 1:** You must first remove the drive-shaft. See **Job 6**.

**Step 2:** Remove the gaiter retaining clip...

**Step 3:** ...and pull the gaiter clear.

**Step 4:** Remove the circlip and pull the shaft from the CV joint.

**Step 5:** Carefully wash the CV joint with engine degreaser and make sure the balls and their seats are perfectly smooth and free from signs of seizing or grooves. If there are any faults, the CV joint must be replaced.

IMPORTANT NOTE: You are advised to replace the gaiter with a new one each time it is removed.

**Step 6:** Fit the new gaiter onto the shaft, followed by the CV joint and circlip. Pack the joint with **FL Tutela MRM2** grease. If you are fitting a new joint, use the grease supplied with it.

**Step 7:** Pull the gaiter over the joint and secure with the retaining band. The drive-shaft assembly is now ready for refitting.

## Job 8. Left inner spider joint - replacement.

**Step 1:** Note the arrangement of the inner drive-shaft components.

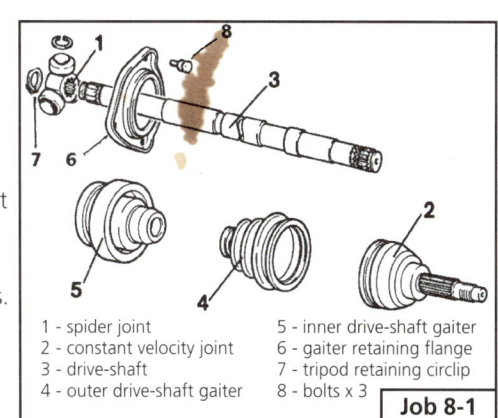

1 - spider joint
2 - constant velocity joint
3 - drive-shaft
4 - outer drive-shaft gaiter
5 - inner drive-shaft gaiter
6 - gaiter retaining flange
7 - tripod retaining circlip
8 - bolts x 3

**Step 2:** With the drive-shaft removed from the car (see **Job 6**), remove the circlip and pull the spider joint from the drive-shaft, or press the shaft out.

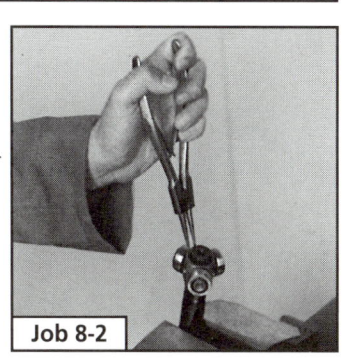

**Step 3:** Remove the inner gaiter and retainer flange from the drive-shaft.

IMPORTANT NOTE: You are advised to replace the gaiter with a new one each time it is removed.

**Step 4:** Inspect the spider joint for wear and obtain a new one from your FIAT dealer if necessary. Fit the new gaiter and its retainer to the shaft, followed by the spider joint and circlip. No lubrication is required prior to refitting the drive-shaft to the transmission.

## Job 9. Right inner spider joint - replacement.

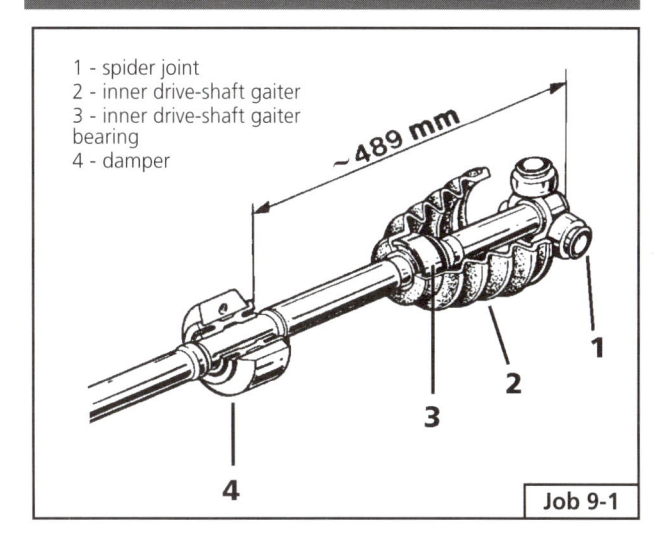

1 - spider joint
2 - inner drive-shaft gaiter
3 - inner drive-shaft gaiter bearing
4 - damper

**Step 1:** Familiarise yourself with the components of the right-hand drive shaft. This is the same as the left drive shaft except that it has the following additional components.
- gaiter bearing (**3**)
- damper (**4**)

☐ **Step 2:** Removal of the spider joint and gaiter is the same as *Job 8*, except that you need to remove the bearing to remove the gaiter from the shaft. Use a universal extractor if you have one. Make a note of the position of the bearing on the shaft so you can replace it at the same position.

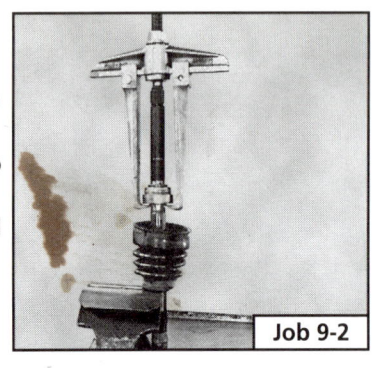

☐ **Step 3:** If you remove the damper, make sure you replace it at the correct position on the shaft. See illustration *Job 9-1, part 4*.

**IMPORTANT NOTE:** You are advised to replace the gaiter with a new one each time it is removed.

☐ **Step 4:** Inspect the spider joint and bearing for wear and obtain replacements from your FIAT dealer if necessary.

☐ **Step 5:** Fit the new gaiter and bearing to the shaft, making sure the bearing is at the correct position. The illustration shows the position of the NADELLA type bearing. Use the following special tools to help you fit get the bearing in the correct position - have your FIAT dealer do it for you:
- Tool no. 1870448000 for the INA bearing.
- Tool no. 1870499000 for the NADELLA bearing.

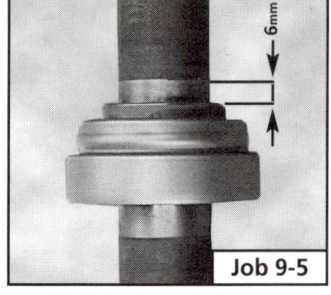

☐ **Step 6:** Fit the gaiter retaining flange, followed by the spider joint and circlip, as shown in *Job 8*. No lubrication is required prior to refitting the drive-shaft to the transmission.

## Job 10. Front hub bearings - replacement.

For details of how to replace the front wheel hub bearings, see **PART F: STEERING AND SUSPENSION, Job 8**.

# PART C: COOLING SYSTEM

### PART C: Contents
Job 1. Cooling fan and switch.
Job 2. Radiator - removal and refitting.
Job 3. Thermostat housing - replacement.
Job 4. Water pump - replacement.

## Job 1. Cooling fan and switch.

**IMPORTANT NOTE:** The cooling system for both OHV and FIRE OHC engines has two thermostats - the mechanically operated coolant thermostat which acts as a by-pass valve mounted on the engine block, and the thermostatically controlled switch in the radiator which controls the cooling fan.

1 - radiator
2 - radiator bleed pipe
3 - expansion tank
4 - hose from injector turret to expansion tank
5 - hose from thermostat to injector turret
6 - hose from heater radiator to pump
7 - heater radiator
8 - thermostat housing
9 - hose from thermostat to heater radiator
10 - water pump
11 - hose from radiator to pump
12 - hose from thermostat to radiator
13 - radiator cooling fan
14 - radiator thermostatic switch

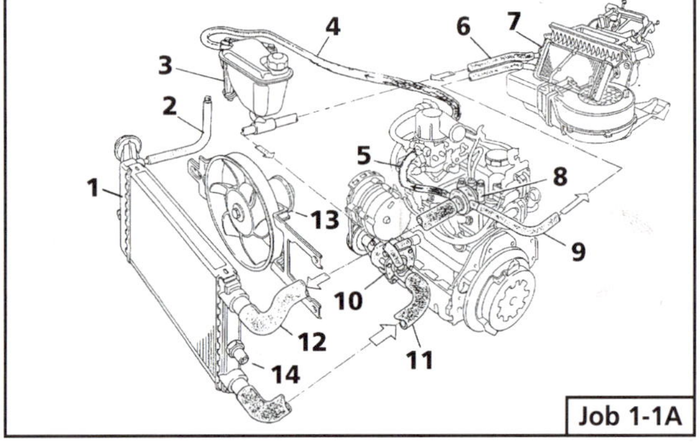

☐ **Step 1A:** Familiarise yourself with the OHV engine's cooling system components shown here.

The FIRE OHC engine has the following important differences:
- The thermostat housing has a different design and fits on the end of the cylinder block. See illustration *Job 4-B1, part 9*.
- The injector turret is mounted on an injection manifold, instead of being directly on top of the engine. Both the turret and manifold are heated by water from the engine. The water gets to the manifold first, then goes out through a hose which divides into two and feeds both the turret and heater radiator. This means the thermostat housing has only a single outlet hose, feeding water back to the cooling radiator. When the thermostat valve closes (because the engine is cold), the outlet path for the water is through the injection manifold.
- The water pump is driven by the timing belt instead of the alternator belt.

☐ **Step 1B:** The cooling fan assembly (*part a* for OHV engines; *part b* for OHC engines) bolts on to the radiator housing and on to the bodywork in the case of OHV engines. Part (**e**) is the thermostatic switch, with it's sealing washer (**d**). Part (**c**) is one of the mounting bolts.

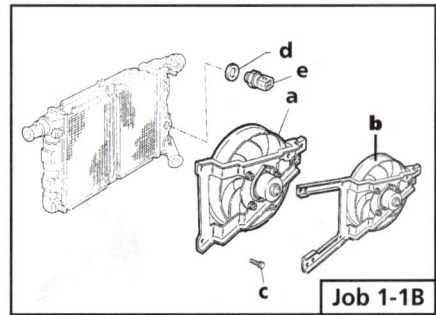

☐ **Step 2:** Disconnect the battery negative earth lead.

## COOLING FAN REPLACEMENT

☐ **Step 3:** Disconnect the wires from the cooling fan (see illustration *Job 1-1A, part 13*) and radiator thermostatic switch (*Job 1-1A, part 14*).

☐ **Step 4:** Undo the bolts from the bracket which holds the cooling fan to the radiator, and remove the cooling fan and bracket.

## THERMOSTATIC SWITCH REPLACEMENT

☐ **Step 5:** Drain the cooling system, while the engine is cold, by loosening the bottom (outlet) hose (see illustration *Job 1-1A, part 11*).

☐ **Step 6:** Unscrew the ic switch from the radiator.

☐ **Step 7:** *i* INSIDE INFORMATION: Test the switch using a test bulb and two leads. Connect one lead to a 12 volt battery terminal and the other to one of the switch terminals. Now connect a wire between the remaining switch terminal and the other battery terminal. *i*

☐ **Step 8:** Lower the switch into a saucepan of water until the thread is just covered and the terminals remain dry.

☐ **Step 9:** Heat the water slowly. The bulb should light just below boiling point (90 to 94 degrees Celsius) and go out when the temperature falls below 85 to 89 degrees Celsius.

☐ **Step 10:** Fit a new O-ring to the ic switch. Do not over-tighten when refitting the switch to the radiator.

☐ **Step 11:** Refit the components in reverse order and fill the cooling system with the correct 50/50 **Paraflu** anti-freeze solution. See *Chapter 3, Facts and Figures* and *Chapter 5, Servicing Your Car*.

## Job 2. Radiator - removal and refitting.

☐ **Step 1:** Disconnect the battery negative earth lead.

☐ **Step 2:** Disconnect the wires from the cooling fan and radiator ic switch, as in *Job 1*, but leave the fan bolted to the radiator.

☐ **Step 3:** Drain the cooling system while the engine is cold, by loosening the thumbscrew at the bottom of the radiator, or by loosening the outlet hose (**a**).

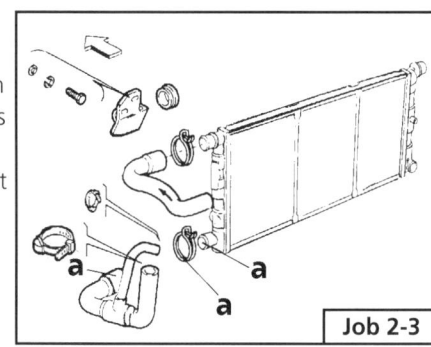

☐ **Step 4:** Disconnect all the radiator hoses.

☐ **Step 5:** Undo the fittings that connect the radiator to the bodywork, and remove both the radiator and fan from the car.

☐ **Step 6:** Refit in reverse order and fill the cooling system with the correct 50/50 **Paraflu** anti-freeze solution. See *Chapter 3, Facts and Figures* and *Chapter 5, Servicing Your Car*.

## Job 3. Thermostat housing - replacement.

☐ **Step 1:** Drain the cooling system while the engine is cold, by loosening the thumbscrew at the bottom of the radiator, or by loosening the outlet hose (illustration *Job 1-1A, part 11*).

☐ **Step 2:** Disconnect the hoses from the housing, undo the nuts and remove the assembly.
- The housing for an OHV engine is shown in illustration *Job 1-1A, part 8*.
- On the FIRE OHC engine it is on the end of the cylinder block as shown in illustration *Job 4-B1, part 9*. The and housing are a complete unit and have to be replaced as one.

☐ **Step 3:** Clean the mating surfaces, fit the new unit and a new gasket.

☐ **Step 4:** Reconnect the hoses and refill the cooling system with the correct 50/50 **Paraflu** anti-freeze solution. See *Chapter 3, Facts and Figures* and *Chapter 5, Servicing Your Car*.

## Job 4. Water pump - replacement.

### PART A - OHV ENGINES

☐ **Step A1:** Drain the cooling system while the engine is cold, by loosening the bottom (outlet) hose (illustration *Job 1-1A, part 11*).

☐ **Step A2:** Remove the right front wheel and support the front of the car on axle stands.

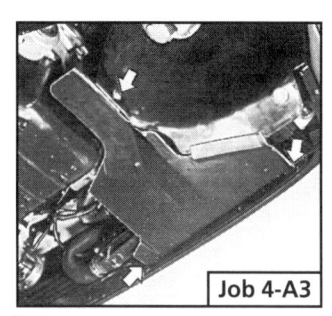

☐ **Step A3:** Remove the radiator shield from under the car, below the right headlight - fixings arrowed.

☐ **Step A4:** Remove the right front plastic wheel arch liner - fixings arrowed.

❑ **Step A5:** Loosen the alternator fixing bolts to release the tension on the drivebelt.

❑ **Step A6:** Disconnect the pipes from the water pump.

❑ **Step A7:** Disconnect the water pump from the engine block by removing the bolts.

❑ **Step A8:** Discard the old gasket and clean off the mating surfaces.

❑ **Step A9:** Refit in the reverse order, using a new gasket.

❑ **Step A10:** Adjust the drivebelt tension. See **Chapter 5, Servicing Your Car**.

❑ **Step A11:** Fill the cooling system with the correct 50/50 **Paraflu** anti-freeze solution. See **Chapter 3, Facts and Figures** and **Chapter 5, Servicing Your Car**.

**PART B - FIRE OHC ENGINE**

1 - water pump
2, 3, 4 - fixings
5 - bolt
6 - seal
7 - pipe
8 - gasket
9 - thermostat
10 - bolt

Job 4-B1

❑ **Step B1:** Drain the cooling system while the engine is cold, by loosening the thumbscrew at the bottom of the radiator, or by loosening the outlet hose (illustration **Job 1-1A, part 11**).

❑ **Step B2:** Remove the right front wheel and support the front of the car on axle stands.

❑ **Step B3:** Remove the radiator shield from under the car, below the right headlight. See illustration **Job 4-A3**.

❑ **Step B4:** Remove the right front plastic wheel arch liner. See illustration **Job 4-A4**.

❑ **Step B5:** Disconnect the metal transfer pipe (**Job 4-B1, part 7**) from the water pump (**Job 4-B1, part 1**).

❑ **Step B6:** Remove the timing belt cover.

❑ **Step B7:** Slacken the timing belt tensioner.

❑ **Step B8:** Disconnect the water pump from its mounting by removing the fixings (**Job 4-B1, parts 2, 3, 4**).

❑ **Step B9:** Discard the old gasket and clean off the mating surfaces.

❑ **Step B10:** Refit in the reverse order, using a new gasket. Before you re-tension the timing belt, make sure the yellow lines on the belt are correctly aligned with the timing marks on the camshaft and crankshaft sprocket, as described in **PART A: ENGINE, Job 11**.

❑ **Step B11:** Fill the cooling system with the correct 50/50 **Paraflu** anti-freeze solution. See **Chapter 3, Facts and Figures** and **Chapter 5, Servicing Your Car**.

# PART D: ELECTRICAL, INSTRUMENTS & HEATER

## PART D: Contents

Job 1. System checks.
Job 2. Alternator - removal and refitting.
Job 3. Starter motor - removal and refitting.
Job 4. Instrument panel - removal and refitting.
Job 5. Speedometer cable - replacement.
Job 6. Windscreen wiper motor - replacement.
Job 7. Tailgate wiper motor - replacement.
Job 8. Windscreen washer pump - replacement.
Job 9. Radio aerial - replacement.
Job 10. Lights - replacement.
Job 11. Fuel pump and fuel gauge sender unit - replacement.
Job 12. Electric window motors - replacement.
Job 13. Heater/ventilation component - dismantling.

## Job 1. System checks.

See **FACT FILE: DISCONNECTING THE BATTERY** in **Chapter 5, Servicing Your Car, Job 4 page 5-5**.

❑ **Step 1:** Decide whether you have enough knowledge or information to do this work yourself, or whether to consult your FIAT dealer or auto-electrician. You can waste money and cause further damage if you don't know what you're doing! PORTER MANUALS *Auto-Electrics Manual* explains everything in a simple-to-follow style.

❏ **Step 2:** Before assuming that a flat battery is 'dead', have the charging system checked. This is the set-up for checking the maximum charge rate on Cinquecento models which all have a built-in electronic regulator.

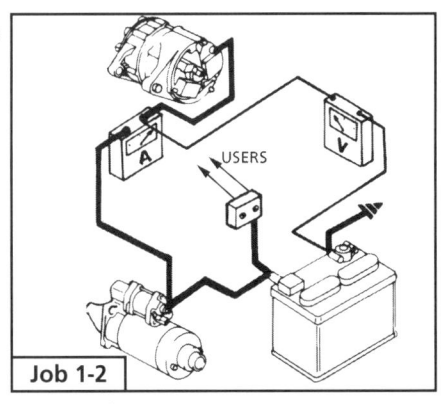

Job 1-2

❏ **Step 3:** You should check the battery voltage only after it has been unused for at least two hours.

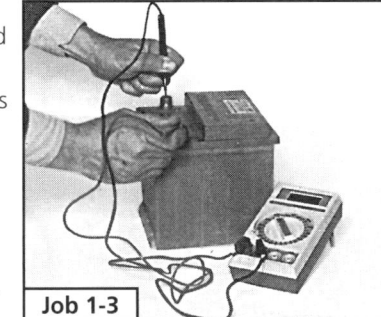

IMPORTANT NOTE: For information on battery charging see **FACT FILE: FUEL INJECTION/ELECTRONIC IGNITION PRECAUTIONS in PART E: FUEL, IGNITION AND EXHAUST**.

Job 1-3

## Job 2. Alternator - removal and refitting.

Refer to **Chapter 5, Servicing Your Car, Job 13** for information on alternator positions, access and belt tensioning.

❏ **Step 1:** Disconnect the battery earth lead, then disconnect the leads from the threaded terminals (arrowed) on the back of the alternator.

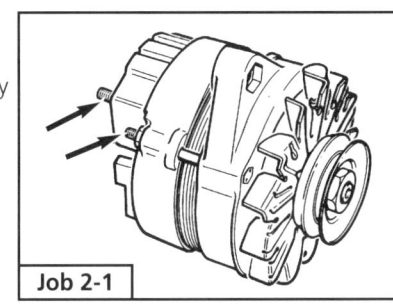

Job 2-1

*making it easy* • If any of the leads are capable of being replaced the wrong way round, tag them as you remove them.

❏ **Step 2:** Slacken the alternator mounting nuts and bolts, including the adjuster, and push the alternator towards the engine to remove the drive belt. Then undo the bolts and remove the alternator from its mountings.

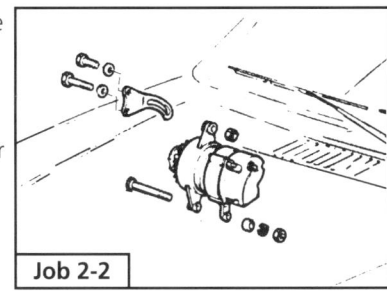

Job 2-2

❏ **Step 3:** Refit in the reverse order and adjust the drive belt. See **Chapter 5, Servicing Your Car, Job 13**.

## Job 3. Starter motor - removal and refitting.

❏ **Step 1:** Disconnect the battery earth (negative) lead.

Job 3-2 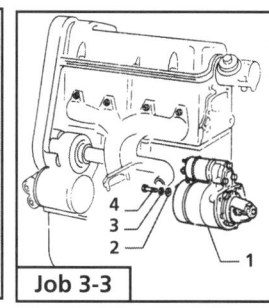    Job 3-3

❏ **Step 2:** Disconnect the cables from the rear of the starter motor solenoid (arrowed).

❏ **Step 3:** Undo the mounting bolts and washers (**2**, **3** and **4**) and remove the starter motor from the transmission.

❏ **Step 4:** Refit in the reverse order, ensuring that all electrical connections are clean and sound.

## Job 4. Instrument panel - removal and refitting.

IMPORTANT NOTE: Several of the following illustrations feature left-hand drive models. Right-hand drive vehicles are the same, but 'reversed'.

❏ **Step 1:** Disconnect the battery negative earth lead.

❏ **Step 2:** It may help to first remove the steering wheel. Set the steering in the straight-ahead position. Remove the centre cap, then undo the retaining nut and pull the wheel off the column.

### SAFETY FIRST!

• As you bang the steering wheel towards you with your hands to get it off the splines, take care not to bash yourself in the face!
• Leave the nut on the end of its thread and remove it once the wheel is loose on the splines.

Job 4-3     Job 4-4

❏ **Step 3:** Undo the screws (arrowed) and remove the cowling from the dashboard.

❏ **Step 4:** Undo the screws (arrowed) and carefully pull the instrument panel towards you until you can access the connections behind it, but without pulling connections adrift.

**CHAPTER 6 PART D: ELECTRICAL**

6-33

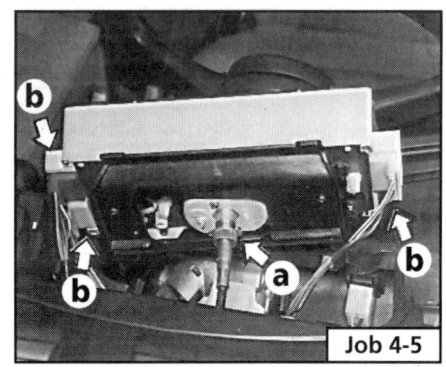

CHAPTER 6  PART D: ELECTRICAL

☐ **Step 5:** Disconnect the speedometer cable (**a**) and electrical connections (**b**) from behind the instrument panel. Take note of the electrical connections so you know where to refit them.

Job 4-5

☐ **Step 6:** With the cowling removed, you can remove the switches by levering them out from the rear with a screwdriver.

Job 4-6

☐ **Step 7:** Refit in the reverse order, and reconnect the battery.

## Job 5. Speedometer cable - replacement.

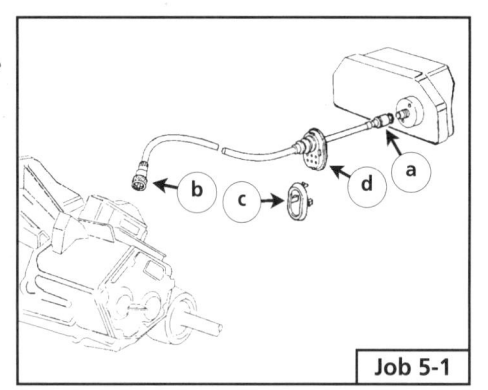

☐ **Step 1:** Disconnect the cable (**a**) from the instruments - see **Job 4**.

☐ **Step 2:** At the gearbox end of the speedometer cable, undo

Job 5-1

the knurled nut securing the cable to the gearbox. See illustration **Job 5-1, part b**.

☐ **Step 3:** Remove grommet clip and grommet from the bulkhead. See illustration **Job 5-1, parts c and d**.

IMPORTANT NOTE: ☐ **Step 4:** Some speedometer cables come in two parts with a union between the bulkhead and gearbox. If this is the case, you will need to disconnect the union from its mounting bracket.

☐ **Step 5:** Withdraw the cable and its fittings.

☐ **Step 6:** Refit in the reverse order.

## Job 6. Windscreen wiper motor - replacement.

☐ **Step 1:** Disconnect the battery negative earth lead.

☐ **Step 2:** Undo the screws (arrowed) and remove the insulating partition.

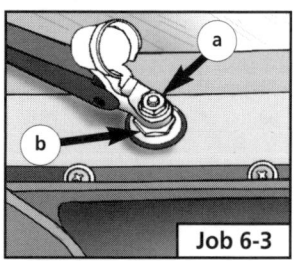

Job 6-2

☐ **Step 3:** Remove the windscreen wiper arm by lifting the cover, undoing the retaining nut (**a**) and carefully pulling it off the splined shaft. Then undo the bezel nut (**b**).

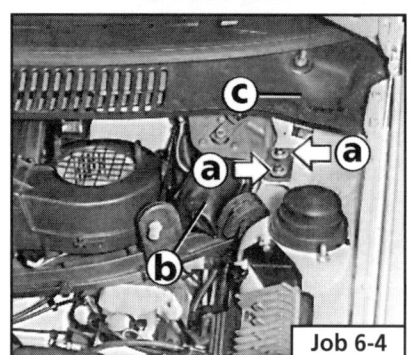

Job 6-3

☐ **Step 4:** Remove the two fixing screws (**a**), and remove the wiper motor and its weather shield (**b**) from under the ventilation grille (**c**). Disconnect the electrical connector from the wiper motor.

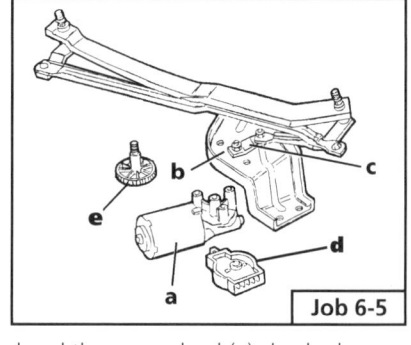

Job 6-4

☐ **Step 5:** Disconnect the wiper motor (**a**) from the support bracket (**b**) and mechanism (**c**).

☐ **Step 6:** If necessary, the motor gear cover (see illustration **Job 6-5,**

Job 6-5

**part d**) can be removed and the gear wheel (**e**) checked or replaced.

☐ **Step 7:** Refit in the reverse order, making sure the wiper arm position is correct.

## Job 7. Tailgate wiper motor - replacement.

☐ **Step 1:** Disconnect the battery earth lead.

☐ **Step 2:** Undo the nut securing the wiper arm to its shaft and remove the arm and blade.

☐ **Step 3:** From under the tailgate, remove the electrical connector from the wiper motor, then undo the mounting screws (arrowed) and remove the motor.

Job 7-3

6-34

❑ **Step 4:** Refit in reverse order.

## Job 8. Windscreen washer pump - replacement.

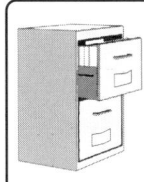

> **FACT FILE: WINDSCREEN / REAR SCREEN WASHER ASSEMBLY**
> • The washer reservoir and pump are mounted under the right front wheel arch with the cap (arrowed) protruding upwards through the bodywork, to make it accessible from the engine compartment.
> • The windscreen washer nozzle is mounted on the bonnet.
> • The rear window washer nozzle is mounted on the tailgate, above the window.
> • The nozzles are connected to the pump by plastic tubes which might need to be cleaned if a nozzle fails to work. Usually it is sufficient just to unblock the nozzle with a pin.

❑ **Step 1:** Disconnect the battery negative earth lead.

❑ **Step 2:** Disconnect the electrical connection/s from the washer pump/s.

❑ **Step 3:** Undo the bolts connecting the assembly to its mountings and remove it from the car.

❑ **Step 4:** Pull out the pump/s and replace as necessary.

Job 8-3

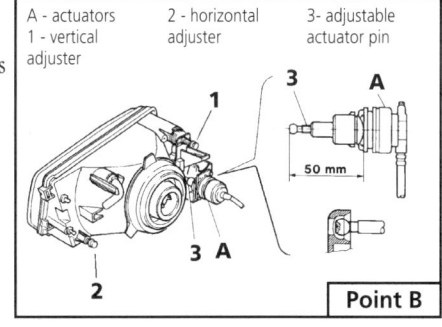

❑ **Step 5:** Refit in reverse order, using a new pump, then reconnect the battery.

## Job 9. Radio aerial - replacement.

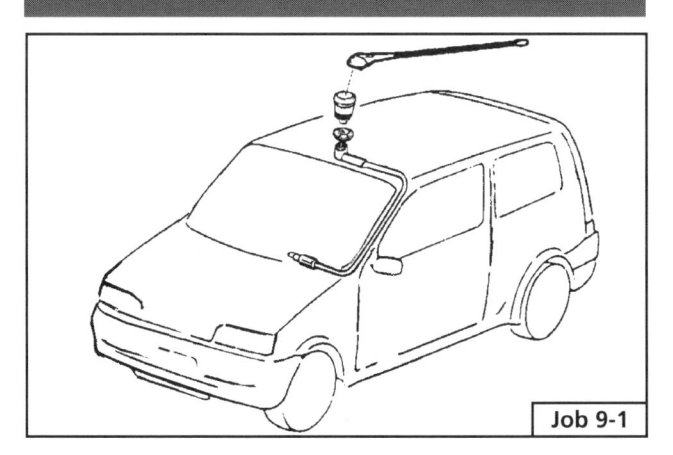

Job 9-1

❑ **Step 1:** ℹ INSIDE INFORMATION: When replacing the aerial, to make cable-routing as easy as possible, unplug the old aerial cable from the radio and leave it in place. ℹ

❑ **Step 2:** Cut the old cable where it joins the aerial. Use insulation tape to attach the new aerial cable's radio-end and use the old cable to pull it through the correct route. Plug the new cable into the radio.

## Job 10. Lights - replacement.

You should check on a regular basis that all the lights are working. If a light fails, check the fuse before replacing the bulb. When a bulb blows, a fuse might also blow in sympathy.

See **Chapter 5, Servicing Your Car, Job 7** for the following topics:
• headlights
• front side lights
• front direction indicators
• indicator side repeaters
• rear light unit
• number plate light
• interior light
• fuses and relays

Dashboard light bulbs are mounted in the back of the instrument panel and are a quarter-turn fit. For details of how to remove the instrument panel, see **Job 4**.

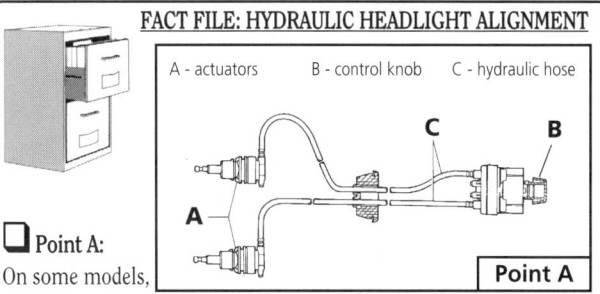

> **FACT FILE: HYDRAULIC HEADLIGHT ALIGNMENT**
>
> A - actuators    B - control knob    C - hydraulic hose
>
> Point A
>
> ❑ **Point A:**
> On some models, the headlight alignment can be vertically adjusted to compensate for load on the vehicle by turning a knob under the dashboard. The alignment device consists of the following components:
> • A hydraulic actuator (**A**), fixed to each of the two front headlights.
> • A manually operated knob (**B**) located under the dashboard.
> • A hydraulic circuit (**C**) with antifreeze (glycol) at a pressure of between 3 and 3.5 bar.
>
> A - actuators    2 - horizontal adjuster    3 - adjustable actuator pin
> 1 - vertical adjuster
>
> 50 mm
>
> Point B
>
> ❑ **Point B:** The control knob gives the correct load-compensated alignment only after the general alignment has been correctly adjusted. This is required in the UK as part of the MOT test and should be done by your FIAT dealer who has the required beam-setting equipment.
> • The headlights should be aligned with the car unladen and the control knob at the zero position.
> • Alignment is achieved using the vertical adjusters (**1**) and the horizontal adjusters (**2**).
> • If the headlights cannot be aligned correctly, remove the actuators (**A**) and turn the adjustment pin (**3**). The factory-set distance between the end of the pin and the actuator body is 50 mm.
>
> IMPORTANT NOTE: The electrical adjustment mechanism fitted to some Sporting models is not covered here.

CHAPTER 6  PART D: ELECTRICAL

6-35

## CHAPTER 6 PART D: ELECTRICAL

### PART A: HEADLIGHT UNIT REPLACEMENT

☐ **Step A1:** Remove the indicator unit by pulling on the spring (**a**).

*Job 10-A1*

☐ **Step A2:** Remove the wiring plug from the bulb. See **Chapter 5, Servicing Your Car**. Disconnect the headlight adjuster (**a**), if fitted.

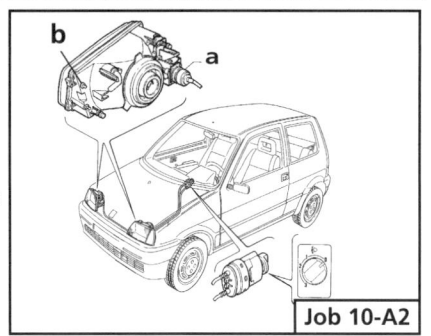

*Job 10-A2*

☐ **Step A3:** Unscrew the nut (see illustration **Job 10-A2, part b**) holding the headlight unit in place and remove.

☐ **Step A4:** IMPORTANT NOTE: The headlight adjuster mechanism (see illustration **Job 10-A2**) contain pressurised fluid. It is only replaceable as a complete unit - no dismantling is possible.

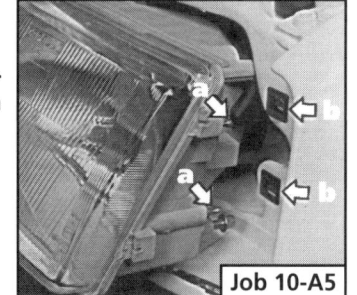

☐ **Step A5:** When refitting the headlight, ensure that the location pegs (**a**) fit into their sockets (**b**).

*Job 10-A5*

### PART B: REAR LIGHTS

☐ **Step B1:** After removing the lens retaining screws (**a**) and lifting away the lens...

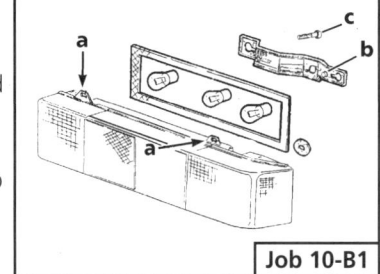

☐ **Step B2:** ...the bulb holder support and printed circuit (illustration **Job 10-B1, part b**) can be removed by unscrewing the two bolts (**part c**).

*Job 10-B1*

### PART C: SIDE INDICATOR LIGHTS

☐ **Step C1:** The unit is removed by detaching the wheelarch liner compressing the spring clips (arrowed) from behind the wiring, and releasing the lights.

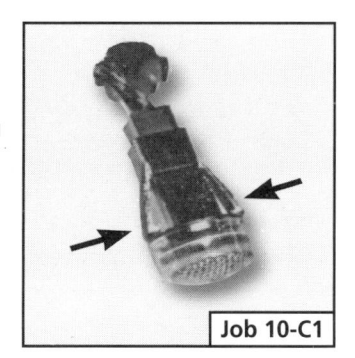

*Job 10-C1*

## Job 11. Fuel pump and fuel gauge sender unit - replacement.

IMPORTANT NOTE: Read **Chapter 1, Safety First!** before carrying out any work on the fuel system.

☐ **Step 1:** Disconnect the battery negative (earth/ground) lead.

☐ **Step 2:** Lift the luggage compartment floor covering and take out the two screws holding the cover in place.

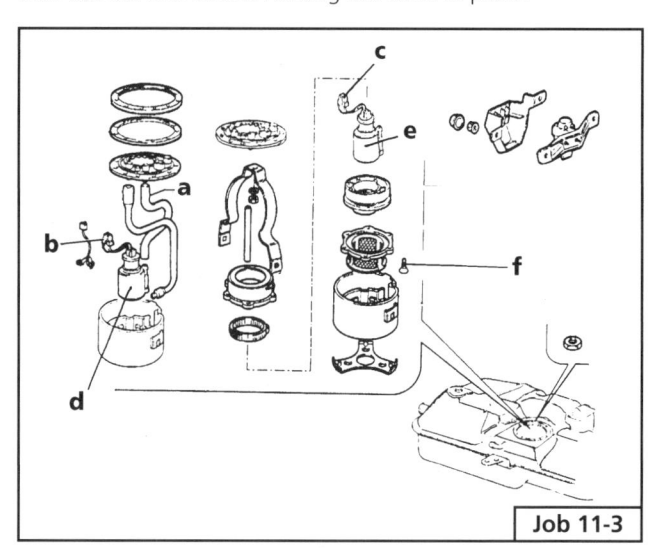

*Job 11-3*

☐ **Step 3:** Remove the two fuel pipes from the top of the pump/sender unit (**a**) and note the following:
- The block connector with two wires (**b**) goes to the fuel pump (**d**).
- The block connector with three wires (**c**) goes to the sender unit (**e**).

### PART A: FUEL GAUGE SENDER UNIT REMOVAL

☐ **Step A4:** The sender unit can be removed without dismantling the pump. It fits in place with a bayonet fitting: the further you turn the cap (**1**), the tighter it gets. Loosen and remove it by turning it anti-clockwise before lifting it out. The tool (**2**) is the FIAT special tool, but you could easily fabricate your own version.

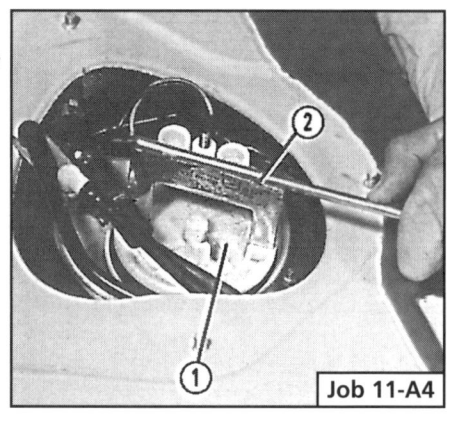

*Job 11-A4*

### PART B: FUEL PUMP REMOVAL

☐ **Step B4:** To remove the fuel pump, you have to strip the unit down, unbolting the line of screws (see illustration **Job 11-3, part f**) before dismantling the various components.

6-36

## Job 12. Electric window motors - replacement.

See **PART H: BODYWORK AND INTERIOR, Job 8**.

## Job 13. Heater/ventilation component - dismantling.

IMPORTANT NOTE: Before carrying out any of the following work, disconnect the battery negative (earth/ground) cable.

### PART A: HEATER RADIATOR REMOVAL

☐ **Step A1:** Disconnect and remove the battery from the engine bay.

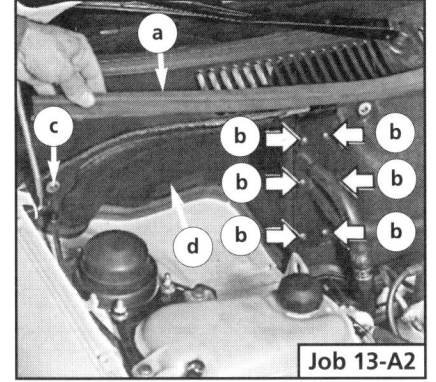

☐ **Step A2:** Pull off the bonnet compartment seal (a)...

☐ **Step A3:** ...and remove the screws (see illustration **Job 13-A2, parts b**) holding the water pipe support. Slide the support a little way forwards, along the pipes.

☐ **Step A4:** Remove the screw (see illustration **Job 13-A2, part c**) holding the sound insulating shield (d) in place, and remove the insulating shield.

☐ **Step A5:** You now have access to the heater radiator. Take out the screws (arrowed).

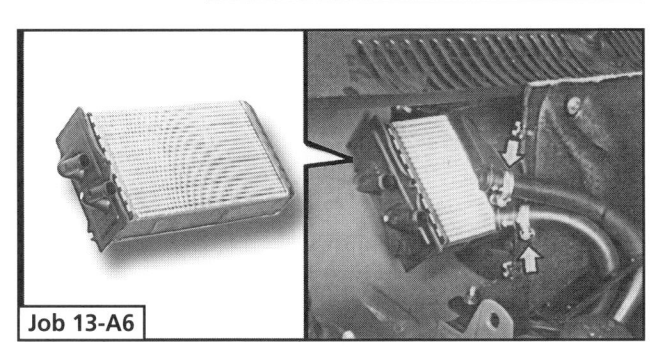

☐ **Step A6:** If you wish to disconnect the pipes, drain down the system. See **PART C: COOLING SYSTEM**. Extract the radiator (inset) from its housing.

### PART B: ELECTRIC FAN REMOVAL

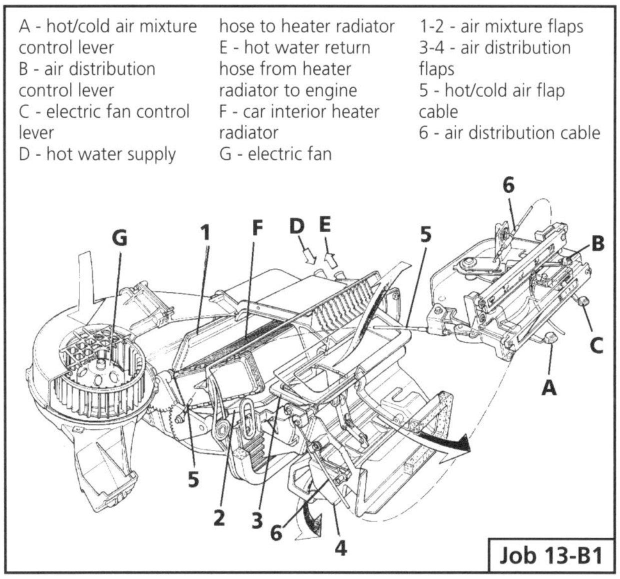

A - hot/cold air mixture control lever
B - air distribution control lever
C - electric fan control lever
D - hot water supply
E - hot water return hose from heater radiator to engine
F - car interior heater radiator
G - electric fan
hose to heater radiator
1-2 - air mixture flaps
3-4 - air distribution flaps
5 - hot/cold air flap cable
6 - air distribution cable

☐ **Step B1:** These are the heater/ventilation components.

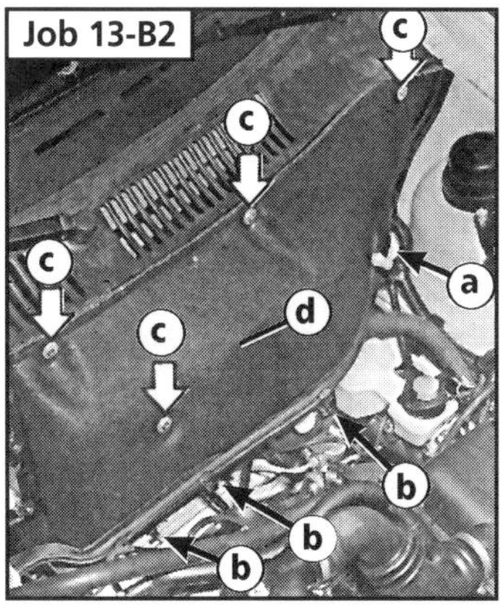

☐ **Step B2:** Disconnect and/or remove the following:
• the speedometer cable, at point (a)
• the vacuum pipe from its clips (b)
• the sound insulating shield screws (c)
• the shield itself (d).

☐ **Step B3:** Remove the screws (c)...

☐ **Step B4:** ...and remove the heater shield (d).

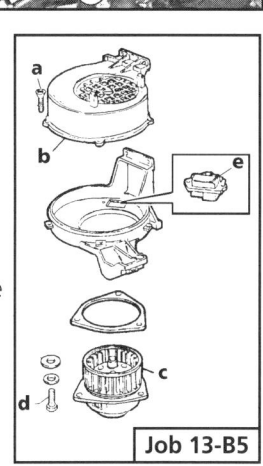

☐ **Step B5:** You may now be able to gain sufficient access to the fan unit. Remove the screws (a), take off the cowl (b) and you will be able to see the fan blades (c). To gain access to the fixing screws (d), the complete heater/ventilation unit must be removed. Part (e) is the fan speed control resistor.

### PART C: HEATER/VENTILATION UNIT REMOVAL

☐ **Step C1:** Remove the cowling from the dashboard. See **Job 4-3**.

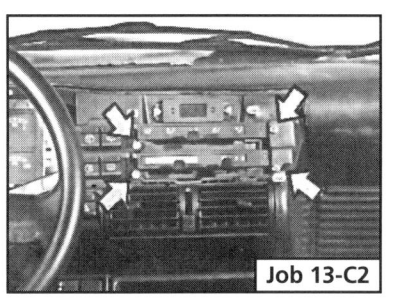

☐ **Step C2:** Remove the screws (arrowed) holding the heater/ventilation controls to the dashboard.

☐ **Step C3:** Carry out the work described in **PART A** and **PART B**.

CHAPTER 6 PART D: ELECTRICAL

☐ **Step C4:** Remove the windscreen wiper motor and mechanism, complete. See **Job 6**.

☐ **Step C5:** Disconnect the electrical connector to the car interior heater, from under the dash.

☐ **Step C6:** Undo the fixing screws (see spanner position and arrows) and remove the heater unit from the car.

*Job 13-C6*

ℹ INSIDE INFORMATION: Most heater problems are caused by seized quadrant controls, cables or pivots, or because of broken springs. Check, lubricate or replace, as necessary. ℹ

☐ **Step C7:** These are the dashboard control levers (**a**). Their relationship to the operating cables can be seen in illustration **Job 13-B1**. Part (**b**) is the fan speed operating switch.

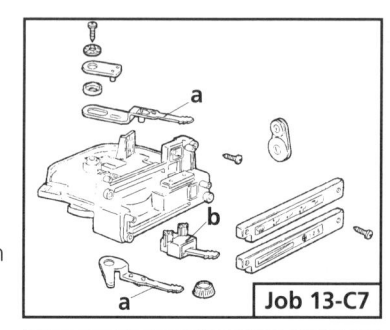

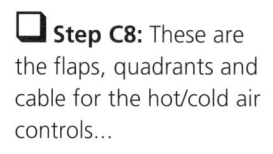

*Job 13-C7*

☐ **Step C8:** These are the flaps, quadrants and cable for the hot/cold air controls...

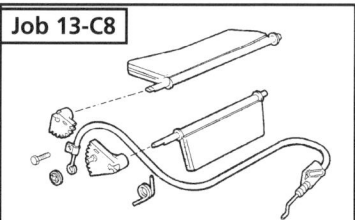

*Job 13-C8*

☐ **Step C9:** ...and these are the flaps, linkages and cable for the air distribution control. All of the parts illustrated here should be available from your FIAT dealer

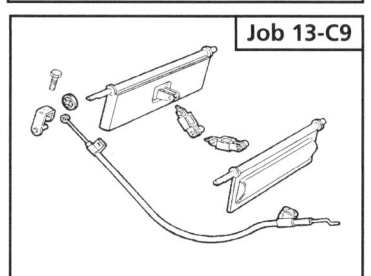

*Job 13-C9*

# PART E: FUEL, IGNITION AND EXHAUST

## PART E: Contents
Job 1. The Electronic Injection/Ignition System.
Job 2. OHV engine - air filter assembly.
Job 3. FIRE OHC engine - air filter assembly.
Job 4. Injection unit - removal and refitting.
Job 5. Accelerator cable - replacement and adjustment.
Job 6. Fuel pump - replacement.
Job 7. Fuel tank - removal and refitting.
Job 8. Lambda sensor - replacement.
Job 9. Fuel evaporation system.
Job 10. Exhaust system - replacement.
Job 11. High pressure injection systems - safety first!

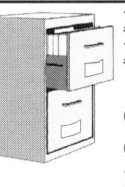

### FACT FILE: FUEL INJECTION/ELECTRONIC IGNITION PRECAUTIONS

Observe The Following Precautions When Working On Petrol-Engined Vehicles With Fuel Injection - Electronic Ignition Systems:

• never start the engine when the electrical terminals are poorly connected or loose on the battery poles;
• never use a quick battery charger to start the engine;
• never disconnect the battery with the engine running;
• when charging the battery quickly, first disconnect the battery;
• if the vehicle is placed in a drying oven after painting at a temperature of more than 80 degrees Celsius, first remove the electronic control unit (ECU);
• never connect or disconnect the ECU multiple connector with the ignition key in MARCIA position;
• always disconnect the battery negative lead before carrying out electrical welding on the vehicle.

The system contains stand-by memory as follows:
• Memory that stores learnt self-adaptive values. This data is lost when the battery is disconnected, so you should disconnect the battery as infrequently as possible.
• Memory that stores diagnostic information in the event of a fault. This data is retained even if the battery is disconnected.

## Job 1. The Electronic Injection/Ignition System.

Both the OHV and FIRE OHC Cinquecento models have a sophisticated Weber-Marelli single-point injection (SPI) system with electronic ignition. The system can be serviced only by a FIAT dealer, although components can be removed and replaced by the user in the context of other jobs.
Illustration **Job 1-1B** shows the FIRE OHC engine. The following differences occur between the OHV and FIRE OHC engines:
• Different injector turret mountings are used:
The turret is mounted directly on top of the OHV engine.
The turret is on a manifold behind the FIRE OHC engine.
• Different Electronic Control Units (ECUs) are used: - a 6F.SO on (early) OHV engines. - an I.A.W. 16F.E0 on (later) OHV engines. - an I.A.W. 16F.ER on FIRE OHC engines.
• The air inlet ic valve exists only on FIRE OHC engines.
• The turret is heated by water from the cooling system (not shown in illustration **Job 1-1B**). The water inlet is from different sources on OHV and FIRE OHC. See **PART C: COOLING SYSTEM**.

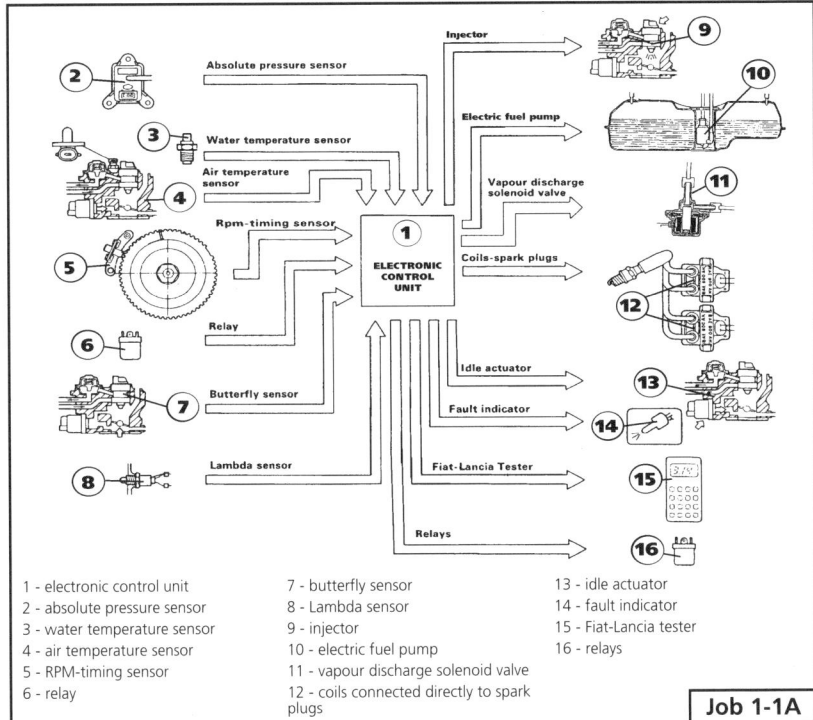

- 1 - electronic control unit
- 2 - absolute pressure sensor
- 3 - water temperature sensor
- 4 - air temperature sensor
- 5 - RPM-timing sensor
- 6 - relay
- 7 - butterfly sensor
- 8 - Lambda sensor
- 9 - injector
- 10 - electric fuel pump
- 11 - vapour discharge solenoid valve
- 12 - coils connected directly to spark plugs
- 13 - idle actuator
- 14 - fault indicator
- 15 - Fiat-Lancia tester
- 16 - relays

**Job 1-1A**

☐ **Step 1A:** Familiarise yourself with the system components shown in illustrations **Job 1-1A**...

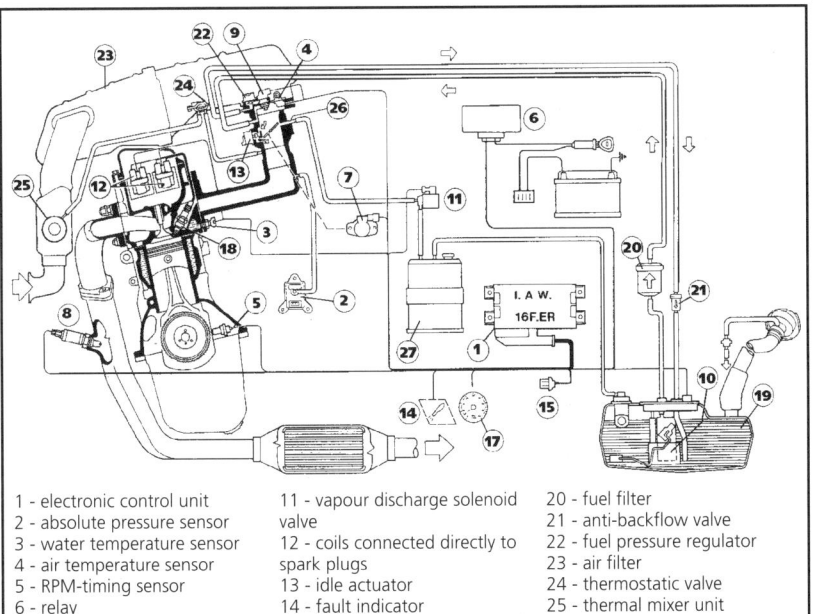

- 1 - electronic control unit
- 2 - absolute pressure sensor
- 3 - water temperature sensor
- 4 - air temperature sensor
- 5 - RPM-timing sensor
- 6 - relay
- 7 - butterfly sensor
- 8 - Lambda sensor
- 9 - injector
- 10 - electric fuel pump
- 11 - vapour discharge solenoid valve
- 12 - coils connected directly to spark plugs
- 13 - idle actuator
- 14 - fault indicator
- 15 - Fiat-Lancia tester
- 17 - rev counter (if present)
- 18 - spark plugs
- 19 - fuel tank
- 20 - fuel filter
- 21 - anti-backflow valve
- 22 - fuel pressure regulator
- 23 - air filter
- 24 - thermostatic valve
- 25 - thermal mixer unit
- 26 - fuel vapours connector
- 27 - active carbon filter.

**Job 1-1B**

☐ **Step 1B:** ...and **Job 1-1B**. These two illustrations have a common numbering system and the components (as far as **part 16**) are as follows:

● The Electronic Control Unit (**1**) is a microprocessor which collects data from a variety of sensors and uses it to control the injection and ignition components.

● The absolute pressure sensor (**2**) measures the pressure in the inlet manifold. When the engine is off, and the ignition is turned on, this gives the barometric pressure which depends on altitude. When the engine is running, the difference between the manifold pressure and the barometric pressure gives the vacuum created by the engine within the inlet manifold.

● The water temperature sensor (**3**) measures the temperature of the cooling water in the engine.

● The air temperature sensor (**4**) measures the air temperature at the top of the injector turret, underneath the cover.

● The RPM-timing sensor (**5**) is mounted on the timing cover, on the periphery of the crankshaft pulley which has two missing teeth. The sensor measures the rotation of the crankshaft as the gap left by the missing teeth passes the sensor.

● The relay (**6**) activates the electronic control unit when the ignition is on. Some systems have a double relay so that parts (**6**) and (**16**) are a single unit. Illustration **Job 1-1B** shows part (**6**) as a double relay so that (**16**) is missing.

● The butterfly sensor (**7**) detects the angle of the butterfly valve underneath the injector.

● The Lambda sensor (**8**) detects the amount of oxygen in the exhaust gases, giving a measure of the completeness of combustion.

The above measurements are fed to the control unit which continuously evaluates a set of complex algorithms, which are beyond the scope of this manual, to determine how the fuel injection and ignition components should operate for maximum performance. The list of components continues as follows:

● The injector (**9**), mounted on the turret, is an electromagnetic valve and spray nozzle which injects fuel into the inlet manifold above the butterfly valve.

● The electric fuel pump (**10**) is mounted in the fuel tank and pumps fuel to the injector. Excess fuel is returned to the tank via a pressure regulator which is mounted in the turret alongside the injector.

● The vapour discharge solenoid valve (**11**) feeds petrol vapours from the active carbon filter to the inlet manifold. The carbon filter accumulates vapours from the tank which would otherwise be discharged to the atmosphere.

● The coils and spark plugs (**12**) provide ignition for the fuel in the engine. There is no distributor. Instead the ignition is controlled electronically.

● The idle actuator (**13**) controls a supplementary air inlet, underneath the butterfly valve, so that the engine can run under idling conditions with the butterfly valve closed.

● The fault indicator (**14**) is a light on the control panel that indicates the failure of any one of the system components. Information about the fault is stored in the control system memory and remains in place even after the vehicle has stopped and the battery has been disconnected.

- The FIAT Lancia Tester socket (**15**) enables your FIAT dealer to analyse the system and diagnose faults using specialised equipment.

- The relays (**16**) supply power to the petrol pump, coils, injector, Lambda sensor and vapour cut-off solenoid. Part (**16**) is shown in illustration *Job 1-1A* only, as a separate component from part (**6**).

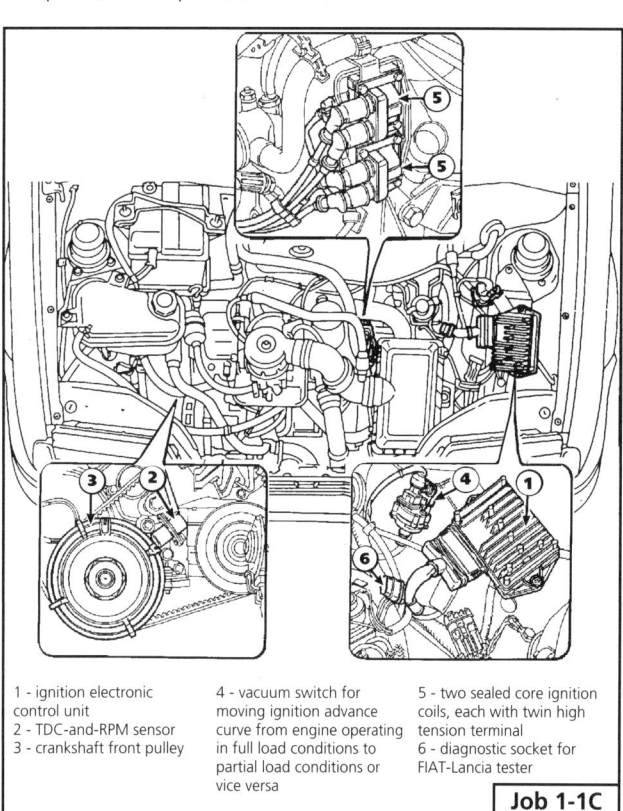

1 - ignition electronic control unit
2 - TDC-and-RPM sensor
3 - crankshaft front pulley
4 - vacuum switch for moving ignition advance curve from engine operating in full load conditions to partial load conditions or vice versa
5 - two sealed core ignition coils, each with twin high tension terminal
6 - diagnostic socket for FIAT-Lancia tester

**Job 1-1C**

☐ **Step 1-1C:** This is the location of the components of the (non-UK) Digiplex 2/S electronic ignition system.

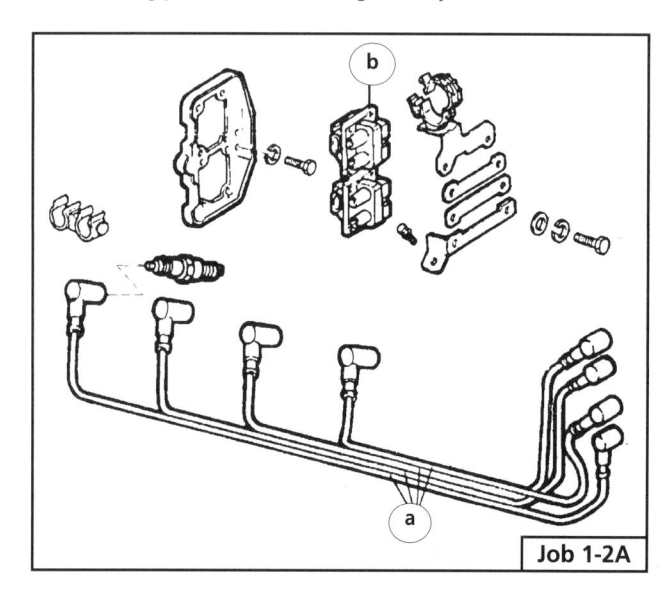

**Job 1-2A**

☐ **Step 2A:** The only repairs that can be carried out, other than by a FIAT dealer are:
- replacement of HT cables (**a**)
- replacement of coils (**b**)
- checking of rubber vacuum pipe from the vacuum switch (see illustration *Job 1-1C, part 4*) and replacement if necessary.

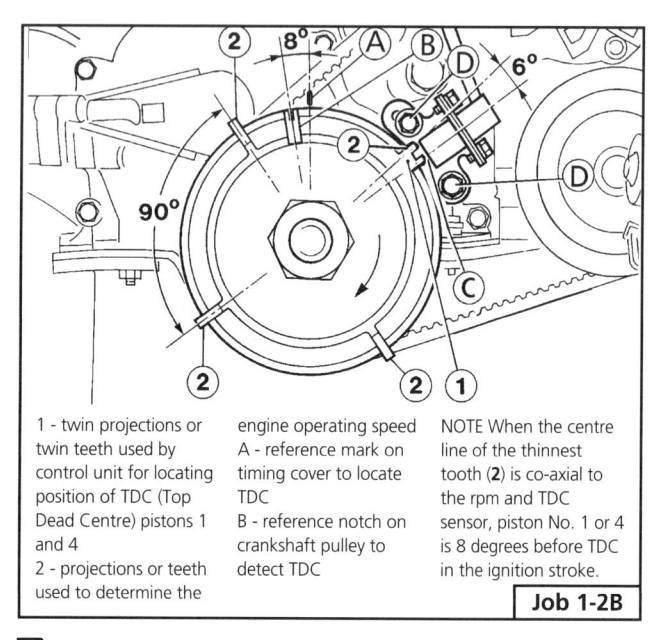

1 - twin projections or twin teeth used by control unit for locating position of TDC (Top Dead Centre) pistons 1 and 4
2 - projections or teeth used to determine the engine operating speed
A - reference mark on timing cover to locate TDC
B - reference notch on crankshaft pulley to detect TDC

NOTE When the centre line of the thinnest tooth (**2**) is co-axial to the rpm and TDC sensor, piston No. 1 or 4 is 8 degrees before TDC in the ignition stroke.

**Job 1-2B**

☐ **Step 2B:** You may also check the gap (**A**) between the TDC-and-RPM sensor and each of the projections, or teeth, on the crankshaft pulley.
- if the gap is not between 0.4 mm and 1 mm at each projection (**2**), replace the pulley, if any of the projections are damaged, or have the gap adjusted by your FIAT dealer.
- DO NOT slacken the bolts (**D**), which would disturb the factory-set timing.

**FACT FILE: FUEL SYSTEM INERTIAL SWITCH**

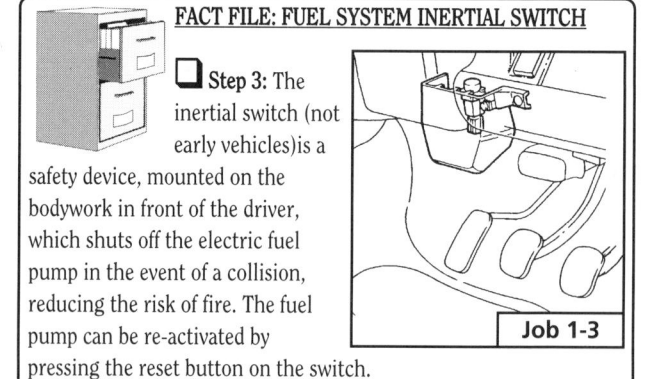

☐ **Step 3:** The inertial switch (not early vehicles) is a safety device, mounted on the bodywork in front of the driver, which shuts off the electric fuel pump in the event of a collision, reducing the risk of fire. The fuel pump can be re-activated by pressing the reset button on the switch.

**Job 1-3**

- If you can smell fuel, or if you notice there are fuel leaks after an apparently minor collision, do not reset the switch.
- First repair the leaks to avoid the risk of fire, then reset the switch.

## Job 2. OHV engine - air filter assembly - removal and refitting.

This Job shows you how to remove the air filter components so that you can access the injector turret.

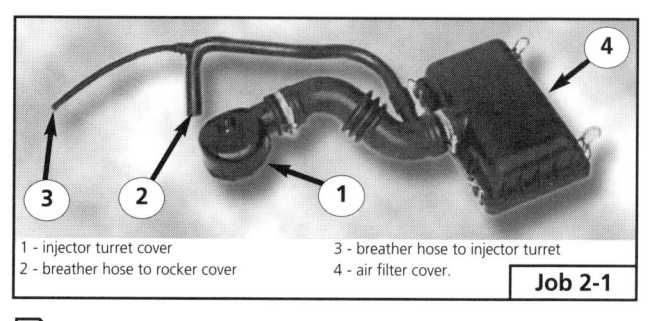

1 - injector turret cover
2 - breather hose to rocker cover
3 - breather hose to injector turret
4 - air filter cover.

**Job 2-1**

☐ **Step 1:** Undo the bolt and remove the injector turret cover (**1**). Disconnect the breather hoses (**2**) and (**3**) from the rocker cover and injector turret respectively. If you are removing only the assembly shown here, undo the clips and detach the air filter cover (**4**) from its base.

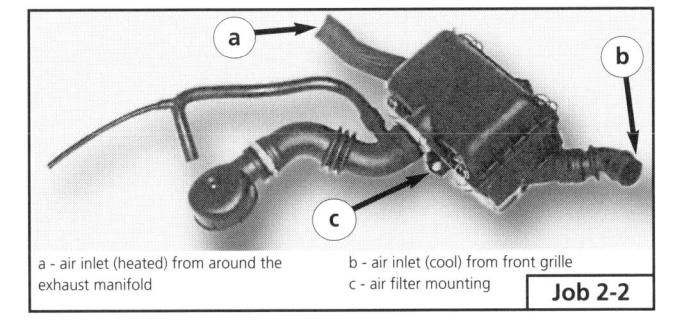

*a - air inlet (heated) from around the exhaust manifold*
*b - air inlet (cool) from front grille*
*c - air filter mounting*
**Job 2-2**

❑ **Step 2:** If you wish to remove the complete air filter assembly shown here, remove the inlet hoses (**a**) and (**b**), then remove the bolts from the mountings (**c**).

❑ **Step 3:** Remove the assembly from the vehicle.

❑ **Step 4:** Refit in reverse order.

## Job 3. FIRE OHC engine - air filter assembly - removal and refitting.

This Job shows you how to remove the air filter components so that you can access the injector turret. The air filter on the FIRE OHC engine is so big, you can do hardly any work on the engine without removing it.

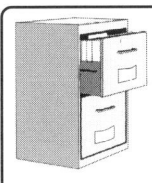

**FACT FILE: AIR FILTER THERMOSTATIC VALVE AND HOSES**
● The air filter cover contains a thermostatic valve which responds to changes in temperature and operates a thermal mixer on the air inlet, using vacuum from the injector turret.
● The thermal mixer adjusts the proportion of air that comes from the front grille (cool air) and exhaust manifold (heated air).
● The good operation of the thermostatic valve relies on air hoses that are in good condition. Replace any that are doubtful before suspecting the valve to be faulty. These valves give little trouble and usually only suffer from sticking, caused by dirt.
● This type of air inlet control exists only on FIRE OHC models. The OHV model has a different type of thermal mixer as a self-contained unit upstream of the air filter and does not connect to any external units.

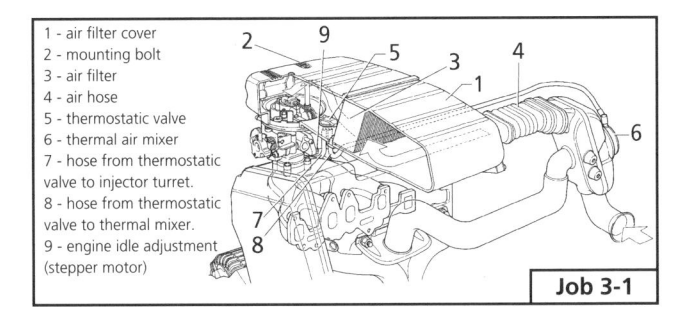

1 - air filter cover
2 - mounting bolt
3 - air filter
4 - air hose
5 - thermostatic valve
6 - thermal air mixer
7 - hose from thermostatic valve to injector turret
8 - hose from thermostatic valve to thermal mixer
9 - engine idle adjustment (stepper motor)
**Job 3-1**

❑ **Step 1:** Disconnect the air hose (**4**) from the air filter cover (**1**).

❑ **Step 2:** Undo the clip at the front of the air filter cover and remove the bolts (illustration **Job 3-1, part 2**).

❑ **Step 3:** Gently lift the air filter assembly so you can access the hoses underneath.

❑ **Step 4:** Disconnect the hoses (illustration **Job 3-1, part 7**) and (**part 8**) from the ic valve (**part 5**).

❑ **Step 5:** Remove the air filter assembly from the vehicle.

❑ **Step 6:** Refit in reverse order, replacing any damaged thermostatic valve hoses (illustration **Job 3-1, part 7**) and (**part 8**) with new ones.

## Job 4. Injection unit - removal and refitting.

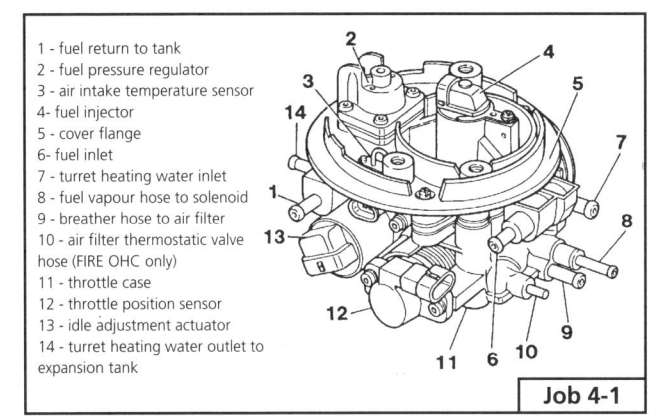

1 - fuel return to tank
2 - fuel pressure regulator
3 - air intake temperature sensor
4 - fuel injector
5 - cover flange
6 - fuel inlet
7 - turret heating water inlet
8 - fuel vapour hose to solenoid
9 - breather hose to air filter
10 - air filter thermostatic valve hose (FIRE OHC only)
11 - throttle case
12 - throttle position sensor
13 - idle adjustment actuator
14 - turret heating water outlet to expansion tank
**Job 4-1**

Illustration **Job 4-1** shows details of the injector turret.

The following differences occur between OHV and FIRE OHC engines:

● The turret heating water inlet (**7**) connects to:
the thermostat housing on the OHV
the injection manifold pre-heater on the FIRE OHC.
See **PART C: COOLING SYSTEM**.
● The air filter thermostatic valve connection (**10**) exists on FIRE OHC models only. On OHV models there is no thermostatic valve in the air filter and this connector is blanked off.

**SAFETY FIRST!**

*● The petrol injection units on Cinquecento models operate at a pressure of 1 bar and do not need to be de-pressurised before removing fuel hoses. However, do not become complacent. If you subsequently decide to work on a high pressure injection system, you need to de-pressurise it first. See **Job 11**.*

❑ **Step 1:** Disconnect the battery negative earth lead.

❑ **Step 2:** Remove the air cleaner assembly and the rubber sealing ring from around the top of the injection unit. See **Job 2 (OHV engine)** or **Job 3 (FIRE OHC engine)**.

*making it easy* ● When removing electrical connections and hoses from the injector turret, identify them for refitting in their correct positions, and label them if necessary.

❑ **Step 3:** Disconnect all electrical connections from the injector turret. The connections are:

- air intake temperature sensor (illustration **Job 4-1, part 3**).
- throttle position sensor (*part, 12*).
- idle adjustment actuator (*part, 13*).

☐ **Step 4:** Release the clips, disconnect the fuel hoses and plug the ends. The hoses are:

- fuel return to tank (*part, 1*).
- fuel inlet to turret (*part, 6*).

☐ **Step 5:** Disconnect the vapour hoses. These include:

- fuel vapour hose to solenoid (*part, 8*).
- breather hose to air filter (*part, 9*), if not disconnected already.

☐ **Step 6:** Drain the cooling system while the engine is cold by loosening the thumbscrew at the bottom of the radiator, or by loosening the radiator bottom hose.

☐ **Step 7:** Disconnect the injector turret water inlet hose (illustration **Job 4-1, part 7**) and outlet hose (*part, 14*).

☐ **Step 8:** Disconnect the throttle cable from the lever arm and bracket on the turret. See **Job 5.**

☐ **Step 9:** Remove the through-bolts from the top of the injector turret, then lift the turret and its base gasket from the manifold.

*Job 4-9*

☐ **Step 10:** Refit in the reverse order, making sure the mating faces are clean and the base gasket is new.

☐ **Step 11:** Fill the cooling system with the correct 50/50 Paraflu anti-freeze solution. See **Chapter 3, Facts and Figures** and **Chapter 5, Servicing Your Car**.

☐ **Step 12:** Reconnect the battery earth lead.

## Job 5. Accelerator cable - replacement and adjustment.

☐ **Step 1:** Disconnect the end of the throttle cable (**1**) from the lever arm on the injector turret. Slacken the two locknuts (**2**) and disconnect the adjuster (**3**) from the bracket.

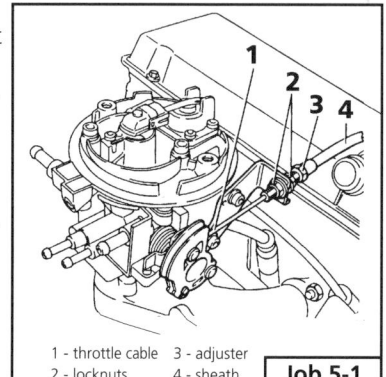

☐ **Step 2:** Working from inside the car, disconnect the other end of the cable from the fork at the top of the accelerator pedal arm.

1 - throttle cable   3 - adjuster
2 - locknuts   4 - sheath
*Job 5-1*

☐ **Step 3:** Pull the cable out through the bulkhead.

*making it easy* • There are so many different types of cable that you are strongly advised to take the old one with you, when buying a replacement to ensure that the new one is exactly the same,.

☐ **Step 4:** Refit in reverse order, using a new cable.

☐ **Step 5:** Ask an assistant to operate the accelerator pedal. Adjust the cable by slackening the locknuts (illustration **5-1, part 2**) and turning the adjuster (*part 3*) to achieve the correct adjustment, then tighten the locknuts. The correct adjustment is as follows:
• The throttle should be fully open when the pedal is fully depressed.
• The cable should neither be under tension, nor excessively slack when the pedal is released.

IMPORTANT NOTE: It is not possible to adjust the engine idle speed on the injection system because it is self-setting. The correct idle speeds are given in **Chapter 3, Facts and Figures**. If the idle speed needs adjustment, there is a fault and you will need to see your FIAT dealer.

## Job 6. Fuel pump - replacement.

IMPORTANT NOTE: Read **Chapter 1, Safety First!** before carrying out any work on the fuel system.

### FACT FILE: FUEL PUMP TYPE AND LOCATION
• Both the OHV and FIRE OHC models have an electric fuel pump mounted in the tank, accessible from under the rear seat. The fuel pump is integrated with the fuel level sender as a single unit.
• The fuel pump is mounted in a basket with a mesh fuel filter on the inlet side.
• The pump is of the turbine type with plastic impeller. It houses a non-return valve and operates at a pressure of 1 bar. It has a pressure relief valve calibrated at 2.6 bar.
• The pump is operated directly by the electronic control unit whenever the engine is running, and responds to the following special conditions:
It operates for about 15 seconds whenever the ignition is switched on, without the engine being started.
It stops if the engine falls below a minimum RPM threshold.

• The pump, which includes a connection for a fuel return hose, is mounted on a removable plate, fixed to the top of the tank.

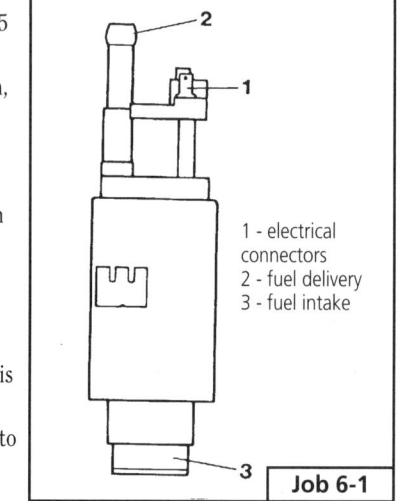

1 - electrical connectors
2 - fuel delivery
3 - fuel intake
*Job 6-1*

6-42

### SAFETY FIRST!

- The petrol injection units on UK Cinquecento models operate at low pressure. If you subsequently decide to work on a high pressure injection system (not fitted to UK Cinquecentos), you need to de-pressurise it first. See **Job 11**.

❏ **Step 1:** Switch off the ignition and disconnect the battery leads, starting with the earth lead.

❏ **Step 2:** Lift the rear seat cushion (3) and pull it forward to access the pump shield (1). Remove the shield by undoing the nuts (2), to expose the cover plate and connections.

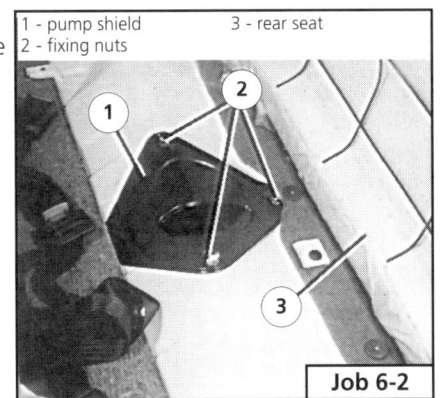

1 - pump shield
2 - fixing nuts
3 - rear seat

Job 6-2

❏ **Step 3:** Detach the electrical connection from the cover plate.

❏ **Step 4:** Detach all the fuel hoses from the cover plate, noting their position for correct refitting later. Plug the ends of the hoses.

❏ **Step 5:** Undo the nuts and remove the fuel pump/sender assembly.

❏ **Step 6:** Refit in reverse order using a new gasket, making sure that all connections are secure.

❏ **Step 7:** Reconnect the battery leads.

## Job 7. Fuel tank - removal and refitting.

### SAFETY FIRST!

- We recommend that you carry out all of this work out of doors.
- Read **Chapter 1, Safety First!** before carrying out this work!

*making it easy* — • Plan ahead! Before starting this work, run the car's fuel level as low as possible.

❏ **Step 1:** Disconnect the battery leads, starting with the earth lead.

❏ **Step 2:** Detach the electrical connection and fuel hoses from the fuel tank cover plate under the rear seat, but do not remove the fuel pump. See **Job 6**.

❏ **Step 3:** Syphon any remaining fuel from the tank into a suitable closed container.

❏ **Step 4:** Disconnect the filler and breather hoses from the tank, working from underneath the car.

❏ **Step 5:** Free the handbrake cable from its bracket at the side of the tank.

❏ **Step 6A: STEEL FUEL TANKS:** Using a trolley jack to support the tank (fitted with a wooden plank across its lifting pad to prevent damage) undo the peripheral mounting brackets.

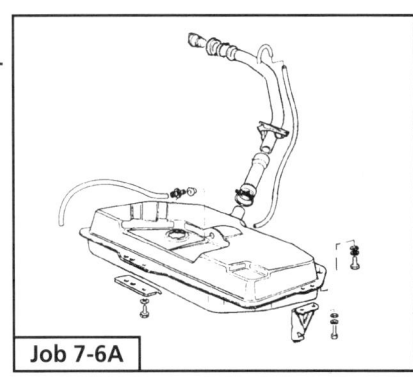

Job 7-6A

❏ **Step 6B: PLASTIC FUEL TANKS:** The tank is held in place with steel straps (arrowed). Undo the strap securing bolts and remove the straps.

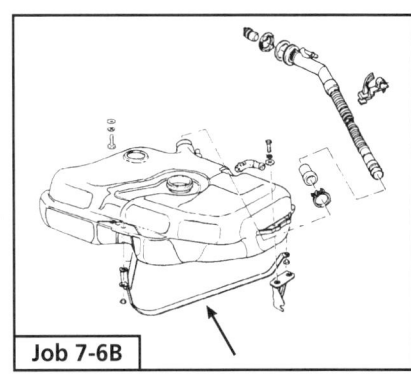

Job 7-6B

❏ **Step 7:** Lower the tank enough to check whether any hoses remain attached, then lower it fully to the ground.

❏ **Step 8:** Refit in the reverse order, making sure all connections are sound.

❏ **Step 9:** Reconnect the battery leads.

## Job 8. Lambda sensor - replacement.

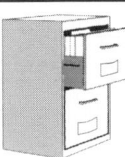

### FACT FILE:

- The Lambda sensor continuously monitors the amount of oxygen in the exhaust gases, to determine the completeness of combustion. The value is fed back to the electronic control unit and is used to adjust the amount of fuel injected, to maintain a fixed fuel-to-air ratio under all operating conditions.
- The sensor is very fragile and should not be knocked or dropped.
- The sensor can quickly be put out of action by small amounts of lead in the petrol.
- We recommend that, if necessary, a new sensor is fitted by your FIAT dealer, who can test the old one to see whether it is working properly.
- No cleaners should be used on the sensor.

**CHAPTER 6 PART E: FUEL AND EXHAUST**

6-43

❏ **Step 1:** Raise the front of the car and support on axle stands. See **Chapter 1, Safety First!** You will find the Lambda sensor screwed into the exhaust front downpipe. On OHV models it is just in front of the catalytic converter. On FIRE OHC models it is further forward, in front of the engine.

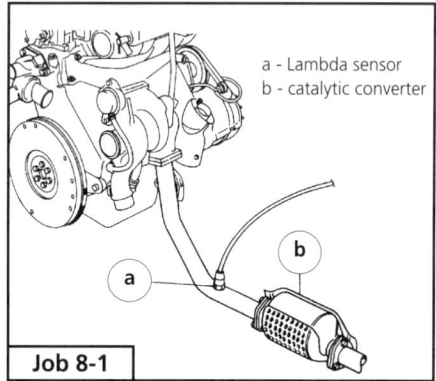

a - Lambda sensor
b - catalytic converter

Job 8-1

a - Lambda sensor
b - connector to ECU
c - sensor heater power supply

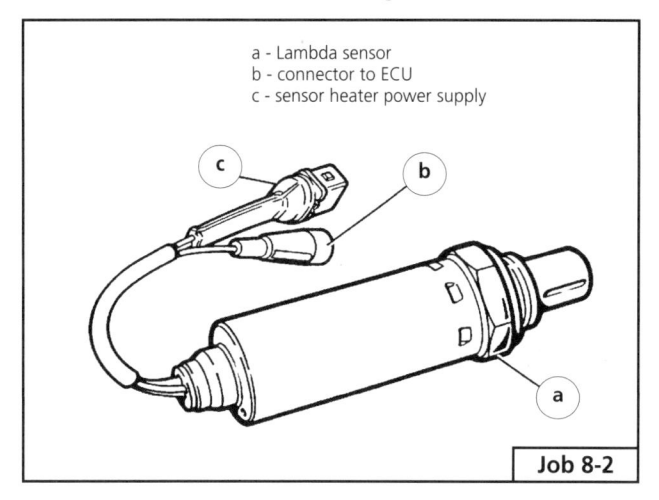

Job 8-2

❏ **Step 2:** Trace the wiring back from the sensor and release it from any securing clips until you reach the main loom and then disconnect it.

❏ **Step 3:** Before refitting, check that the sensor sealing ring is in good condition, and lubricate the thread of the sensor with a high-temperature anti-seize compound.

❏ **Step 4:** When re-fitting the sensor, tighten it to the specified torque. See **Chapter 3, Facts and Figures**.

## Job 9. Fuel evaporation system.

**FACT FILE: HOW THE SYSTEM WORKS**

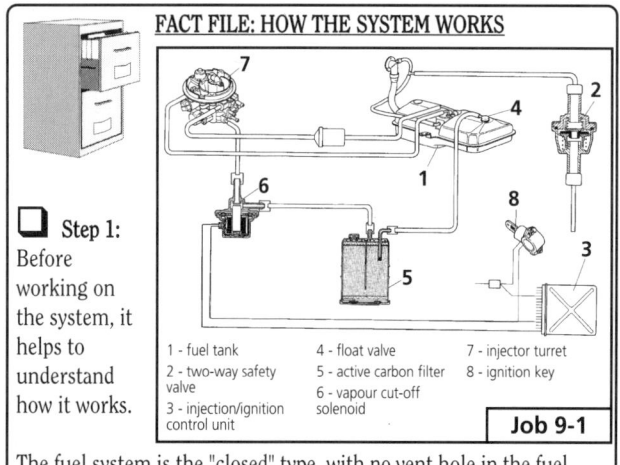

❏ **Step 1:** Before working on the system, it helps to understand how it works.

1 - fuel tank
2 - two-way safety valve
3 - injection/ignition control unit
4 - float valve
5 - active carbon filter
6 - vapour cut-off solenoid
7 - injector turret
8 - ignition key

Job 9-1

The fuel system is the "closed" type, with no vent hole in the fuel tank filler cap. Fuel vapour emissions to the atmosphere are controlled according to the following conditions:

*FACT FILE Continued...*

*...FACT FILE Continued*

• When the fuel level in the tank (**1**) is average or low, and the pressure exceeds a certain value because of hot weather, the float valve (**4**) opens and the vapours are absorbed by the active carbon filter (**5**).

• When the fuel level in the tank is high, the float valve remains closed regardless of the pressure, to prevent liquid fuel from reaching the carbon filter. If the pressure gets too high, the two-way safety valve (**2**) opens releasing vapour to the atmosphere.

• If a vacuum occurs in the tank, the two-way safety valve opens in the opposite direction to ventilate it.

• When the engine is running, the vapours absorbed by the active carbon filter are fed to the inlet manifold under controlled conditions via the solenoid cut-off valve (**6**). To prevent the mixture from becoming too rich, the solenoid is operated by the electronic control unit (**3**).

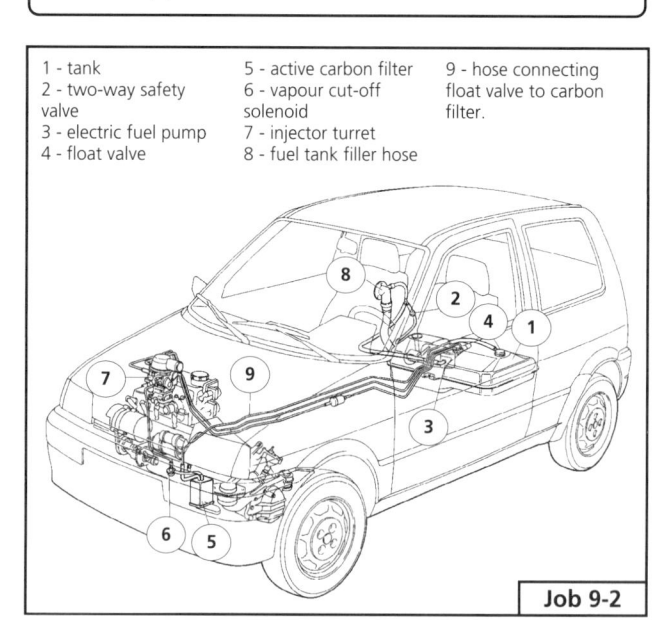

1 - tank
2 - two-way safety valve
3 - electric fuel pump
4 - float valve
5 - active carbon filter
6 - vapour cut-off solenoid
7 - injector turret
8 - fuel tank filler hose
9 - hose connecting float valve to carbon filter.

Job 9-2

❏ **Step 2:** This shows where the anti-evaporation system components are located. Other than occasional replacement of the carbon filter, no system maintenance is needed. However, a fault with the system can lead to problems running the car, and if so, you will need to see your FIAT dealer.

## Job 10. Exhaust system - replacement.

**SAFETY FIRST!**

• All exhaust systems can cause burns if they are touched when hot.
• Catalytic converters become especially hot when the engine is running and should only be touched when cold.

6-44

CHAPTER 6 PART E: FUEL AND EXHAUST

1 - Lambda probe
2 - catalytic converter
3 - connection for measuring exhaust gases upstream of catalytic converter

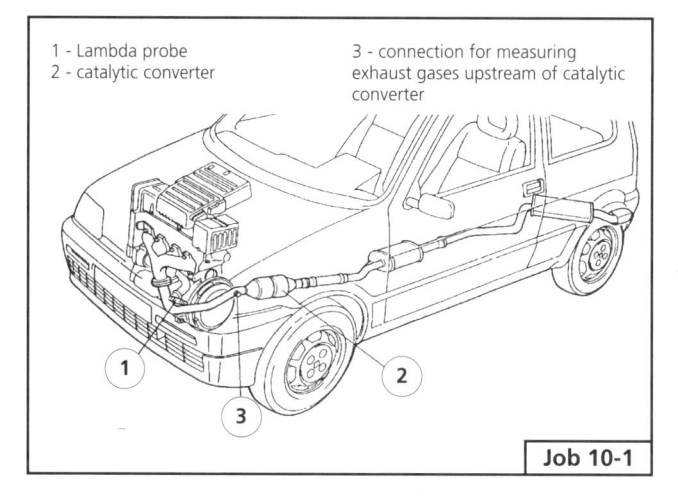

**Job 10-1**

Illustration **Job 10-1** shows the exhaust system for the FIRE OHC engine. The exhaust for the OHV engine is the same except that the front section, which connects to the manifold, is shorter because the manifold is behind the engine, as shown in **illustration Job 8-1**.

**ℹ️ INSIDE INFORMATION:**
- The exhaust manifold is mounted on the side of the cylinder head, secured by studs, nuts and washers. When refitting it, always use a new gasket and tighten all retaining nuts evenly.
- There is a hose attached to a flange close to the exhaust manifold, feeding hot air to the air inlet.
- The catalytic converter is replaced the same as any other section of the exhaust system, if it is damaged or becomes ineffective. ℹ️

☐ **Step 1:** Raise the front of the car and support on axle stands. See **Chapter 1, Safety First!**

☐ **Step 2:** Disconnect the exhaust downpipe from the manifold.

☐ **Step 3:** Remove the nuts and undo the clamps from the exhaust mountings on the entire length of the system, or from the sections to be replaced.

*making it easy*
- Use penetrating oil and tap with a hammer to loosen the sections.
- If this doesn't work, apply several doses of penetrating oil over a couple of days.

☐ **Step 4:** Refit by loosely assembling the complete system and attaching it to its rubber hangers and to the manifold.

Align the system, ensuring sufficient clearance along its length, then (and ONLY then!) tighten all the clamps and nuts.

*making it easy*
- When reconnecting the system, use a heatproof exhaust joint sealer.
- This both seals the joints and makes it easier to separate them again later.

☐ **Step 5:** Lower the car to the ground, run the engine and check for exhaust leaks.

### Job 11. High pressure injection systems - safety first!

Before you disconnect any of the pipework on a high pressure injection system, you should de-pressurise it for safety reasons.

**SAFETY FIRST!**
- *The high pressure pipework on a fuel injection system can retain its pressure for days, even after the engine has been switched off.*
- *When you disconnect the pipework, a jet of fuel can be emitted under very high pressure - strong enough to penetrate the skin or damage the eyes.*
- *NEVER work on the fuel pipework when the engine is running, except when bleeding air from the injectors.*
- *ALWAYS place a rag over a housing while it is being undone until all the pressure has been let out of the system.*
- *You are recommended to wear strong rubber gloves and goggles when disconnecting the fuel injection system's high pressure pipework. Always disconnect VERY slowly, letting pressure out progressively.*
- *See the appropriate vehicle documentation for details of how to depressurise the system. Usually it means removing the fuel pump relay and running the engine until it 'dies'.*
- *Disconnect the battery negative earth before working on the fuel system.*
- *Work outdoors and away from sources of flame or ignition.*
- *ALWAYS wear rubber gloves - don't let your skin come into contact with fuel.*

# PART F: STEERING AND SUSPENSION

## PART F: Contents
Job 1. The systems explained.
Job 2. Steering wheel - removal and refitting.
Job 3. Track rod end (TRE) balljoint - replacement.
Job 4. Steering rack gaiter - replacement.
Job 5. Steering rack - replacement.
Job 6. Front track control arm - replacement.
Job 7. Front suspension-strut and anti-roll bar - replacement.
Job 8. Front wheel bearing - replacement.
Job 9. Rear shock absorbers and coil springs - replacement.
Job 10. Rear track control arm - removal and replacement.
Job 11. Rear wheel bearings - replacement.

CHAPTER 6 PART F: SUSPENSION

## Job 1. The system explained.

**Point 1A:** This is the front suspension assembly for all Cinquecento models. The layout shown here is left-hand drive - the right-hand drive system is essentially the same but 'reversed'.

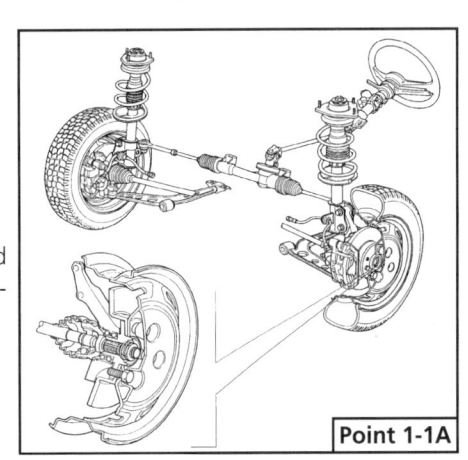

Point 1-1A

### SAFETY FIRST!

- Never remove the central nut holding the coil spring at the top of the front suspension strut without using a purpose-made coil spring compressor, as described in **Job 7**.
- We recommend that dismantling the shock absorber assembly is carried out by your FIAT dealer.

**Point 1B:** This is the front shock absorber strut and its attachments to the hub carrier (two bolts - one arrowed) and to the bodywork, at the top. The shock absorber is surrounded with a coil spring.

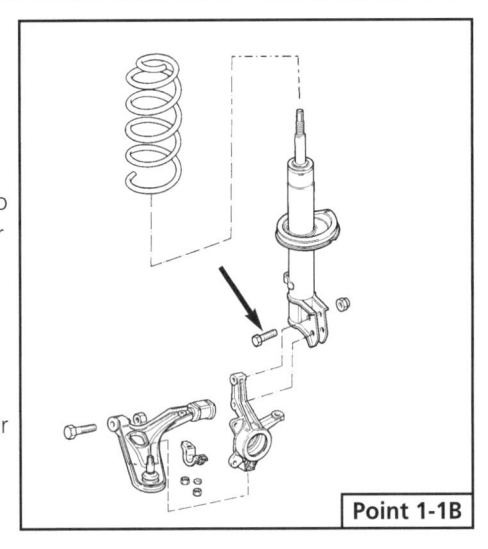

Point 1-1B

**Point 2:** This is the rear suspension assembly for all Cinquecento models.

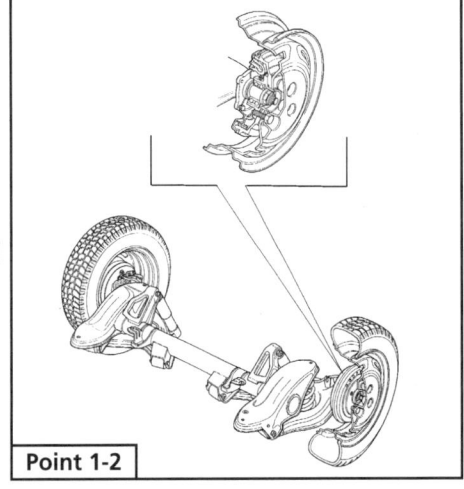

Point 1-2

## Job 2. Steering wheel - removal and refitting.

**Step 1:** Set the steering in the straight ahead position.

**Step 2:** Remove the steering wheel centre cap. Lever out the centre insert, or remove the retaining screws from behind the steering wheel, if fitted. Undo the retaining nut and pull the steering wheel towards you so it comes off its column. Refit in reverse order.

Job 2-2

### SAFETY FIRST!

- As you bang the steering wheel towards you with your hands to get it off the splines, take care not to bash yourself in the face!
- Leave the nut near the end of its thread and only remove it once the wheel is loose on the splines.
- If an airbag is fitted, it must be removed first. This must only be done by a FIAT dealer

## Job 3. Track rod end (TRE) balljoint - replacement.

**Step 1:** Slacken the bolts of the front wheel on the relevant side of the car, raise the front of the car and support on axle stands. See **Chapter 1, Safety First!**

**Step 2:** Undo the nut on the track rod end until it is near the end of the TRE stud, but do not remove it. Release the TRE stud from its taper in the steering arm using a suitable splitter.

**Step 3:** *i* INSIDE INFORMATION: A sharp blow with a hammer to the side of the eye (see illustration **Job 3-4, part e**) often momentarily distorts the eye and releases the ballpin from its taper. *i*

**Step 4:** Remove the nut (**a**) and disconnect the TRE balljoint (**e**) from the steering arm (**b**).

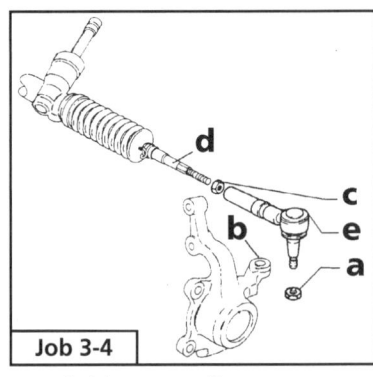

Undo the locknut (**c**) which secures the TRE to the steering tie rod. Unscrew the TRE from the tie rod (**d**), counting the exact number of turns needed to remove it.

Job 3-4

**Step 5:** Clean and grease the tie bar threads before fitting the new balljoint to prevent future seizure. Fit the new balljoint in reverse order screwing it on by exactly the same number of turns as it took to remove the old one. This will provide wheel alignment that is roughly correct, but before using the car further, take it to your FIAT dealership or tyre specialist to have the front wheel alignment set. This is NOT a

6-46

job you can do at home but it DOES need doing as soon as possible to avoid severe tyre wear and potentially dangerous braking and steering!

☐ **Step 6:** Refit and tighten the wheel, and lower the car to the ground.

## Job 4. Steering rack gaiter - removal.

☐ **Step 1:** Remove the Track Rod End (TRE) balljoint. See **Job 3**.

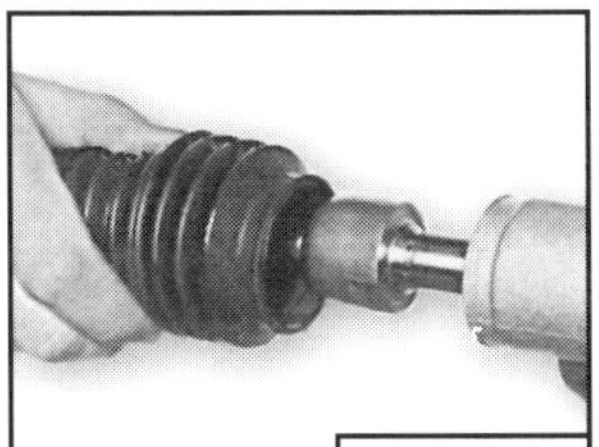

☐ **Step 2:** Undo the securing clip from each end of the gaiter and pull the gaiter off the tie rod.

☐ **Step 3:** Wipe away contaminated grease and replace with new lithium-based molybdenum disulphide grease. Secure the new gaiter in position at both ends with new bands or screw-type clips.

☐ **Step 4:** Complete the reassembly in the reverse order.

☐ **Step 5:** Refit the TRE balljoint. See **Job 3**.

## Job 5. Steering rack - replacement.

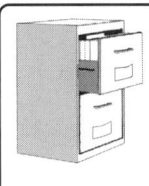

**FACT FILE: STEERING RACK AND COLUMN**
The steering rack and column are connected to each other through the floor of the vehicle. The steering rack is bolted to the floor, from underneath, and has a pinion that protrudes upwards through the floor. The pinch joint at the lower end of the steering column connects to the pinion from inside the car.

☐ **Step 1:** Slacken the front wheel bolts, raise the front of the car and support on axle stands. See **Chapter 1, Safety First!** Remove the front wheels.

☐ **Step 2:** Undo the Track Rod End (TRE) balljoint nuts then separate the balljoints from the steering arms with a splitter tool. See **Job 3**.

☐ **Step 3:** Undo the pinch bolt and nut (arrowed) from the coupling at the lower end of the steering column inside the car.

☐ **Step 4:** On OHV models, disconnect the exhaust front downpipe from the manifold. FIRE OHC models have a longer front downpipe which connects to the manifold at the front of the engine.

☐ **Step 5:** Undo the two rack mounting bolts (arrowed) from under the floor.

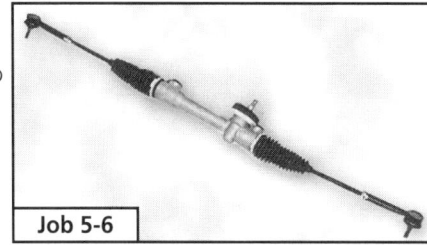

☐ **Step 6:** With an assistant inside the car, helping to separate the steering column pinch-joint from the rack pinion, pull the rack assembly away from under the floor and withdraw it from beneath a wheel arch.

*making it easy!* ● ☐ **Step 7:** The replacement rack should be centred before installation.
● Measure the total travel of a TRE when the steering is moved from lock to lock.
● Go back half this distance and your rack is centred.

☐ **Step 8:** Place the steering wheel in the dead ahead position and engage the rack and pinion splines with the column coupling. Ensure the pinch bolt engages in the slot between the two sets of splines.

☐ **Step 9:** Continue refitting in the reverse order of removal.

☐ **Step 10:** Take your car to your nearest FIAT dealership or tyre specialist to have the front wheel alignment set before using the car further. This is NOT a job you can do at home but is DOES need doing as soon as possible to avoid severe tyre wear and potentially dangerous braking and steering!

## Job 6. Front track control arm - replacement.

IMPORTANT NOTE: If the arm bushes or the arm balljoint (strut bottom balljoint) are worn, the entire arm assembly must be replaced.

*i* INSIDE INFORMATION: It may be possible to disconnect the track control arm outer balljoint from the hub carrier without removing the hub from the car. However, you will probably damage the balljoint gaiter - which will mean having to buy a complete, new track control arm! Avoid this very real risk by following **PART B**. *i*

**PART A: HUB REMAINING IN PLACE**

☐ **Step A1:** Slacken the relevant front wheel bolts, raise the front of the car and support on axle stands, then remove the front wheel. See **Chapter 1, Safety First!**

**CHAPTER 6 PART F: SUSPENSION**

6-47

## CHAPTER 6 · PART F: SUSPENSION

☐ **Step A2:** Remove the nut (**f**) from the track control arm balljoint (**a**).

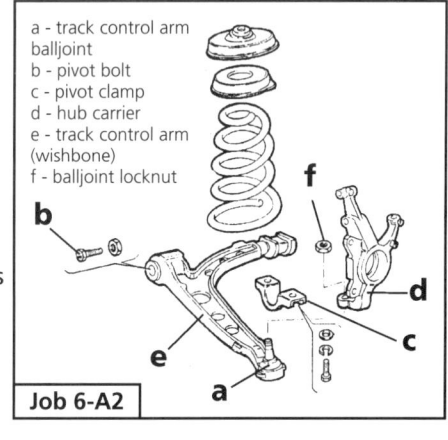

ℹ **INSIDE INFORMATION:** Some mechanics refer to the track control arm as the lower wishbone. ℹ

**Job 6-A2**
a - track control arm balljoint
b - pivot bolt
c - pivot clamp
d - hub carrier
e - track control arm (wishbone)
f - balljoint locknut

☐ **Step A3:** Using a splitter tool, part the balljoint from the hub carrier (see illustration *Job 6-A2, part d*).

☐ **Step A4:** Remove the track control arm pivot bolt (see illustration *Job 6-A2, part b*) and pivot clamp (*part c*).

☐ **Step A5:** Remove the track control arm (see illustrations *Job 6-A2, part e*) from the car. Now go to **Step 6**.

### PART B: HUB REMOVED FROM CAR

☐ **Step B1:** With the road wheels on the ground, lift the staking on the relevant front hub nut and slacken it, but leave it in place for the time being. Then slacken the wheel bolts, raise the front of the car and support on axle stands, and remove the wheel.

> **SAFETY FIRST!**
> ● Do not attempt to slacken the hub nut while the car is on a jack or on axle stands.
> ● This requires an enormous force to be tightened or released (see **Chapter 3, Facts and Figures**) and there is a risk of pulling the car off its supports.

☐ **Step B2:** Remove the hub nut, together with its washer, then refit the nut by a couple of turns and tap on it with a mallet to free the outboard drive-shaft joint from the hub.

☐ **Step B3:** Remove the track control arm pivot bolt (see illustration *Job 6-A2, part b*) and pivot clamp (*part c*).

☐ **Step B4:** Pull the suspension strut and wheel hub outwards while pulling the drive-shaft out of the hub carrier from the rear.

☐ **Step B5:** Undo the track control arm ball joint retaining nut (behind the hub carrier - see illustration *Job 6-A2, part f*), and use a ball joint splitter to separate the ball joint from the bottom of the hub carrier. Remove the arm from the car.

☐ **Step 6:** Inspect the track control arm balljoint for damage. If inner bushes or the rubber shroud are damaged, you will need to replace the entire arm with a new FIAT part.

☐ **Step 7:** Refitting is the reverse of removal.

☐ **Step 8:** Lower the car to the ground and tighten the wheel bolts.

## Job 7. Front suspension strut and anti-roll bar - replacement.

### PART A: FRONT STRUT/SHOCK ABSORBER REPLACEMENT

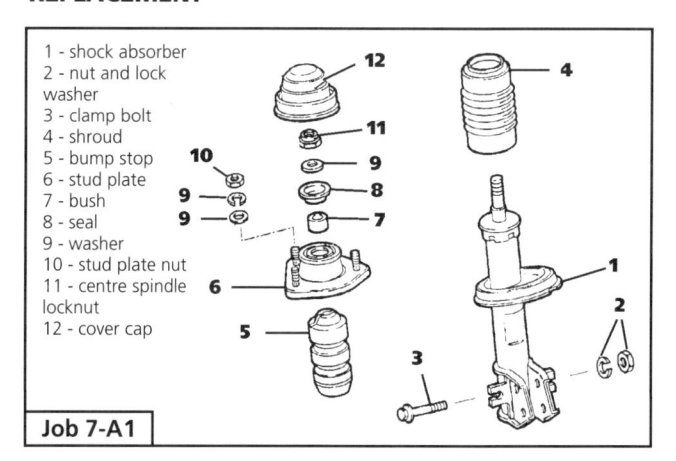

**Job 7-A1**
1 - shock absorber
2 - nut and lock washer
3 - clamp bolt
4 - shroud
5 - bump stop
6 - stud plate
7 - bush
8 - seal
9 - washer
10 - stud plate nut
11 - centre spindle locknut
12 - cover cap

☐ **Step A1:** Familiarise yourself with the components of the front shock absorber/strut which shows the shock absorber assembly without the spring. See illustration **Point 1-1B** for the spring and other associated components.

☐ **Step A2:** Slacken the bolts of the relevant front wheel, then raise the front of the car and support on axle stands, so that the front wheels hang free. See **Chapter 1, Safety First!** Remove the wheel, then detach the brake hose from the suspension strut.

☐ **Step A3:** Remove the two bolts (see illustration *Job 7-A1, parts 2* and *3*) which secure the hub carrier to the base of the strut. Separate the hub carrier and strut.

☐ **Step A4:** Remove the cover cap and then remove the three strut top mounting nuts and washers (arrowed). Note that on some models, ancillary components may be attached to the strut-top fixings and these will have to be removed first.

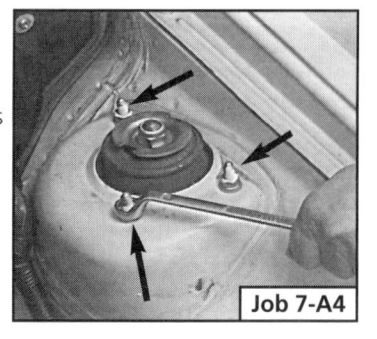

**Job 7-A4**

> **SAFETY FIRST!**
> ☐ **Step A5:** ● Do not remove the central nut (arrowed, and also see illustration *Job 7-A1, part 11*) holding the coil spring onto the strut without using a purpose-made coil spring compressor. See **Steps 7** and **8**.
> ● The power contained within the spring is enormous and potentially dangerous.

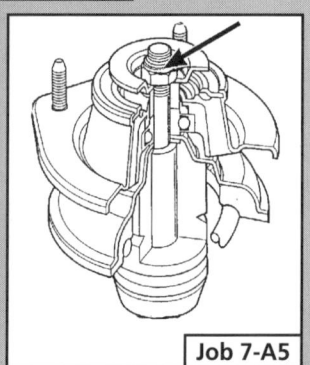

**Job 7-A5**

6-48

Job 7-A6

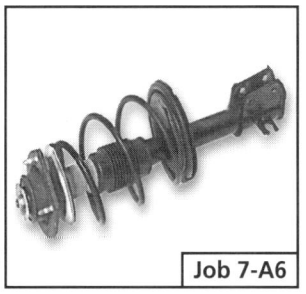

Job 7-A7

☐ **Step A6:** Lower the suspension strut to the ground.

☐ **Step A7:** Using two coil spring compressors spread over as many spring coils as possible, compress the spring, tightening each compressor a little at a time, in turn, until the spring ends are free of their seats.

☐ **Step A8:** Use an open-ended spanner - or the FIAT special tool, if available (**a**) - to hold the strut centre rod to prevent it from turning, while undoing the large nut (**b**) securing the rod to the top mounting assembly.

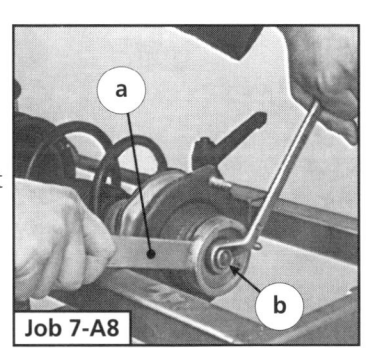

Job 7-A8

### SAFETY FIRST!

• Because of the irregular shape of the top end of the spring coils, it can be difficult to use spring compressors safely.
• Unless you are trained and experienced in this part of the job, and you have the correct tools, we recommend that you take the shock absorber assembly to your FIAT dealer to have it dismantled.

☐ **Step A9:** Pull off the mounting together with its bearing, the spring seat, seat cushion, coil spring and rubber bellows.

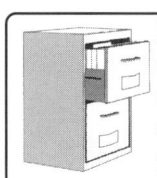

### FACT FILE: COIL SPRINGS
• If a coil spring is cracked, sagged or heavily rusted, replace the front springs AS A PAIR. FIAT springs are colour-coded with a stripe of either yellow or green paint. Use only a matching pair.

☐ **Step A10:** Refit all components in reverse order, making sure the coil spring is properly seated with the large coil at the bottom, and the end of the coil tight against the stop in the spring seat. Tighten to the specified torques

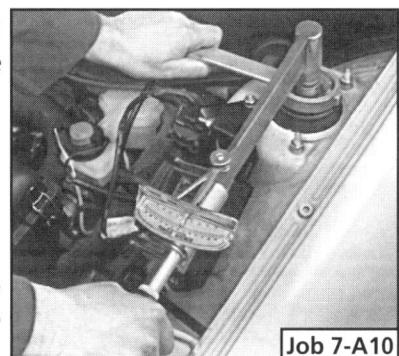

Job 7-A10

(see **Chapter 3, Facts and Figures**) only when the strut is back in place and the car is back on its wheels.

## PART B: FRONT ANTI-ROLL BAR REPLACEMENT

A front anti-roll bar was fitted as standard to 'Sporting' models only.

☐ **Step B1:** Examine the rubbers (**4** and **10**) and replace if necessary.

☐ **Step B2:** The two outer clamps (illustration **Job 7-B1, part 3**) are removed by removing the locknuts and washers (**parts 6** and **7**) and

Job 7-B1

removing from the track control arm (**part 12**).

☐ **Step B3:** The two inner clamps (illustration **Job 7-B1, parts 9** and **11**) are split by undoing the mounting lock nuts and washers (**parts 6** and **7**) and sliding off the rubbers (**part 10**).

## Job 8. Front wheel bearing - replacement.

IMPORTANT NOTE: When disconnecting the outer end of the track control arm (or bottom wishbone) from the balljoint mounting on the hub carrier, you may have the greatest difficulty in removing the balljoint without destroying the gaiter. If you do so, you will have to fit a complete, new track control arm! You will probably be better off removing the hub carrier and track control arm, still connected together, then splitting the ball joint when off the car. See **Job 6**.

☐ **Step 1:** *i* INSIDE INFORMATION: • The hub nut requires a great deal of torque to undo!
• Lever off the dust cap and slacken the centre hub nut (shown being staked in illustration **Job 8-13A**) while the car is still on the ground. *i*

### SAFETY FIRST!

• Do not attempt to slacken the hub nut while the car is on a jack or on axle stands.
• This requires an enormous force to be tightened or released (see **Chapter 3, Facts and Figures**) and there is a risk of pulling the car off its supports.

☐ **Step 2:** Remove the hub nut.

☐ **Step 3:** Remove the brake caliper, brake disc and disc shield. See **PART G: BRAKES**.

*making it easy!* • The hub and bearing can be drifted out from the hub carrier.
• If you have difficulty doing so, you could remove the hub carrier and take it to your FIAT dealer for bearing replacement.

**CHAPTER 6 PART F: SUSPENSION**

6-49

## CHAPTER 6 PART F: SUSPENSION

☐ **Step 4:**
Remove the hub carrier as follows:
● Disconnect the track rod end balljoint. See **Job 3**.
● Disconnect the track control arm from its mounting

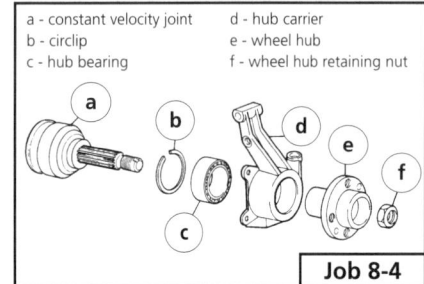

a - constant velocity joint
b - circlip
c - hub bearing
d - hub carrier
e - wheel hub
f - wheel hub retaining nut

*Job 8-4*

by removing the pivot bolt and pivot clamp. See **Job 6, Step B3**.
● Disconnect the hub carrier from the suspension strut. See **Job 7, Step 3**.
● Pull the hub carrier away from the constant velocity joint.
● Separate the track control arm from the hub carrier by disconnecting the balljoint. See **Job 6, Step B5**.

☐ **Step 5:** Support the hub carrier horizontally across the open jaws of a large vice, or a pair of supports on the bench. Carefully drift the wheel hub (see illustration, **Job 8-4**) out of the bearing.

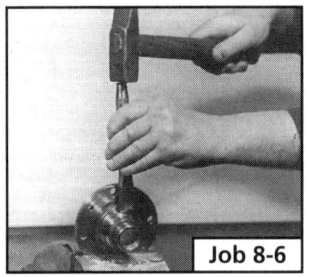

*Job 8-6*  *Job 8-7*

☐ **Step 6:** If the bearing inner race comes off with the driveshaft, carefully separate them, working all the way round with a cold chisel, as shown.

☐ **Step 7:** Undo the bolt (arrowed) and remove the dust shield from the hub carrier.

☐ **Step 8:** Remove the outer race circlip (illustration **Job 8-4, part b**) from the hub carrier.

☐ **Step 9:** Place the hub carrier back onto the vice, or supports, and carefully drift

*Job 8-8*

out the outer race, taking GREAT CARE not to mark the bearing housing.

☐ **Step 10:** Fit the new bearing as a complete assembly (inner and outer races together) to the hub carrier. Press or drift on the OUTER RACE ONLY, inserting the bearing EVENLY until it is fully seated.

IMPORTANT NOTE: The bearing is 'sealed for life' and needs no additional grease.

*making it easy* ● *If you have a large enough vice, start the bearing off - until it is flush with the carrier - by pressing it in with the jaws of the vice.*
● *Finish off with a drift, tapping at evenly spaced positions around the bearing.*

☐ **Step 11:** Refit a NEW outer race circlip.

☐ **Step 12:** Reassemble the front suspension and brakes in the reverse order of removal. See relevant Jobs for detailed information. Use a NEW hub nut.

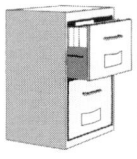

### FACT FILE: STAKING THE HUB NUT

☐ **Step 13A:** Use a cold chisel with an edge ground to an angle of about 60 degrees to stake the collar of the nut. USE A NEW NUT EACH TIME IT IS REPLACED.

*Job 8-13A*

☐ **Step 13B:** Make sure the staked-down section of the collar fits in the stub axle slot in the opposite direction to the direction of the nut rotation, as shown.

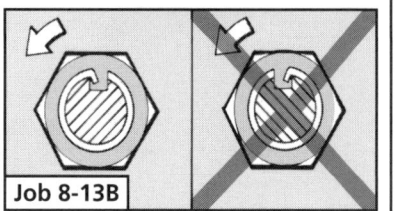

*Job 8-13B*

## Job 9. Rear shock absorbers and coil springs - replacement.

☐ **Step 1:**
Familiarise yourself with the components of the rear suspension assembly. The rigid axle comes as a single unit, complete with

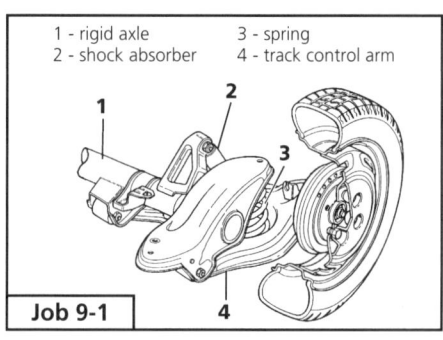

1 - rigid axle
2 - shock absorber
3 - spring
4 - track control arm

*Job 9-1*

the mountings that attach it to the bodywork.

☐ **Step 2:** Slacken the rear wheel bolts, raise the rear of the car and support on axle stands under the body or the rigid axle. See **Chapter 1, Safety First!** Remove the rear wheels.

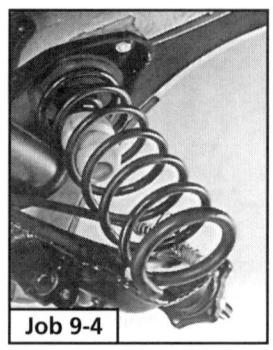

*Job 9-3*  *Job 9-4*

☐ **Step 3:** Use a trolley jack to lift the track control arm and compress the suspension, then undo the bolts (arrowed) and remove the shock absorber.

☐ **Step 4:** Slowly and carefully lower the jack so that the spring becomes fully decompressed. Remove the spring by pulling the lower end out of the recess in the track control arm.

**Step 5:** Inspect the coil spring to make sure there are no cracks or distortions that could adversely affect its operation and obtain a new one from your FIAT dealer if necessary.

IMPORTANT NOTE:
● Coil springs are subdivided into two categories, identifiable by a stripe of either yellow or green paint. Springs of the same category must be fitted in pairs.
● If there are any problems with the shock absorber, replace it as a complete unit.

**Step 6:** Refit in reverse order.

## Job 10. Rear track control arm - removal and replacement.

**Step 1:** Familiarise yourself with the components of illustration *Job 9-1*.

**Step 2:** Slacken the rear wheel bolts, raise the rear of the car and support on axle stands under the body or the rigid axle. See *Chapter 1, Safety First!* Remove the rear wheels.

**Step 3:** Remove the bolts (**4**) and washers (**3**) and remove the shock absorber (**2**) and spring. See illustration *Job 9-1, parts 2* and *3*.

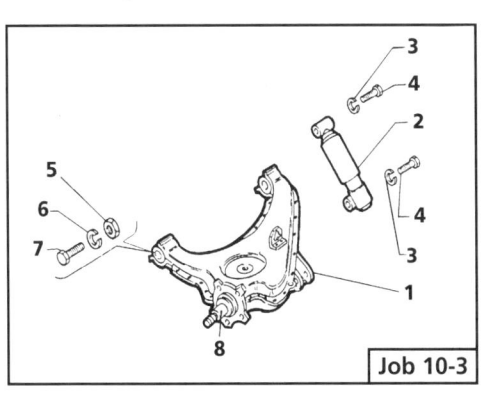

**Step 4:** Disconnect the brake pipe from its mounting on the track control arm, and disconnect the handbrake cable from the brake back plate.

**Step 5:** Remove the axle bush bolts washers and nuts (see illustration *Job 10-3, parts 5, 6* and *7*) which connect the track control arm (*part 1*) to the rigid axle. Remove the track control arm and wheel hub from the vehicle. The illustration shows the track control arm separated from the hub, i.e. with the axle stub (*part 8*) bare.

**Step 6:** Inspect the track control arm as follows:
● Make sure there are no cracks or distortions.
● Check that the flexible bushes are intact and have not gone soft.
● If necessary, separate the track control arm from the wheel hub and inspect the axle stub. See *Job 11*.

If necessary, replace the complete track control arm.

**Step 7:** Refit in the reverse order. Tighten the axle bush bolts to the specified torque (see *Chapter 3, Facts and Figures*) only when the car is back on its wheels with the equivalent of four occupants and 40 kg of luggage on board. (If not accessible, this will have to be done on a garage ramp.)

## Job 11. Rear wheel bearings - replacement.

IMPORTANT NOTE: FIAT hub bearings have a long service life because they are factory built into the hub. The bearing races cannot be replaced separately.

**Step 1:** With the road wheels on the ground, lever off the hub centre grease cap from the centre of the brake drum at the appropriate rear wheel, then lift the staking on the hub nut (as far as possible - see *Job 8*) and slacken it, but leave the nut in place for the time being.

### SAFETY FIRST!
● Do not attempt to slacken the hub nut while the car is on a jack or on axle stands.
● This requires an enormous force to be tightened or released (see *Chapter 3, Facts and Figures*) and there is a risk of pulling the car off its supports.

**Step 2:** Slacken the wheel bolts, raise the front of the car and support on axle stands, then remove the wheel. See *Chapter 1, Safety First!*

**Step 3:** Remove the brake drum.

**Step 4:** Remove the previously slackened hub nut and the thrust washer from beneath it.

**Step 5A:** Pull the hub from the stub axle, using a slide hammer, shown here connected to FIAT special tool number 1847017004. Alternatively, use a two or three-leg puller.

**Step 5B:** If the bearing pulls apart, leaving the inner race on the stub axle, it should be removed using a suitable puller.

*i* INSIDE INFORMATION: In rare, extreme cases, the inner race just won't budge! Try pouring boiling water over it, then try again. DON'T heat with a flame. In the worst possible case, the inner race can be cut off with a cutting wheel on an angle grinder. *i*

**CHAPTER 6 PART G: BRAKES**

❏ **Step 6:** Inspect the axle stub. If it is worn you will need to replace the complete track control arm. See **Job 10**.

❏ **Step 7:** Lightly grease the axle stub, then tap on the new hub assembly (complete with ready-assembled bearing) using a tubular drift in contact with the wheel bearing inner track.

Job 11-7

IMPORTANT NOTE: The bearing is 'sealed for life' and needs no additional grease.

❏ **Step 8:** Refit the hub nut washer, and fit a NEW hub nut. Tighten it while rotating the hub flange, but not to torque.

**SAFETY FIRST!**

• Do not tighten the hub nut to its correct torque until the wheel is in place and the car is on the ground.

❏ **Step 9:** Refit the remaining components in the reverse order (referring also to **PART G: BRAKES**). Lower the car and tighten the wheel bolts.

❏ **Step 10:** Tighten the hub nut to the specified torque (see **Chapter 3, Facts and Figures**). Stake the nut locking collar into the slot in the stub axle, using a drift. See **Job 8**. Replace the hub centre grease cap.

## PART G: BRAKES

### PART G: Contents
Job 1. Understanding Cinquecento brakes.
Job 2. Front brake pads - replacement.
Job 3. Front brake caliper - replacement.
Job 4. Front brake disc - replacement.
Job 5. Rear brake shoes - replacement.
Job 6. Rear wheel cylinder - replacement.
Job 7. Master cylinder and pressure regulators - replacement.
Job 8. Servo - check, remove and refit.
Job 9. Flexible hoses - replacement.
Job 10. Metal pipes - replacement.
Job 11. Brake bleeding.
Job 12. Handbrake cable - replacement.

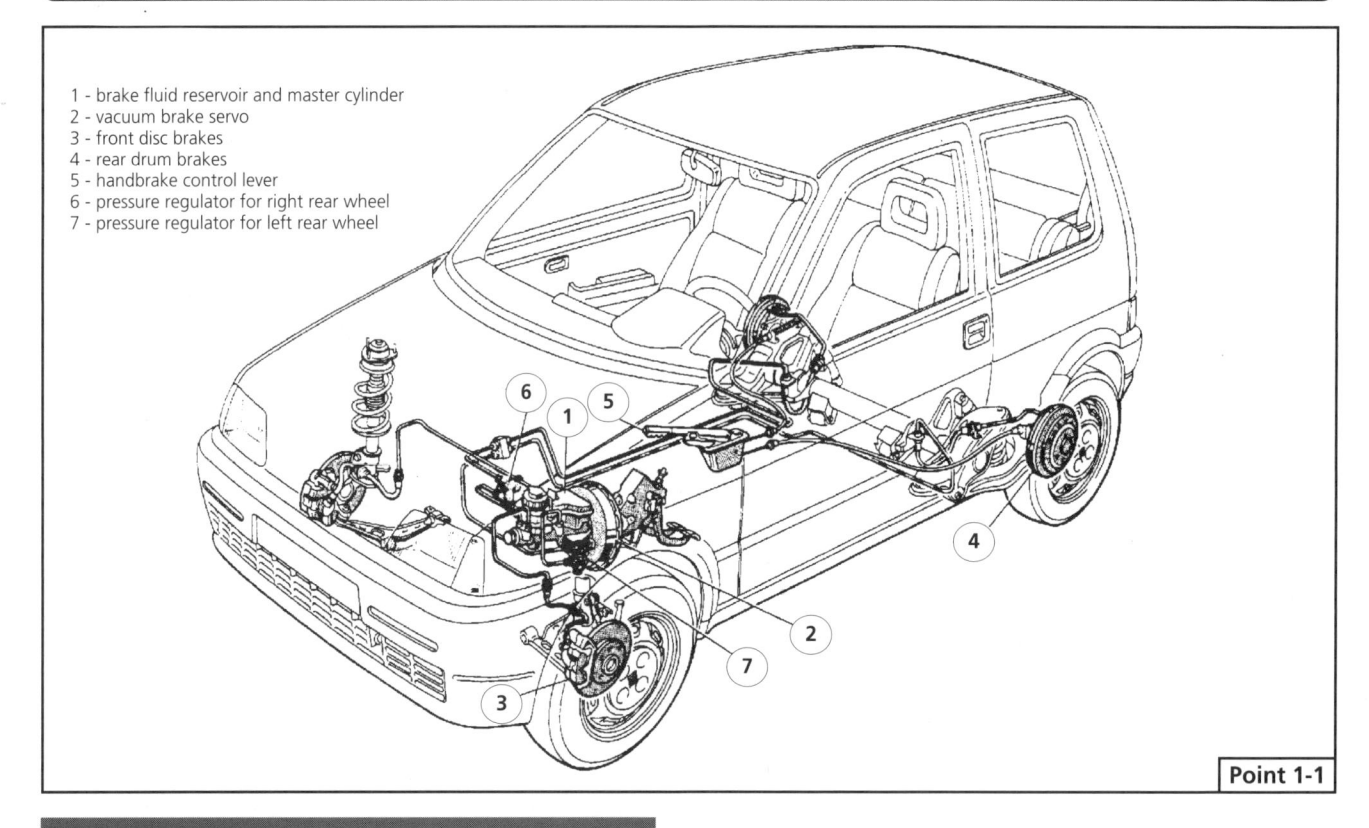

1 - brake fluid reservoir and master cylinder
2 - vacuum brake servo
3 - front disc brakes
4 - rear drum brakes
5 - handbrake control lever
6 - pressure regulator for right rear wheel
7 - pressure regulator for left rear wheel

Point 1-1

### Job 1. Understanding Cinquecento brakes.

❏ **Point 1:** This is the layout of the standard model braking system. Obviously, the brake pedal is on the other side on right-hand drive cars. The hydraulic system is split into two separate sets of pipes:

• left front and right rear brakes

• right front and left rear brakes

• if there is a loss of fluid from one part of the system, emergency braking should be available from other parts.

6-52

## Job 2. Front brake pads - replacement.

Checking and replacing the front brake pads is part of regular servicing. See **Chapter 5, Servicing Your Car, Job 40**.

## Job 3. Front bake caliper - replacement.

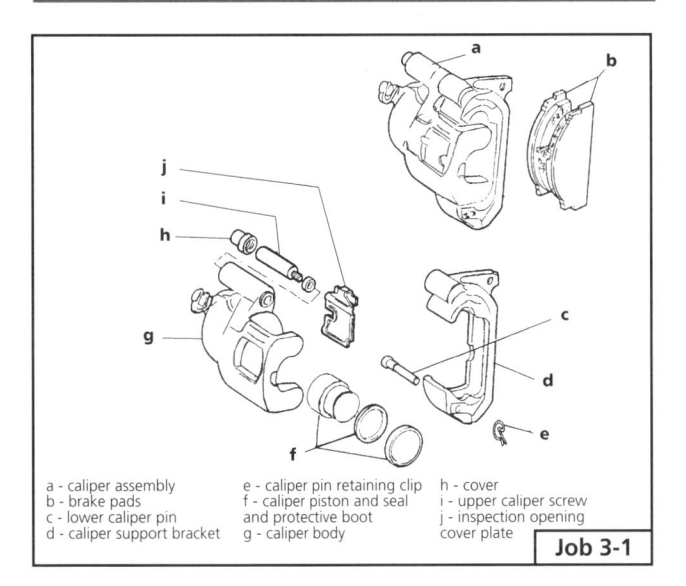

a - caliper assembly
b - brake pads
c - lower caliper pin
d - caliper support bracket
e - caliper pin retaining clip
f - caliper piston and seal and protective boot
g - caliper body
h - cover
i - upper caliper screw
j - inspection opening cover plate

Job 3-1

❏ **Step 1:** These are the front brake caliper components.

❏ **Step 2:** Slacken the front wheel bolts, raise the front of the car and support on axle stands. See **Chapter 1, Safety First!** Remove the front wheels.

❏ **Step 3:** Remove the clip and pin (see illustration **Job 3-1, parts c** and **e**) at the bottom of the brake caliper, and remove the brake pads. Also, see **Chapter 5, Servicing Your Car, Job 40**.

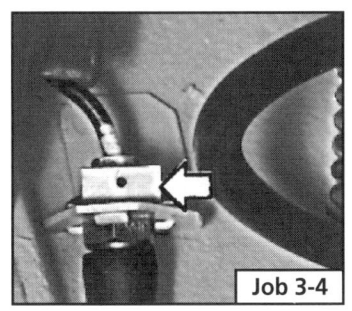

Job 3-4   Job 3-5

❏ **Step 4:** Disconnect the flexible brake hose from the metal hose, where they meet on the wheel arch bracket. Disconnect the flexible brake hose from its bracket on the suspension strut.

❏ **Step 5:** Remove the cover, and then the screw (see illustration **Job 3-1, parts h** and **i**) from the top of the brake caliper, then remove the caliper from its support bracket (**part d**). Also, remove the cover (see illustration **Job 4-1, parts 3** and **6**).

❏ **Step 6:** Check the piston seals (see illustration **Job 3-1, parts f**) for cracking, splitting or leaks, and both the piston and bore for signs of corrosion or sticking. If in doubt, replace the caliper with a new unit. We do NOT recommend the overhaul of an old unit, for safety reasons.

❏ **Step 7:** Check the flexible brake hose for signs of cracking, perishing or chafing against other components. If there is any damage, replace the hoses on both sides of the vehicle.

❏ **Step 8:** Fit the new caliper in reverse order, replacing the cover, and bleed the brakes. See **Job 11**.

❏ **Step 9:** Refit the wheels, lower the car to the ground, and tighten the wheel bolts.

## Job 4. Front brake disc - replacement.

❏ **Step 1:** Refer to the parts shown here and to the relevant parts of the dismantling sequence in **Job 3**, but leave the caliper attached to its carrier.

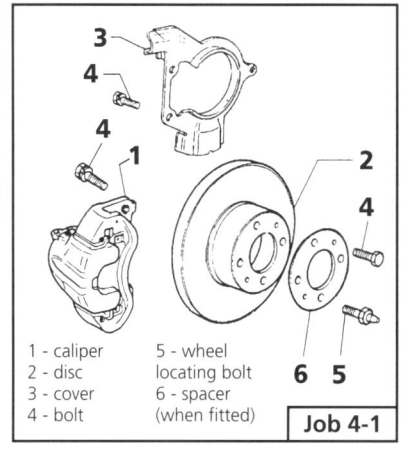

1 - caliper
2 - disc
3 - cover
4 - bolt
5 - wheel locating bolt
6 - spacer (when fitted)

Job 4-1

❏ **Step 2:** Slacken the front wheel bolts, raise the front of the car and support on axle stands. See **Chapter 1, Safety First!** Remove the front wheels.

❏ **Step 3:** Remove the clip and pin at the bottom of the brake caliper, and remove the brake pads. See **Chapter 5, Servicing Your Car, Job 40**.

❏ **Step 4:** Knock back the locktabs (where fitted) and undo the bolts connecting the caliper support bracket to the hub carrier.

Job 4-4

❏ **Step 5:** Remove the brake caliper assembly and hang it on a suitable support inside the wheel arch to avoid damaging the flexible hose.

Job 4-5

*making it easy* • Hang the caliper from one of the upper spring coils with a piece of bent wire.

**CHAPTER 6 PART G: BRAKES**

6-53

☐ **Step 6:** Remove the bolts connecting the disc to the wheel hub.

*Job 4-6*

☐ **Step 7:** Remove the disc from the hub, and the spacer if there is one.

☐ **Step 8:** Thoroughly clean the disc mating face on the hub drive flange, and its counterpart on the disc, then reassemble in reverse order. Degrease the disc surfaces with alcohol before fitting the brake pads.

*Job 4-7*

## Job 5. Rear brake shoes - replacement.

*i* INSIDE INFORMATION! When the lining thickness is down to a minimum of 1.5 mm, replace the shoes as a complete axle set. *i*

*making it easy* / • Before removing the shoes, mark them F(ront) and R(ear) respectively, so that you can compare old and new shoes and ensure refitting in the correct positions.
• Complete work on one side at a time so that you have always got the other side as a visual guide.

☐ **Step 1:** Jack up the rear of the car and support on stands.

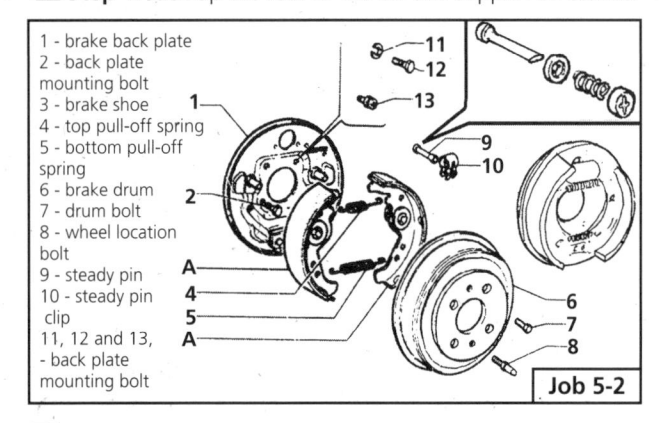

1 - brake back plate
2 - back plate mounting bolt
3 - brake shoe
4 - top pull-off spring
5 - bottom pull-off spring
6 - brake drum
7 - drum bolt
8 - wheel location bolt
9 - steady pin
10 - steady pin clip
11, 12 and 13, - back plate mounting bolt

*Job 5-2*

☐ **Step 2:** Unscrew the drum securing bolts (**7** and **8**) and remove the drum (**6**).

*making it easy* / If the drum sticks try the following:
• Disconnect the handbrake cable from beneath the car.
• Tap carefully around the drum with a hide mallet to help loosen it.

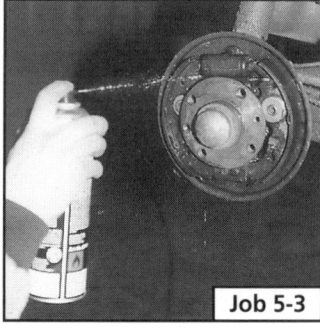

☐ **Step 3:** Wash the brake dust away with a proprietary brand of spray-on brake cleaner, taking care not to inhale any brake dust.

☐ **Step 4:** *i* INSIDE INFORMATION: Either fit the correct special tool now or, as soon as the shoes are removed, wrap strong wire around the wheel cylinders, to prevent the pistons from 'popping' out which they otherwise will! *i*

*Job 5-3*

*Job 5-5*   *Job 5-6*

☐ **Step 5:** Undo the shoe steady pin by levering off the clip. (see illustration **Job 5-2, part 10**)...

☐ **Step 6:** ...and removing the pin through the rear of the backplate.

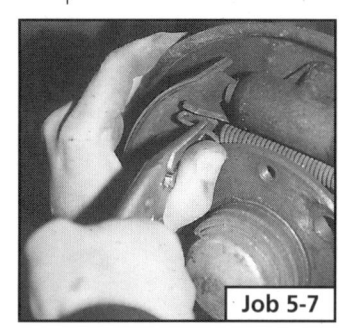

*Job 5-7*   *Job 5-8*

☐ **Step 7:** Use self-locking grips to hold the top spring while you disengage it.

☐ **Step 8:** Use larger grips to unhook the bottom of the shoe - to take the pressure off the spring - and remove the spring.

*Job 5-9*   *Job 5-10*

☐ **Step 9:** You now have to turn the cut-outs on the hub flange (arrowed) so that the auto-adjusters clear the flange as the shoes are removed.

☐ **Step 10:** *i* INSIDE INFORMATION: While the shoes are off, check the wheel cylinder for leaks - peel back each rubber shroud - and push the pistons to-and-fro to make

6-54

sure that they move freely. Replace them if any problems are found. See **Job 6**. *i*

☐ **Step 11:** When reassembling, put a smear of lithium-based brake grease (not ordinary grease!) on all the working contact surfaces including those shown on the backplate, except the wheel cylinder piston ends.

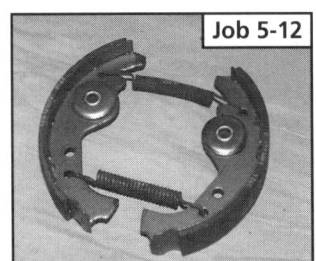

☐ **Step 12:** Ensure that the springs are in the correct positions.

☐ **Step 13:** Do not forget to refit the shoe retaining pins and securing clips.

*Job 5-12*

*making it easy!* ☐ **Step 14:** • Compare with the other side for correct assembly.
• Repeat the whole operation on the second side using your first one as a guide if necessary.

☐ **Step 15:** Centralise and align the shoes by tapping them towards the centre of the hub with a soft mallet. This moves them against the pressure of the self adjuster springs.

☐ **Step 16:** Clean the dust from the drums and check their condition. Use a piece of fine emery cloth to de-grease them. Refit the brake drums and securing bolts.

☐ **Step 17:** Pump the brake pedal vigorously, several times to bring the linings into contact with the drums. Refit the road wheels and lower the car to the ground. Check the wheel bolts for tightness.

## Job 6. Rear wheel cylinder - replacement.

☐ **Step 1:** Remove the brake shoes. See **Job 5**.

☐ **Step 2:** Disconnect the brake pipe from the back of the wheel cylinder (**a**) and seal the pipe end.

☐ **Step 3:** Undo the fixing bolts (see illustration **Job 6-2**, arrowed) and remove the wheel cylinder from the backplate.

*Job 6-2*

☐ **Step 4:** Fit the new cylinder to the backplate and connect the brake pipe. We strongly recommend that you do not attempt to overhaul a seized, leaking or damaged wheel cylinder. Replace it with a new unit from your FIAT dealer.

☐ **Step 5:** Refit the brake shoes, drum and road wheel.

☐ **Step 6:** Bleed the brake hydraulics. See **Job 11**.

## Job 7. Master cylinder and pressure regulators - replacement.

*i* INSIDE INFORMATION:
• Pressure regulators are fitted in the pipes connecting the master cylinder to the rear brake control cylinders.
• They prevent the rear wheels locking during emergency stops when the car's weight shifts to the front wheels.
• Two pressure regulators are required because a crossover braking system is used. *i*

☐ **Step 1:** Familiarise yourself with the master cylinder and regulator assembly.
• The master cylinder and the two pressure regulators are mounted on a bracket attached to the brake servo unit.
• The brake fluid reservoir is mounted immediately above the master cylinder
• See also illustration **Job 1-1**.

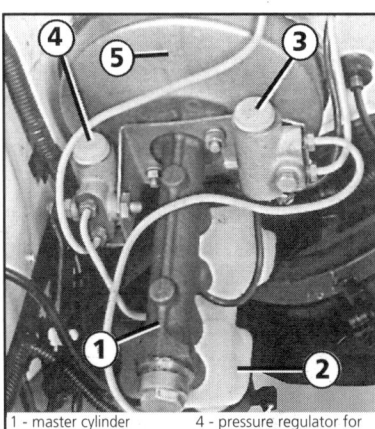

1 - master cylinder
2 - fluid reservoir
3 - pressure regulator for right rear wheel
4 - pressure regulator for left rear wheel
5 - vacuum brake servo unit
*Job 7-1*

☐ **Step 2:** Raise the bonnet and protect the wings from brake fluid spillage.

☐ **Step 3:** Disconnect the electrical leads from the reservoir cap, then remove the cap and level float.

☐ **Step 4:** Remove the brake fluid reservoir from the master cylinder by pulling it upwards.

☐ **Step 5:** Unscrew the pipe unions from the master cylinder and the two pressure regulators.

☐ **Step 6:** Undo the two nuts connecting the mounting bracket to the servo unit and remove the cylinder assembly.

☐ **Step 7:** Separate the master cylinder and pressure regulators from the mounting bracket and replace with new units as required.

☐ **Step 8:** Refit in reverse order ensuring sound connections of the fluid pipe unions.

☐ **Step 9:** Bleed the brake hydraulics. See **Job 11**.

## Job 8. Servo - check, remove and refit.

*i* INSIDE INFORMATION: • Before condemning the servo for lack of efficiency, check the condition of the one-way valve and vacuum pipe connecting it to the inlet manifold.
• Ease the valve out of the front of the servo and disconnect the pipe from the inlet manifold.
• Check that you can only blow one way through the valve - from the servo end towards the inlet manifold.

**CHAPTER 6 PART G: BRAKES**

**6-55**

- The vacuum pipe can suffer failure in many ways. Age can harden it until it cracks, causing an air leak which sometimes results in a whistling noise and rough slow-running.
- Loose connections could also produce the same result.
- The other type of vacuum hose failure is an implosion - where the hose is sucked flat by the vacuum - often because oil has softened the hose.
- This is not so easily detected, as it rarely upsets the engine performance and resumes its normal shape shortly after the engine is stopped.
- The inner lining can also deteriorate, causing a blockage. *i*

For location of the servo unit, see illustration **Job 1-1**.

☐ **Step 1:** Remove the master cylinder. See **Job 7**.

☐ **Step 2:** From inside the car, disconnect the servo pushrod (arrowed) from the pedal by removing the split pin or circlip securing it to the pedal peg.

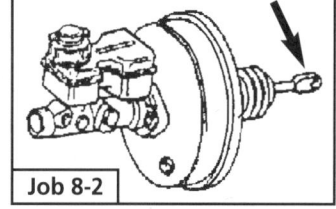

Job 8-2

☐ **Step 3:** Undo the four servo mounting nuts and washers

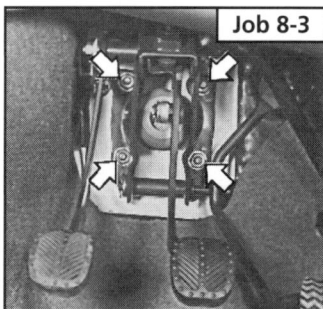

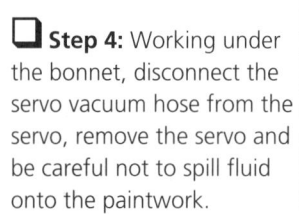

Job 8-3

☐ **Step 4:** Working under the bonnet, disconnect the servo vacuum hose from the servo, remove the servo and be careful not to spill fluid onto the paintwork.

☐ **Step 5:** Measure the projection of the servo piston pushrod (arrowed). With the master cylinder fitted there should be a clearance of between 0.825 and 1.025mm between the primary piston face and the end of the pushrod. Use the mating surfaces of the master cylinder and servo as the reference point.

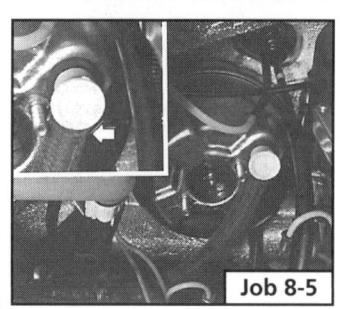

Job 8-5

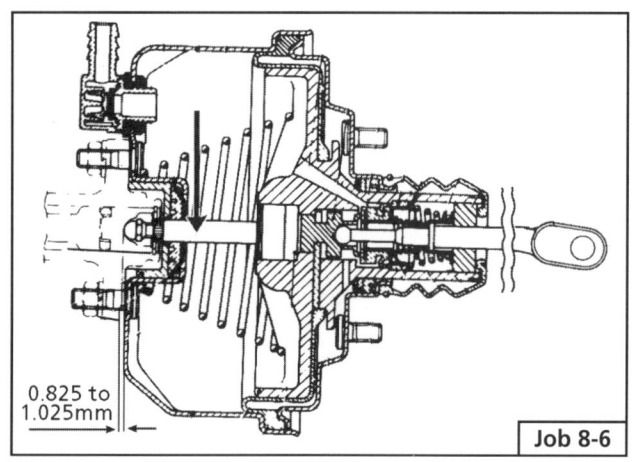

0.825 to 1.025mm

Job 8-6

☐ **Step 6:** Turn the adjusting screw on the servo as necessary and apply locking fluid to the thread when finished.

☐ **Step 7:** Complete reassembly in the reverse order and bleed the brake hydraulics. See **Job 11**.

## Job 9. Flexible hoses - replacement.

*i* INSIDE INFORMATION: When disconnecting brake pipes or hoses, it is essential to minimise brake fluid loss. This can be done by unscrewing the master cylinder reservoir cap, laying a sheet of plastic across the opening, and refitting the cap. This will prevent atmospheric pressure from pushing the fluid out of opened lines. *i*

☐ **Step 1:** Undo the rigid pipe union (**a**) connecting to the hose where hose and pipe join at the support bracket. Take care not to damage the bracket or tear it off the body.

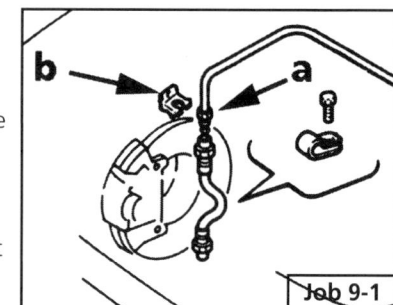

Job 9-1

☐ **Step 2:** Pull out the clip (see illustration **Job 9-1, part b**) which secures the hose to the bracket, then unscrew the hose union at its other end.

*making it easy*
- If the pipe starts to twist with the union, grip the pipe as lightly as possible, and see if you can stop it from turning.
- If not, cut through the pipe with a junior hacksaw and replace the length of rigid pipe.

☐ **Step 3:** Fit the new hose in reverse order, making sure that the hose is not twisted when refitting the rigid pipe.

☐ **Step 4:** Check that the hose cannot chafe anywhere over the whole range of steering and suspension movement.

☐ **Step 5:** Bleed the brake hydraulics. See **Job 11**.

## Job 10. Metal pipes - replacement.

*i* INSIDE INFORMATION: When disconnecting brake pipes or hoses, it is essential to minimise brake fluid loss. This can be done by unscrewing the master cylinder reservoir cap, laying a sheet of plastic across the opening, and refitting the cap. This will prevent atmospheric pressure from pushing the fluid out of opened lines. A pipe spanner makes the job *much* easier! *i*

☐ **Step 1:** Undo the unions at each end of a pipe length. Patience is often required because of the union seizing both in its threads and on the pipe. See **Making it Easy!** after **Job 9, Step 2**. Use penetrating oil to help free seized unions, and use a split-ring spanner rather than an open-ended one, to reduce the risk of rounding off the union nuts.

☐ **Step 2:** Detach the pipe length from its securing clips and remove it.

*making it easy!* ☐ **Step 3:** Where possible, use the old pipe as a pattern to shape the new one prior to fitting.

☐ **Step 4:** Follow the original route and secure the pipe in the body clips.

☐ **Step 5:** Connect the unions and bleed the brake hydraulics. See **Job 11**.

## Job 11. Brake bleeding.

**FACT FILE: BRAKE BLEEDING SEQUENCE**
When any part of the brake hydraulic system has been opened, causing loss of fluid, you need to bleed the complete system, either clockwise starting from the bleed nipple behind the right front wheel, or anti-clockwise starting from the left front bleed nipple. The two sequences are:

| EITHER, Clockwise: | OR, Anti-Clockwise: |
|---|---|
| right front | left front |
| right rear | left rear |
| left rear | right rear |
| left front | right front |

Go round the sequence at least twice.

The engine needs to be running while bleeding the brakes to operate the vacuum brake servo unit.

☐ **Step 1:** Start the engine and leave it ticking over in neutral.

**SAFETY FIRST!**

• Carry out this operation in the open air or in a well-ventilated area to avoid breathing dangerous exhaust fumes.
• You will need an assistant, working within the car, to help you bleed the brakes. Make sure your assistant does not touch the gearstick while the engine is running.

☐ **Step 2:** Push a tight fitting length of plastic or rubber tubing onto the first bleed screw and immerse the other end in a small quantity of brake fluid in a glass jar so that no air can be accidentally pulled up the tube.

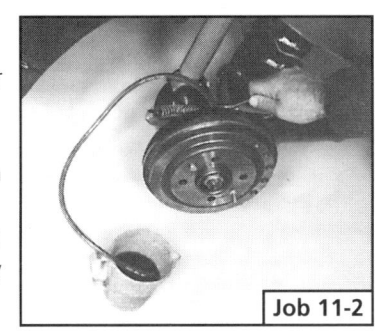

**Job 11-2**

☐ **Step 3:** Undo the bleed screw by half a turn. Have your assistant push the brake pedal to the floor and hold it there while you lock up the bleed screw. Then release the pedal slowly. Repeat several times, with the following suggested dialogue:

YOU. *(Open bleed screw)* "Open!" *(called out loud)*
HELPER. *(Pushes pedal down)* "Down!"
YOU. *(Close bleed screw)* "Closed!"
HELPER. *(Lets pedal up)* "Up!" - repeated, as necessary.

**IMPORTANT NOTE:** Take great care not to let the master cylinder run out of brake fluid. Otherwise you will introduce fresh air into the system and have to start again. Use ONLY fresh brake fluid from a previously unopened container.

☐ **Step 4:** Top up the fluid reservoir frequently while repeating the bleeding operation until all air is expelled from the brake line (no bubbles appear in the tube or jar).

☐ **Step 5:** Bleed each remaining brake in the same way, going round the sequence at least twice.

**SAFETY FIRST!**

• After completing the bleeding operation, and with your helper's foot firmly on the brake pedal, check all connections for leaks.
• Remember to top up the fluid, replace the master cylinder cap and reconnect the wires to it.

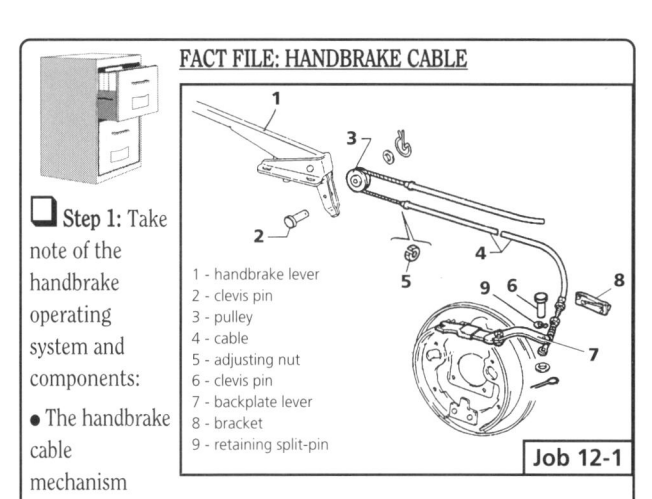

## Job 12. Handbrake cable - replacement.

**FACT FILE: HANDBRAKE CABLE**

☐ **Step 1:** Take note of the handbrake operating system and components:

1 - handbrake lever
2 - clevis pin
3 - pulley
4 - cable
5 - adjusting nut
6 - clevis pin
7 - backplate lever
8 - bracket
9 - retaining split-pin

**Job 12-1**

• The handbrake cable mechanism consists of a single cable that does a U-turn round a pulley under the handbrake lever and operates both of the rear brakes. See illustration *Job 12-1*.

• The handbrake is adjusted from an adjusting nut underneath the car. See illustration *Job 12-1, part 5*.

• If the handbrake won't hold even though it is properly adjusted, check the rear brake mechanism for seizure or for oil or fluid contamination or severe wear of the brake shoes.

**CHAPTER 6 PART G: BRAKES**

6-57

☐ **Step 2:** Chock the front wheels at front and rear, raise the rear of the car and support on axle stands. See **Chapter 1, Safety First!**

☐ **Step 3:** From under the floor, remove the cover that contains the handbrake pulley mechanism. Remove the clevis pin and pulley. See illustration **Job 12-1, parts 2** and **3**.

☐ **Step 4:** Undo the adjuster nut and remove the cable from the bodywork.

Job 12-4

☐ **Step 5:** Working at each brake backplate in turn, straighten out the retaining split-pin (**a**), remove the clevis (**b**) from the handbrake mechanism lever, then pull back the spring around the cable end to free the cable from its bracket on the suspension strut. See illustration **Job 12-1, parts 6, 7** and **9**.

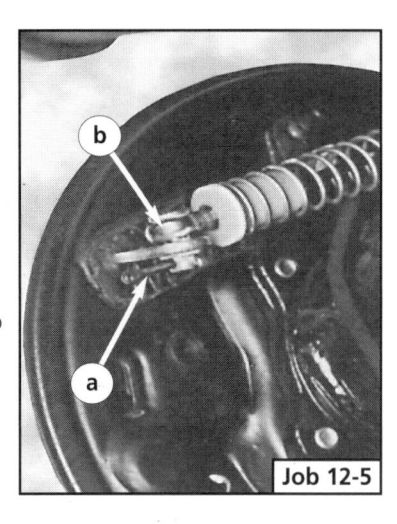

Job 12-5

Job 12-6

☐ **Step 6:** The handbrake shoe-control lever can only be removed with the brake shoes detached. See **Job 5**.

☐ **Step 7:** Disconnect the cable from all other fittings on the bodywork.

☐ **Step 8:** Refit in reverse order, using new split pins. In addition:
• renew the clevis pins and the backplate lever if wear is apparent
• lubricate the cables and ensure that inners move smoothly in the outer cable
• lubricate both clevis pins
• always use new split-pins
• lubricate the backplate lever pivot (keep grease away from braking surfaces)
• clean and lubricate the pulley (see illustration **Job 12-1, part 3**).

## PART H: BODY AND INTERIOR

### PART H: Contents
Job 1. Bonnet - removal, refitting and adjustment.
Job 2. Bonnet release - adjustment and removal.
Job 3. Tailgate - removal, refitting and adjustment.
Job 4. Tailgate release - adjustment and removal.
Job 5. Front bumper - removal and refitting.
Job 6. Rear bumper - removal and refitting.
Job 7. Door trim removal and refitting.
Job 8. Door glass & window mechanism - removal and refitting.
Job 9. Door lock/handle - removal and refitting.
Job 10. Door mirror - replacement.
Job 11. Door - removal and refitting.
Job 12. Seat - removal and refitting.
Job 13. Front wing - replacement.

### Job 1. Bonnet - removal, refitting and adjustment.

☐ **Step 1:** Using the prop, support the bonnet in the open position.

☐ **Step 2:** Undo the fixing buttons from the sound-insulation lining and detach the windscreen washer tube (arrowed) from the bonnet.

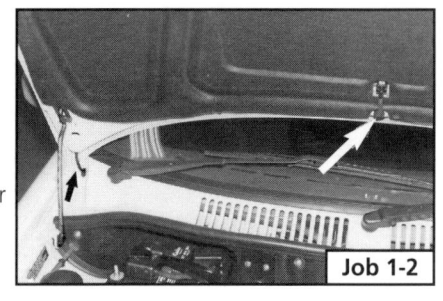

Job 1-2

☐ **Step 3:** Use a felt pen or masking tape to mark out the hinge positions, then get a helper to support the bonnet while you undo the four hinge bolts (two at each side). Lift the bonnet clear.

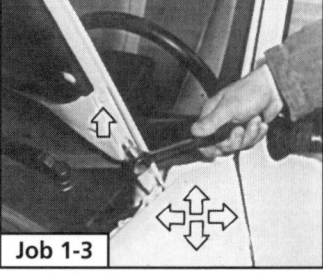

Job 1-3

IMPORTANT NOTE: The arrows show the movements available for adjustment of the bonnet lid when refitting.

☐ **Step 4:** Refit in the reverse order but tighten the bolts just enough to position the bonnet, then lower it carefully and check for an equal gap between wings and bonnet, and for proper alignment of its leading edge. Make any minor adjustments and when you are satisfied, fully tighten the hinge bolts to the correct torque. See **Chapter 3, Facts and Figures**.

*making it easy* / ☐ **Step 5:** When you and your assistant replace the bonnet, place a piece of cloth under each back corner so that it doesn't damage your car's bodywork.

IMPORTANT NOTE: Removing and replacing the bonnet might affect the adjustment of the release mechanism. See **Job 2**.

## Job 2. Bonnet release - adjustment and removal.

☐ **Step 1:** Open the bonnet and adjust the position of the bonnet release mechanism using the two nuts (**1**).

☐ **Step 2A:** Adjust the height of the bonnet, where it closes at the front, by raising or lowering the rubber buffers at the left and right of the front bodywork.

☐ **Step 2B:** The rubber buffers have a series of ridges on the pegs which fit into the bodywork. Select the appropriate position.

*making it easy* / • Lubricate the buffer with washing up liquid.
• Each one is an extremely tight fit!

☐ **Step 3:** To remove the release mechanism, undo the adjusting nuts and the cable nut and bolt. See illustration **Job 2-1, parts 1** and **2**.

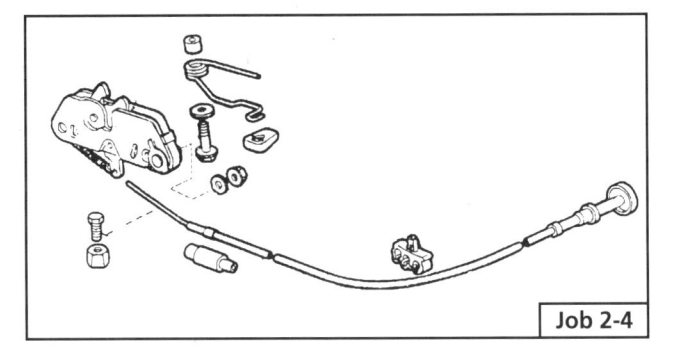

☐ **Step 4:** To remove the cable, release it from its mounting bracket (illustration **Job 2-1, part 3**), then detach the bonnet release cable from its fittings under the dashboard. Detach it from any other fittings and pull it out from inside the car.

☐ **Step 5:** To remove the safety catch from the front of the bonnet, push a screwdriver into the slot under the button and remove the button from the spring. Then undo the bolt (arrowed) and remove the spring.

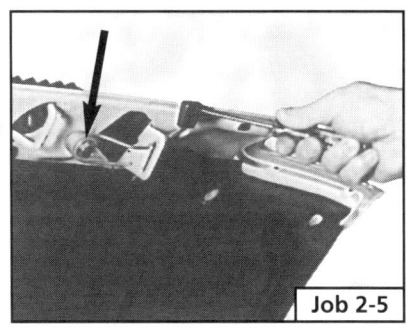

☐ **Step 6:** Refit in reverse order of removal, and re-adjust.

**SAFETY FIRST!**

• Do not drive the car unless both the bonnet release and safety catch systems are fitted and working properly.

## Job 3. Tailgate - removal, refitting and adjustment.

☐ **Step 1:** The tailgate fits to the bodywork via a pair of top-mounted hinges and is held aloft with hydraulic struts.

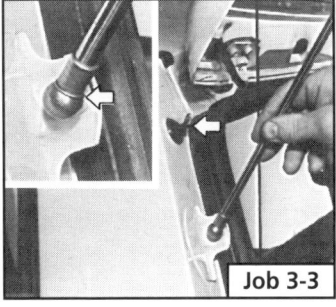

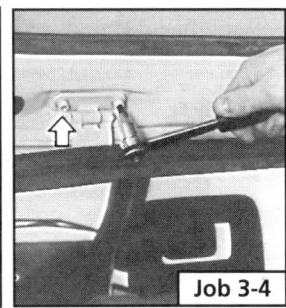

☐ **Step 2:** Disconnect the battery negative earth lead.

☐ **Step 3:** Raise the tailgate and ask an assistant to support its weight. Remove the retaining ring and disconnect the supporting shock absorbers from the lower anchorages (see inset). Disconnect the window washer pipe, shown by the arrow in the main illustration.

*making it easy* / • Use a felt pen to draw round the hinge plates so you can refit them later at exactly the same position.

☐ **Step 4:** Remove the hinge bolts and carefully lift away the tailgate.

*making it easy* / ☐ **Step 5:** When you and your assistant replace the tailgate, place a piece of cloth under each top corner so that it doesn't damage your car's bodywork.

☐ **Step 6:** Refit all components in the reverse order, making sure that the tailgate sits correctly and that its release latch works correctly.

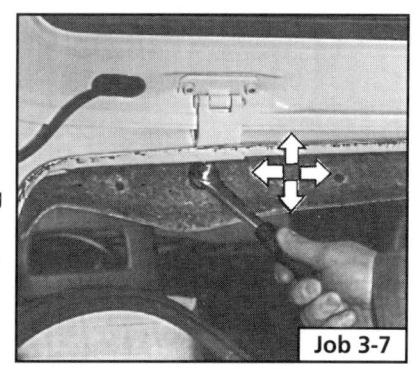

☐ **Step 7:** If the tailgate needs to be adjusted, remove the upper part of the trim, lower the rear part of the roof lining and loosen the bolt connecting the hinge to the roof. Do the same on both sides, then adjust the tailgate position in the direction shown by the arrows. When the position is correct, tighten the bolts to the correct torque. See **Chapter 3, Facts and Figures**.

## Job 4. Tailgate release - adjustment and removal.

☐ **Step 1:** Note the tailgate closing devices:
- striker plate (**a**)
- tailgate door latch (**b**)
- anti-vibration device (**c**)

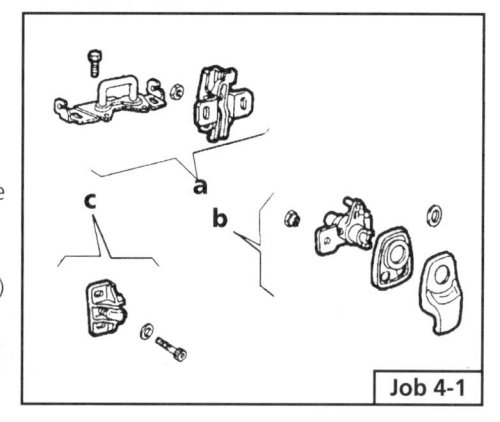

ℹ **INSIDE INFORMATION:** Don't loosen and try to adjust both the latch and striker at the same time! Do them one at a time, leaving the other one tightly fixed in place. ℹ

☐ **Step 2:** Open the tailgate, loosen the two bolts and adjust the tailgate door latch in the direction shown by the arrows. When the position is correct, tighten the bolts.

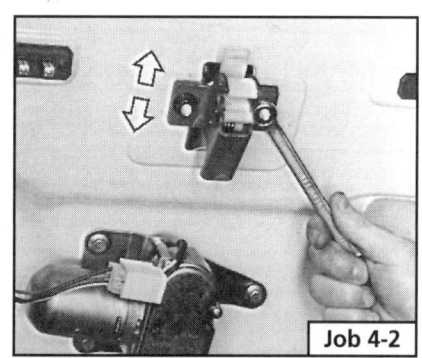

☐ **Step 3:** Loosen the two bolts and adjust the lock striker in the direction shown by the arrows. When the position is correct, tighten the bolts to the correct torque. See **Chapter 3, Facts and Figures**.

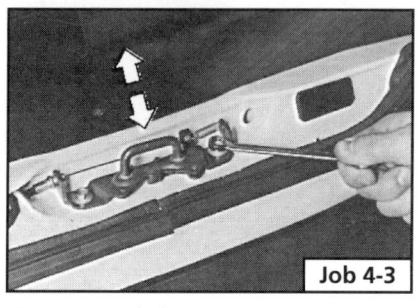

☐ **Step 4:** To adjust the closure position, raise or lower the rubber buffers at the left and right of the tailgate...

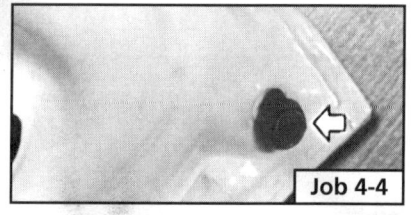

☐ **Step 5:** ...and adjust the anti-vibration device on the bodywork. Loosen the bolts, move the device in the direction of the arrows, then tighten the bolts again.

☐ **Step 6:** To remove the tailgate door latch, undo the two bolts. See illustration **Job 4-1, part b**. The lock comes out complete with the barrel.

☐ **Step 7:** To remove the tailgate lock striker, disconnect the cable from the lever, and the cable sheath from the bracket, then undo the two bolts. See illustration **Job 4-2**.

☐ **Step 8:** To remove the cable, peel back the carpet and undo the screws which secure the remote release handle to the floor between the driver's door and seat. Detach all other cable fittings and pull the cable out from inside the car.

☐ **Step 9:** Refit in reverse order of removal, and re-adjust.

## Job 5. Front bumper - removal and refitting.

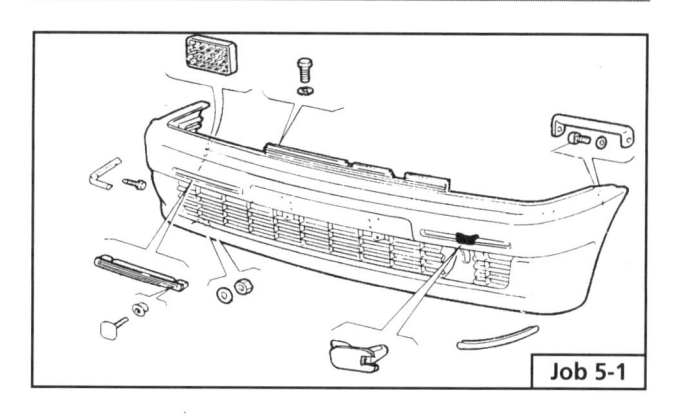

☐ **Step 1:** These are the front bumper components and mountings.

> *making it easy* • The front bumper is quite heavy and you will need a second person to help you remove it.

☐ **Step 2:** Separate the wheel arch liner from the bumper on the left side.

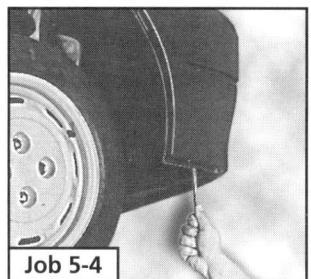

☐ **Step 3:** Undo the bolt (arrowed) fixing the radiator shield on the right side, then separate the wheel arch liner from the bumper.

☐ **Step 4:** Undo the lower side nut fixing the bumper to the bodyshell.

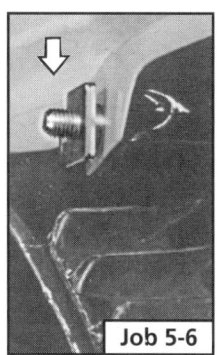

☐ **Step 5:** Undo the upper bolts (arrowed) and then remove the bumper.

☐ **Step 6:** Refit in reverse order, making sure the side fixing plates (arrowed) are correctly engaged in the guides in the bumper.

## Job 6. Rear bumper - removal and refitting.

☐ **Step 1:** These are the rear bumper components, fixings and support brackets.

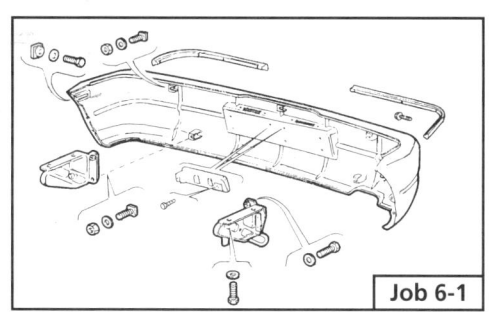

*making it easy* ● *The rear bumper is quite heavy and you will need a second person to help you remove it.*

☐ **Step 2:** Undo the two lower nuts (arrowed), one on each side of the bumper.

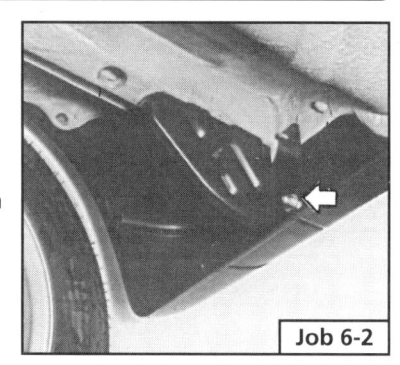

☐ **Step 3:** Raise the cover in the luggage compartment. Undo the upper nuts (arrowed) fixing the bumper to the bodyshell.

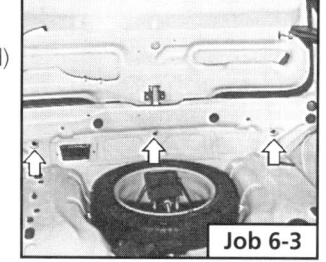

☐ **Step 4:** Remove the bumper from the vehicle and disconnect the electrical connectors from the number plate lights.

☐ **Step 5:** Refit in reverse order, making sure the side fixing plates are correctly engaged in the guides in the bumper. See illustration **Job 5-6**.

## Job 7. Door trim - removal and refitting.

☐ **Step 1:** These are the trim components and fixings.

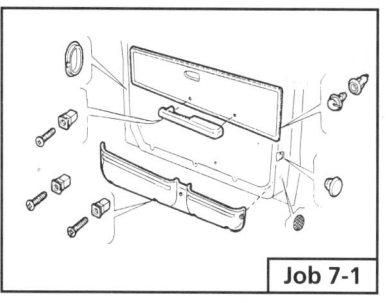

IMPORTANT NOTE: For cars with manually operated window winders you will first have to remove the winder handle. See illustration **Job 8-B3-A**. Push inwards on the trim to compress the ring (*part 5*), and with a piece of thin wire, hook out the clip (*part 6*). The winder handle (*part 7*) will now slide off.

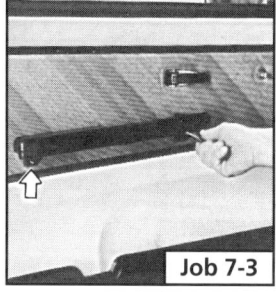

☐ **Step 2:** Undo the bolt and remove the door lever trim.

NOTE: The window winder pin for the window winder, shown in this illustration, does not exist on models which have electric windows.

☐ **Step 3:** Undo the screws and remove the door-pull handle.

☐ **Step 4:** Remove the door trim panel by levering it off its studs with a suitable flat blade. Take care not to over-force the studs and rip them out of the trim panel.

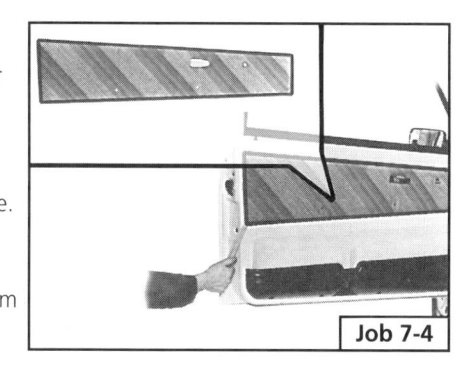

CHAPTER 6 PART H: BODY AND INTERIOR

6-61

☐ **Step 5:** Undo the screws (arrowed) and remove the tidy bin.

☐ **Step 6:** Refit in reverse order.

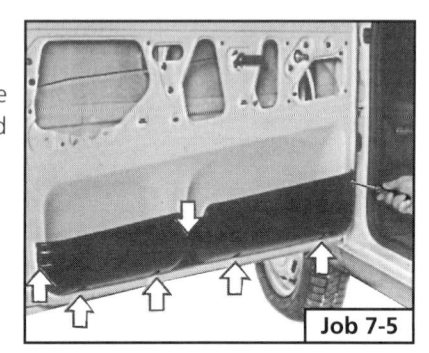

## Job 8. Door glass & window mechanism - removal & refitting.

☐ **Step 1:** Disconnect the battery negative (earth/ground) lead.

☐ **Step 2:** Remove the door trim panel and tidy bin see *Job 7*.

IMPORTANT NOTE: For cars with manually operated window winders you will first have to remove the winder handle. See illustration *Job 8-B3-A*. Push inwards on the trim to compress the ring (*part 5*), and with a piece of thin wire, hook out the clip (*part 6*). The winder handle (*part 7*) will now slide off.

### PART A: DOOR GLASS REMOVAL

☐ **Step A1:** Remove the screws (arrowed)...

☐ **Step A2:** ...and remove the front window guide.

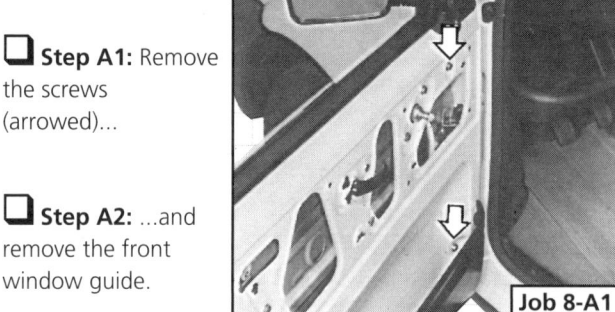

☐ **Step A3:** With the window lowered, detach the inner and outer window glass trims. Here, the FIAT special tool is shown being used, but it is possible to manage without it.

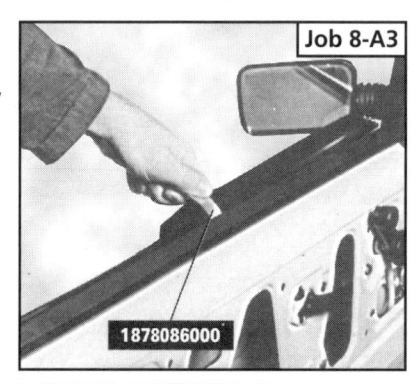

☐ **Step A4:** Remove the rubber trim from the door frame. Temporarily fit the window winder mechanism and position the glass so that the screws (arrowed) can be reached through the aperture shown. Remove the screws and separate the window glass from the window opening device.

☐ **Step A5:** Rotate the glass to the angle shown and slide it upwards and out of the door frame.

### PART B: WINDOW WINDER MECHANISM REMOVAL

☐ **Step B1:** Remove the trim as described in *Job 7*.

☐ **Step B2:** Remove the door glass as described in *PART A*.

It is now a simple job of disconnecting and removing the window winder (regulator) mechanism.

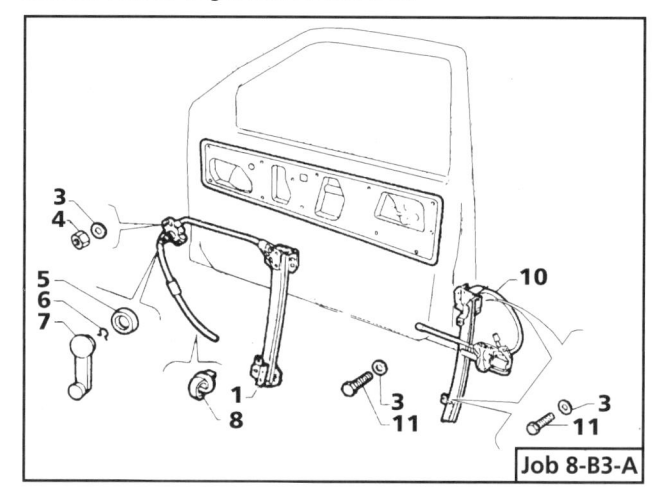

☐ **Step B3-A: MANUALLY OPERATED WINDOWS:** Take out the screws (**11**) and nuts (**4**) holding the mechanism in place and unclip the outer cable from the clip fitted to the door (**8**). The entire mechanism (**1**) can now be lifted away.

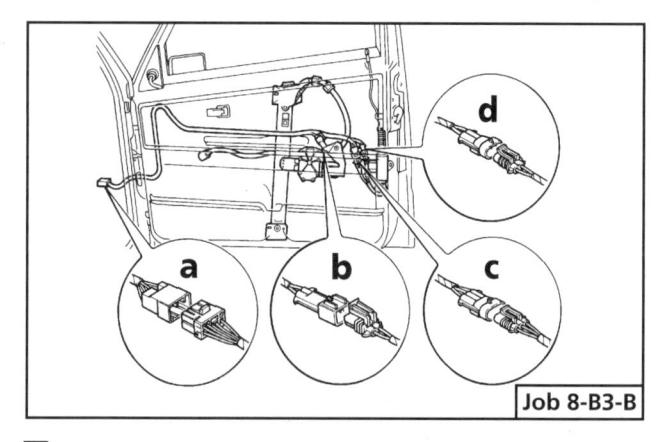

☐ **Step B3-B: ELECTRICALLY OPERATED WINDOWS:** Disconnect the sockets (**b, c** and **d**) adjacent to the window winder motor. Leave the socket (**a**) in place, along with the wiring loom, unless the door is to be removed. Remove the fixing screws (see illustration *Job B-3A, part 11*) and lift away the complete assembly (*part 10*).

6-62

# Job 9. Door lock/handle - removal and refitting.

## PART A: EXTERIOR HANDLE AND LOCK

**Step A1:** The exterior door handle and lock can be removed without removing the door trim panel. Undo the screw and pull the assembly away from the door, then detach the rod from the pin (arrowed - see inset).

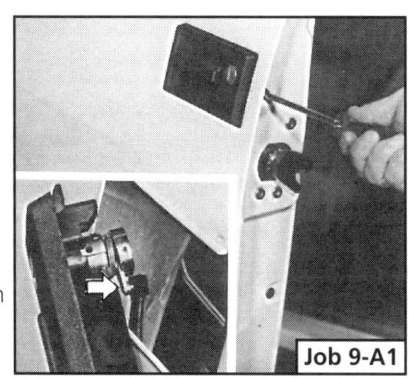

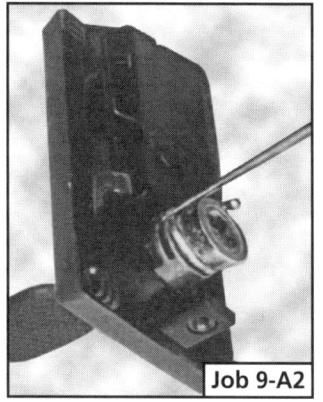

*Job 9-A1*

*Job 9-A2*

*Job 9-A3*

**Step A2:** To remove the barrel:
- insert the key in the lock
- extract the retaining ring, as shown.

**Step A3:** Press on the barrel retaining the tab and withdraw it.

## PART B: INNER LATCHING MECHANISM

**Step B1:** To detach the inner mechanism, you first need to remove the door trim panel and tidy bin. See **Job 7**.

**Step B2:** These are the door lock/latch control levers.

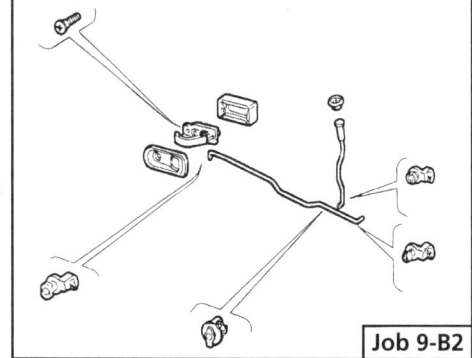

*Job 9-B2*

**Step B3:** Undo the screws fixing the rear window glass guide to the door...

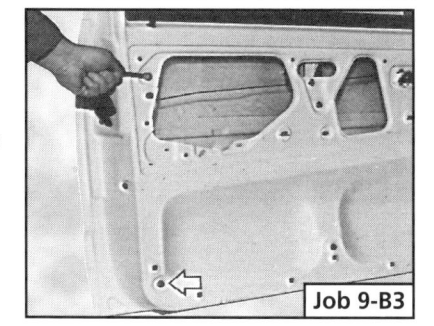

*Job 9-B3*

**Step B4:** ...and remove the guide.

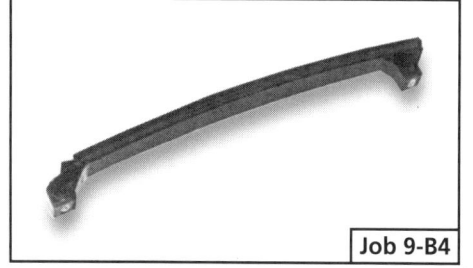

*Job 9-B4*

**Step B5:** Detach the door handle rods from inside the door (see *inset*), then undo the screws on the outer edge of the door...

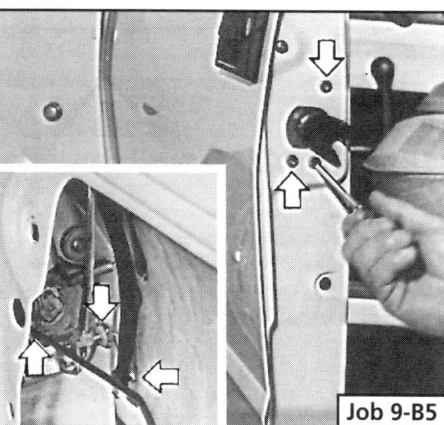

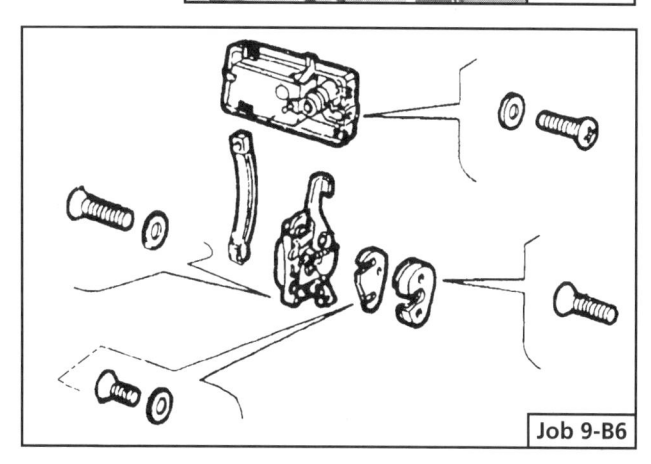

*Job 9-B5*

*Job 9-B6*

**Step B6:** ...and remove the latching mechanism from the door. These are the components of the door latch.

**Step B7:** Refit in reverse order.

## PART C: CENTRAL LOCKING MOTOR

**Step C1:** Disconnect the electrical supply connectors (**a**).

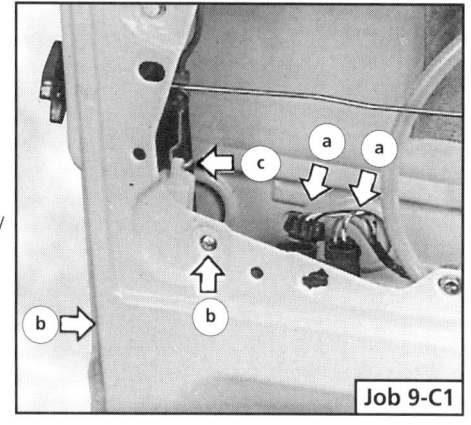

*Job 9-C1*

**Step C2:** Remove the fixing screws (see illustration **Job 9-C1, parts b**) and unhook the operating rod (**part c**). Remove the motor.

**CHAPTER 6 PART H: BODY AND INTERIOR**

6-63

CHAPTER 6 PART H: BODY AND INTERIOR

## Job 10. Door mirror - replacement.

☐ **Step 1:** Lower the window and support the mirror from the outside while undoing the fixings (arrowed) on the trim.

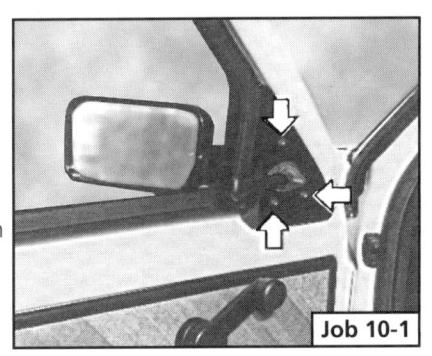

Job 10-1

☐ **Step 2:** The same fixings hold both the trim and mirror in place. Remove the mirror and trim together.

Job 10-2

☐ **Step 3:** Refit in reverse order.

## Job 11. Door - removal and refitting.

☐ **Step 1:** Disconnect the battery negative earth lead.

☐ **Step 2:** Remove the door trim panel. See **Job 7**.

☐ **Step 3:** Disconnect the electrical connectors from the central locking mechanism and electric window winder motor (when fitted), then pull the cables completely out of the door, from the hole near the door hinge.

☐ **Step 4:** Remove the pin (**a**) from the door check strap (**b**), located between the two hinges.

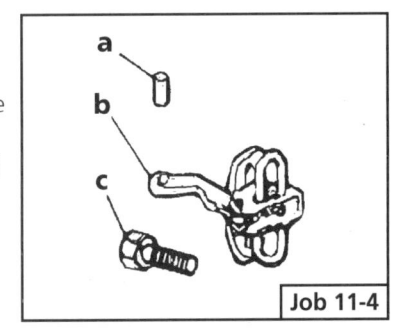

Job 11-4

☐ **Step 5:** With an assistant helping you to support the door, remove the bolts (arrowed) fixing the hinge pins, then lift up the door until the tapered pins can be extracted from their seats. Remove the door from the vehicle.

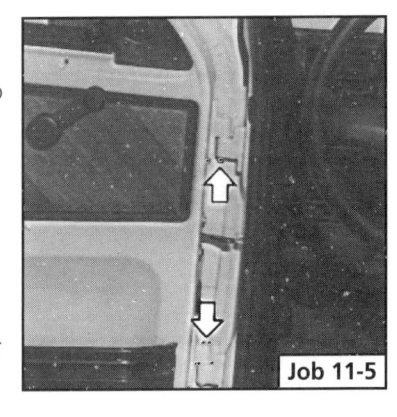

Job 11-5

☐ **Step 6:** Refit in reverse order and tighten the hinge pin bolts to the correct torque of 49 Nm.

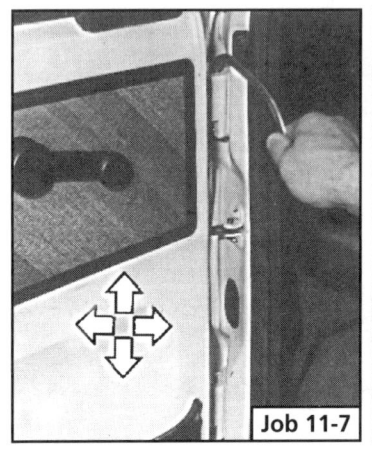

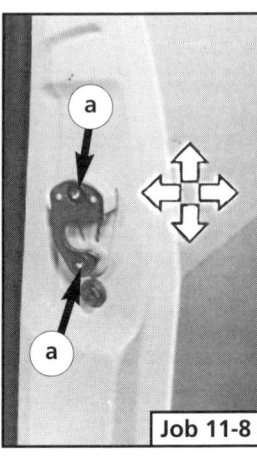

Job 11-7

Job 11-8

☐ **Step 7:**
To adjust the position of the door:
• loosen the bolts fixing the hinges to the bodyshell;
• adjust the position of the door; the arrows show the movement allowed;
• fully tighten the bolts fixing the hinges to the bodyshell - see **Step 6**.

☐ **Step 8:** To adjust the position of the door lock striker, slacken the screws (**a**). The larger arrows show the possible movement for the adjustment.

## Job 12. Seat - removal/replacement.

**PART A: FRONT SEATS**

Some Cinquecentos have an optional driver's air bag and front seat belt pre-tensioners. They are NOT suitable for owner servicing and MUST be attended to by a FIAT dealer.

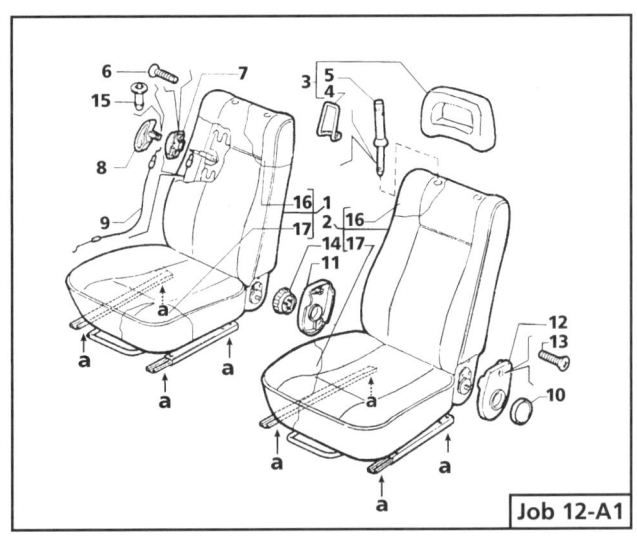

Job 12-A1

☐ **Step A1:** Each front seat is held down with four bolts screwed through the seat guides to the bodyshell.

☐ **Step A2:** The backrest adjustment knob (see illustration **Job 12-A1, part 14**) is a push fit and can be levered off (carefully) with a screwdriver. The lower covers (**parts 11** and **12**) are held on with crosshead screws (**part 13**).

6-64

❑ **Step A3:** IMPORTANT NOTE: On many cars the headrests are not easily removed and it is necessary to get underneath the upholstery to release the retaining clips. To remove the easy-to-remove type of headrests, rotate the headrest supports (see illustration *Job 12-A1, part 5*) through 90 degrees to release them from the seat frame. With the headrests removed from the seat, rotate the supports through 90 degrees to release them from the headrest, if necessary.

❑ **Step A4:** Replacing the seats into the car is the reversal of the fitting procedure but check that:
• the seat mountings in the floor are in good condition
• the threads are clear so that the bolts will screw right down
• insert all four bolts loosely before tightening any of them.

**PART B: REAR SEAT REMOVAL**

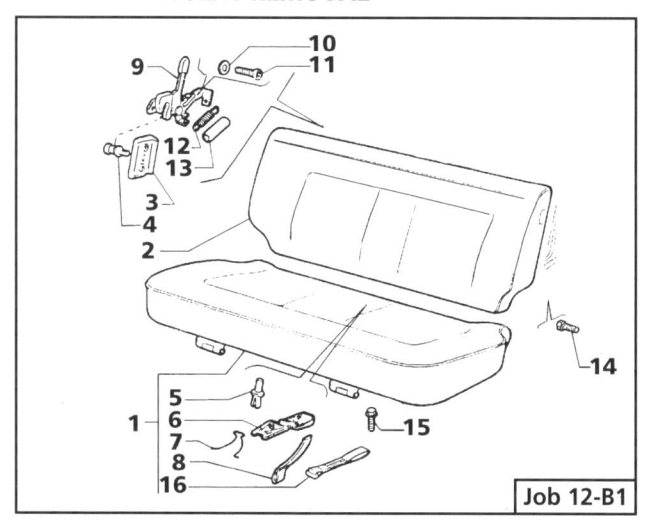

Job 12-B1

❑ **Step B1:** To remove the rear seat base, tip it forwards and take out the screws holding the hinges to the floor.

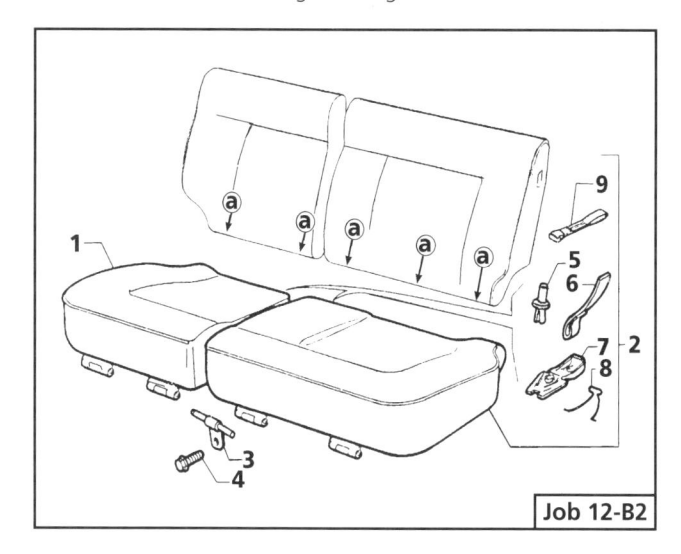

Job 12-B2

❑ **Step B2:** Split rear seats (non-UK cars) are the same, except that there are twice as many hinge fittings.

❑ **Step B3:** To remove the backrest, tip the backrest forwards, and remove the fixing screws from the positions (shown in illustration *Job 12-B2, positions a*).

## Job 13. Front wing - replacement.

❑ **Step 1:** Release the six screws holding the wing to the inner panel.

Job 13-1

❑ **Step 2:** Carefully lever the wing flanges away from the adhesive sealant around the entire perimeter in contact with the bodyshell.

Job 13-2

❑ **Step 3:** Clean all of the old sealant from the bodyshell.

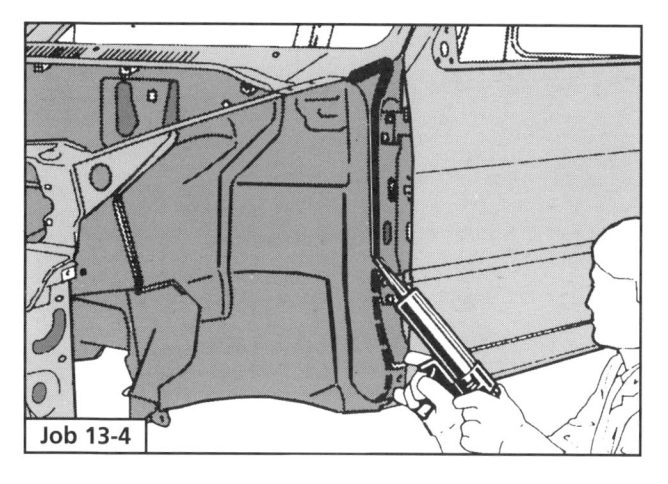

Job 13-4

❑ **Step 4:** Before fitting the new wing, apply fresh sealant, using a suitable sealant medium available from your FIAT dealer or automotive body parts specialist.

❑ **Step 5:** IMPORTANT NOTE: Fit the new wing but before tightening the screws and before the sealant becomes hard, check the gaps against the position of the closed bonnet and the door and ensure that:
• gaps are constant and even all the way along
• neither the bonnet nor the door rubs on the wing as each of them is opened
• check with a straight edge that the wing is on the same level as the door
• note that the height of the bonnet can be adjusted - see *Job 1*
• the position of the door can be adjusted - see *Job 11*.

# CHAPTER 7
# WIRING DIAGRAMS

**IMPORTANT NOTE:** Not all of the components listed here are fitted to all models.

**KEY:**

|  |  |
|---|---|
| 1 | Left front light cluster |
| 2 | NANOPLEX electronic ignition control unit |
| 2A | DIGIPLEX 2S electronic ignition control unit |
| 2B | M.I.W. electronic injection control unit (903cc) |
| 2B | Electronic fuel injection control unit (1108cc Sporting) |
| 3 | Left front engine compartment earth |
| 4 | Engine cooling fan |
| 5 | Engine cooling fan thermal switch |
| 6 | Engine coolant temperature sender unit |
| 9 | Switch signalling insufficient engine oil pressure |
| 10 | Switch for moving NANOPLEX DIGIPLEX 2S ignition curves |
| 11 | Horn |
| 12 | Starter motor |
| 13 | Spark plug |
| 13A | Spark plug |
| 14 | Spark plug |
| 14A | Spark plug |
| 15 | Alternator with built in regulator |
| 16 | Ignition coil |
| 16A | Ignition coil (for 903cc only) |
| 17 | Right front engine compartment earth |
| 18 | Electric windscreen washer pump |
| 19 | Right front light cluster |
| 20 | Left front side direction indicator |
| 21 | Fuse carrier and relay control box: |
| A | Heated rear windscreen relay |
| B | Ignition discharge relay (903cc) |
| B | Horn relay (1108cc Sporting) |
| C | Direction indicators and hazard warning lights flasher unit |
| E | Relay for exterior lights and engine cooling |
| 22 | Windscreen wiper motor |
| 23 | Insufficient brake fluid level sensor |
| 24 | Car interior heater fan |
| 25 | Battery |
| 26 | Battery earth |
| 27 | Right front side direction indicator |
| 28 | Left front speaker |
| 29 | Connection between front and rear cables |
| 30 | Connection between front and rear cables |
| 31 | Connection for courtesy light |
| 32 | Connection between front and rear cables |
| 33 | Earth on passenger side strut (903cc) |
| 33 | Earth on steering wheel (1108cc Sporting) |
| 34 | Instrument panel |
| A | Insufficient engine oil pressure warning light |
| B | Battery recharging warning light |
| C | Hazard warning lights warning light |
| D | Dipped headlights warning light |
| E | Main beam headlights warning light |
| F | Handbrake and insufficient brake fluid level warning light |
| G | Fuel reserve warning light |
| H | Choke warning light |
| I | Fuel level gauge |
| L | Instrument panel light bulbs |
| M | Heated rear windscreen warning light |
| N | Rear fog lights warning light |
| O | Direction indicators warning light |
| P | Water temperature gauge |
| Q | Electronic injection failure warning light (903cc) |
| Q | Fuel injection fault warning light (1108cc Sporting) |
| R | Rev. counter |
| 35 | Connection between front cables and heater cable |
| 36 | Ignition switch |
| 37 | Heater controls light bulb |
| 37A | Heater controls light bulb |
| 38 | Steering column switch unit |
| A | External lights switch (903cc) |
| A | Main beam/dipped beam headlights switch (1108cc Sporting) |
| B | Windscreen wash/wipe - rearscreen wash/wipe control switch |
| C | Direction indicators switch |
| D | Horn button |
| E | Windscreen washer button |
| F | Flasher button |
| 39 | Choke switch |
| 40 | External lights switch |
| 41 | Brake lights switch |
| 42 | Rear fog lights switch |
| 43 | Hazard warning lights switch |
| 44 | Courtesy light bulb |
| 45 | Switch signalling handbrake applied |
| 46 | Push button for courtesy light on front left pillar |
| 47 | Push button for courtesy light on front right pillar |
| 48 | Heater fan control switch |
| 48A | Additional resistor |
| 49 | Cigar lighter |
| 50 | Radio |
| 51 | Heated rear windscreen switch |
| 52 | Right front speaker |
| 53 | Reversing lights switch |
| 54 | Fuel level gauge |
| 55 | Left rear light cluster |
| 56 | Left rear earth |
| 57 | Left number plate light |
| 58 | Right number plate light |
| 59 | Heated rear windscreen |
| 59A | Contact for heated rear windscreen (903cc) |
| 59A | Boot contact assembly (1108cc Sporting) |
| 59B | Boot contact assembly (1108cc Sporting) |
| 60 | Right rear earth |
| 61 | Right rear light cluster |
| 62 | Rearscreen washer switch |
| 63 | Rearscreen wiper switch |
| 64 | Digital clock |
| 65 | Electric pump for rearscreen washer |
| 66 | Rearscreen wiper motor |
| 100 | Wiring for ignition or injection cable |
| 102 | Connection between fuel injection cable and electric fuel pump supply cable |
| 103 | Electric petrol pump |
| 106 | Relay for electric windows and central locking |
| 107 | 15A fuse for central locking circuit |
| 108 | Central locking control unit |
| 109 | Connection for dashboard cable, driver's side |
| 110 | Connection for dashboard cable, passenger side |
| 111 | Dashboard connection, passenger side |
| 114 | Switch for left electric window |
| 115 | Switch for right electric window |
| 116 | 25A fuse for electric windows circuit |
| 118 | Left electric windows ideogram light bulb |
| 120 | Headlight alignment and right electric windows ideogram light bulb |
| 121 | Left electric window motor |
| 122 | Left central locking geared motor |
| 123 | Right electric window motor |
| 124 | Right central locking geared motor |
| 125 | Contact for boot locking geared motor |
| 126 | Boot locking geared motor |
| 127 | DIM-DIP circuit additional resistor |
| 128 | DIM-DIP circuit remote control switch |
| 129 | 7.5A fuse for DIM-DIP circuit |
| 130 | Left rear light cluster (903cc only) |
| 131 | Right rear light cluster (903cc only) |
| 132 | Idle cut-out device |
| 133 | Connection between battery cable and injection cable (903cc S.P.I. only) |
| 134 | Connection between battery cable and front cable |
| 135 | Connection between front cable and dashboard cable |
| 136 | 5A fuse for injection system |
| 137 | Engine coolant temperature sender unit |
| 138 | Air temperature sender unit |
| 139 | Connection with AISAN cable |
| 140 | Receiver for central locking remote control adevice |
| 141 | Injector |
| 142 | Canister solenoid valve |
| 143 | Relay for electronic injection system |
| 144 | Absolute pressure sender unit |
| 145 | 20A fuse for electronic injection |
| 146 | Solenoid air valve (903cc) |
| 146 | RPM and TDC sensor (1108cc Sporting) |
| 147 | Lambda sensor |
| 148 | Electric fuel pump relay |
| 149 | Injection earth |
| 150 | Thermal switch on water thermostat |
| 151 | Connection with AISAN cable |
| 152 | NANOPLEX diagnostic socket |
| 152A | DIGIPLEX 2S diagnostic socket |
| 152B | Diagnostic socket |
| 153 | Sensor on pulley |
| 154 | Connector block |
| 155 | Connector block |
| 156 | Connector block |
| 157 | Connector block |
| 158 | Connector block |
| 159 | Connector block |
| 160 | Connector block |
| 161 | Throttle position sensor |
| 162 | Idle adjustment stepping actuator |
| 163 | Diagnostic socket |
| 171 | Lambda probe |
| 179 | Condenser cooling fan |
| 180 | Electromagnetic connection for switching on air conditioning compressor |
| 181 | Remote control switch for electromagnetic coupling |
| 182 | Electric fan remote control switch |
| 183 | Fuel injection cable/air conditioner cable connection |
| 184 | 3-stage pressure switch for air conditioner |
| 186 | 7.5A fuse for protecting electromagnetic coupling remote control switch |
| 187 | 25A fuse for protecting electric fan remote control switch |
| 188 | Air conditioner cable/compressor cable connection |
| 189 | Relay for switching on air conditioner switch |
| 190 | Anti-frost thermostat |
| 191 | Car interior air recirculation switch |
| 192 | Motor for controlling opening/closing of car interior air recirculation flap |
| 193 | Air condition fan |
| 194 | 25A fuse for protecting air conditioning system |
| 196 | Air conditioning switch |
| 197 | Switch controlling opening/closing of car interior air recirculation flap |
| 198 | Air conditioner controls illumination bulbs |
| 200 | Earth on control unit |
| 201 | Anti-theft device control unit |
| 202 | Inertial switch |
| 203 | Reverse cables connection |
| 204 | Earth on dashboard attachment |
| 205 | Diagnostic socket for anti-theft device |
| 206 | 15A fuse protecting anti-theft device |
| 207 | Switch on book for switching on anti-theft device |
| 208 | Anti-theft device warning light |
| 209 | Switch on bonnet for switching on anti-theft device |
| 210 | Connection with front cables |
| 211 | Ignition coils assembly |
| 212 | Ignition coils assembly |
| 213 | RPM and TDC sensor |
| 214 | Multiple relay |

Cable colour code:

| | | | |
|---|---|---|---|
| A | Light blue | M | Brown |
| B | White | N | Black |
| C | Orange | R | Red |
| G | Yellow | S | Pink |
| H | Grey | V | Green |
| L | Blue | Z | Violet |

Most wires have two colours, shown as, for example, CN, which means Orange and Black.

List of fuses in the fusebox 21:

| Fuse 1 | 15A | Fuse 9 | 10A |
| Fuse 2 | 15A | Fuse 10 | 7.5A |
| Fuse 3 | 25A | Fuse 11 | 7.5A |
| Fuse 4 | 10A | Fuse 12 | 7.5A |
| Fuse 5 | 10A | Fuse 13 | 7.5A |
| Fuse 6 | 10A | Fuse 14 | 20A |
| Fuse 7 | 15A | Fuse 15 | 15A |
| Fuse 8 | 10A | | |

# Relay and Fuse Box

## 1. LOCATION ON VEHICLE

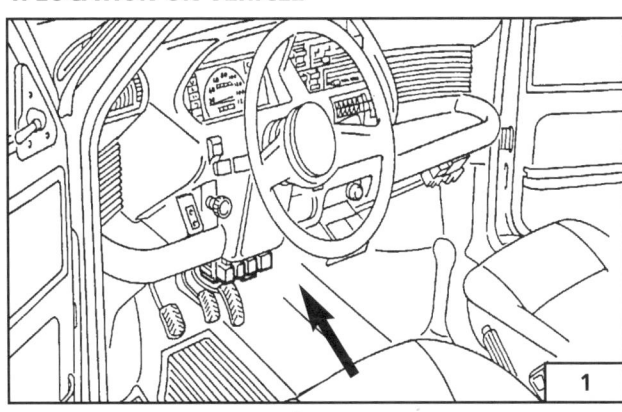

## 2. RELAY TYPES:
1 - relay for dipped headlights and radiator cooling fan
2 - heated rear windscreen relay
3 - horn relay
4 - intermittent device for direction indicators/hazard warning lights

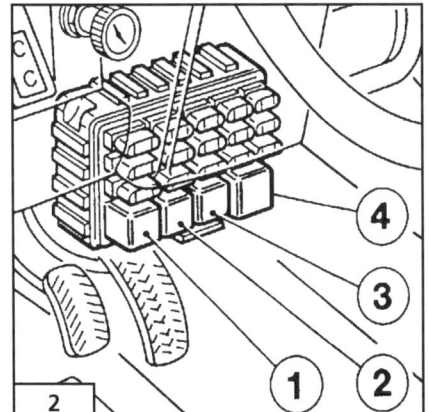

## 3. REMOVING-REFITTING RELAY AND FUSE BOX

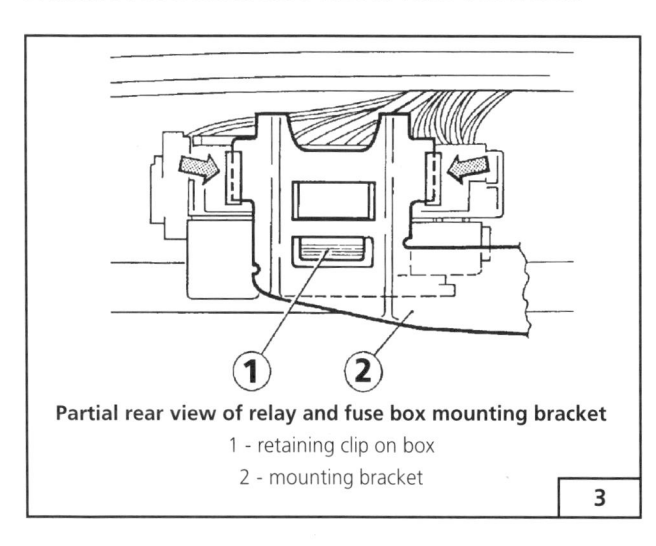

**Partial rear view of relay and fuse box mounting bracket**
1 - retaining clip on box
2 - mounting bracket

To remove the relay and fuse box, press on the retaining lip (**1**) and remove the box from the anchoring guides shown by the arrows.

## 4. FUSE TYPES AND REPLACEMENT

For information on fuse types and replacement, see **Chapter 5, pages 5-8 and 5-9**.

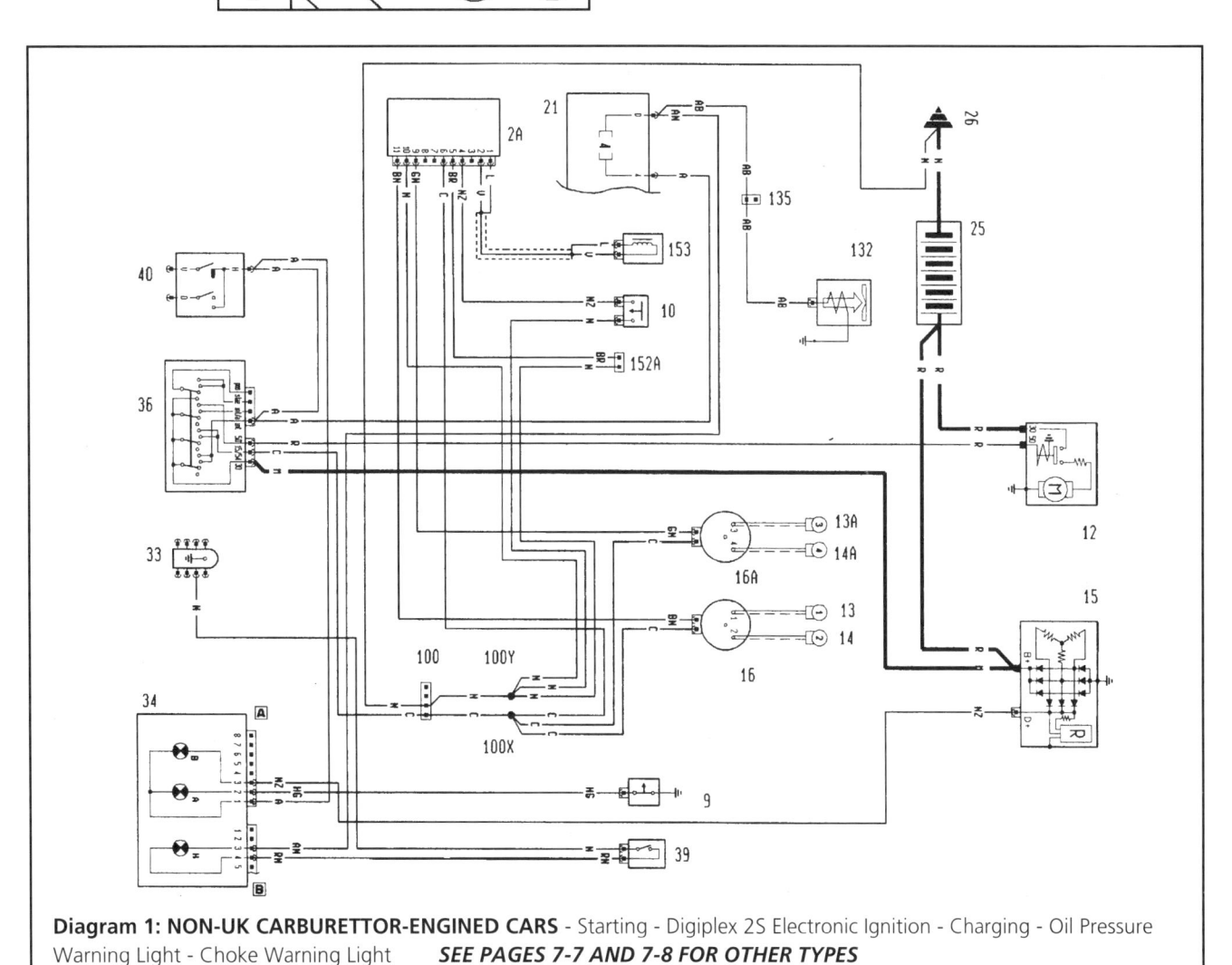

**Diagram 1: NON-UK CARBURETTOR-ENGINED CARS** - Starting - Digiplex 2S Electronic Ignition - Charging - Oil Pressure Warning Light - Choke Warning Light  *SEE PAGES 7-7 AND 7-8 FOR OTHER TYPES*

**CHAPTER 7 WIRING DIAGRAMS**

7-2

# CHAPTER 7 WIRING DIAGRAMS

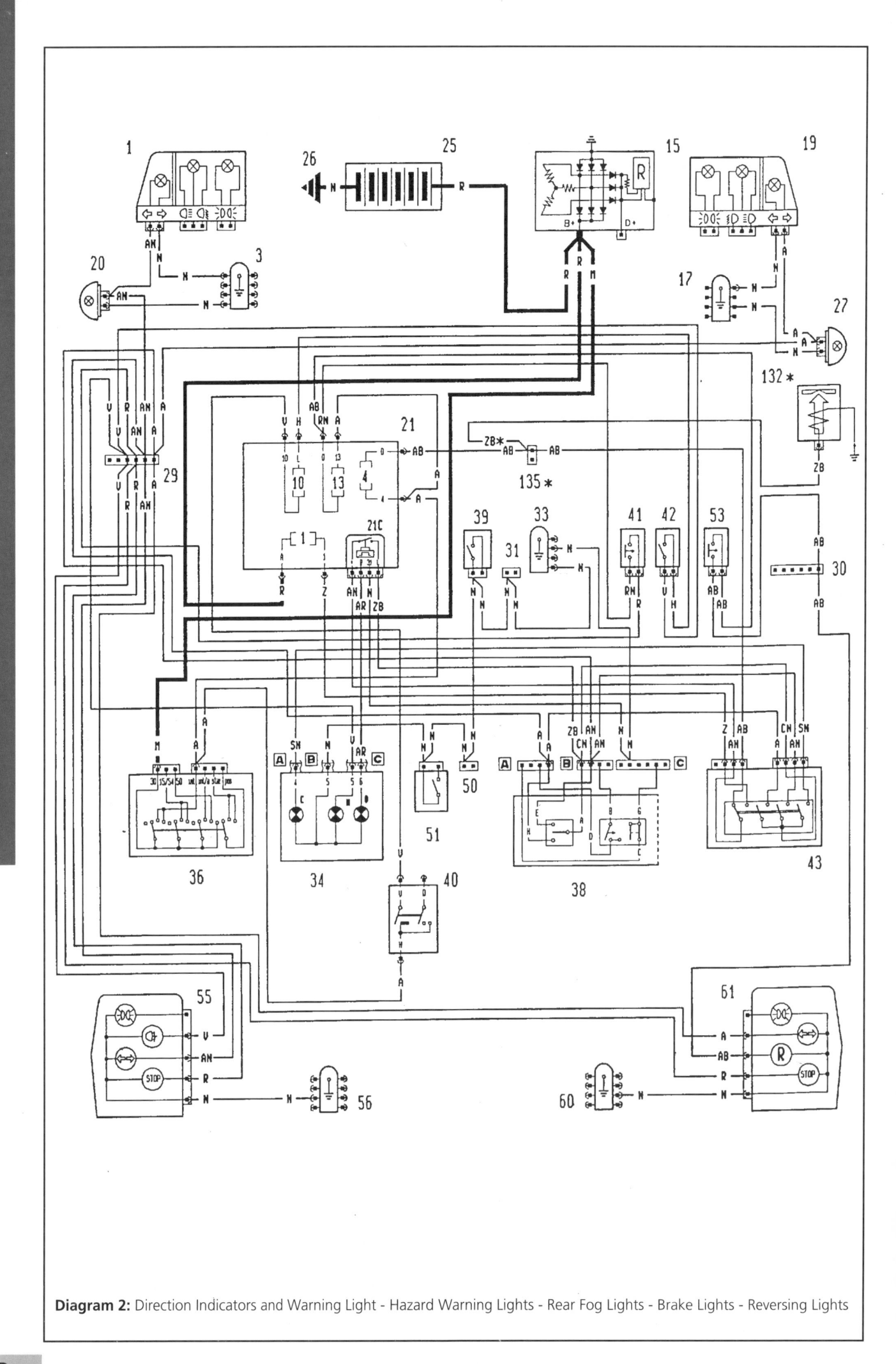

**Diagram 2:** Direction Indicators and Warning Light - Hazard Warning Lights - Rear Fog Lights - Brake Lights - Reversing Lights

7-3

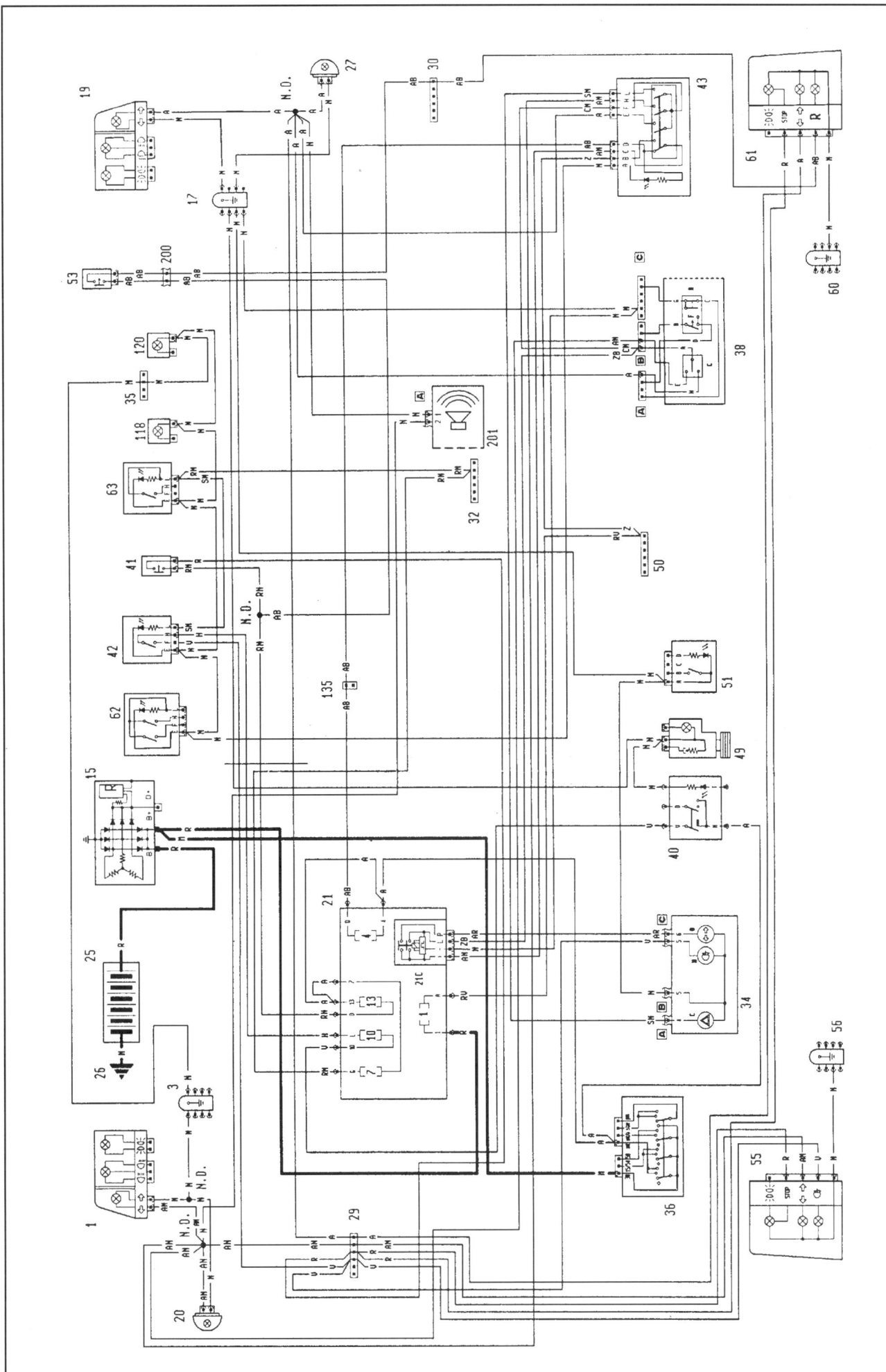

**Diagram 3:** Direction Indicators and Warning Light - Hazard Warning Lights and Warning Light - Rear Fog Lights - Stop Lights - Reversing Lights

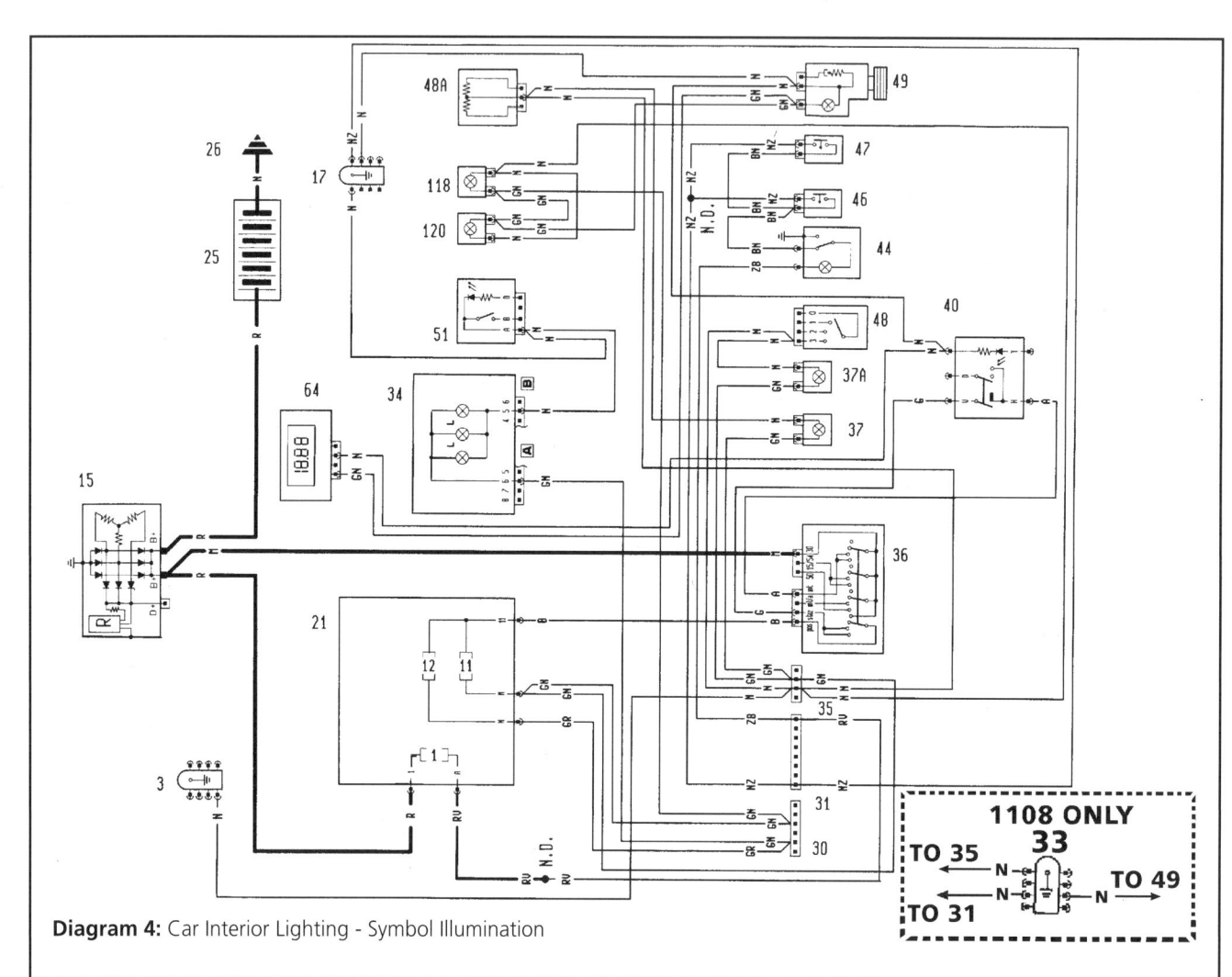

**Diagram 4:** Car Interior Lighting - Symbol Illumination

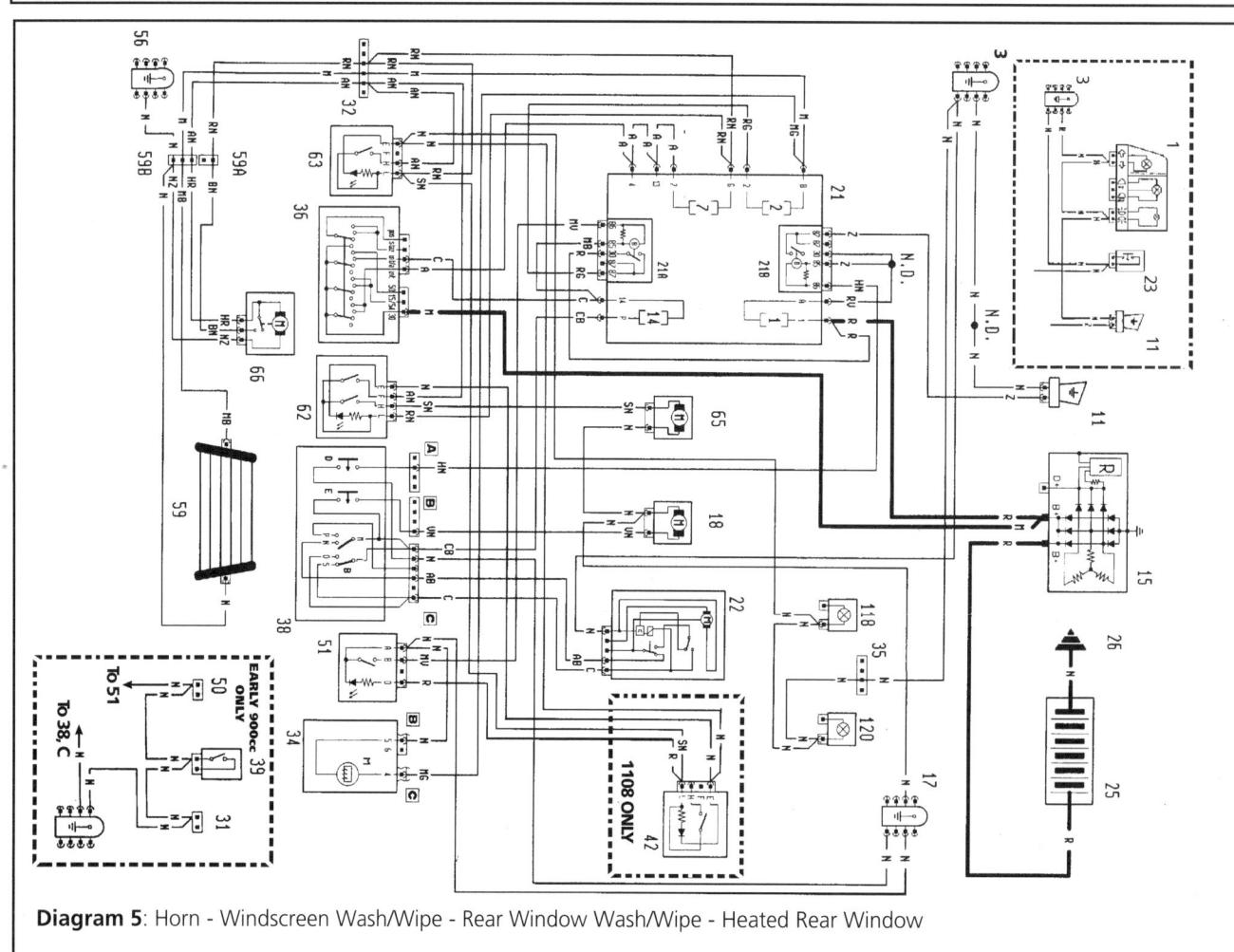

**Diagram 5:** Horn - Windscreen Wash/Wipe - Rear Window Wash/Wipe - Heated Rear Window

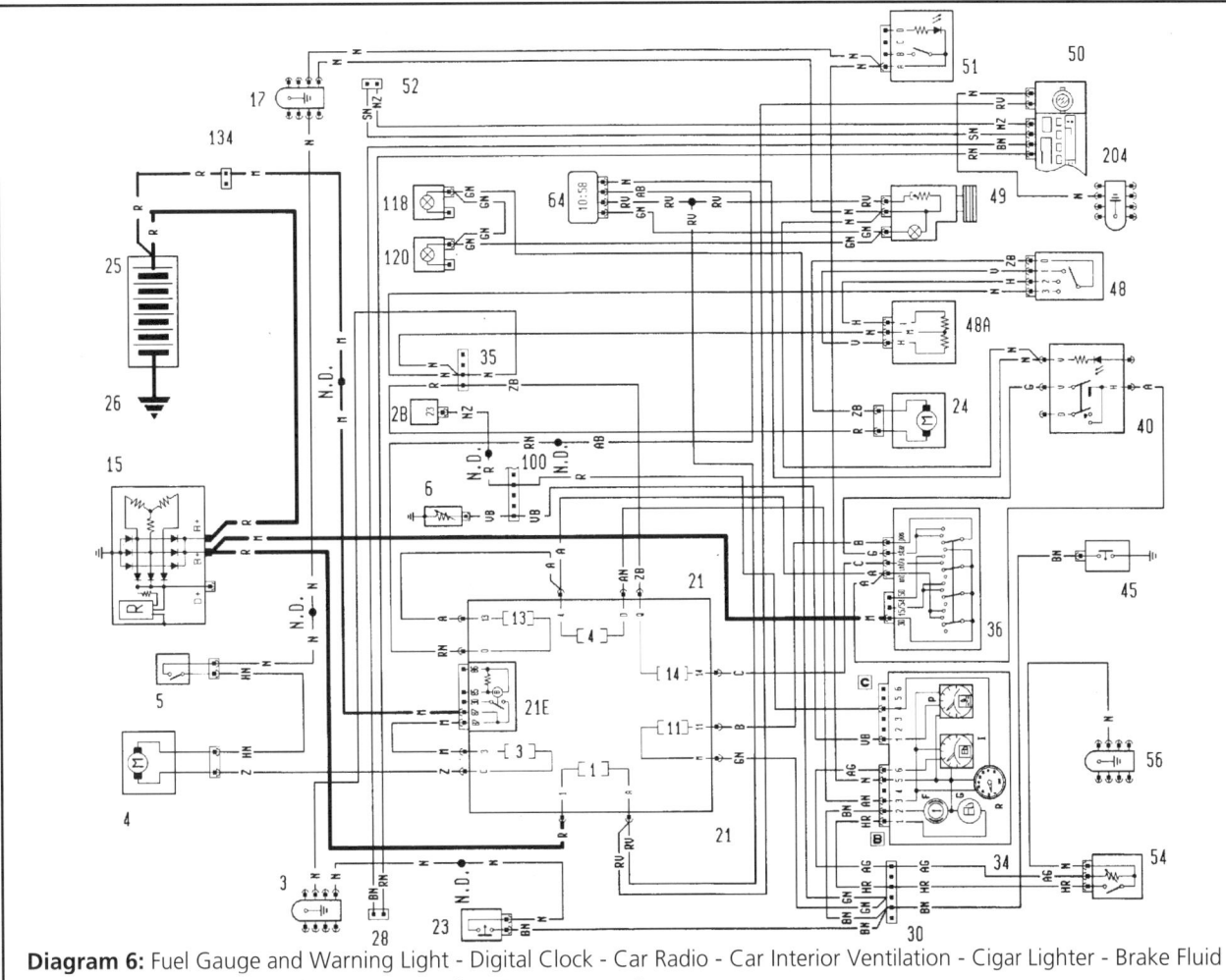

**Diagram 6:** Fuel Gauge and Warning Light - Digital Clock - Car Radio - Car Interior Ventilation - Cigar Lighter - Brake Fluid and Handbrake Warning Light - Engine Coolant Temperature Gauge

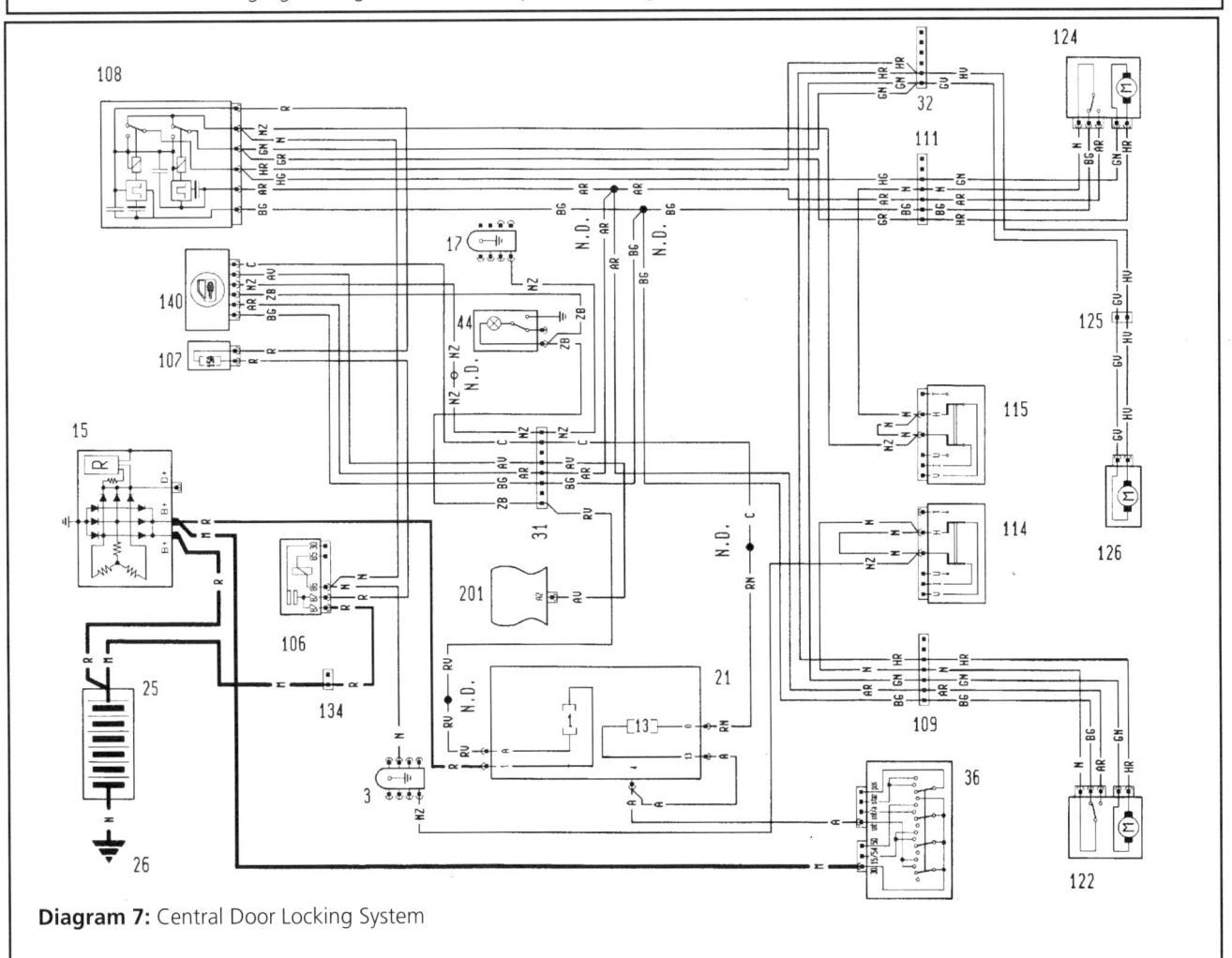

**Diagram 7:** Central Door Locking System

CHAPTER 7 WIRING DIAGRAMS

7-6

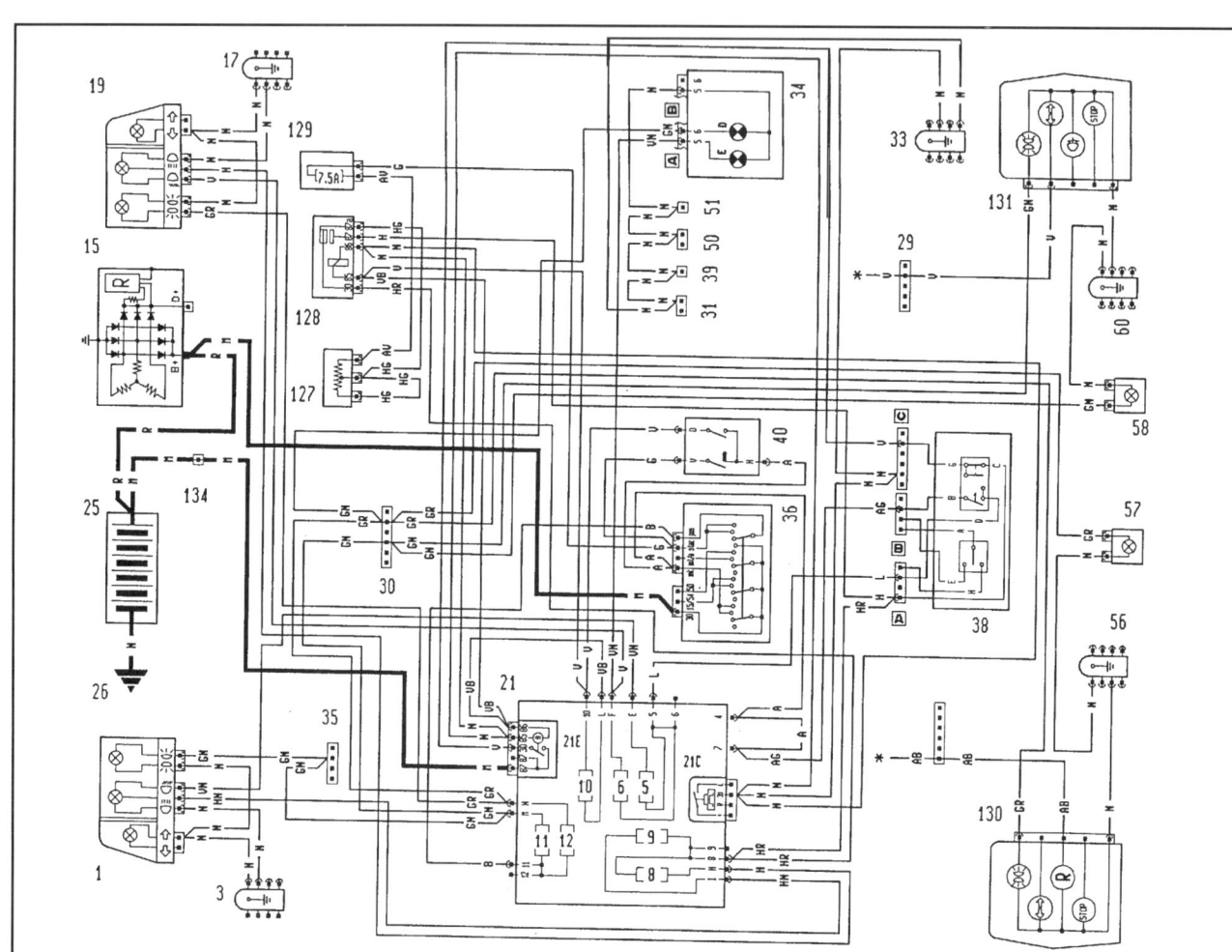

**Diagram 8**: Parking Lights and Warning Light - Dipped Beam Headlights - Dimmed Beam Headlights - Main Beam Headlights and Warning Light - Headlight Flashers - Number Plate Lights

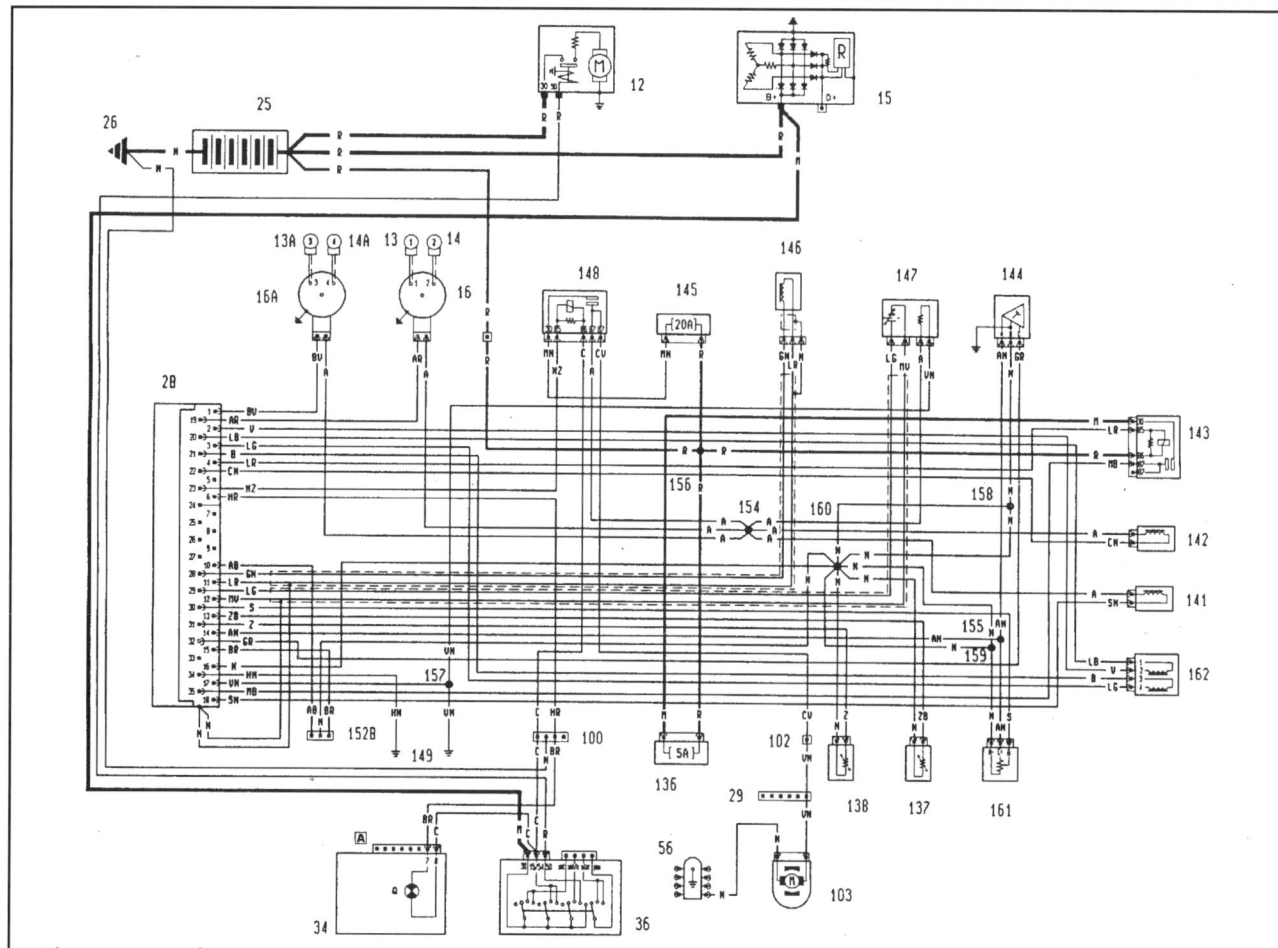

**Diagram 9:** Early 900cc Starting - Ignition - Charging - Oil Pressure Warning Light - MIW Electronic Injection/Ignition - Electronic Injection Failure Warning Light *SEE PAGES 7-2 FOR OTHER EARLIER 903cc TYPE*

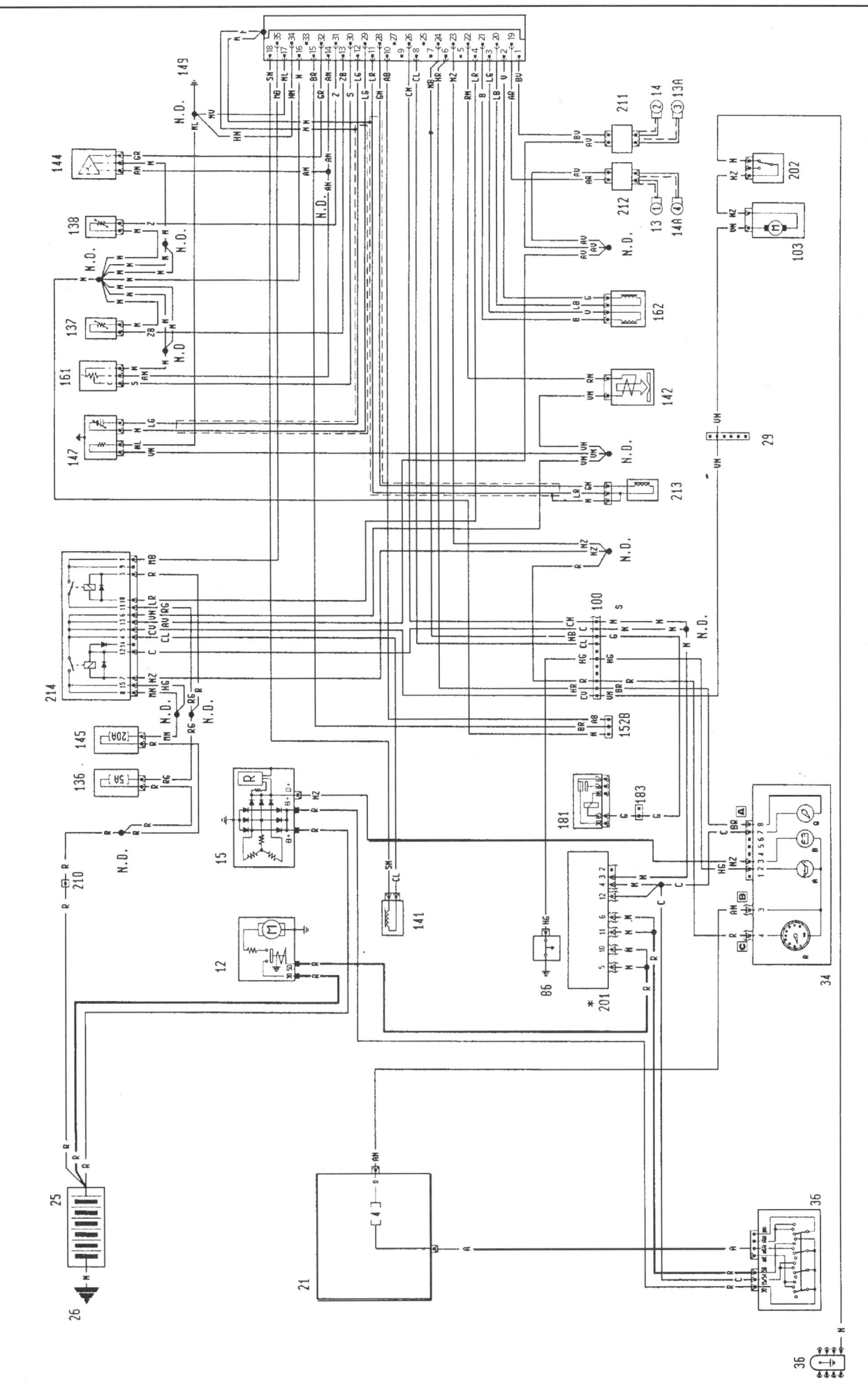

**Diagram 10: 1108 SPORTING** - Starting System - Electronic Ignition and Fuel Injection - Charging System - Oil pressure Warning Light - Electronic Fuel Injection Fault Warning Light

# CHAPTER 7 WIRING DIAGRAMS

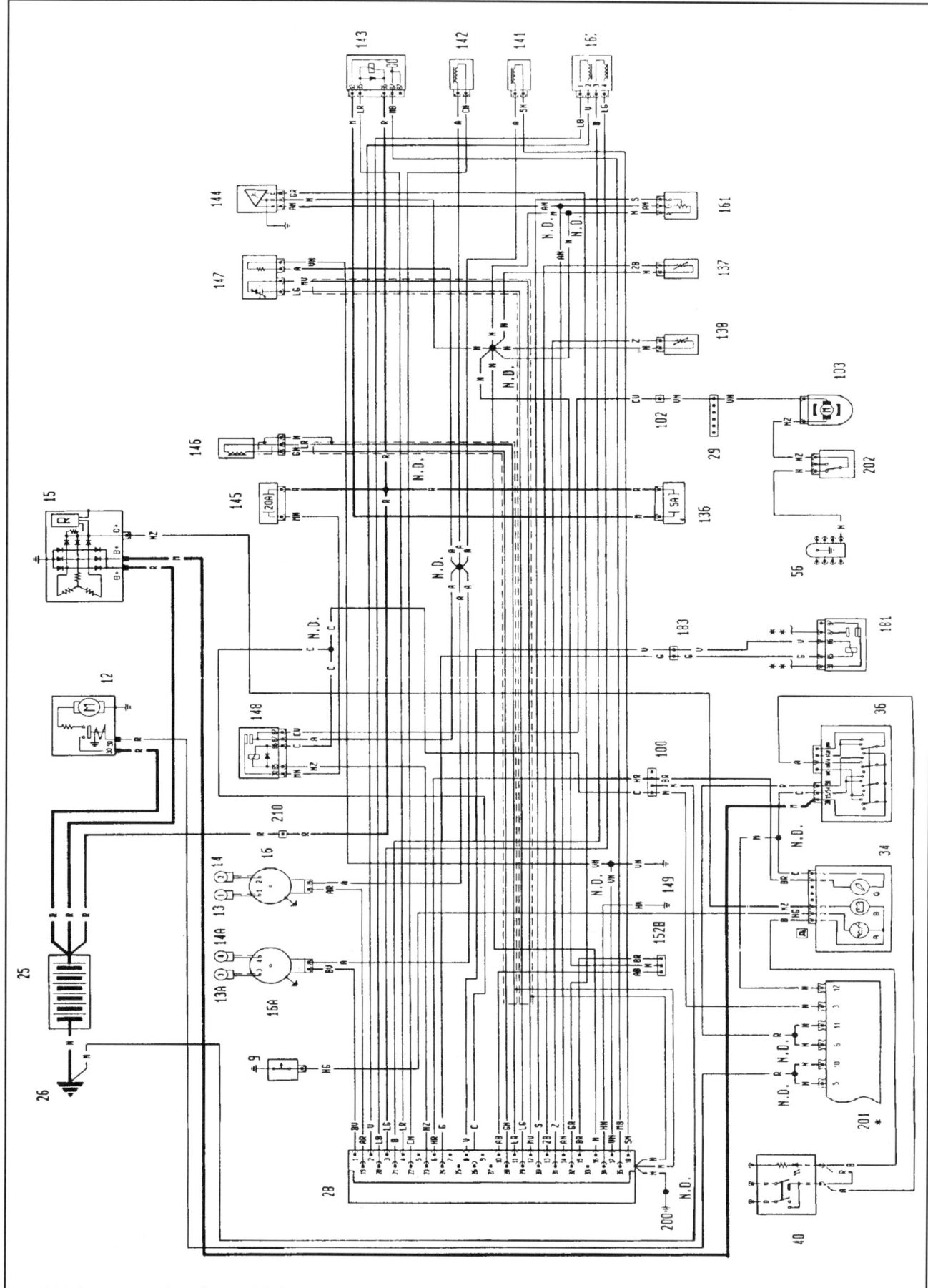

*Variant connections for models fitted with anti-theft device  **See diagram for air conditioner

**Diagram 11: 900 LATE TYPE** - Ignition - Recharging System - Low Engine Oil Pressure Warning Light - MIW Electronic ignition/Fuel Injection - Electronic Injection Fault Warning Light

# INDEX

## A
**Accelerator**
  linkages and cables . . . . . . . . 6-45
**Aerial**, maintenance . . . . . . . 6-35
**Air bag** . . . . . . . . . . . . . . . . . 2-5
**Air cleaner/filter**
  OHC. . . . . . . . . . . . . . . . . . . . 6-40
  OHV. . . . . . . . . . . . . . . . . . . . 6-41
  air temperature control . . . . . . 2-2
  air conditioning . . . . . . . . . . . . 2-2
**Alternator**
  drive belt . . . . . . . . 5-3, 5-11, 6-33
**Antifreeze** . . . . . . . . . . . . . . . 5-4
**Anti-roll bars** . . . . . . . . . . . . 6-49
**Auto-Biography** . . . . . . . . . . . . i

## B
**Ball-joints**
  steering and suspension . 6-46, 6-47
**Battery**
  disconnecting. . . . . . . . . . . . . . 5-5
  electrolyte . . . . . . . . . . . . . . . . 5-5
  jump starting . . . . . . . . . . . . . . 2-8
  safety. . . . . . . . . . . . . . . . . . . . 1-3
**Bellows**, steering gear (see 'Gaiters')
**Bonnet** . . . . . . . . . . 2-6, 6-58, 6-59
  removal and refitting . . . . . . . 6-58
**Brake** 3-4, 5-22 to 5-24, 6-52 to 6-58
  bleeding. . . . . . . . . . . . . . . . . 6-57
  caliper. . . . . . . . . . . . . 5-22, 6-53
  cylinder (master). . . . . . . . . . . 6-55
  discs. . . . . . . . . . . . . . . . . . . 6-53
  drums . . . . . . . . . . . . . . . . . . 6-54
  fluid, check level. . . . . . . . . . . . 5-4
  handbrake . . . . . . . . . . . . . . . 5-24
  hoses/pipes . . . . . . . . . . . . . . 6-56
  pads . . . . . . . . . . . . . . . . . . . 5-22
  safety. . . . . . . . . . . . . . . . . . . 1-3
  servo . . . . . . . . . . . . . . . . . . 6-56
  shoes. . . . . . . . . . . . . . . . . . 6-54
**Bulb renewal** (see 'Lights')
**Bushes**. . . . . . . . . . . . . 5-20, 6-47
**Bumper**
  removal and refitting. . . . 6-60, 6-61

## C
**Cables**
  accelerator. . . . . . . . . . . . . . . 6-42
  clutch. . . . . . . . . . . . . . . . . . 6-27
  handbrake . . . . . . . . . . . . . . . 5-24
**Caliper**, brakes (see 'Brakes')
**Camshaft belt**. . . . . . . . . . . . 5-11
**Capacities**. . . . . . . . . . . . . . . . 3-2
**Catalytic converter** 5-18, 5-19, 6-44
  safety . . . . . . . . . . . . . . 1-2, 6-44
**Clutch** . . . . . . . . . . . . . . 6-26, 6-27
  adjustment. . . . . . . . . . . . . . . 6-27
  replacement. . . . . . . . . . . . . . 6-27
  cable . . . . . . . . . . . . . . . . . . 6-27
**Coil spring** . . . . . . . . . . . . . . 5-20
**Constant Velocity** (C.V.) joints
(see 'Driveshaft')
**Contents** . . . . . . . . . . . . . . . . . iv
**Controls and switches**. . . 2-3 to 2-5
**Cooling system** . . . . . . . . . . . . 5-4
  change coolant . . . . . . . . . . . . 5-4
  radiator pressure cap . . . . . . . . 5-4
**Crankcase ventilation system**. 5-10
**Cylinder head**
  OHC 'FIRE'. . . . . . . . . 6-14 to 6-21
  OHV . . . . . . . . . . . . . 6-1 to 6-14

## D
**Data** . . . . . . . . . . . . . . . . 3-1 to 3-6
**Disc**, brakes (see 'Brakes')
**Distributor** (see ECU)
**Doors**
  hinges . . . . . . . . . . . . . . . . . 6-64
  locks and handles. . . . . . . . . . 6-62
  trim panels. . . . . . . . . . . . . . . 6-61
**Drivebelts**
  alternator. . . . . . . . . . . . . . . . 5-11
  camshaft. . . . . . . . . . . . 5-11, 6-10
**Driveshaft**
  C. V. joints . . . . . . . . . . . . . . 6-29
  gaiters . . . . . . . 5-13, 5-21, 5-23, 6-47
  removal and refitting. . . . 6-29, 6-47
**Drum** (see 'Brakes')

## E
**Electrical system** . . . . . . . 7-1 to 7-9
**Electronic control module**. . . . 6-38
  safety. . . . . . . . . . . . . . . . . . . 1-3
**Emergency starting** . . . . . . . . . 2-8
**Emissions** . . . . . . . . 4-4, 5-17, 5-18
  legal limits . . . . . . 4-4, 5-16 to 5-19
**Engine bay layouts** . . . . . . . . . 5-3
**Engine dismantling**
  OHC 'FIRE'. . . . . . . . . 6-20 to 6-21
  OHV . . . . . . . . . . . . . 6-11 to 6-12
**Engine mountings** . . . . . . . . . 6-24
**Engine oil** (see 'Oil')
  check level. . . . . . . . . . . . . . . . 5-3
**Engine refitting**
  OHC 'FIRE'. . . . . . . . . . . . . . 6-21
  OHV . . . . . . . . . . . . . 6-12 to 6-14
**Exhaust manifold**. . . . . . . . . . . 6-3
**Exhaust**. . . . . . . . . . . . . . . . . 6-45
  system . . . . . . . . . . . . . . . . . 6-45
**Expansion tank** . . . . . . . . . . . . 5-4

## F
**Facts & Figures**. . . . . . . . 3-1 to 3-6
**Fan** . . . . . . . . . . . . . . . . . . . . 5-15
**Fast idle**
  carburettor. . . . . . . . . . . . . . . 5-17
  fuel injection . . . . . . . . . . . . . 5-18
**Filter**
  air . . . . . . . . . . . . . . . . . . . . 5-16
  fuel . . . . . . . . . . . . . . . . . . . 5-17
  fuel injection . . . . . . . . . . . . . 5-17
  oil (see 'Oil filter')
**Fire Extinguisher** . . . . . . . . . . . 1-2
**Fluoroelastomers**, safety . . . . . . 1-4
**Fuel gauge** . . . . . . . . . . . . . . 6-36
**Fuel injection** . . . . . . . . . . . . 6-38
**Fuel lines/pipes** . . . 5-16, 6-36, 6-45
**Fuel pump**
  electric . . . . . . . . . . . . . . . . . 5-18
  mechanical . . . . . . 6-9, 6-10, 6-11
**Fuel system** . . . . . . . . 6-38 to 6-44
  evaporation control system. . . . 6-44
**Fuel tank** . . . . . . . . . . . . . . . . 6-43
**Fumes**, safety . . . . . . . . . . . . . 1-2
**Fuses** . . . . . . . . . . 5-8 to 5-9, 7-1, 7-2

## G
**Gaiters**. . . . . . . 5-13, 5-21, 5-23, 6-47
**Gearbox** (transmission) . 6-24 to 6-26
  oil (manual) . . . . . . . . . . . . . . 5-13
**Generator drive belt** (see 'Alternator, drive belt')

## H
**Handbrake** . . . . . . . . . . . 6-57, 6-58
**Headlights** (see 'Lights')
  adjustment. . . . . . . . . . . . . . . 5-25
  bulb replacement. . . . . . . 5-6 to 5-8
**Heater** . . . . . . . . . . . 2-3, 6-37, 6-38
**Hoses/pipes** (see 'Pipes and hoses')
**HT leads** . . . . . . . . . . . . . . . 5-15
**Hub**
  front . . . . . . . 6-30, 6-48, 6-49, 6-50
  rear . . . . . . . . . . . . . . . . . . . 6-51

## I
**Identification numbers** . . . . . . . 3-6
**Ignition system** 5-14 to 16, 6-38 to 40
  coil . . . . . . . . . . . . 5-18, 6-4, 6-39
  safety. . . . . . . . . . . . . . . . . . . 1-3
**Ignition timing** 3-2, 5-15 to 16, 6-38
**Instruments** . . . . . . . . . 6-33 to 6-34
  panel lights . . . . . . . . . . . . . . . 2-2

## J
**Jacking** . . . . . . . . . . . . . . 2-7 to 2-8
  safety. . . . . . . . . . . . . . . . . . . 1-1
  wheelchange . . . . . . . . . . . . . 2-7
**Jump leads** (Jump starting) . . . . 2-8

## L
**Lambda sensor** 5-18, 5-19, 6-39, 6-44
**Lights**
  fog lights . . . . . . . . . . . . . . . . 2-5
  hazard warning . . . . . . . . . . . . 2-5
  headlights . . . . . . . . . . . . 2-4, 5-6
  indicators . . . . . . . . . . . . 2-4, 5-7
  interior . . . . . . . . . . . . . . . . . 5-8
  number plate . . . . . . . . . . . . . 5-7
  rear lights. . . . . . . . . . . . . . . . 5-7
  reversing lights . . . . . . . . . . . . 5-7
  sidelights. . . . . . . . . . . . . 2-4, 5-6
**Locks and latches** . 2-1, 2-2, 2-6, 6-3
**Lubricants** (see inside back cover)

## M
**Mirrors**. . . . . . . . . . . . . . . 2-5, 6-64
**Model years** . . . . . . . . . . . . . . 3-1
**MoT**, getting through . . . . 4-1 to 4-4

## N
**Number plates** (lights) . . . . . . . 5-7

## O
**Oil change**
  disposal. . . . . . . . . . . . . . 1-2, 1-3
  engine. . . . . . . . . . . . . . . . . . 5-3
  transmission. . . . . . . . . . . . . 5-13
  safety. . . . . . . . . . . . . . . . . . . 1-2
**Oil filler cap** . . . . . . . . . . . . . . 5-4
**Oil filter** . . . . . . . . . . . . . . . . . 5-9
**Oil level**
  engine. . . . . . . . . . . . . . . . . . 5-3
  gearbox . . . . . . . . . . . . . . . . 5-13
  topping up . . . . . . . . . . . . . . . 5-3

## P
**Pads**, brake (see 'Brakes')
**Pipes and hoses**
  brakes . . . . . . . . . . . . . . . . . 6-56
  hot air. . . . . . . . . . . . . . 6-37, 6-38
  radiator (cooling system) . . . . . 5-4
**Plastics**, safety. . . . . . . . . . . . . 1-3
**Production changes**. . . . . . . . . 3-1

## R
**Radiator** . . . . . . . . . . . . . . . . . 5-4
**Raising the car** . . . . . . . . 1-1, 2-7
**Repair data** . . . . . . . . . . . . . . 3-3
**Road test**, brakes . . . . . . . . . 6-55

## S
**Safety First!** . . . . . . . . . . 1-1 to 1-4
**Seats**. . . . . . . . . . . . . . 2-5, 6-64, 6-65
**Servicing Your Car**. . . . . 6-1 to 6-65
**Shock absorbers**. 5-20, 6-48 to 6-50
**Shoes**, brake (see 'Brakes')
**Sidelights** (see 'Lights')
**Spark plugs** (see inside back cover)
**Specifications** (see 'Facts & Figures')
**Speedometer cable** . . . . . . . . 6-34
**Starter motor** . . . . . . . . . . . . 6-33
**Steering** . . . . . 5-20, 5-21, 6-46, 6-47
  rack gaiters (see 'gaiters')
**Steering wheel**. . . . . . . . . . . . 6-46
**Sunroof operation** . . . . . . . . . 2-6
**Suspension** . . 5-20, 5-21, 6-46, 6-47
  front . . . . . . . . . . . . . . . . . . 6-48
  rear . . . . . . . . . . . . . . . . . . . 6-50
  strut. . . . . . . . . . . . . . . . . . . 6-48

## T
**Tailgate wiper** (see 'Windscreen wipers')
**Tailgate and strut** . . . . . . . . . 6-61
**Thermostat** . . . . . . . . . . 6-3, 6-31
**Throttle cable and pedal** (see 'Accelerator, linkage and cables')
**Timing belt** . . . . . . . . . . 5-11, 6-10
**Torque wrench settings** . . . . . 3-4
**Track control arm**. . . . . . . . . . 6-47
**Track rod ends (TRE)**. . . . 5-20, 6-46
**Transmission** . . . . . . . . . 6-24, 6-26
  removal . . . . . . . . . . . . . . . . 6-24
  separation/reconnection . 6-24 to 26
**Transmission fluid** . . . . . . . . . 5-13
**Tyre**
  checking. . . . . . . . . . . . . . 4-2, 5-5
  pressures . . . . . . . . . . . . . . . 3-2

## U
**Universal joints**. . . . . . . . 5-21, 6-29
**Using your car** . . . . . . . . 2-1 to 2-8

## V
**Valve clearances** . . . . . . . . . . 5-10
**Vehicle Identification Numbers**
(VIN). . . . . . . . . . . . . . . . . . . . 3-6

## W
**Washer fluid reservoir**. . . . . . . 5-44
**Water pump** . . . . . . . . . . 6-30, 6-31
**Wheel alignment**. . . . . . . . . . . 4-1
**Wheel bearings**. . . . . . . . 5-20, 5-21
**Wheel bolts**. . . . . . . . . . . 2-7, 5-22
**Wheel changing** . . . . . . . . . . . 2-7
**Wheel cylinder** . . . . . . . . 6-54, 6-55
**Wheel sizes** . . . . . . . . . . . . . . 3-2
**Windscreen, damage**. . . . . . . . 4-2
**Window regulator**. . . . . . . . . 6-62
**Windscreen washers** . . . . . . . 6-35
**Windscreen wipers** . . . . . . 2-4, 6-34
**Wiring diagrams** . . . . . . . 7-1 to 7-9

# WHY DOUBLE COPPER IS BETTER FOR YOUR ENGINE

Champion Double Copper plugs are the first in the world to have copper core in both centre and earth electrode. This innovative design means that they run cooler by up to 100°C - giving greater efficiency and longer life. These double copper cores transfer heat away from the tip of the plug faster and more efficiently. Therefore, Double Copper runs at cooler temperatures than conventional plugs giving improved acceleration response and high speed performance with no fear of pre-ignition.

- Faster cold starting
- For unleaded or leaded fuel
- Electrodes up to 100°C cooler
- Better acceleration response
- Lower emissions
- 50% bigger spark area
- The longer life plug

**EARTH ELECTRODE TEMPERATURE vs. ENGINE SPEED**

### PLUG TIPS/HOT AND COLD
Spark plugs must operate within well-defined temperature limits to avoid cold fouling at one extreme and overheating at the other.

Champion and the car manufacturers work out the best plugs for an engine to give optimum performance under all conditions, from freezing cold starts to sustained high speed motorway cruising.

Plugs are often referred to as hot or cold. With Champion, the higher the number on its body, the hotter the plug and the lower the number the cooler the plug. For the correct plug for your car refer to specifications below.

### PLUG CLEANING
Modern plug design and materials mean that Champion no longer recommends periodic plug cleaning. Certainly don't clean your plugs with a wire brush as this can cause metal conductive paths across the nose of the insulator so impairing its performance and resulting in loss of acceleration and reduced m.p.g.

However, if plugs are removed, always carefully clean the area where the plug seats in the cylinder head as grit and dirt can sometimes cause gas leakage.

Also wipe any traces of oil grease from the plug leads as this may lead to arcing.

### SPARK PLUG APPLICATION TABLE

| CINQUECENTO | | | | | |
|---|---|---|---|---|---|
| Engine | Models | Year | Champion Type | Fiat Type | Fiat Stock Code |
| 900 OHV (and 704cc engines) | All models | 1992-on | RN9YCC | 9FYSSR | 5894587 |
| 1.1 FIRE OHC | Sporting | 01/95-on | RC9YCC | 9GYSSR | 5893486 |

**CHAMPION DOUBLE COPPER**

- SAC-9 resistor (where fitted)
- Ultraseal zinc-plated shell protection
- Extruded copper-cored centre electrode
- Unique copper-cored earth electrode operating at up to 100°C less than conventional earth electrodes